Our Common Life

Music in American Life

For a list of books in the series,
please see our website
at www.press.uillinois.edu.

Our Common Life

Folksong from the Front Porch to the Concert Hall

STEPHEN WADE

UNIVERSITY OF ILLINOIS PRESS
Urbana, Chicago, and Springfield

Manufactured in the United States of America
C 5 4 3 2 1
∞ This book is printed on acid-free paper.

Publication of this book was supported in part by grants
from the L. J. and Mary C. Skaggs Folklore Fund.

Library of Congress Cataloging-in-Publication Data

Names: Wade, Stephen author
Title: Our common life : folksong from the front porch to the concert hall / Stephen Wade.
Description: Urbana : University of Illinois Press, 2026. |
Series: Music in American life | Includes bibliographical references and index.
Identifiers: LCCN 2026008506 (print) | LCCN 2026008507 (ebook) |
ISBN 9780252059865 hardcover | ISBN 9780252049262 ebook
Subjects: LCSH: Folk music—United States—20th century—History and criticism |
Folk songs, English—United States—20th century—History and criticism |
Folk musicians—United States | Folk singers—United States |
Folk music—Social aspects—United States—History—20th century |
Folklore—United States | Music and race—United States—History—20th century |
LCGFT: Biographies
Classification: LCC ML3551.5 .W33 2026 (print) | LCC ML3551.5 (ebook) |
DDC 781.62/13—dc23/eng/20260423
LC record available at https://lccn.loc.gov/2026008506
LC ebook record available at https://lccn.loc.gov/2026008507

The manufacturer's authorized representative in the EU for product safety is
Mare Nostrum Group B.V., Mauritskade 21D, 1091 GC Amsterdam, The Netherlands.
Email: gpsr@mare-nostrum.co.uk

For Michaelle

I have driven 29,000 miles in twenty states in the last eighteen months and I feel as if I had discovered, not America, exactly, but Americans.

—SIDNEY ROBERTSON, NOV. 6, 1937

Contents

Preface

ON MAY 15, 1979, my life as a musician utterly changed. That date marks not only the first but the most consequential performance I ever gave of *Banjo Dancing, or the 48th Annual Squitters Mountain Song, Dance, Folklore Convention & Banjo Contest and How I Lost.* The show, a solo stage piece that I performed nightly for nearly twenty years, premiered in the smallest of the three spaces at Chicago's Body Politic, the city's first off-Loop theater. As the theater had scheduled the piece to open three days later for a four-weekend run at the close of their annual season, both time and finances dictated no audience previews. In other words, even though I had never publicly performed this show, Chicago's theater critics, including its major metropolitan newspaper reviewers, all planned to attend this May 15th performance.

The morning of the show's premiere, I listened to Bill Monroe's *Bluegrass Instrumentals* album. His rusty-throated mandolin scraped with fearless assertion, and his accompanists restated his tunes with intricacy and resonance, filling me with a reservoir of inspiration I knew I would soon require. Then, heading outside, I slowly walked under gray skies in the quiet of Lincoln Park, rehearsing my lines, distracted at times by sights from my childhood: the lagoon, the zoo rookery, and the Victorian glass curvature of the conservatory, whose atmosphere within breathed with a tropical moistness unlike Chicago's temperate zone aridity. On the way back, just up the street from the theater where I would play that night, I passed the hospital where I was born. A few blocks later, I passed my elementary school.

Late that afternoon I took supper at a small restaurant in the basement of a residential hotel not far from the lakefront. The kindly if concerned waitress asked me if anything was wrong, my nerves apparently visible as I struggled through the meal. Then I made my way to the theater. A half-hour or so before the curtain, I crossed the street, at that point fully attired in the three-piece suit I would wear during the show. By now, parched with fear, I trembled from my clogging boots to my collar. There, at that neighborhood bar, my friends—whose amber drinks seemed umbilically attached to their wrists—assured me with good cheer that all would go well. Their tipsiness aside, this was Chicago, and such convivial taverns had long provided the setting for those of us who had taken the stage for our profession.

Finally, it came time for the inaugural performance. The show begins with a mythical banjo contest, one whose elongated name I modeled after Bascom Lunsford's annual folk festival in Asheville, North Carolina.[1] I took on the role of a hapless banjoist, who, after playing a trio of three instrumentals, each set in different tunings, including one played with just one hand, and another with simultaneous clog dancing, then loses the contest. If downcast in that defeat, he soon finds uplift as one of the judges kindly tells him, "Keep on practicing."

Other stories, also set to banjo, followed. One, "The Far-Famed Fairy Tale of Fenella," derived from an alliterative piece of nineteenth-century street literature that retells the "Beauty and the Beast" story, its every word beginning with the same letter.[2] Another, a participatory number, enlisted the audience to clank on their chairs with their pocket change, tapping out a beat with a suggested quarter they might have in their pockets or purses. While accompanying them on a small, wooden-hooped, fretless banjo made in the Southern Highlands, and conducting their rhythms with a ballpoint pen used as a baton, I reached into a cabinet overstuffed like Fibber McGee's hall closet. Scores of identical pens poured out, and I ran along the risers and through the aisles, selling these 25-cent items. Its sales pitch originated from a sidewalk vendor recorded in New York in 1952, a cry that I enriched with additional snippets of hard-pavement philosophy. Here in Chicago, where decades earlier the Industrial Workers of the World had first organized, I thought it only appropriate to end the piece with a call to literary arms: "Poets of the world, ignite!"[3] The second act included a traditional tale about a nocturnal creature, whose voice I projected through the open back of my banjo, coupling its reverberant

FIGURE 1. F. O. Darley's 1858 illustration for "The Far-Famed Fairy Tale of Fenella."

sound with the totemic appearance that facelessness created, and which the stage lighting, a dark green follow spot, accentuated. Beyond these moments, I recall that evening in fragments: an unplanned ad-lib that went over well and the comforting physicality that permeated me when, early on, I assumed a character's walk. "Get it in your legs," I had been coached. "The attitude, the voice, the rest will follow."

Immediately after the curtain, the theater's publicist offered Planter's Punch for those who attended the opening. She thought its deep-South legacy somehow appropriate for my mountain banjo song-and-story presentation. While I dimly remember a toast being raised, I fully recall some well-meaning musician friends of mine balefully commenting on the serious demeanor adopted by the reviewers, not knowing this poker-faced mien was a requirement for that job. Though I'd planned this appearance for years, its future now seemed all the more uncertain. Later that night, I wrestled with sleep on my best friend's couch, where I had roosted in the weeks leading up to the opening. I feared that I had squandered this opportunity by lapses of concentration, let alone larger failures of artistry. No matter my misgivings over those next few days until the reviews came out, I knew this much to be true: *Banjo Dancing* was not just mine; it came from a gallimaufry of the past, of writers, musicians, actors, and orators.

That past included many of the people who appear in this book, some of whom even came to see *Banjo Dancing.* In a sense, one could review this book's index and find that nearly every person in it substantively shaped these stage works. From opening night onwards, playgoers could read a dedication to my teacher, Fleming Brown, and a salute to his teacher and my musical partner, Doc Hopkins, in *Banjo Dancing*'s program notes. Beyond these closest of preceptors, other players cited in this book, including Thaddeus Willingham, Dick Burnett, Uncle Dave Macon, Dock Boggs, Sam and Kirk McGee, Frank Proffitt, and Hobart Smith all figured prominently in the show. In *Banjo Dancing*'s 1989 sequel, *On the Way Home,* I recalled a young Earl Scruggs leveling audiences at the *Grand Ole Opry* with what its host, George D. Hay, called his "fancy banjo." The chiming music of Omer Forster and Dee Hicks, roustabout singers like those remembered in the chapter "Archie's 'Old Man,'" Dakota Jack's medicine show spiel that captivated a young Doc Hopkins, the fiddle tunes of Jewel Fagan Haynes that she performed with Uncle Dave Macon, the barre chords I learned from Jim Schwall, the route taken from Mississippi to Chicago that formed its down-home blues scene, a few choruses of "Secret Agent Man" and "Dancing in the Street" played on a Sears Silvertone electric guitar of the sort described in this book's second chapter, the guitar shops set along Chicago's music row, WLS radio's moniker, the precedent of display pieces

FIGURE 2. Odell Thompson at home, Mebane, North Carolina, Nov. 3, 1987. Photo by Stephen Wade.

and talking banjo music, and a closing story about visiting Joe and Odell Thompson, who knew about and were delighted with their role in that show—all these histories found expression, however truncated, over the course of this performance and its predecessor.

This book now extends that work, focusing on a handful of American musicians, storytellers, singers, educators, and advocates. Those among them who figure most prominently here appear in the table of contents. They witnessed, and in many instances, performed rural Southern folksongs, spoken-word pieces, and instrumentals of the sort captured on English-language, vernacular music recordings that proliferated between 1890 and 1943. The ensuing chapters, while written as stand-alone studies, explore a set of allied themes. Much of this material is guided by first-person contact with individuals of that era, many born in the last years of the nineteenth century or the first quarter of the twentieth. They bear lessons from tradition, and like tradition itself, defy monolithic characterization. Their observations extend from pieces they knew to values they held, from persons they remembered to methods they employed.

Nor did these artists, patrons, and their works stay confined to their communities. Repeatedly, they leaped across cultural registers, reaching new audiences and inspiring new adherents. I include myself as one such beneficiary. This book draws from those who taught me to play and educated me to hear. Its sequence loosely represents stages in my own learning, evoking persons and pieces central to that development. Nearly all these song studies, biographies, and essays arise from promises I made to the subjects, their families, and friends to try to tell their stories. Archivists entrusted with their materials and scholars devoted to these subjects also counted among those pledges. I wanted to explore this music less from its reception by outsiders and more from working practices held among these artists themselves. How did these players learn? What are they telling us? What precedents did they draw upon? What sets their performances apart by way of resourcefulness and originality? Back when I made my first album in 1990, I ended its liner notes with something Fleming Brown told me that applies to all these questions. He was describing the five-string banjo and its music as a vehicle of expression. "It's not just pyrotechnics and it's not hickory-dickory-dock either," he said. "It's a thing of beauty, and each piece of music is like a jewel full of facets. Turn it around and try it again."[4] *Our Common Life: Folksong from the Front Porch to the Concert Hall* addresses this creative freedom.

• • •

In the present era of cultural studies, many thoughtful and painstaking accounts have emphasized social, political, and market forces that have surrounded this music and its performers. Increasingly, these works investigate, or in current parlance, "interrogate," institutional structures, in particular racism, that have denied due credit to the original makers. Along with this historical restitution, much related writing includes artist biographies, genre studies, regional styles, and monographs on folksong collectors. That collectors typically leave institutionally accessible written records couched in culturally familiar language no doubt furthers the popularity of those monographs. Comparatively fewer books focus on folksong case studies, reflecting a general academic shift in interest from art to artist. In an illuminating study of the banjo tune "Coal Creek March," scholar Neil V. Rosenberg observed that the

> most committed of the young revivalists [by the 1960s] had begun to move toward a new aesthetic perspective. In searching for song and music, they found singers and musicians. Their aesthetic involvement underwent a shift of focus from appreciation of the artistic product to fascination with the life of the producer. . . . *Humanitas* has replaced *communitas* as the focus.[5]

He also anticipated that this orthodoxy would change again in subsequent generations, as evidenced in present-day scholarship in which the frame more than the picture itself draws attention, leading the study of America's folk cultural traditions into increasingly theoretical constructs. The addition to the title of the *Journal of American Folklore* reflects these new emphases, now describing itself on its cover, "A Global Quarterly."

Yet this new globalism has not displaced the local, which in some ways has become more accessible than ever before. As record stores have closed, digital resources have grown. Resources such as eBay allow purchasers to effortlessly find sheet music and pictures long submerged. Many of these relics come from persons numbered among the last generation to have lived in America before the coming of electricity, and counted among the first to have experienced it. Their kerosene-lit cultural past is, in myriad ways, irretrievable to us. But sensibilities persist and artifacts survive. Modern folklore thrives in abundance. Urban legends, songs about the latest antiheroes and outlaws, moralizing scandals, and fake news reports transmitted over the Internet recall broadside printers from London's Seven Dials district. Like their American counterparts who contemporaneously published pocket songsters of forbidden liaisons, lurid trials, and gallows confessions, these single-sheets, in turn, were succeeded by latter-day tabloids like the *Weekly World News*. Once displayed at grocery store checkout lanes, this now-shuttered publication recounted UFO abductions and illustrated giant-sized babies and household vampires, perennial subjects that currently traverse computer screens and occupy YouTube and TikTok animators.[6] Media may change, but patterns endure. As Ben Botkin wrote in 1944, "But if folklore is old wine in new bottles, it is also new wine in old bottles. It says not only, 'Back where I come from,' but also, 'Where do we go from here?'"[7]

Examples readily come to mind. The personnel in a gospel group will inevitably transition, but these ensembles often extend over generations. Church practices, particularly those that foreground vernacular music and older forms of folk preaching, persist, resonating with older traditions on Sunday mornings. Narrative ballads once sung among family members gathered by the hearth have also proved resilient, as musically inclined descendants, taking pride in their great-grandparents, sing these songs anew. Still others use digital tools to retrieve nearly vanished sounds from emulsifying discs and employ computer programs to slow down those performances so they might learn from them. New perceptions, for instance, surround the rural five-string banjo. From having arrived on these shores via slavery and found decades of representation in derogatory imagery, the banjo now represents, for some younger Black devotees, a sign of cultural achievement.

From a distance, folksong can appear like a superorganic process, an artistic product modeled by many and whose change slowly occurs through time, akin to an abstract force of nature or the evolution of biological species. In that light, its development resembles a force that can only be seen by comparing very early examples of its effects with very recent ones. In such a scheme of things, the individual inheritors of a song could change it, but generally not in obvious and dramatic ways. However, opportunities arise when we can see the changes as they occur. In this book, for instance, E. C. Ball's adaptation of "Pretty Polly," with his memorable guitar figure after each verse, provides one example.[8] There, the convergence in the Southern mountains of the five-string banjo, which he translated to the guitar, itself a recent arrival in his community, couples with an unaccompanied singing tradition. This marks a dramatic change in which two parallel musical traditions come together. E. C. Ball was seen during his

FIGURE 3. Gerald E. Parsons Jr. with Delilah, Washington, D.C., summer 1994. Photo by Margaret Parsons.

lifetime as both representative and exceptional.[9] This book centers on persons like Ball, whose art hinges "on exchanges between creative individuals and community-shaped meaning."[10]

Not surprisingly, the principal methodology I have followed is that of a participant-observer. Back in 1991, Gerald E. Parsons Jr. (1940–1995), longtime reference librarian of the Library of Congress's Archive of Folk Culture, described the multi-format, unpublished, ethnographic works that constitute his office's collections.[11] From an array of field notes, maps, sound recordings, and pictures, a collector seeking to represent human experience assembles a body of documentation. It is a complicated business, and Gerry took pains to understand it. At the heart of what Gerry found was an idea articulated by Suzanne Langer in *An Introduction to Symbolic Logic.*[12] She discussed two kinds of knowledge—knowledge *of* a thing and knowledge *about* a thing. In recounting Langer's idea, Gerry spoke of how a baby crawling around her room can have intimate knowledge of it: every corner, the spaces under her crib and dresser, or the patterns she finds on the linoleum floor of her nursery. This is one kind of knowledge, again, knowledge *of* a thing. Another kind of knowledge comes from the ethnographer, who views the room in relation to other rooms of the same house, describing how the place is organized, who lives elsewhere in the house, and how the baby behaves within it. Here, then, is knowledge *about* a thing.

Gerry found value in both kinds of knowledge—the private, subjective world of the child, and the public, denotative accounts of the ethnographer. The pitfalls of the former, its possible ambiguities, faced the pitfalls of the latter, with its possible irrelevance. Gerry cautioned against those who, in their single-minded pursuit of "methodological refinement," find that "in eliminating ambiguity they have nearly succeeded in eliminating reality as well."[13] On the other hand, personal experiences might not constitute testable statements. Even though the proverb tells us "Experience is the best teacher," we still prefer, in Gerry's words, "the opinions of the criminologist to those of the criminal, the chronicles of the historian to the memoirs of the general, the analysis of the psychiatrist to the proclamations of the patient."[14] But one who might be able to relate "the living concerns of one group of people to the professional concerns of another" might be the fieldworker who is also a participant.[15]

In the last years of his life, Gerry borrowed a banjo of mine. We sometimes spoke of the ways one might interpret this deeply vernacular instrument, how the experiences of a chord played on a fingerboard could open up a whole way of understanding the idiom and its adherents. From the physical control of the banjo, as fingers close themselves around a chord, to the songs an individual chooses to perform, much can be learned using a participatory experience honed by the tools of scholarship. Ethnomusicologist Mantle Hood termed this approach "bi-musicality," having found that his students benefited from playing the instruments they studied.[16] A phenomenological approach is not a shortcut, nor is it the only avenue one can validly pursue, but it can be a starting point in the study of a cultural setting, in reaching for what Gerry Parsons called "inspiration born of real experience."[17]

• • •

Looking back at the individuals and their art detailed in this book, I also look ahead. In 1979, an LP titled *Laugh Your Blues Away* went into print, featuring seventeen previously unreleased recordings and air checks of *Grand Ole Opry* star Uncle Dave Macon.[18] Four recently discovered, pristine-condition 1930 test pressings, performances never issued and long thought vanished, prompted its publication. Even before the album, which received a Grammy nomination later that year, came out, word of its existence amounted to a major archeological discovery in the world of old-time music. These records consisted of sides that Uncle Dave and his accompanist, Sam McGee, recorded at the Edwards Hotel in Jackson, Mississippi, on December 17, 1930.

Only months earlier, educator David Ramsey Macon (1931–2016), a high school science and math teacher, as well as a founder of the Uncle Dave Macon Banjo Picking Contest, and his wife, librarian and genealogist Edna Shewcraft Macon (1928–2013), had come upon this hatbox of unreleased test pressings made by his grandfather.[19] Ramsey was the son of Uncle Dave's oldest child, Archie Macon, with whom this material had earlier resided. When Ramsey and Edna invited me to their home in the summer of 1979, they let me open this precious container they had kept dry and away from light on a closet shelf. My reverence for these dormant treasures that Uncle Dave had preserved, coupled with visits I made through the years with other Macon family members, friends, and colleagues evidently didn't escape their notice. On a tape-recorded cassette that Ramsey titled "Banjo Heritage," that he and Edna sent me two years later, he said:

> We certainly appreciate the fact that you carry on Uncle Dave's heritage. And we stop and think sometimes of how maybe that another fifty or more years from now, it'll be sort of the other way. Somebody will be learning the heritage from you, knowing that you came as direct as you could to learning from the source, and carrying on what we like to think of as "the banjo heritage."[20]

These words, and the trust they bequeath, surface now nearly a half century after they were first uttered. I join Ramsey and Edna Macon in the hope that the heritage they so intimately knew, like all the inheritances and inheritors named in these pages, that these sources might teach us still, refulgent in their vitality, their directness, and their light.

Acknowledgments

FOLKLORE AS BOTH a social reality and a scholarly pursuit repeatedly comes back to the personal. These acknowledgments accordingly begin with mentors who gave so freely, schooling me in the entwined realms of folklore lived and folklore contemplated.

These souls include Judith McCulloh, the longtime editor of the Music in American Life series at the University of Illinois Press. As a folklorist, Judy subscribed to what she and others before her called the "God's Truth" school of scholarship. Its converse she termed the "Hocus Pocus" school. There, one starts with a hypothesis and selects data that suits it. In the former model, however, life furnishes the plot, taking one wherever the evidence might lead. Judy applied that principle throughout her 1970 doctoral dissertation about "In the Pines," in which she documented 160 versions of that well-traveled song. Judy writes, "My feeling is that a person steeped in the tradition being studied can make valid subjective judgments about the identity of tunes." She trusted the folk as witnesses to their arts, without devaluing folklorists in their methods.

By that light, I thank first the performers, their families, and neighbors who fill these pages. Their presence, from bluesman David Edwards to music store proprietor Charlie Grano, from string band musicians Joe and Odell Thompson to storyteller Helen Marie Rowe, from my childhood guitar teacher Jim Schwall to old-time pianist Jewell Fagan Haynes, from Thaddeus Willingham's daughters, beginning with Jeana Willingham Dodge, to Will Keys and those who lovingly surrounded him, all of these persons and more give this book its substance. These people not only understood folklore and folksong, they embodied it.

Among the scholars, who no less thoughtfully threaded the fibers of folklore, and who abetted this effort that, in truth, began years ago, I gratefully name Archie Green, Dena Epstein, Alan Jabbour, Charles K. Wolfe, Bess Lomax Hawes, Alan Lomax, Norm Cohen, Dick Spottswood, Kip Lornell, Tony Russell, Doug Seroff, Carl S. Smith, Abbott Ferriss, Herbert Halpert, Ed Kahn, Douglas Wixson, and Chris Smith. Their names, and still more, appear in the book's endnotes. Lasting gratitude to them all.

Reference librarians repeatedly demonstrate what their colleague Gerry Parsons termed "a high coefficient of reality." Among those who brought that perspicacity to this undertaking are Alan Stoker of the Country Music Foundation (with thanks also to Paul Kingsbury); Matthew Barton, Curator of Recorded Sound at the Library of Congress, and Todd Harvey of the Library's Archive of Folk Culture; Steve Weiss and Aaron Smither of the Southern Folklife Collection, University of North Carolina–Chapel Hill; Lesley Martin at the Chicago History Museum; Greg Reish and the Center for Popular Music at Middle Tennessee State University; Allison Schein of the WFMT Studs Terkel Radio Archive; Anne L. Webster and the Mississippi Department of Archives and History; Greg Adams and Jeff Place at Smithsonian Folkways archives; Mark Davidson of the Woody Guthrie Center; staffers at the Bancroft Library, University of California, League of American Writers Archives; Christine Colburn of the University of Chicago, Hannah Holborn Gray Special Collections Research Center; Jennifer M. Jackson and Gretchen Neidhardt of the University Library at the University of Illinois, Chicago; Alison Hinderliter and Martha Briggs of the Modern Manuscripts and Archives, Newberry Library; Michael Gary Zeliff of the McKeldin Library, University of Maryland; and Tricia Greenstein of the George Washington University Library.

Friends who have contributed to this work in myriad ways include Barbara Ryan, Jack Beuthin, Andy Braunfeld, Leonard Rapport, Tom Mindte, Michael Doubler, Kevin Enoch, Mike Monseur, Todd Treadway, Jim Craig, Peggy Browning, Myron Gabbard, Raun MacKinnon Burnham, Craig Gill, John Cowley, Terika Dean, Don Huber, Clay Eals, Peter Jackson, Juel Ulven, Michael Roux, Matt Brown, Jay Bruder, Frantisek Frantik, Marc Nathan, Douglas Goodhart, Irwin Nash, Bob Sayers, Larry Maltz, Marina Bokelman, Paul Garon, Eddie Holstein, Jack Wright, Michael Melford, J. David Miller, Fred Ordower, Barb Kuhns, Doug Smith, and Donald and Spencer Nitchie.

Mariah Mendes Schaefer of the University of Illinois Press tirelessly guided this work into print, imbuing the entire process with joy and clarity. Doug Hood likewise brought his time-tested artistry to all the book's visual images with the photographic restorations that appear in these pages, extending anew the labors he made more than a decade earlier in *The Beautiful Music All Around Us*. Outside reviewers Erika Brady and Norm Cohen drew upon years of folklore study, personal insight, and immense stores of goodwill, to propel this book forward. Independent copy editor Allison Torres Burtka and the press's associate editor Megan Donnan readied the text, reference notes, and captions for publication.

Four individuals worked closest with this manuscript, and in thinking of them now, a fondly whimsical image comes to mind: Sam Gross's *New Yorker* cartoon of three people watching a housecat shredding their living room easy chair. The caption reads, "We believe that in a former life she was an editor." Here, Jean Murphy, equipped with equally sharp critical talons, contemplated every sentence in this book. I think of her as this book's closest companion, and my gratitude to her is boundless. At a wider rung, the historian and my longtime friend, Elliott Gorn, advised this project at its start, offering his thoughtful suggestions and authorial experience when these chapters first began to come. Folklorist David Evans then took this project home, bringing his knowledge and watchfulness to all its pages. David is an inheritor of the comparativist approach, and his preceptors, who include Wayland Hand, D. K. Wilgus, and Albert Lord, join the God's Truth school in searching songs, tunes, and tales—the items of folklore—within their living contexts. Finally, thank you to the past director of the University of Illinois Press and editor of the Music in American Life series, Laurie Matheson. She unfailingly lent her encouragement and counsel throughout this book's development. Laurie was Judy McCulloh's colleague at the press and served as her worthiest inheritor.

Always and ever, I dedicate with love *Our Common Life* to my wife, Michaelle LaFond Wade. This book's writing began early in the pandemic when we could barely venture outside our home, only to find that time of social distancing also brought familial closeness.

ABOUT THE COVER: Thomas Hart Benton's 1943 egg tempera on canvas, titled "The Music Lesson," portrays his neighbor, Gale Huntington, with his daughter, Emily. The elder Huntington played in Benton's band on Martha's Vineyard, in addition to working as a school teacher and a fisherman. He was also an author, singer, and prolific collector of whaling songs.

·1·

Our Common Life

When Saul Bellow recalled the Chicago neighborhood of his childhood, Humboldt Park of the mid-1920s, with its lodge halls and speakers' forums, he summoned up a pungent cultural scene: aging anarchists and garment-worker poets holding strong against the night, "Tolstoyan vegetarians, Swedenborgians, Single-taxers . . . health faddists, bulging physical culturists, dentists' wives who danced the Isadora Duncan style, and a considerable variety of self-taught and often cranky theoreticians . . . [where] peculiar autodidacts and philosophers in ragged trousers brooded and raged."[1] Nearby, at another outdoor plaza, one still known as Bughouse Square, Bellow observed regulars who included orator Facts-and-Figures Taylor. Equipped with a voice that apparently rivaled Paul Robeson's sonorities and the demeanor to match, he intoned what Bellow called "statistical recitals": "'And in nineteen-ought-four, Argentina exported in beef . . . now I'm goin' to tell you folks the figure in tons.'" Bellow then records the listeners' response, which equally echoing this revivalist fervor, called out, "'Go on now, Facts-and-Figures, you tell 'em.'"

In Bellow's evocation of Facts-and-Figures Taylor, as with the diapason of characters who peopled Humboldt Park, he took from their mottled roar a realization: "This common life, our life, our very common selves, astonishingly enough contained important meanings, that we belonged to that same human species which had supplied Sophocles with his Oedipus, Shakespeare with his Lear."[2] His appreciation for the humanity evident in his Bruegelesque tableau of sidewalk artistry gives this book its title and forecasts its subject matter.

The word *common,* as Bellow uses it, shows up in words like *commonality* and *commoner, commonweal,* and *common sense.* Its earliest usage denotes a social bond, of being "together under obligation."[3] This meaning survives in our current understanding of *community,* as well as in *the commons,* which encompass shared natural resources from the sky overhead to the oceans we traverse. The idea of the commons also arises in cultural inheritances, such as the gifts bequeathed to us in folklore, itself a creative property held in public trust.[4] Yet *common* also reflects, Janus-like, a contrary sense, denoting the lowly and the vulgar. Not surprisingly, the last of these social attitudes connects, as cultural historian Raymond Williams has found, to "*vulgus,* the common people."[5] This word and its associations, like folklore, carry meanings both positive and pejorative.

Certainly, affirmation greeted those local types who appeared on *The Tonight Show* during Johnny Carson's tenure. They sat between sidekick Ed McMahon, who squared off on one side, and Johnny, who bordered them on the other, from behind his desk. These individuals, while known among their neighbors, were none of them professional celebrities. More often than not, they charmed their hosts during the interview by steadfastly remaining themselves. No guest chair, however, could confine folk artist and musician Howard Finster of Pennville, Georgia, as he sang an *a cappella* number he wrote for his grandchildren and their friends. At one point during the piece, this former Baptist minister, whose outsider art has reached collectors across the nation, pictures this younger generation intently watching him: "I thought I heard them say, 'Did you come from space?'" Then he played the banjo, performing in a solidly traditional North Georgia two-finger style, another of his compositions, a paean to family titled, "Just a Little Tack in the Shingle of Your Roof."[6] To the delight of all, Johnny Carson included, and with camera glare and mass audience notwithstanding, Howard Finster brought to late-night America home truths and personal gumption.

More recently, a similar feeling of local unity emerged when the Democratic Party chose to name its 2020 presidential nominee. Due to COVID-19 restrictions that downsized the customary quadrennial convention hall gathering, the event announced its tallied votes from points throughout the United States and its territories. Like roadside postcards one might send home from a long trip, the delegates' roll call brought attention to their respective locales in the regional accents in which they spoke, settings where they stood, and sometimes in the garb they wore. In the case of Rhode Island, they did all that, plus extolled the virtues of its calamari appetizer.

In like spirit, the common life that Saul Bellow identified calls attention to vernacular creativity. By the seventeenth century, *vernacular* was tied to locale and came "to express the rootedness of a given cultural expression within a particular nation, region, or province."[7] The word stems from *verna*, a Latin name for a home-born slave, and broadened to describe colloquial speech, unschooled literature, self-taught art, idiomatic architecture, local landscapes, and grassroots music. Its connection to someone of low estate—the bondsman, the native, the disinherited—runs through these forms, sustaining their core sense of the nonstandard and the unofficial. As these usages have expanded, so, too, has this voice resounded in ever-widening arcs from the cries of the watermelon seller to the chants of children at play, from the bell of the scissors grinder to the fanciful code of the hash-house waiter yelling orders into the kitchen, "Gimme a half-smoke and put a suit on it."[8] Vernacular artistry, spanning frontier boast and street corner rap, enriches everyday existence in often uncommon ways, yet ineluctably remains a product of the common life.

While not everything deemed vernacular is inherently traditional—the Sunday funnies, the Manhattan skyline, the T-Model Ford, chewing gum—nothing keeps these materials from entering tradition, a concept understood here as knowledge handed down informally that communities appropriate. Throughout this process, sundry forms of cultural expression, even those most fanciful and innovative, fit within familiar patterns. They become incorporated into what Constance Rourke calls the "large common storage of experience and character."[9] By the time five-string banjoist Earl Scruggs began recording with Bill Monroe in September 1946, he had evolved a playing method for his instrument so compelling that it inspired others to learn and vary it for themselves. What began as his approach, based on earlier models and elaborated according to his talents, became canonized. His distinctive system, transmitted on radio, recordings, and by live performance, became known as "Scruggs-style." It yielded a new folk tradition that has reached countless emulators, players with proficiencies reaching from the front porch to the concert hall.

A definition proffered over seventy years ago by Pennsylvania musicologist and collector Samuel P. Bayard obtains in Scruggs's case as it applies to so many more: "The primary materials of folklore must be certain categories of creative ideas which have become traditional among the people of any society and which may be recognized as their common property."[10] Neighborhood codes, ethnic customs, shop floor knowledge, homespun patterns, and handicraft skills variously reflect folk solutions that informal musicians likewise incorporate into their songs and styles.[11] Just as Earl Scruggs achieved a creative compromise of the inherited and the invented in his playing, early country music prior to World War II can be described as "a commercialized form of folk music," folklorist Bill Ivey explained during his tenure as director of the Country Music Foundation. "The degree of 'traditionality' or 'commercialization,'" he continued, "in any one performance varies."[12] This fluid proportion, he added, similarly occurs in blues and jazz, popular idioms also varyingly drawing from folk precedents.

In 1996, I worked as a performer and presenter at an outdoor festival that afforded an unexpected opportunity to contrast vernacular culture with traditional folklore. The event, a cultural component of the 1996 Summer Olympics, was principally sponsored by the Smithsonian Institution and called *Southern Crossroads: A Festival of the American South.*[13] Held at Atlanta's Centennial Park, it presented over 130 ensembles and soloists in seventeen days beginning that July. Its musical roster ran from gospel to blues, rockabilly to jazz, Native American to Cajun, hip hop to brass band, jump rope to line dancing, bluegrass to reggae. During a single afternoon, one could enjoy a virtuoso, Cuban-born trombonist from Miami or an anvil-playing blacksmith from Spruce Pine, North Carolina. Then, you could see Rufus Thomas, creator of the "Funky Chicken," garbed in a phosphorescently glowing matched leisure suit and shorts, charming everyone within sight of the stage. His song-and-dance performance took place in an area ringed with replica General Motors cars suspended overhead on moving cantilevers that created an intermittently jiggling automobile ballet as the music played. Amidst a barrage of similarly clamorous displays stationed around Centennial Park, *Southern Crossroads* lived out its purpose to "provide a complex portrait of the cultural landscape."[14] Program director George Holt added in a letter to the stage presenters, tasked with introducing the performers:

> It's my own view, though, that we shouldn't focus exclusively on the heterogeneity of the region's makeup. We also need to explain, as best we can, that southern culture has a unifying aspect, the result of the sometimes extraordinary assimilation of Anglo/European, African, and Native cultural streams through many generations.

Another evening, I stood, along with thousands of others, listening to Ray Charles, this vernacular artist of global repute, sing "Georgia" with aching beauty. Meanwhile, only a few feet away stood a makeshift folk memorial to the pipe bombing victims of the week before. Over those days, I also observed a ritual behavior, certainly less solemn but no less communal and customary than that assemblage for the slain. The *Southern Crossroads* program included not only studio accompanists who had appeared on Elvis Presley's earliest recordings for the Sun record label, but also two Elvis impersonators, each performing on successive weeks. Certainly, they, too, lay claim to Southern culture, in both the music they performed and the musician they honored, let alone the phenomenon they embodied. Anyone who has attended an afternoon of local Elvis imitators will encounter an array of interpretations, a procession of body types, hairstyles, and homemade costumes that defy standardization, despite their single focus. A similar balance of the commercial and the communal arose at the Olympics.

Here in Atlanta, following an excerpt from *Also sprach Zarathustra* as its fanfare, the performer I introduced began with a few of the karate kicks and angular hand gestures that Elvis famously employed.[15] By then, from the first notes of the soundtrack, and before he began singing "See See Rider," the Atlanta audience knew their role. They crowded close to the stage, participating in a collective act of imagination. Central to Elvis's shows was the physical bond he had with his fans, in which kissing, handshaking, and hugging repeatedly took place. By 1970, he had begun conferring silk scarves on them too, sometimes tossing these items into the audience, but sometimes sliding them from his neck and individually conferring them on recipients. Video clips show that he would occasionally touch his perspiring face with the diaphanous fabric, apart from whatever moisture it might absorb from being on his person.

The same contact happened in Atlanta. Throughout the show, the performer interacted with those listeners nearest him all the while singing to the audience. Admittedly, a moment of opéra bouffe transpired when the scarf supply ran out, and with an offstage glare that would burn a hole in a saddle blanket, Atlanta's Elvis indicated the immediate need for more linen. This sent me scurrying to the backstage trailer, where the only textiles in sight amounted to an armful of face towels. Due to the performer's grace and the audience's willingness, this improvisation met the show's needs that day. Afterward, my co-presenter, Choctaw artist Gary White Deer of Ada, Oklahoma, summed up this ceremonial transfer of perspiration with its implicit fertility rites that we had just witnessed as "Elvis as Harvest King." Here, the figure perhaps most emblematic of popular culture at the *Southern Crossroads* festival summoned the most ancient of theatrical rituals at the Olympics, itself of ancestral origin. On the concrete demesne of Centennial Park, amid flashing displays for Coca-Cola, Budweiser, and Nike, with police helicopters cruising overhead and snipers stationed at the overlooking buildings, vernacular artistry and folk tradition held their own.

These Atlanta experiences demonstrate the larger reality: folkways are all around us, no matter one's social standing or professional attainment. Families, ethnicities, occupations, religions, and regions all generate informal, customary expression in countless signs, symbols, and images. Contemporary trial lawyers, for instance, have evolved on-the-job strategies about jury selection and admit to verbally crafting their closing summations attuned to their sense of their impaneled listeners, rather than solely reciting the legalistic discourse girding their arguments.

How different are these courthouse rhetoricians from "sand hogs," those 1930s tunnel builders who built the passageways beneath the East River, while making up site-specific initiation pranks for recently hired greenhorns?[16] Every group, to the extent they make themselves available to it, Elvis imitators included, participates in this expressive dimension. From hand skills to verbal yarns, proverbs to playing styles, folklore occurs, "patterned by common experience; varied by individual repetition."[17] From craft apprenticeship to personal savvy, schoolyard games to old-world jests recast in an industrial age, these perceptions form, in Bayard's words, "a fund of folk ideas," storehouses of customs, knowledge, and attitudes that remain fluid, renewing, borrowing, dropping some items while incorporating others.[18]

Folklore, however, is not always charming and beguiling. While it carries for many intrinsic value as a cultural treasure, it also freights negative meanings, and like the shame attached to *common*, it signifies the narrowly provincial, the naïve, the false, and the misinformed. On a still darker level, it has served doctrines such as *Herrenvolk*, whose master race adherents wrap themselves in folkloristic notions of ancestral nationhood. ("Jews will not replace us," chanted the torch-bearing marchers in Charlottesville in 2017.) Yet these morally repugnant interpretations also reveal the essential nature of folklore's transmission. In all these instances, both benign and malignant, writes Benjamin Botkin, folklore is "a species of living literature which has no fixed form . . . and which is constantly shifting back and forth between written and unwritten tradition."[19]

An item, once in folk use, can assume myriad shapes. At Centennial Park, a Hank Williams honky-tonk tune became reworked into a Cajun standard, while B. B. King's hit "The Thrill Is Gone" gained new meanings when an electric blues band of Native Americans garbed in full ceremonial dress played it during their sets. Such combinations never cease. I can't help but think of an analogy to Southern music that historian Charles Wolfe drew from *Huckleberry Finn*. It appears early in the novel, in the book's third paragraph, when Huck sits down to eat with Widow Douglas.

Here, the book's hero looks down at his plate of "victuals" and observes, " . . . there warn't really anything the matter with them—that is, nothing only everything was cooked by itself. In a barrel of odds and ends it is different; things get mixed up, and the juice kind of swaps around, and the things go better."[20] Huck's appraisal speaks to more than the intercultural stew that produced the folk and folk-based musical forms that filled the 1996 Olympics Arts Festival in Atlanta. His admixture poses an alternative to present-day divides in which we face a resurgence of ethnonationalism and blood-and-soil populism.

In 1892, a few years before Saul Bellow first heard the soapboxers at Bughouse Square, his fellow Chicagoan, reformer Jane Addams, spoke at the School of Applied Ethics in Plymouth, Massachusetts. She made these remarks just three years after she and Ellen Gates Starr had founded Hull-House, the nation's pioneering social settlement. In her talk, she grappled with how young people "long to give tangible expression to the democratic ideal." She continued:

> These hopes may be loosely formulated thus: that if in a democratic country nothing can be permanently achieved save through the masses of the people, it will be impossible to establish a higher political life than the people themselves crave; that it is difficult to see how the notion of a higher civic life can be fostered save through common intercourse . . . that the good we secure for ourselves is precarious and uncertain, is floating in mid-air, until it is secured for all of us and incorporated into our common life.[21]

In speaking of the common life, Addams proposed a civic vision that depended on the participation of its citizenry. At Hull-House, a receiving point for thousands of immigrants, she repeatedly faced questions about assimilation and pluralism.[22] No closer illustration of these currents arises than the words of Hilda Satt Polacheck (1882–1967), a self-described "Hull-House girl." A Jewish, Polish-born immigrant, Hilda came to the United States, specifically Chicago, in 1892. She lived three blocks from Hull-House with her recently widowed mother, who was consigned to sell groceries

FIGURE 4. A young Hilda Satt Polacheck at Hull-House, Chicago, Illinois, ca. 1895. Hilda Satt Polacheck papers, Special Collections and University Archives, University of Illinois at Chicago.

door to door while Hilda and her sisters sewed cuffs ten hours a day in a shirtwaist factory. At age thirteen she attended a Christmas party at the settlement house with an Irish playmate. She approached the event with trepidation because in Poland, it had not been safe for a Jewish child to be on the streets at Christmas. Hilda described the prospects of going to such an event now:

> So when I was told that I could go to a Christmas party at Hull-House, I instinctively shrunk at the very thought. I told my little Catholic friend that I never go to Christmas parties. "Why not?" she asked . . . I told her I might get killed. "Get killed!" She stared at me. "I went to the Hull-House Christmas party last year, and the year before, and no one was killed."[23]

Without telling her mother beforehand, Hilda went to the party. Her memoir describes the candles on the Christmas trees, the singing of carols. She continues:

> After the singing, Jane Addams told us how glad she was that we had all come to her party. The sincerity of her words shone in her eyes. I knew that she meant every word she was saying.
>
> I became an American at this party. I was with children who had been brought to America from all corners of the earth. The fathers and mothers of all of us had come in search of a free and happy life. And we were having a good time at a party.
>
> We were all poor. Most of us were underfed. Some of us had torn shoes. But we were not afraid of each other.

Hilda's experience contrasts with a set of values, equally emblematic, that ensued at the Virginia Folklore Society. Since its founding in April 1913, the society, one of the nation's earliest such organizations, acted on the belief that a time-honored artistry singularly dwelt in British and Scottish antiquities identified in Francis James Child's multi-volume collection completed in 1898. The premise for their ballad quest soon went nationwide. In January 1914, P. P. Claxton, the U.S. Commissioner of the Bureau of Education, sent out a ballad-hunting bulletin to some 30,000 teachers, encouraging them to gather from their students those works that had helped mold "the character of men and women who made up the larger part of the Colonial population of this country."[24] In the same document, Virginia Folklore Society founder C. Alphonso Smith added historical context and a list of titles, enthusiastically reminding collectors "that two versions of the same ballad are almost as valuable as two different ballads."[25] Shortly afterwards a similar request went out to members of Virginia's State Teachers' Association, again with Smith's argument for the collecting to proceed with haste. "It is now or never," he warned:

> Many influences are tending to obliterate them. Catchy, but empty, songs not worthy of comparison with them, the decadence of communal singing, the growing diversity of interests, the appeal to what is divisive and separative in our national life, the presence of the artificial and self-conscious in modern writing.[26]

Within a month of the circular's initial release, *The Nation* took this ballad rescue message positively:

> It ought to lend an impulse to the collection of Servian, Polish, Czech and a score of other national folk-songs, of which recent immigration must have brought great store. Finally, it should add interest to a new movement, already of strength—that for the collection of American made ballads of folk-origin, like the cowboy songs, on American themes.[27]

As for embracing the folksongs of America's recent arrivals in a time when nativist sentiments and melting pot anxieties figured high in the national life, *The Nation* liberally favored inclusion.

The Child ballad collection endeavor continued into the following year, with *Harper's Monthly Magazine* focusing again on Alphonso Smith's plea. After noting the original circular, the writer quotes Hubert Shearin, a folk-song collector from Kentucky, who added his urgency to Smith's prediction of Anglo balladry extinction:

> In another generation or two, they [ballads] will be but a memory in the Kentucky highlands; the clank of the colliery, the rattle of the locomotive, the roar of the blast-furnace, the shriek of the factory whistle, and, alas, even the music of the school-bell, are already overwhelming the thin tone of the dulcimer and the quavering voice of the Last Minstrel of the Cumberlands, who can find scant heart to sing again the lays of older years across the seas.[28]

Machine-age changes to the countryside and the rising volume of these new technologies notwithstanding, Smith himself wrote in 1916 that balladry in America had not entirely become a "lost art."[29] His passion for recovering Child ballads in living practice, while undiminished, focused on their transmission. He ventured that present-day Black camp meeting songs might reveal the compositional method of the Child ballads.[30] He also noted the work of collectors Phillips Barry in the Northeast, John Lomax in Texas, Hubert Shearin in Kentucky, and Henry M. Belden of Missouri, who, in 1912, pointed to recently composed outlaw ballads such as "Jesse James," and the assassination songs that arose after President Garfield's killing, as proof of a continuing folk creativity.[31]

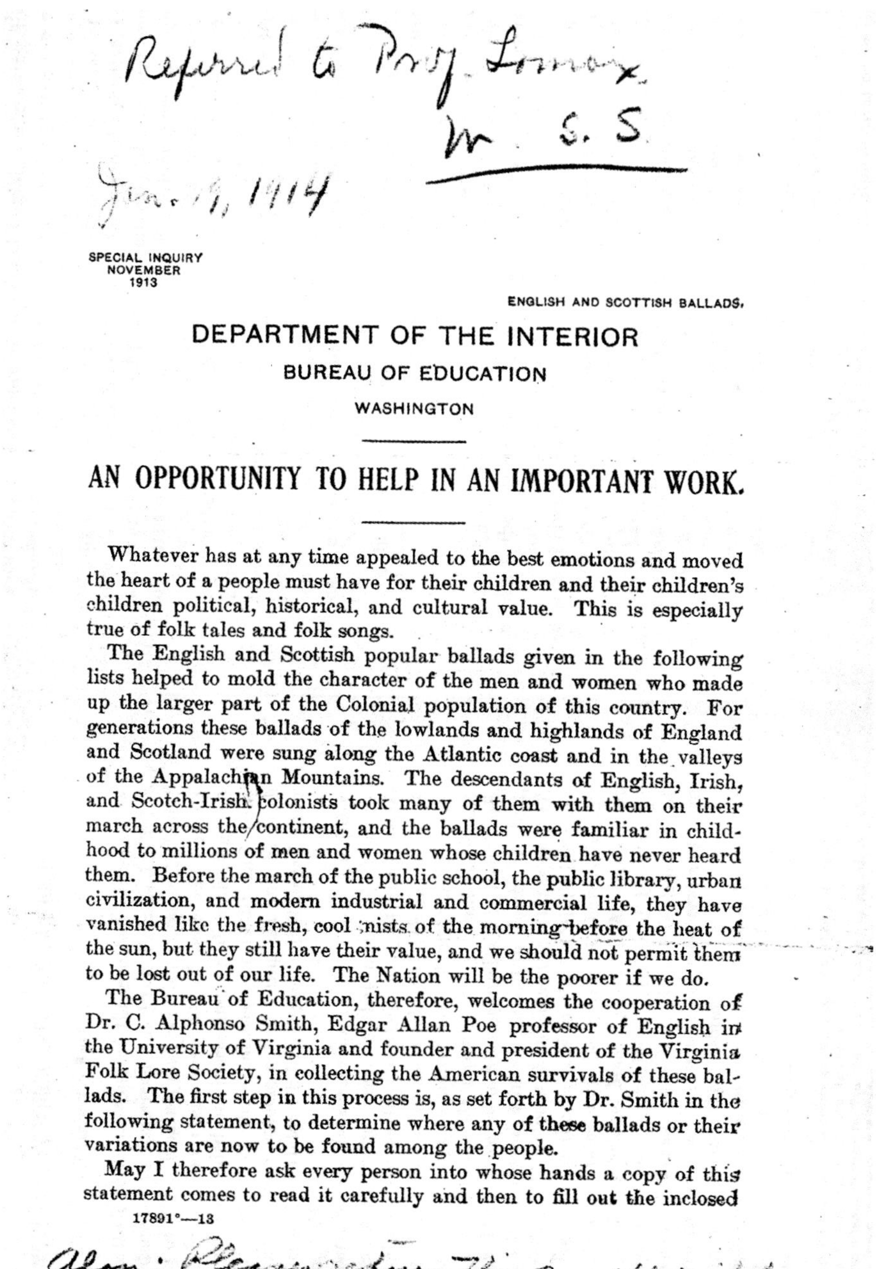
Referred to Prof. Lomax.
W. S. S.

SPECIAL INQUIRY
NOVEMBER
1913

ENGLISH AND SCOTTISH BALLADS.

DEPARTMENT OF THE INTERIOR

BUREAU OF EDUCATION

WASHINGTON

AN OPPORTUNITY TO HELP IN AN IMPORTANT WORK.

Whatever has at any time appealed to the best emotions and moved the heart of a people must have for their children and their children's children political, historical, and cultural value. This is especially true of folk tales and folk songs.

The English and Scottish popular ballads given in the following lists helped to mold the character of the men and women who made up the larger part of the Colonial population of this country. For generations these ballads of the lowlands and highlands of England and Scotland were sung along the Atlantic coast and in the valleys of the Appalachian Mountains. The descendants of English, Irish, and Scotch-Irish colonists took many of them with them on their march across the continent, and the ballads were familiar in childhood to millions of men and women whose children have never heard them. Before the march of the public school, the public library, urban civilization, and modern industrial and commercial life, they have vanished like the fresh, cool mists of the morning before the heat of the sun, but they still have their value, and we should not permit them to be lost out of our life. The Nation will be the poorer if we do.

The Bureau of Education, therefore, welcomes the cooperation of Dr. C. Alphonso Smith, Edgar Allan Poe professor of English in the University of Virginia and founder and president of the Virginia Folk Lore Society, in collecting the American survivals of these ballads. The first step in this process is, as set forth by Dr. Smith in the following statement, to determine where any of these ballads or their variations are now to be found among the people.

May I therefore ask every person into whose hands a copy of this statement comes to read it carefully and then to fill out the inclosed

17891°—13

FIGURE 5. 1913 Virginia ballad circular with John A. Lomax's handwritten margin note to Alan Lomax.

By 1929, the Virginia Folklore Society had achieved its goal of locating Child ballads sung in every county throughout the state. In the ensuing volume titled *Traditional Ballads of Virginia,* the Society's Archivist-Secretary, Arthur Kyle Davis Jr., raised the "patriotic" question of what identifies a folksong as American. He rejected:

> . . . the tribal and ceremonial songs of the Red Indian, which are American in no sense except the geographical, or the folk-songs of the Negro, which, beautiful as they often are, are obviously the heritage of the "Homo Africanus" transplanted in America, not the possession of our white majority.[32]

Instead, he asserted that "the American stock is European in origin." He elaborated that the "patriotic preference for one hundred per cent American ballads," rather than those that came to America from Europe, "is based on ignorance of the nature of folk-song, perhaps also on ignorance of the true meaning of Americanism, as well as upon an indifference to artistic standards."[33] American balladry was shaped by "long adoption, by adaptation, sometimes by almost complete re-creation."[34] Davis developed his judgments in an undated essay, handwritten in pencil, found among his papers. In this conclusion, he was more liberal in his approach:

> At any rate, America may be proud to have nurtured within its boundaries three such lusty folk of song: the Anglo-Saxon, whose contribution is the authentic racial inheritance of a plurality of Americans; the Negro, whose songs half African, half American are the authentic expression of the black minority of America; and the autochthonous Indian whose songs belong to the American soil.
>
> The collecting of these traditional ballads and folk songs then, far from being an attempt to emphasize the Western European caste of American civilization, is a patriotic duty and an artistic obligation of the highest sort.[35]

Members of the society had also, by 1929, recognized that their state possessed more than just Child ballads thriving in oral tradition. Five years before the publication of *Traditional Ballads,* the society's membership charged Davis with a new direction: to gather "all the songs of the people traditionally known and varied, especially those of American origin and adaptation."[36] Davis embraced this "polyhedral character of folksong."[37] By

1949, *Folk-Songs of Virginia* contained a checklist of 974 songs with 2,454 variants. Davis had cataloged both this enlarged repertory and named folksingers within the state whose renditions formed the collection.

The quest for ballads that Virginia's collectors pursued so passionately more than a century ago anticipates cultural currents of the present day. Then and now, advocates assert what best represents the nation's voice. "Appalachian music conjures up simpler and time-honored notions of purity and ancient moorings," country music historian Bill Malone has observed, "appealing to those who envision a culture unspoiled by urban conceits and machine technology."[38] He recognizes the sustaining appeal of that romance, "real or imagined."[39] However, this romantic view, he explains, obscures the multiplicity of sources that created mountain music. Hilda Polacheck's experience, in contrast with the Anglo-American emphasis that initially guided Virginia's tireless ballad hunters (one of whom suggested a bandaged foot as their symbol in those years, for all the walking and attendant bruises they endured in their quest). Instead, she evokes a composite and pluralistic view of society.

Folklorist Archie Green, discussed in chapter five, implicitly extended this idea when he told me, "The vernacular is the cultural face of pluralism."[40] Archie's connection of democracy with grassroots creativity formed a linkage he tirelessly pursued in his work, one that he also envisioned for this book. His efforts, particularly during his Washington-based lobbying on behalf of American folklife—much like Jane Addams when she spoke of "our common life"—attested to the close relationship of culture and cultural policy. For seven years, he and like-minded cohorts contacted some 435 congressional offices representing the fifty states, conducting tutorials with staffers and legislators alike, introducing them to the folklore of their constituents back home. As Archie cautioned during a 1974 Senate hearing when called on to speak extemporaneously, "We must tune our ears to the understated voice."[41] He emphasized the imperative: "to reach out to very ordinary people doing ordinary things at a quiet level—the Tarheel banjo picker, the rodeo rider." He beseeched the gathered lawmakers to consider legislation creating a national center to preserve and present American folklife "in terms of your commitment to the American scene."

Later, reflecting on that hearing, Archie noted how most legislators sympathetic to the bill took "a common-sense view of the folk as members of enclaved groups, retaining special traditions, expressing special styles."[42] In time, Archie's arguments prevailed, with support from congressional aides, professional colleagues, fellow advocates, and voting members of the House and Senate themselves. Their ardency resulted in the passage of Public Law 94-201, the American Folklife Preservation Act.

This 1976 legislation, signed by President Ford at the start of the nation's Bicentennial year, established the American Folklife Center in the Library of Congress. By then, the Ethnic Heritage Studies Act of 1972, a multi-million-dollar education bill, had already passed into law. Like the Folklife Act, its advocates sought what they termed "a new pluralism in America."[43] The ethnic studies bill supported elementary and secondary school programs that addressed the multiple heritages of students in their home communities. The language its sponsors used, specifically the historical and metaphorical references they cited, corresponded with those invoked by the folklife proponents. Repeatedly, witnesses and congressional representatives alike contrasted assimilation with pluralism, pivoting between the melting pot metaphor they largely scorned to the patchwork quilt they favored. Or, as Archie noted concerning whatever was congealing in the cultural melting pot, he still treasured "its discarded slag."[44] Advocates for both bills connected the nation's many-peopled milieu with its democratic vision. "Our American civilization," said Congressman Thomas Downey of New York, "signed up all kinds for its ranks."[45]

Opponents included those who found unity in assimilation, envisioning only social fracture and division under multicultural strategies. During one 1974 debate in the House of Representatives, Iowa Congressman Harold Royce Gross felt that the bill, beyond its cost to taxpayers and what he considered its essentially frivolous subject matter, worked against national purpose. Gross cited Theodore Roosevelt, who said that "there is no room in this country for hyphenated Americans [who would leave] a tangle of squalling nationalities."[46] Elsewhere, Roosevelt balefully warned during a period that witnessed intensive European emigration to the United States, of the country becoming "a polyglot boarding-house."[47]

Fifty years later, this unitary view of America's common life helped fuel the 2024 election of Donald Trump. Often, during campaign rallies, Trump's supporters reacted to his podium fusillades as platform entertainment, while he invoked darker currents of shared discontent. "He's got to say what people want to hear," remarked Chuck Mills, a towing operator and auto repair service owner in Whitewater, Wisconsin, "so that they'll vote for him."[48] During a probing radio essay that aired on election day, Mills admitted how his earlier fears that his town might become "a sanctuary city" had shifted. He had moved from formerly screaming imprecations at recent arrivals from Central America to respectfully embracing those same immigrants. He came to recognize them as persons reaching for similar goals that he held, with a committed work ethic and fealty to family. He realized that they had enriched the Whitewater community with their presence. All the while, he remained committed to Donald Trump, promising him his vote, the candidate's avowed deportation programs notwithstanding. Florida Senator Marco Rubio's post-election commentary explained this duality that attracted recent Hispanic support for Trump as it did long-settled citizens: "He appealed to Americans, as Americans, irrespective of your background, or your customs or the music you listen to or how your last name is pronounced."[49] According to Rubio, sublimating those qualities translated into patriotism. "For voters in the United States of America," he continued, "their primary identity is not their ethnicity, it's not their race. It's what they do for a living, it's who they are in their daily lives."

Yet a resolution of this perennially repeated antinomy lies within reach. During the years that Congress debated the Ethnic Studies and Folklife Center bills, and the American public continued to navigate its way through competing ideas about identity, writer Ralph Ellison grappled with the melting pot imagery, but from another perspective than those of temperament similar to his own might have anticipated:

> Today that [melting pot] metaphor is noisily rejected, vehemently disavowed. In fact, it has come under attack in the name of the newly fashionable code word "ethnicity." . . . So today, before the glaring inequities, unfulfilled promises, and rich possibilities of democracy, we hear heady evocations of European, African, and Asian backgrounds accompanied by chants proclaiming the inviolability of ancestral blood. Today blood magic

> and blood thinking, never really dormant in American society, are rampant among us, often leading to brutal racial assaults in areas these seldom occurred before. And while this goes on, the challenge of arriving at an adequate definition of American cultural identity goes unanswered.[50]

Ellison was a liberal pluralist who found that Americans continually absorbed and integrated diverse elements using what he considered their "most characteristic style . . . the vernacular."[51] No one group, he contended, possesses the whole of the nation's culture. "Indeed," he wrote, "it was through the process of cultural appropriation (and misappropriation) that Englishmen, Europeans, Africans and Asians *became* Americans.[52] From these transfers and possibilities comes "One of the most precious of American freedoms . . . our freedom to broaden our personal culture by absorbing the cultures of others."[53] Individuals drawing from this ceaselessly mobile, variegated pool of traditions and precedents exercise their personality and, in doing so, make their experience available to others.[54] Ellison, ardent in his conviction to separate matters of race from matters of culture, credited this awareness to Hazel Harrison, the renowned head of the piano department at Tuskegee during his college years. At that time, before he turned to literature, he entertained hopes of playing classical trumpet as his profession. Recalling discussions they had in her studio at school, Ellison reconstructed her advice to him:

> Look, baby, the society beyond this campus is constantly trying to confuse as to the relationship between culture and race. Well, if you ask me, artistic talent might have something to do with race, but you do *not* inherit culture and artistic skill through your genes. No, sir. These come as a result of personal conquest, of the individual's applying himself to that art, that music—whether jazz, classical or folk—which helps him to realize and complete himself. And that's true *wherever* the music or art of his choice originates.[55]

In folklore, and its expression in folk music, philosophical clashes over background and birthright still play out against cultural sharing and acceptance. Yet history shows that segregation never really keeps musicians apart. They learn from one another, no matter the prohibitions around them. By its very nature, tradition depends on renewal and chooses its sources where it may. Ralph Ellison's sense of personal agency, Hilda Polacheck's story of

becoming an American, the Virginia Folklore Society's embrace of a polyhedral heritage, the Atlanta Olympics wanting its presenters to publicly express how individual uniqueness and regional unities marked the artists they were assigned to introduce, and the demotic ideal instilling the folklife bill, emblematically speak for the individuals and ideas that occupy this book. In the following chapters, we see people laboring under compulsion as they hoist cumbrously weighted cotton bales onto riverboat steamers and singing to survive as much as to amuse themselves. Others seek out and even pester the senior musicians they most admire, each of them living up to Hazel Harrison's admonition to apply themselves in their art.

In doing so, they fulfill the vision Saul Bellow found among the denizens of his Chicago neighborhood. There he discovered a sacredness borne within those souls who crowded the city's sidewalks. Bellow's recognition of his neighbors' inherent worth fits with Ellison's *Invisible Man* who, in the last words of the novel, asks, "Who knows, but that, on the lower frequencies, I speak for you?"[56] Collectively, these voices tell us that in the artistries of daily life dwells an unruly splendor. For all who make the time to listen, this vernacular dimension, palpable and pungent, offers a way of understanding the world while fulfilling a portion of this nation's democratic promise.

• • •

This book repeatedly pivots from the historically shared to the personally crafted. Here I recall an experience of my own, one that, I hope, brings together the public and the private in keeping with those who fill the pages that follow.

In January 1987, at Chicago's Orchestra Hall, I performed a piece about my childhood that I had written for that occasion. Essentially a string of

FIGURES 6 AND 7. (*facing*) In October 1935, on assignment for the Farm Security Administration, Ben Shahn took this photograph of the Musgrove brothers in Westmoreland County, Pennsylvania. Five years later, Shahn painted the scene, naming his work "Pretty Girl Milking the Cow" after a traditional Irish song the brothers had played. The music traveled from the roadside to the art gallery.[57]

Ben Shahn, *Pretty Girl Milking the Cow*, 1940.

anecdotes eight and a half minutes long, it began with my playing the opening notes of the song "Chicago (That Toddlin' Town)" on the five-string banjo, a melody easily recognizable to the 2,500 persons gathered in this august setting, assembled to support the Old Town School of Folk Music's building fund.[58]

My story, *Chicago,* tells how my friends and I rode the elevated train around the Loop, responding to its whoosh and roll, jumping between cars, and leaning into the screeching curves. It describes how we made a giant snowball that filled the width of a nearby side street and then cheered as a big green moving van merrily smashed through it. The audience that night recognized a downtown department store I also mentioned, and whose floors variously mirrored the stages of our lives: initially, we sought out its fourth-floor toys; then, over time, perused its third-floor books; then, older still, patronized its seventh-floor restaurants.

However, this audience's greatest reaction came in response to a telephone number that apparently none of us had forgotten. It belonged to Boushelle Carpet Cleaners, a local firm founded in 1903. Cast in a three-second jingle, the number consisted of "HUdson 3-2700," an announcement sung in the deepest *basso-profundo* voice imaginable. It appeared at the tail end of the company's commercials, and for decades beginning in the post-war era, it played over Chicago's airwaves and on its television screens.

Boushelle's longtime owner, Cecil Treadway, later told me that the jingle was likely written by its singer, Val Sherman, for a one-time payment of $62.00. It first aired on radio in 1948, soon followed by a preliminary series of 20-second TV spots that showed the factory, its rug cleaning equipment, and its delivery service. With these ads positioned during showings of *I Remember Mama* as well as Arthur Godfrey's several variety shows, it emerged during a time when entire families still gathered around the TV, the refrain forming a tiny part of the domestic soundscape.

By the early 1970s, the telephone company wanted to drop all alphabet-driven exchanges such as "HUdson 3" from the Yellow Pages and just display numbers. However, "the digits didn't work," Treadway noted. "Everyone knew that phone number more than any other market in the country."[59] So no matter how it came to appear in print listings, the jingle did not change throughout its broadcasts.

That night at Orchestra Hall, after mentioning the rug cleaner's name, I began singing it, and without any prompting from me, the entire crowd joined in. They *knew* this jingle. In that soaring moment, the listeners recast this advertisement into a tiny piece of public art, made it their own, fusing community with creativity. A local trademark, imprinted in all our minds, translated into a piece of the city's folk experience and brought us together in a resounding testimonial, to a history both evergreen and alive. With an aged five-string banjo serving as its soundtrack, our common life had reached from the front porch to the concert hall.

·2·

Catching the Music

Music has to be caught.

In July 1866, Long Island genre painter William Sidney Mount (1807–1868) began one of his final canvases. Titled *Catching the Tune*, the completed 22-by-27-inch oil painting shows a whistler, his lips pursed, passing along a melody to a raptly listening fiddler. The whistler's fingers bear the delicacy of someone reading braille. They tap the musician's leg while his other hand motions like a conductor, signaling a peak moment in the score. Meanwhile, the fiddler looks off into the distance, his left hand poised on the fingerboard, finding the notes he will soon play. Three other people, two women and one man, stay close by, the youngest of them, possibly the fiddler's daughter, touching his shoulder. Their reposeful eyes and expectant postures suggest the confidence they place in him and the interest they hold for what may soon emerge from his instrument.

Twenty-six years earlier, in an 1840 letter, Mount's older brother, Robert, then a traveling dance master and music instructor in Georgia, had suggested that his artistic sibling depict this tableau, one so common that he termed it "hacknied" yet still worth the effort to render: "I saw recently a

FIGURE 8. William Sidney Mount, *Catching the Tune*, 1866, oil on canvas, 21 3/4" H x 26 5/8" W (unframed). The Long Island Museum Collection.

scene which I think would make a good Picture. One was whistling a tune, and the other was sitting in a listening attitude with violin in hand ready to commence playing when his crony had finished his part."[1] A year later, the two communicated about a tune called "Possum Up a Gum-Tree."[2] This well-known piece had figured in Black folk use as well as on the popular stage. It even served as the finale in the 1824 ballad opera *The Saw Mill or, A Yankee Trick*, composed by Mount's maternal uncle, Micah Hawkins. Mount's diary reveals that the day he began work on the painting, these memories had remained steadfast through the years, as he wrote: "Catching a tune, 'Possum up a gum tree.'"[3]

The painting evokes a familiar transaction in Mount's life. He also includes a fiddle of his own design. For years, Mount performed at country dances, and his writings show his yearning for better self-amplification that he believed this instrument, which he patented in 1852, would provide. Like others in his family, he played the fiddle (as well as flute), hand notating some 500 pieces in his manuscript books, many of them taken from oral tradition. Yet *Catching the Tune*'s theme of learning by ear does more than reflect Mount's own experience. Whether acquired in person or by proxy, in written form or through recorded sound, "catching" is a core element of informal tradition. Across the years, the whistler depicted in Mount's painting who confides his tune into the fiddler's ear, communicates, as Alan Jabbour has written of folklore as a whole, "the passing along of cultural knowledge in a personal way."[4]

• • •

William Sidney Mount credited his initial violin training to a freedman named Anthony Hannibal Clapp (1749–1816). In 1853, Mount recalled, "I have sat by Anthony when I was a child— to hear him play his Jigs & Hornpipes—He was a master in that way—and acted well his part."[5] Despite the limited personal autonomy granted him in that era (implicit in Mount's letter), he overcame these barriers with his knowledge and expertise, which he readily shared. His impact on the youngster vivifies the core idea of tradition, whose Latin root, *tradere*, signifies a handing across, a giving, a delivering.[6] Mount's painting captures the workings of that transfer, which is memorialized in its title.

The phrase *to catch a tune*, meaning to hear it and absorb it, has long appeared in everyday usage as well as scholarly commentary. The verb suggests both the immediate and the fleeting, and the whole phrase suggests resourcefulness and informality. For example, blues pianist Jimmy Walker (1910–1997), recalling his youthful entry into music, spoke of a former accompanist for Gloria Swanson whose piano skills he much admired. Although Walker no longer remembered his preceptor's name, he explained, "I always wanted to play. Well, he taken a liking to me and I was running around and, see, sometimes when he wasn't playing, well I go where he was at and I'd learn, too. Caught on a little bit, then I'd drop back."[7]

Sometimes the role models freely shared their art with their acolytes, but other times they had to be pursued. Emmett Lundy (1864–1953), a fiddler from Grayson County, Virginia, spoke of his resolve to learn from musician Green Leonard, who was born in the early decades of the nineteenth century, a man Lundy described as "an old mountain boomer."[8] Lundy continued, "He didn't want everyone to catch his tunes, he wanted to keep ahead, and practically bear the honor of bein' the best fiddler." When asked if Leonard had taught him his old pieces, Lundy replied, "No, he didn't teach them to me, I catched them from him." He added that in Leonard's final days, he applauded the younger man's determination to capture his playing. "He told me that I was the only one that had tracked him down, and he wanted to learn me some old pieces before he died—he didn't want 'em to be buried—and live after he was gone."

This kind of catching arose, too, when the celebrated western Kentucky guitarist Mose Rager detailed how a locally based, white string band musician named Paul Landrum showed some chords to young Arnold Schultz (1886–1931), the seminal Black musician whom Rager, Merle Travis, Ike Everly, and Bill Monroe would forever credit as a principal inspiration. "Paul," said Rager, "used these chords and said Arnold caught 'em just like that."[9] In yet another tradition, Chicago-based Sacred Harp singer Ted Mercer, describing the ideal mode of instruction, recommended that "Sacred Harp singing can be *taught*, but it's more easily, and more naturally, *caught*. . . . Think of it as a bit of an apprenticeship. Go to Georgia, go to Alabama. . . . *Listen and absorb*."[10]

In 1940, when folksong collector John A. Lomax asked Alabama singer Vera Hall for "Another Man Done Gone," a blues that she previously had only heard her husband sing, she replied, "I ain't never sung it except to myself, but maybe I can catch it up."[11] Here, she uses *catch* in yet another way, as *recall*, describing how she summoned the song in her mind before making what soon became a celebrated recording.

At its heart, the word *catch* in these examples refers to a purposeful choice. Mountain banjoist and banjo maker Kyle Creed describes how he learned his tunes:

> Well, it depended on whether I liked the way it sounded, when the other guy was playing it. If I liked it, I'd learn it. If I didn't, I didn't even bother

> with it. You just get it in your head. If you like it, then you'll catch it. If you don't, you won't. Then, of course, you got your lick at it; you won't be like the other guy no-how.[12]

North Carolina musician John Snipes (1899–1983), a Black banjoist, spoke of his beginnings, of how he would "catch" tunes from his mentor, Will Baldwin (1873–ca.1943), who in turn caught tunes while playing at white dances.[13] Snipes's chronicler, folklorist Cecelia Conway, reprises the term *catch* throughout her discussion of early minstrelsy, explaining how aspiring white players of the 1840s cultivated first-hand contact with Black musicians. In following these exemplars, in catching their music, younger players developed repertory and acquired instrumental technique. When Conway indexed her study, she subsumed "'catching' songs" within a larger category of "apprenticeship," locating this process alongside "mentor." She added, "*see also* cultural exchange."[14] There she embedded still another idea: "*see also* . . . crossroads."[15] Common to all these affiliated realities dwells the movement of culturally distinctive materials becoming culturally shared.

The living musicians Conway documented also drew on a body of older tunes and songs, which they, in turn, transmitted to others. She included fiddler Joe Thompson (1918–2012) and his banjo-playing cousin, Odell Thompson (1911–1994), the last Black traditional banjo and fiddle team still active in the United States. They formed a living link that reached back before William Sidney Mount's time to the cross-racial music-making of post-Revolutionary America. In November 1987, I first visited the Thompsons in Mebane, North Carolina, and there, too, the term arose. One of the pieces they played was "Old Corn Liquor," an extended reel enlivened by Joe's old-time dance calls. When it ended, Joe asked, with his attention fixed as much on my cassette recorder as on me, "You catching it?"[16] Here, the word *catch* expresses the piece's transfer not only between us, from one player to another, but also towards its documentation. Joe valued this song for its history as well as its sound. He and Odell had acquired it from their fathers, in Joe's words, from "watching, listening, admiring." Having it caught on tape served not just practical, instructional ends, but possessed intrinsic, conservational value.

Catching the music accordingly means more than hearing a song and learning it. It also means recording and preserving it for others.[17] Folklorist

Dorothy Scarborough, describing herself as a "song hunter," wrote of her delight "at hearing a folk song put across in such a way that I could capture it."[18] Her posthumous collection, *A Song Catcher in the Southern Mountains*, published in 1937, more pointedly expresses this idea. She found "sometimes they [her sources] write the words which they call 'ballets,' and their name for a singer is 'song-catcher.'"[19] Scarborough warmed to this homegrown name and adopted it for her title. According to a reviewer at the time of the book's publication, she "'caught' about 600 of these songs." The 2000 film *Songcatcher* is indebted to this usage, as well as to the work of Scarborough's predecessor, Olive Dame Campbell. It features a fictional collector named Doctor Lily Panleric, who hauls, sometimes loses, and repeatedly tends her recording machine for her ballad collecting in the Appalachian uplands.

Earlier, nineteenth-century ethnologists had also begun using recording technology to document traditional culture and its bearers. Just thirteen years after Thomas Edison invented the cylinder phonograph, Jesse Walter Fewkes, the first person to publish on folk music field recordings, wrote in 1890:

> The collector may not have a musical ear, as in my own case, and may not be able to write out songs, no matter how many times they are repeated. He can in that case collect the records, and submit them at some favorable time to one who is able to catch the song and set it to music.[20]

Likewise, the emerging commercial record companies gave rise to their own songcatchers, music scouts who sought out musicians to meet the sales opportunities that had arisen with the phonograph. These A&R (artist and repertoire) representatives identified, selected, and signed performers with local and sometimes national appeal. By the 1920s, these included vernacular musicians and singers such as Bessie Smith, the Carter Family, Jimmie Rodgers, and Blind Willie Johnson, along with thousands more who appeared on nationally marketed blues, gospel, and country music releases.[21]

An early Columbia records circular characterized its rural music list as "familiar tunes old and new," and this description could equally apply to the foreign language catalogs that they and others produced from the industry's earliest years.[22] Non-English speakers spanning some thirty languages, from Welsh to Persian to Icelandic to Yiddish, bought records playing their own familiar music and bought the phonographs to play them. Department stores, general stores, phonograph and radio repair shops, and mail-order catalogs all sold records. Ethnically oriented vendors stocked them among other culture-related goods. First-person accounts left by local retailers and music dealers reveal them as acting as songcatchers in their own right. They knew where the community talent resided among them and recommended performers worthy of recording, sometimes by simply promising the labels to buy enough product in advance that it became a worthwhile business venture. Between 1893 and 1942, the body of ethnic recordings produced in the United States included more than eleven thousand performers. In sum, vernacular music caught on phonograph records by collectors, both academic and commercial, reflected a treasury of creative expression.

Though different motivations—from ethnography to commerce—inspired these recordists, their songcatching recalls the exchange depicted

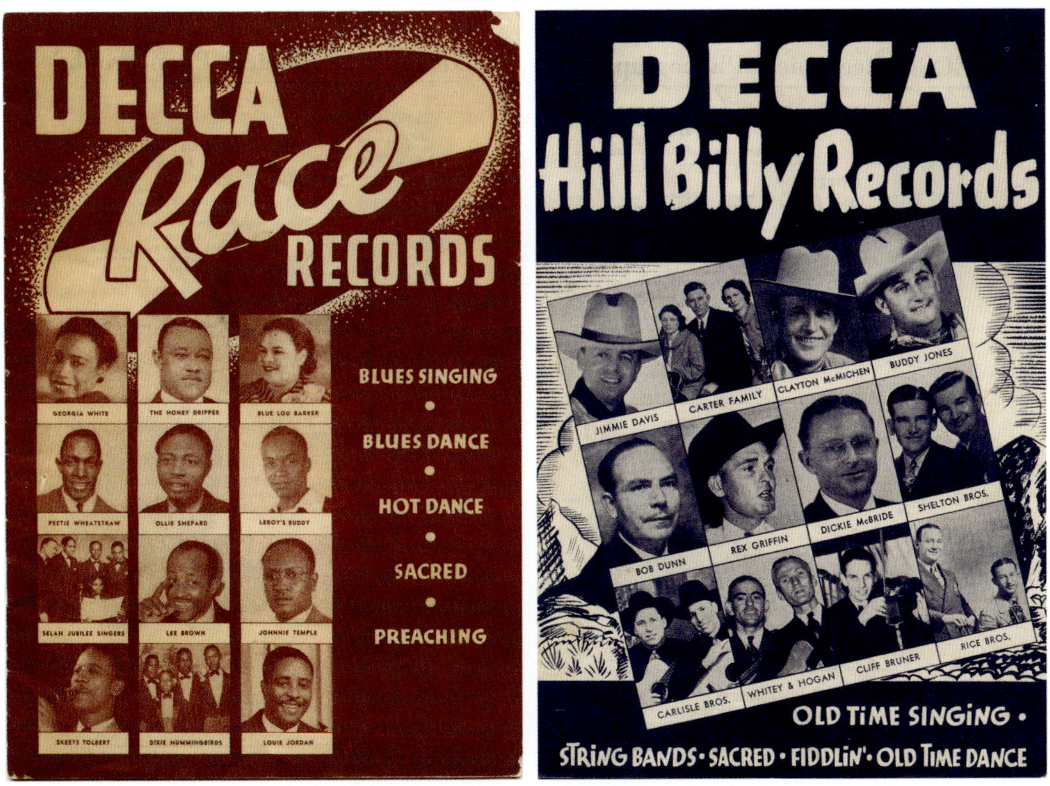

FIGURE 9. Decca race and hillbilly releases, May 1940.

in Mount's painting. For countless musicians, sound recordings operate like Mount's whistler. Recordings allow players, however dispersed by time and location, to retain and reproduce the nuances they hear. At the same time, folklorist David Evans reminds me, "in learning from records one loses the entire visual side of the performance. Also the record tends to become the fixed version of a tune that might have varied considerably in performance."[23] These limitations notwithstanding, Limerick-born folklorist/performer Mick Maloney describes this means for the transmission of Irish traditional music in America as an inevitable but practical alternative to "the Old World method of learning from family, friends, and neighbors."[24]

To catch a tune from a disc, musicians have to place the stylus down in a given spot and strain after a given passage. In the early 1930s, Virginia bluesman Archie Edwards and his brother would borrow 78-rpm records and work out on their guitars what they heard on the discs. At first, they found the music daunting. Speaking of Mississippi John Hurt's deft performances of "Stack O' Lee" and "Candy Man," Edwards noted, "the speed he was playing was a little too fast for us to catch all the sound and all."[25] So they slowed down the phonograph to "just about a mumble," and acted in tandem, each advising the other through the rough spots. "When my brother carried the record back to the owner, my brother and I had stolen all the music."

Edwards's fellow Virginian, songster John Jackson, described, too, how he gleaned most of his repertory from recordings.[26] He cited the releases of blues and ragtime guitar player Blind Blake, his avowed favorite. To match the tones he heard, Jackson improvised a guitar capo with a pencil stick and attached it with a rubber band cut from an inner tube. Then, "I played behind the record. That's the way I mostly learned to play, was playing behind the 78 records."[27]

Some two decades older than either Edwards or Jackson, multi-instrumentalist Hobart Smith (1897–1965) of Saltville, Virginia, voiced in late 1963 what they all shared in this learning. Mastery depended on desire as much as memory:

> I get around the old folks that played a banjer and I'd listen to that, and I was just full of music as I could be. It'd just register on me up and down just like a thermometer. And you see, I'd get that in my ear, and then I'd

get ahold of that banjer. You've got to get a-hold of that banjer. You've first got to get it on your mind . . . and then find it with your fingers. Keep on, till you find what you want on that neck. That's the main part of it. But keep that tune in your mind just like you can hear it a-playing.

Really, I've been to the cornfield many of a time—I was a farmer—and I'd hear a good fiddle tune or a good banjer piece, and I'd commence whistling it. And I'd whistle that till my mouth got so tired, and I'd go home to keep it on my mind. I'd go pretty fast, and I'd go home and I'd whistle all the way into the holler on the mountain. And my banjer would be hanging on the wall. . . . I'd kept that right in my mind, and I'd find that tune on them strings before I'd quit. I never stopped. I never stopped till I found it. 'Cause I loved it. I loved it. And I just went for it.[28]

I know what Hobart meant. In 1964, a galvanic wave reached America's shores via Ed Sullivan's long-running Sunday evening variety show. On February 9, 1964, witnessed by some 73 million viewers and extending over the next two Sundays, the Beatles captured one of the largest audiences in the medium's history. Over the ensuing weeks, the group topped the popular music charts and AM radio countdowns. By late February, Chicago's Silver Dollar Survey, a free weekly listing of top forty hits published since 1960 by the city's leading music station, changed its name to the Silver Beatle Survey. Beatlemania reached from bobbleheads and lunch boxes emblazoned with their images, to preteen dance parties that included cakes decorated with their names, to filmgoers screaming during the concert scenes for the band's feature-length movie that opened that September. As *A Hard Day's Night* ended, portraits of the backs of the Beatles' heads flashed across the screen—shapes that, by then, had become so familiar that viewers could accurately identify each one. "The film was so influential," remembered critic Roger Ebert three decades later, "that untold thousands of young men walked into the theater with short haircuts, and their hair started growing during the movie and didn't get cut again until the 1970s."[29] Within the music business, too, it became commonplace to acknowledge that the Beatles did not just sell records, they sold record players.

I had turned eleven and found in that shimmering time a great happiness. Starting that year on Saturday mornings, I began going downtown, taking a city bus for twelve cents, bearing in hand the brown zip-up case that sheltered my cherry red, single-pickup, solid-body electric guitar with its bolt-on neck. Those days typically consisted of two parts: first, an hour-long lesson that took place in a small basement studio of Wurlitzer's Pianos, a room set apart from the formal music trade upstairs and isolated enough to accommodate the clang of fledgling guitarists. Afterward, I traipsed off to the neighboring music stores that occupied this strip along Chicago's south Wabash Avenue, called "music row." The businesses clustered there included instrument dealers and showrooms, as well as brass and violin repair benches, along with the city's principal sheet music purveyor, and its largest record store. Both the city's principal formal music venue, Orchestra Hall, and its largest, the Auditorium Theatre, stood nearby. In earlier years musical commerce and musical training operated side by side, with recording studios as well as conservatories also arrayed along the street. By 1964, these enterprises and institutions still existed both within that district and across the metropolitan region.

My principal interest lay in the electric guitars displayed in the music row shops. The dealers typically promoted specific brands—Gibsons here, Fenders there, Gretsches elsewhere. Each brand bore its own enchantments expressed in the geometry of its designs and the glow of its finishes, from apricot lacquer to satin black cellulose. Wurlitzer's, for instance, set aside wall space for the locally manufactured line of Airline guitars, aglow in red and white acrylic, made by Valco and marketed by Montgomery Ward (while downstairs in the tiny studio where my lessons took place, they left out a sunburst Fender Jazzmaster, a valuable electric guitar for all to use, until one day when it sadly disappeared). These were the tools, like Mount's fiddle (which he named the "Cradle of Harmony"), that like-minded musicians my age sought to acquire, if largely beyond our means.[30]

A few doors away, at 218 S. Wabash Avenue, Charlie Grano oversaw the one-man wind instrument repair shop he had opened in 1960. Charlie had also become the city's principal purveyor of Gretsch guitars. His business was transformed, he told me years later, by George Harrison's playing of the Gretsch's Country Gentleman model. "The Beatles changed the music all around. They changed the whole course of music."[31] These elegant instruments, resplendent in shades of citrus orange to foamy green, from angel white to burnished mahogany, were optionally equipped with a leather pad on the back to prevent buckle scratch. They were so rarefied that Charlie allowed only the most serious of customers to try them. "These weren't," he explained, "guitars for kids." Across the street at Lyon and Healy, the grandest of all the music row stores, a magisterial line of fluted classical harps occupied the same floor as their glass display cases of Gibson electrics. Take the elevator up to three, and a demure woman wearing pearls goes one direction, while an unshaven young man in a leather jacket peels off the other way. Cultural dissonances notwithstanding, the company lived up to its motto, "Everything in music."

Of all the shops that lined music row purveying electric guitars (these included Baldwin, Prager and Ritter's Chicago Guitar Gallery, and Kagan and Gaines), the most welcoming belonged to former dance band trumpeter and violinist Sid Sherman. By the mid-1960s, Sid Sherman's Musical Instrument Company operated as a family business that Sid led, assisted by his wife and son. Alongside them, a handful of employees made floor sales, worked on repairs, and took inventory. They dealt a variety of instruments that spanned big band to string jazz, leaving percussion needs to Franks Drum Shop, located on the floor just above. (As the city's premier drumming outlet, Franks regularly hosted Saturday clinics that players like Gene Krupa or Buddy Rich might lead).[32] Meanwhile, Sid Sherman's, with its peaceable murmur regularly interrupted by the elevated train rattling past its outer windows, welcomed a procession of musical aspirants and professionals. Newly formed bands (you could always tell their drummer by the sticks in his back pocket) bustled past the elderly elevator operator, himself a former musician, as did the veteran players who greeted Sid like an old friend. In 1964, Sid Sherman and his staff allowed me to spend entire Saturday afternoons there. My role consisted of wiping off the guitars that the older customers tried out, after which the salesmen returned them to the glass display cases. From my perch near the shop's entrance, I had a front-row seat as the players dropped by and sometimes plugged in.

There I first recognized people who had caught music. Someone trying out one of the guitars played the biting chords to the Kinks' "You Really

FIGURE 10. Charlie Grano's business card and Sid Sherman's sticker, two of Chicago's music row proprietors in 1964.

Got Me." Another reprised the telltale turn in Roy Orbison's "Oh, Pretty Woman." Still more numbers tumbled out, from the riff that marks "Tobacco Road," to the reprise of "Not Fade Away," to the arpeggios in "House of the Rising Sun"—any or all of these instantly recognizable. What existed before as mythic works of art pouring from my transistor radio suddenly became palpable. The capacity of those young players at Sid Sherman's seemed nothing short of Promethean. They had snatched music from the air itself and caught it. I yearned for this ability to translate those sounds onto the fingerboard of my guitar, to play what I heard.

I also knew that the moves they made on those guitars didn't correspond to the Nick Manoloff method book I had to guide me. Its pedagogy lay in the past, closer to the chord-melody standards of the 1930s and 1940s, as well as its sobering regimen of practice exercises. Nor did my more recent Chuck Berry songbook with its first-position diagrams reveal the pivot points and chord shapes Berry actually used. I had found these folios and others like them on music row either at Carl Fischer's, the street's leading dealer in sheet music, or else filling the main floor bins at Lyon and Healy's. Their attractive covers and full sets of lyrics notwithstanding, these editions too often did not capture the techniques heard in the original songs or what the younger players at Sid Sherman's had replicated. Instead, these works often set the music in piano keys, essentially arranged for copyright. Borrowing terms from linguistics, musicologist Charles Seeger differentiated between "prescriptive" versus "descriptive" notation: "between a blueprint of how a specific piece of music shall be made to sound and a report of how a specific performance of any music actually did sound."[33] Manuals attuned to performers and their methods, let alone close transcriptions (such as those masterfully rendered by Seeger's wife, Ruth Crawford Seeger, who herself had attended the conservatory in Chicago's music row district), certainly existed back then. But those works had so far eluded me.

Happily, my guitar teacher, Jim Schwall (1942–2022) of the soon-to-be-formed Siegel-Schwall Band that would shortly achieve national fame, was an exceptionally well-versed guide. He knew both formal guitar pedagogies and vernacular styles, especially those drawn from blues and hillbilly precedents. In 1964 he could certainly play the figures behind "Johnny B. Goode." While my father hoped I might learn Carlos Montoya's "Malagueña" and gain some musical literacy along the way, he accepted that I would play that piece and those like it on the electric guitar. As a result, Jim taught me some classical rudiments and written notation, but he also answered my pleas for the barre chords to The Ventures remake of "Walk, Don't Run." Mostly, we worked on twelve-bar blues patterns in different keys. Soon, Jim's career took him elsewhere, and our lessons were curtailed. Still, my trips to music row continued.

• • •

In 1964, as a youngster, I hoped to catch that era's music on my electric guitar. My attempts, however, took place within a much larger local (let alone national) context. The music trade centered along south Wabash Avenue in the Beatlemania years reflected a long-standing mercantile infrastructure emblematic of Chicago's role as exporter to the nation. The street's merchandising history points to the kind of informal learning that Mount's painting portrays.

As early as 1836, at Osbourn and Strail, a dry goods/groceries/crockery shop located near the future site of music row, one could obtain "flutes, violins, clarinets, flageolets, accordions, violin strings and bridges, clarinet reeds, tuning forks, and brass post horns" along with "the latest and most fashionable Songs for the Piano and Guitar."[34] Come April 1861 and the commencement of the Civil War, the local firm, Root & Cady, published patriotic marches, recruitment odes, and rallying songs that included George F. Root's own "Battle Cry of Freedom" and "Tramp, Tramp, Tramp." Other hits that emerged from their offices located at the nearby corner of Washington and Clark Streets included Benjamin Hanby's "Darling Nellie Gray," as well as "Kingdom Coming," "Marching through Georgia," "The Ship that Never Returned," and "Grandfather's Clock," all from the pen of local songwriter and printer Henry Clay Work. These songs gained an additional distinction: they thrived, as Norm Cohen has written in his lucid definition of folksong, "without the necessity of commercial media."[35] Countless singers and players thus came to catch this music as well.

Music row, while embryonic in the mid-nineteenth century as a business district, was complemented by Chicago's rise as an instrument manufacturer, further providing sources for catching music. Although no reports of this activity precede 1850, by the following year the city directory listed one G. A. Helmkamp producing organs, pianos, guitars, and violins. Julius Bauer & Company, established in 1857, and similarly broad in its scope—offering banjos, tambourines, melodeons, concertinas, and accordions among its products—prospered with its flute and drum sales to the Union's Army of the West. Kimball's reed organs, founded the same year, became, by 1900, the nation's largest piano and organ maker. The establishment in the music row locale of Lyon and Healy in 1864 by George Washburn Lyon and Patrick J. Healy, was launched, their music publishing efforts coupled with retail instrument sales. As the sole major music publisher to survive the city's great fire of 1871, their stability led them to begin manufacturing under their own names by 1880. Their products included the Washburn line of fretted instruments, recalling George Lyon's middle name, and by decade's end, their celebrated grand concert harps.[36] Nearby, the homegrown brand of Harmony guitars, launched in 1892 and purchased by Sears, Roebuck in 1916, became the largest in the country, and along with Kay guitars, were produced by the millions.

The city's mail-order houses furthered this success. Montgomery Ward was formed in 1872, followed eight years later by Sears, Roebuck and Company. Ward initially affiliated with the Patrons of Husbandry, a rural political and social organization best known as the Grange, to build its customer base, while Richard Warren Sears began his career selling watches via station agents on the Minneapolis and St. Louis Railroad. By the early 1890s both firms were sending out "wish books," hundreds of pages long, that spread across the American countryside. Historian William Cronon writes, "those much-thumbed volumes contained an encyclopedic description of modern life" that tied city and country together, "no matter how remote . . . wherever one made one's home."[37] Just as Chicago received from its rural interior the nation's grain, lumber, and livestock, the city responded with finished products and manufactured goods. Cronon lists some of them: "Chicago Honey Cured Hams. Ladies Fine Shirt Waists. American Chatelaine Watches. Giant Acme Gasoline Stoves. Princess Tonic Hair Restorers. Yukon Gents' Bicycles," and much, much more that the great catalogs offered.

Musicians of that era, especially those who caught their music by living example from others, have repeatedly credited their first store-bought instruments as coming from these mail-order merchandisers via rural free delivery. In time, this distribution system, federally established in 1896, in response to the catalogs' success, extended to records marketed under the Montgomery Ward and Sears, Roebuck imprimaturs. This marketing effort also reached the airwaves. In 1924, Sears launched its high-wattage station at the Sherman Hotel astride Chicago's music row. Its WLS call letters trumpeted its commercial might: "*W*orld's *L*argest *S*tore." Sears hoped their live programming might sell radio sets, let alone phonographs.

• • •

One item that Sears's catalog customers would have found among its offerings was a book of fiddle tunes first published in 1883. At that time, Boston music publisher Elias Howe had announced the release of *Ryan's Mammoth Collection*. This volume, which has since become the single most popular reference source for fiddling repertory in the United States, consisted of 1,050 tunes gathered by Howe's longtime employee, William Bradbury Ryan. Ryan (1831–1910), a Vermont-born musician and Civil War veteran, where he served as a military bandsman, had assembled in this work what its front cover promised: "Reels and Jigs, Hornpipes, Clogs, Walk-arounds, Essences, Strathspeys, Highland Flings, and Contra

Dances, with Figures, and How to Play Them."[38] A contemporaneous trade announcement further revealed Ryan's collecting method, a process that echoes the scene in *Catching the Tune*: "As they have been taken down by hearing them played by Pipers and Violin Players, and often sang or whistled, they being unable to read music, the task has been extremely difficult."[39] In the same notice, attention also centered on the book's surfeit of newly written pieces: "President Grant's Hornpipe," "Telephone Hornpipe," and "President Garfield's Hornpipe."

The entries reflect Ryan's hometown of Boston and his position there as a band leader. The collection's 200-plus jigs, some titles associated with known individuals and local sights, underline the signal role that Irish and Irish-American tunes occupy in his work. Even if Ryan only had commercial rather than ethnographic motivations in creating this collection, scholar Paul Wells has persuasively argued that he should "surely be regarded today as the first great documentarian of Irish traditional music in the United States."[40]

Between the mid-1890s and 1906, the Sears catalog sold *Ryan's Mammoth Collection.* An 1897 caption identifies it as "a very popular collection of lively music for violin," and it stood out as the sole tunebook Sears sold apart from Elias Howe's *Musician's Omnibus*.[41] During this period some of Ryan's tunes also appeared without attribution in Francis J. O'Neill's 1903 *Music of Ireland,* the first of the seven collections he assembled. Published by Lyon and Healy in Chicago, it consists of 1850 tunes gathered by O'Neill, a flute player from County Cork who served as Superintendent of the Chicago Police Department from 1901 to 1905. A publishing landmark, it immediately became the largest printed collection of traditional Irish dance music. The inclusion of Ryan's material within its pages reinforces its front cover vow: "collected from all available sources."[42]

With the dissolution of Elias Howe's businesses in 1931, *Ryan's Mammoth Collection* fell out of publication. Its print life, however, had not ended. Nine years later, as first noted by Alan Jabbour, and then traced by scholars Charles Wolfe, Patrick Sky, and Paul Wells, it returned fully intact with its original plates in 1940 via Chicago music publisher M. M. Cole. Yet this republication bore no mention of either Ryan's or Howe's names, let alone its prior existence. The principal changes M. M. Cole made to the collection, apart from the layout in which the compositor fit more tunes on larger pages, resided in their dropping some fifty tunes and practice exercises to fit its other new title, *One Thousand Fiddle Tunes.* Once again, Sears offered it to their catalog customers, selling it for 75 cents per copy. Players from across North America came to call it "Cole's," and it became known as "The Fiddlers Bible," a popular motto the publisher eventually added to its cover.[43] By 1945, Cole advertised *1000 Fiddle Tunes* as "the most complete book on the market. A terrific value." Soon another aspect of Cole's sales strategy would go into effect.

In 1946, the company undertook a series of recordings (electrical transcriptions) of their copyrighted songs, intended solely for radio broadcast. These appeared on 16-inch discs sent out to stations for which WLS musicians performed both selections from *1000 Fiddle Tunes* and other works Cole had published. WLS *National Barn Dance* star Doc Hopkins contributed hundreds of titles to this effort for the M. M. Cole Transcribed Library.[44] Doc led an ensemble organized for this purpose called the Country Boys. The log sheets identify fiddler Alan Crockett playing on all of Doc's tracks, which included fifty-five "dance calls" taken from the book. He had earlier played in a family band led by his father, John "Dad" Crockett, as a member of Crockett's Kentucky Mountaineers. In the late 1920s, their group began recording for the Brunswick label, which included sessions at its studio located at 623 South Wabash Avenue, near the latter-day music row. By the postwar period, Crockett returned to Chicago to play with the Prairie Ramblers on WLS, making him available for the M. M. Cole transcription sessions. Doc Hopkins remembered those forays, recalling how Crockett, facing a music stand, could read the tunes from the Cole book and play them with ease, one after another.[45]

As a result, the book proliferated in multiple ways. The combination of WLS radio, founded as a Sears, Roebuck enterprise, coupled with publisher M. M. Cole's products, whose sales entwined Sears's catalog merchandising, and augmented by these radio transcriptions, propelled *Ryan's Mammoth Collection* intergenerationally. Meanwhile, performers from across the continent broadcast its content. Professional country radio fiddlers Robert Rutland (best known as Georgia Slim Rutland) and Howdy Forrester, Texas contest fiddlers Benny Thomasson and Mark O'Connor,

Nashville studio fiddlers Tommy Jackson and Buddy Spicher, Canadian fiddlers Angus Chisholm and Graham Townsend—all credited Cole's, bringing its storehouse of tunes to their listeners and then playing them in an array of styles.

These efforts translated to local tune-catching. Fiddler Charlie Walden, raised in Missouri's Little Dixie region, identified the "Missouri Valley style": an "exceptionally clean, notey playing of complex hornpipes and reels, many of which can be traced to Cole's."[46] Elsewhere in Missouri, other fiddlers drew from the book, including stylists as distinctive from one another as Cyril Stinnett, Milo McCubbin, Taylor McBaine, and George Morris.[47] In a statement that speaks for all these fiddlers, Art Galbraith, who likewise learned from Cole's, said, "I think it's the beauty of fiddling; you let ten fiddlers play the same tune and every one of them will have a different stamp on it."[48]

M. M. Cole noted this interpretative breadth, and by the time of the 1984 edition, stated on the back cover, "The tunes have been arranged as close as possible in their original form. The player may vary the tunes to suit individual needs and styles."[49] For many, its pieces formed a template, not a model. They might memorize a tune "note for note," as fiddler Frank Maloy observed, but then "add any personal (subtle) variations only after the basic melody had been committed to memory."[50] Some melodies, too, appear several times in the book, each different from the other, constituting representations of specific performances and not simply generalized outlines of a basic form.[51] Either way, whether by reading the notes themselves or by learning from those who did, fiddlers caught these tunes, much as their predecessors had back when William Bradbury Ryan first committed their music to paper. This combined effort of music and mercantilism reached from the collection's first appearance in 1883 to its republication in 1995, a span of 112 years. Over the years, the book not only served as a source of folk material but became used in a folk manner.

Traditionality depends on neither an item's origin nor age, whether it's taken from a book like Cole's or recently composed for popular purposes. "Fiddle music," writes Missouri scholar/musician Howard Wight Marshall:

> comes through time not only on sheets of paper but through the ancient avenues of apprenticeship and imitation of respected masters. It operates

> by unwritten laws of oral and aural tradition and time-tested custom. Essentially solo music learned by ear, each melody is given special treatment by every fiddler who plays it. Each writing represents merely one particular opinion of music that is fluid, dynamic, and ever changing from one generation to the next and one individual to the next.[52]

Like the early commercially issued vernacular recordings that documented thousands of individualistic performances, the Ryan/Cole book benefited from mechanisms of mass culture, from print to radio to latter-day tape cassettes that circulated among professionals and amateurs alike to communicate its contents. In turn, grassroots musicians have repeatedly reshaped and inflected these pieces anew. In Chicago, this same creative process expressed in *Catching the Tune* was working in another idiom. It, too, reached from music row to the neighborhoods beyond. One need only look at the city's greatest musical export: the blues.

• • •

During the months I took guitar lessons in the Wurlitzer's basement from Jim Schwall, he and his schoolmate, Corky Siegel, became the Siegel-Schwall Band. Over the next ten years, followed by periodic reunion tours, they achieved international acclaim. The group made twelve albums plus five compilation collections, wrote and recorded newly composed works for "Blues Band and Orchestra" with the San Francisco Symphony under Seiji Ozawa, appeared on national television with the Boston Pops, and even produced some of Joni Mitchell's earliest recordings.[53] In 1965 they were installed as the house band at Pepper's Show Lounge, a South Side tavern where local players included Howlin' Wolf, Little Walter, and Sammy Lawhorn (who played in Muddy Waters's band). Sometimes they sat in with Jim and Corky, who initially performed as a duet, the two of them singing to Corky's piano and harmonica, coupled with Jim's acoustically amplified guitar. Proprietor Johnny Pepper, however, insisted on a quartet, adding bass and drums to meet the expectations of a neighborhood clientele who came there to drink, dance, and enjoy themselves on Thursday nights.

The band, racially integrated for most of its years, emerged during Mississippi Freedom Summer, a time when five Southern states left the Demo-

FIGURE 11. Jim Schwall and Corky Siegel, Detroit, Michigan, winter 1966. Photo by Wilson Lindsey.

cratic party in that year's presidential election, beginning a new alignment in American politics. That August, the Gulf of Tonkin resolution passed Congress with near unanimity, irrevocably escalating the Vietnam War. Within these transnational currents, Jim recalled a quiet moment that epitomized those times. When Jim and Corky first organized their quartet at Pepper's, they included Bob Anderson on electric bass. Anderson (1934–1985) was a veteran Black Chicago blues player whom Jim described as "a guy on the scene."[54] He played around town, including a long stint with James Cotton, in addition to accompanying Howlin' Wolf, Koko Taylor, and

Junior Wells. His nickname, "Little Bob Anderson," was no exaggeration, Jim noted, concerning his small frame. While Jim personally felt no unease walking from Pepper's every week back to his car, despite its location in a disadvantaged neighborhood, Bob Anderson turned to him one night:

"Let me walk out to the car with you."

After heading that way for a bit, it suddenly occurred to Jim to ask, "Are you protecting me?"

"No, I'm probably not big enough to protect you," Bob said, "but I can let people know you belong here."[55]

In like spirit, photographer Raeburn Flerlage (1915–2002), who documented that era in the city's South Side clubs and whose camera work distinguished numerous LP covers arising from this scene, spoke of the "Camaraderie of the Blues."[56] A white man who chose to live in the city's Black community for the greater portion of his life, he witnessed a collegiality among these players, a support given to one another and across racial divides. The personal affection expressed by both Muddy Waters and Howlin' Wolf towards Jim and Corky would not have surprised him. Nor the fact that Muddy eventually integrated his own band. At the same time, Flerlage recalled how Eddie "Son" House, an early inspiration and model for Muddy Waters, commented in 1964 after hearing a recording of another young white player sing one of his numbers, "Those are my words all right, but it sure ain't my music."[57] Or, as Muddy said of this coming generation of white musicians, "They play so much, run a ring around you playin' guitar, but they cannot vocal like the black man."[58]

For both learners and listeners, this period marked a shift in the blues. By then the city's postwar players faced a declining market among the Black community, which was increasingly attracted to the soul music of artists like Mary Wells and the Supremes, along with gospel-based crooners like Sam Cooke, let alone the crossover appeal Martha and the Vandellas achieved with their anthemic performance of "Dancing in the Street." Meanwhile, the Beatles' American tour, followed by the Rolling Stones and guitarists like Eric Clapton, cast new light on the city's senior blues players. The Stones drew their band's name from one of Muddy's songs, and their 1964 instrumental, "2120 S. Michigan Avenue," refers to the street address for Chess Records, where they recorded the piece. Their tune stands as an homage to this inner-city label whose stars included Muddy Waters, Howlin' Wolf, Chuck Berry, Bo Diddley, Sonny Boy Williamson No. 2, Little Walter, and Willie Dixon. The British rock musicians' embrace of these elders created opportunities for Chicago's bluesmen to perform in new venues and festivals both stateside and abroad. Admittedly, Muddy and his fellow players recognized that they received less pay than their rock proteges. Yet these interactions marked a welcome development for them. Without this employment, many faced a return to the manual labor they had known before.

Over the July 4, 1964, holiday weekend, a folk music booking at Big John's, a saloon on Chicago's North Side, brought new opportunities for Black players. White harmonica player Charlie Musselwhite accompanied Big Joe Williams (1903–1982), a veteran Mississippi bluesman, in what became a hugely popular engagement. Musselwhite and his musician friends immediately launched a campaign: "We started telling the owners about other blues bands," he recalled. "You know, 'Why don't you book Muddy Waters or Howlin' Wolf?' So they started booking them and eventually it was seven nights a week, live blues, live electric blues from the South Side."[59]

Ray Flerlage, who shot pictures at clubs on both the North and South sides, noted the contrast between the two environments:

> You walked into the Black clubs and you were in a different world. . . . In a Black club, when the performers sang, we were all in it together. You had had that experience, you had had that sorrow. You too had been conned and double-crossed, taken for a ride, had money troubles, been disappointed in love. You were part of the experience. In the White clubs, as wonderful as some of the artists and their performances were, and however knowledgeable some members of the audience might be, the experience was different. Instead of telling *us* about *us*, they were telling *you* about *them*. The identification between the artist and the audience wasn't there.[60]

Different audiences brought different understandings and expectations, and the blues players modified their shows accordingly. The musicians varied their performances depending on their listeners, recalled longtime record producer Michael Melford.[61] No longer at a song's dramatic peak would Muddy Waters spray out a beer bottle concealed in his trousers, simulating male orgasm. "He didn't do that for white kids," Melford explained. Nor were these North Side venues as dangerous for the musicians or as alcoholically drenched. They also paid better. This new work allowed Muddy and Wolf to move to the suburbs and live more comfortably. Wolf's band members came to receive not only a salary but health benefits too.

Blues research also leaped forward in the 1960s. A 1957 article by Yannick Bruynoghe, the Belgian-born biographer of bluesman Big Bill Broonzy, spoke of "this unknown Chicagoan world," describing his visit to the South Side clubs, meeting with Muddy Waters, watching Howlin' Wolf, and listening to Memphis Slim, Willie Dixon, and Magic Sam.[62] He was there, he said, "because Chicago's South Side is and always has been a whole world in itself, and one of the richest musically." Early in the profusion of writings that followed, blues historian Sam Charters, who produced the first Siegel-Schwall albums following his celebrated 1966 trio of records called *Chicago Blues Today!*, also found that at Pepper's and its counterparts "a living music is still played in local bars and neighborhood clubs."[63] Vitality permeated those places, centered in performers Charters called "the everyday working bluesmen who were still part of the life of the South Side."[64]

Jim Schwall recalled how the neighborhood clubs served those everyday players "coming up."[65] The training that took place in the city's neighborhood taverns was "not a system, but [occurred] in an organic way." Someone might first learn bass and then guitar. It might take five years, but Jim saw this practice period as part of working one's way up, from being a backup player "making fourteen dollars a night, if they're lucky." Opportunity lay at hand. "Someone might let you sit in first. Then welcome you the next time," allowing you to "just grow up with the whole thing." Then possibly a key voice "couldn't make it that night, and a new leader emerges . . . to front their own band." He likened this apprenticeship to playing with Bill Monroe, whose bluegrass ensemble with its ever-changing membership became "a rite of passage and [a means to] learn the ropes." Otherwise, for these working bluesmen, "Sometimes you'd just get phone calls."[66] A band leader needed someone to fill in. Since there was "a common fund of songs everyone knew," if "you played in the clubs you already knew what to do."

Among those who developed expertise in these environments, Jim named Luther Tucker (1936–1993), one of the city's most admired guitarists. He never led a band, but had, since adolescence, honed his craft in the neighborhood clubs, guided by mentors who had shown him how to play. "As a second guitar," Jim explained, "he did a lot of different things, depending on the songs, and played in a bunch of different ways."[67] Likewise, over on the city's West Side, Jim would watch guitarist and singer Magic Sam, the nickname of Sam Maghett (1937–1969), learning from his example. Jim took note of how he held his hands, a lesson more illuminating than simply replicating notes heard on a recording. Jim found that Sam liked to play country blues with two fingers, "like the old solo guys, but on an electrified guitar." They both favored that body of earlier work. "We were friends, and I could go sit in with him."

Jim's musical life began early. Once he became big enough to carry one, and in keeping with his German-American upbringing, he played accordion. A steady run of Lawrence Welk and New Orleans jazz records played on his grandfather's phonograph. Swing band orchestras provided the pop music of that time, followed by the harmony singing of Lambert, Hendricks, and Ross, which became a particular favorite among Jim's high school classmates. Midway through those years, his musical horizons widened with the folk revival. This term, *folk revival*, which Jim used, applied to singers and players raised from outside a particular culture presenting the traditional music of that community. Two years before he graduated from New Trier High School, he heard the North Carolina mountain ballad "Tom Dooley," as performed by the Kingston Trio. In 1958, it became the number one hit record in the United States. "It's not hard to figure out that the Kingston Trio didn't make up 'Tom Dooley,'" Jim said.[68] That instinct led him and his schoolmates, like Michael Bloomfield and Michael Melford, to search for earlier sources within the music. Bloomfield (1943–1981), who soon became the first widely recognized electric guitar virtuoso in the blues-rock era, found himself so excited about the blues he heard back then, that during Jim's visits to his home, he would drop the needle on twenty different records, wanting to share them all. Together, Jim and his friends carried the sounds of those records to their parties and song circles, where they played guitars, learning from one another.

In 1961, a year after Jim's high school graduation, the University of Chicago launched its first folk festival, which focused on traditional performers. Ray Flerlage's photographs from the festival's first ten years illuminate the breadth of artists heard at Mandel Hall. Initial performers included the sweet-voiced blind ballad singer Horton Barker from Chilhowie, Virginia. From Beech Mountain, North Carolina, came Frank Proffitt, the source of "Tom Dooley," whose performance of the song led to the Kingston Trio's hit. In subsequent years the festival presented a pantheon of the folk revival: Roscoe Holcomb, Hobart Smith, Bessie Jones, Dock Boggs, Almeda Riddle, Bill Monroe, Jim and Jesse, Doc Watson, Clarence Ashley, Reverend Gary Davis, Elizabeth Cotton, Fred McDowell, Bukka White, Maybelle Carter, Furry Lewis, and Sleepy John Estes, along with greats from Chicago's own blues and gospel community, among them: Big Joe Williams, Arvella Gray, the Staple Singers, Sunnyland Slim, Big Walter Horton, Carl Martin, and Ted Bogan.[69] For Jim Schwall, these festivals brought into focus the music itself. "It wasn't just the Stanley Brothers and something I'd heard on a record. [Now] I'd watch those guys play."

Jim cited three blues artists who affected him most during his formative years: Big Bill Broonzy, Lightnin' Hopkins, and Robert Pete Williams. Jim saw Big Bill play before he died in 1958 and viewed his masterful artistry not as a country bluesman so much as a sophisticated player, which he attributed to Bill's long years of playing and recording in ensembles. He likened him to his close friend, the guitarist Otis Rush, for also having crafted "very smooth, well-thought-out parts."[70] Lightnin' Hopkins offered something else: "a starting place for a lot of guitarists who wanted to play blues." He favored playing in the key of E, which, with its open strings, intensified the pentatonic blues scales that marked so many Deep South blues. His essentially uncomplicated style, Jim found, easily adapted to tackling a range of songs. He also named Robert Pete Williams, whom he found to be "completely loose," to the point that on some songs, he made no chord changes at all. He likened him to Buddy Guy, whose playing he considered "completely unpredictable, where anything could happen." Jim had listened to Williams's records, but it was not until he saw him at the Newport Folk Festival in 1964 that the music became clear to him. "It was eye-opening when I saw what he was doing with his hands. I was making it more complicated than it was."

Jim further noted the different approach taken by earlier country blues guitarists and the direction of the amplified stylists who succeeded them.

For most modern players, their orientation is derived from B. B. King and T-Bone Walker working the treble strings. The structure of King's band and those like his allowed him to occupy this higher range on the neck, while the other instruments covered the lower register, a task that a solo guitarist of an earlier day would need to sustain by himself. Jim watched and learned: catching the music from phonograph records, personal encounters, immersion in the clubs, and contact with fellow players who, in letting him sit in with them, schooled him in the blues.

Sometimes catching the music draws one beyond a single genre. It did not surprise Jim that Ray Charles had made a much-heralded country album. For a singer as wonderful as he was, it made sense that "he would have to try it."[71] He cited, too, a popular story of Charlie Parker listening to country music radio as he and his bandmates traveled by automobile to the next gig. When his fellow players questioned his interest "in that cracker music," he countered by pointing out in those country songs, "They're telling stories." This affectionate acceptance speaks to Jim's own life. From writing ballets, operas, and string quartets during his academic career, to his movement from the Dixieland music of his boyhood to exploring free jazz while working on his doctorate, from his exposure to the saxophone of Jerry Mulligan and the singing of Charles Brown, from cherishing the polka music of Eddie Blazonczyk's Versatones to treasuring the compositions of Igor Stravinsky, from the flatpicking of Doc Watson to discovering a Cajun scene in southwest Louisiana as vital as the blues clubs he had habituated in Chicago, Jim said, "It's all music and you can find something in all of it." While his long career enabled him to play with a dazzling range of musicians—from Clarence White to Chuck Berry—right up until his death at seventy-nine, music excited him as he wondered where it might lead next. He was driven by a desire shared by most musicians: "I just want to get good at this."[72]

In March 1964, after an eleven-year hiatus from recording—his time spent in the interval working as a forklift operator as well as in building construction, and other factory employment in Chicago—bluesman

FIGURE 12. David "Honeyboy" Edwards, Chicago, Illinois, Aug. 6, 1998. Photo by Stephen Wade.

David "Honeyboy" Edwards (1915–2011) sang once again into a studio microphone. The nascent blues revival, an offshoot of its folk counterpart, had created an opening he pursued to the last. Blessed with a prodigious memory and a willingness to describe the life and times of his musical peers framed by his own experiences as a player, he became, in the words of scholar Barry Lee Pearson, "his art form's foremost historian."[73] In his performances, interviews, and published autobiography, Honeyboy's memories reached from the country blues pioneers who first taught him to the players who transformed the music in Chicago. His sagas, like his daily rounds, never lacked vitality. During our first conversation, he had just arrived home at his Chicago apartment, where he had lived since 1952. Then, in his early eighties, yet somehow fresh from an all-night flight from Paris, the following week he would set off for Turkey. "You go all kinds of ways when you're a musician," he said.[74]

Honeyboy, an affectionate nickname given him by his family when he was still a youngster, was born in Shaw, Mississippi, a Delta community. His mother died during childbirth in 1927, her health weakened by dropsy and intensified by the great Mississippi flood. They had been "caught in the high water," and Honeyboy detailed how they, like other families, stayed in railroad boxcars through late May of that year as they waited for the floodwaters to recede.[75] "The water was so tall," he said, and the smell of fish so rank that it permeated every structure. Any homes that did survive required spraying to again become livable. For his family, living in Shaw proved impossible, and his widower father moved them to Greenwood.

Drawn to play by age fourteen, Honeyboy studied under the working blues musicians of his region and came to know an entire generation of players: Robert Johnson, Tommy Johnson, Tommy McClennan, Charley Patton, Robert Petway, and Son House. He embodied the tenacity essential for catching the music, beginning by learning on a mail-ordered Sears, Roebuck guitar that had belonged to his father, Henry Edwards, who also played the fiddle. Honeyboy first learned from watching chords that the older man used for what he called "ragtime stuff."[76] This material included "John Henry," "Railroad Bill," and "Stagolee"—all pieces played in the Black community before the emergence of the blues. Then, in 1932, with his father's permission, Honeyboy left home to follow Big Joe Williams. "I wanted to be Joe Williams," he told me, and a primary way he learned Williams's playing came from seconding him on guitar.[77] He provided a complementary part, typically cast in one of the alternative tunings the older player had shown him. He traveled with Williams for about a year, essentially pursuing an internship with him before coming back to Greenwood. "I was dead on his style. I patterned behind Joe and that's how I learned."[78] Other Delta luminaries, such as Tommy McClennan and Robert Petway, also inspired him, and he played with them soon after his time with Big Joe Williams. He admitted that earlier, when he first came around and was still a boy, both McClennan and Petway found him too eager, too young, and mostly, too unskilled. "I used to run up behind them . . . I was small, and I had a guitar. . . . They used to see me comin' down the streets. They say, 'Yonder comes little old Honey. Let's dodge him.' I was just worrisome. I'd be around every which way they go, they'd turn, I'd be right behind them."[79]

Honeyboy continued to broaden his skills, working in idioms from the country blues to boogie-woogie to jug band music. He played for dances both Black and white. The latter favored songs like "St. Louis Blues" and "Careless Love," but for his Black listeners, Honeyboy emphasized what he called "slow drag and up-shuffle blues." A self-described "walking bluesman," he traveled by foot, freight train, and thumb, hitchhiking throughout the region, and learning tricks of the gambler's trade. In Memphis and outlying towns in west Tennessee, he played with Hammie Nixon, Sleepy John Estes, and Yank Rachell. He described their older style by their choice of chords and keys (C and G), rather than the key of E typically favored in Chicago-style blues, coupled with an "up-tempo beat." His musical knowledge became increasingly formalized at this time through his work back in Greenwood, with a C-melody saxophonist from Clarksdale he called "Little Willie." The duo performed at a riverboat tavern, and Willie's repertory of jazz standards like "Stars Fell on Alabama," "Sophisticated Lady," and "Stardust" led Honeyboy to purchase a guitar book and learn some theory. "I could always make the chords, but I didn't know what I was making. But I knowed they worked together."[80] He added, "You do something long, but you got to learn it." For someone who quit school in fifth or sixth grade, he noted, "I learnt more teaching my own self."

He continued to build his musical identity. His relationship with Robert Johnson, the most fabled of all the Delta's bluesmen, and with whom he spent time on the day of his fatal poisoning, led Honeyboy to say, "I always put some Robert Johnson in my songs, even if they're in my style."[81] He spoke of using the entire fingerboard, of how he favored playing "all of my staff, all of my neck." Thirty years earlier, in a 1968 interview, he explained, "When you first start to play, you got to play like someone, or do something like that . . . You got to pick up somebody's style or something, and then you leave from there."[82] As we sat in his home, his instruments stored in a closet near his bedside, its door handles chained with a bicycle lock, he said, "I had my own thing I wanted to do and had my own style that I wanted to learn." The upshot of this learning, both from records and largely from persons, was "I'm doing it my own ways." As he said in his 1997 autobiography, "I was learning that for me to do my best, to make some headway for myself, I had to learn my own style and hold to that. I think that's the most important thing you can get to. I started to come into my own sound."[83]

Honeyboy's blues mastery, his catching the music, follows a pattern common to his fellow players. Robert Palmer, who wrote the notes to Honeyboy's 1979 album, *Mississippi Delta Bluesman*, noted how bluesmen worked with precedent: "While an artist like Robert Johnson may be highly innovative, many of his lyrics, rhythm patterns, and characteristic vocal and instrumental melodies can be traced to earlier bluesmen or the commercial recordings of his contemporaries. This does not mean individual blues musicians are not creative; to the contrary, they are so creative that no two sound alike."[84]

By the time of his first recordings, Honeyboy had already found his own style. In July 1942, at the recommendation of Son House, folklorist Alan Lomax, representing the Library of Congress in a joint folksong project with Fisk University, went to Clarksdale, Mississippi, where he recorded Honeyboy, who was then mostly working as a street performer and juke joint entertainer. "Worried Life Blues" appeared among the eighteen songs he recorded over two sessions that took place at a nearby schoolhouse. Honeyboy credited Maceo Merriweather's 1941 piano rendition, which had lately appeared on regional jukeboxes. Earlier, Honeyboy had heard the 1935 Decca recording by Sleepy John Estes and Hammie Nixon of "Someday Baby Blues," which they made in Chicago. Here, in his rendition, one man with a guitar becomes an entire orchestra. He takes the song through a succession of single-string runs, bent notes, treble licks, half-chord voicings, and boogie-woogie patterns. Fisk University musicologist John W. Work III, transcribing the field trip's recordings at that time, saw what Honeyboy and his peers Muddy Waters and Son House had achieved. He recognized that with the increasing use of mechanical phonographs, the role of the bluesman as accompanist for social dancing had lessened. Now, he wrote, "patterns copied from the jukebox by the younger men appear to be more melodic and virtuosic, and serve mainly as dazzling cadenzas between phrases or verses of their songs."[85] Honeyboy's "Worried Life Blues" captured that emergent virtuosity.

Though Honeyboy continued to build on this modernized exploration over the decades left to him, he remained forever watchful of prior forms. He spoke poignantly of the motivations for slavery time hollers, how they preserved sanity in a life of ceaseless labor. He prized the range that a fifty-cent Marine Band harmonica could produce, even if it took working "half a day to buy one."[86] He named country reels played by members of his father's generation while staying equally abreast of the increased tempos of the "daytime city blues" heard in Chicago. These built, he said, from slower counterparts, from the "lowdown dirty shame blues" and their dances from an earlier time. His knowledge reached back to blues performers who included Blind Lemon Jefferson, Ida Cox, and Bessie Smith, let alone those who succeeded them. When he purchased his first amplifier in 1946, allowing him to work in tandem with a piano player, he set that development against a historical backdrop. Previously drowned out by the piano's volume, he found that the new loudspeakers created opportunities, and "guitar players started starving the piano players out." In the roadhouses of Mississippi, and soon in the taverns of Chicago, the guitar came into its own. "Once people could hear you, that's when guitar players got big."

Honeyboy Edwards's path toward musical mastery echoed the message of William Sidney Mount's painting. Mount's musical training, like Honeyboy's, started with emulation and admiration. In Mount's case, the exemplar was an ex-slave he had heard in childhood. In time, Mount and Honeyboy both shared a desire for a more formalized music education embodied in Mount's handwritten tune books and Honeyboy's guitar primer for studying chords. Likewise, Honeyboy's first-person contacts with more seasoned players in Mississippi anticipate how Jim Schwall absorbed the blues of Honeyboy's contemporaries and those who followed from their examples. This same kind of learning reflects the myriad ways that musicians took *1000 Fiddle Tunes* across North America.

From a youngster watching and remembering, observing and assimilating, to an adult sitting in with an expert player on a bandstand in a smoky Chicago club, came an ongoing exchange between musicians that Mount's brother termed so common as to be hackneyed. Honeyboy summed up a striving they all shared. At one point during our discussion of "Worried Life Blues," he looked at me with a smile. His rendition, drawn from a song he both knew first-hand and learned from a phonograph record, arose from a molding process: "I put it together myself, but I *used* the song."[87] The song had become a vehicle for his creativity.

Sometimes, though, catching the music may not be enough. Sometimes one might need to steal it. In 1948, harmonica player Junior Wells (1934–1998), a colleague of both Honeyboy Edwards and Jim Schwall, explained why. A couple of years after first coming to Chicago, he spotted a two-dollar mouth organ he desired. He played hooky from school and worked all week on a beverage truck to earn most of its cost, but he lacked the last fifty cents needed to pay the pawnbroker for it whole. He left $1.50 on the counter and pocketed the instrument when the clerk turned away. "When my trial came up the judge asked me why I did it. I told him I *had* to have that harp. The judge asked me to play it and when I did, he gave the man the 50 cents and hollered, 'Case Dismissed.'"[88]

⁂

In 1964 I unknowingly glimpsed my life's course. In that year, the Beatles came to America. Boys in the music store played pop radio hits by ear. I befriended Jim Schwall—the first of my teachers who radiated warmth and led by example. The knowledge and fluency of these boys and Jim embodied the transfer depicted in William Sidney Mount's painting. The tune Mount had in mind as he painted was a fusion of Black and white practices from the Jacksonian era. That same fusion, ninety-eight years later, was taking place in nightspots across Chicago. Here thrived an amalgam that reached from the state of Mississippi to the city of Chicago. It translated into an idea that I could only awkwardly express.

Corky Siegel still remembers my telling him back then that I wanted someday to play "blues banjo." I knew that the two didn't mesh, that the notes of the blues sustained more than the banjo permits. The music differed too, but the instrument and its playing techniques bore qualities that I felt somehow connected to the blues. While I don't recall what prompted me to express this thought, I do remember where we were when I said it: standing outside a Chicago tavern where Corky and Jim were opening for Howlin' Wolf. I was too young to enter, but on that warm day, with the door swung open, I could watch and listen to them.

By then I had heard the five-string banjo, not just as the television theme song from *The Beverly Hillbillies*, but on the radio with Earl Scruggs seconding Paul Warren on fiddle. The two performed instrumental duets, sometimes just titled "Fiddle and Banjo," in which Scruggs provided a pulsing counterpoint to Warren's leads. Their pairings plumbed the oldest reaches of their music via traditional fiddle tunes set within a modern style. In that sense, they paralleled Chicago's postwar bluesmen who also crafted a new amplified music based on older ideas. Producer and historian Sam Charters recognized this continuity, writing in 1966, "The sound of the blues has changed on the South Side, but there's still some of the sound of Mississippi music around the corner in a neighborhood bar or in a lounge near the El tracks . . . driven into a new creative excitement, in the slums of the northern city."[89]

The synthesis I sought did exist in music that arose before the blues. It even reached from the Southern countryside to Chicago's music row. In 1928 both Henry Thomas, a Black songster from Texas, recorded for the Brunswick label located (mentioned earlier in connection with the Crockett family recordings) on south Wabash Avenue, as did his white contemporary, Middle Tennessee banjoist and *Grand Ole Opry* star Uncle Dave Macon.[90] These two players, born in the decades after the Civil War, drew on a repertory of shared dance reels and songs, tonalities, and melodic shapes that this notion of "blues banjo" encompassed. Some of their songs even coincided, being different versions of the same pieces. Admittedly, time passed before I learned about their bodies of work, heard their records, and best of all, got to meet some who had known them or their legatees.[91] My affinity for this blues-inflected quality, of what Bill Monroe called "the old Southern sound," led me to visit Joe and Odell Thompson and others of their generation and earlier who forged this cross-cultural music.[92] Before those travels, I had listened to other Southern home and church musicians caught on folk music field recordings that had appeared on Library of Congress compilations. These weren't readily available, but I found them at the main branch of the Chicago Public Library, located a few blocks past music row. Later, when I edited *A Treasury of Library of Congress Field Recordings* and subsequently wrote *The Beautiful Music All Around Us,* I bore this Deep South sound in mind. Interestingly, the greatest number of those choices and chapters emanated from Mississippi.

I remember being struck in 1964 by the presence of Mississippi in both music and society. In January of that year a book of documentary photography, filled with black-and-white pictures principally taken by recent University of Chicago graduate Danny Lyon and written by Lorraine Hansberry, appeared. Called *The Movement: Documentary of a Struggle for Equality*, it made stark and stunning sense of the brutalities and beauties that marked current civil rights efforts, portraying both its workers and their adversaries. The murders that took place that June in Philadelphia, Mississippi, of James Chaney, Michael Schwerner, and Andrew Goodman added terrifying force to the book's images of segregated drinking fountains, jail cells, and cattle prods. Contemporaneous phonograph albums of the Freedom Riders featured impassioned rewrites of preexisting works. Ray Charles's "Hit the Road, Jack" became "Get Your Rights, Jack." The album that included that particular track was published under the aegis of the Congress of Racial Equality, its jacket showing two horizontal bars of ledger lines.[93] On them the designer inserted telling symbols of the struggle for desegregation: lunch counter seats that serve as musical notes.

Mississippi fixed itself in my consciousness. Musicians I first heard back then and sometimes got to see had come from there: Muddy Waters and Pop Staples, let alone Howlin' Wolf and Honeyboy Edwards. So, too, did a muffled telephone call to our home, making threats over the long-distance wire regarding a family member's contemplated participation in 1964's Freedom Summer. While Mississippi represented what civil rights activist Robert Moses had earlier called "the heart of the iceberg," it also offered in the persons of its blues and gospel musicians the surpassing beauty of their reverberant guitars and chanted rhythmical choruses.[94] In my mind, the civil rights movement's moral purpose and the music's aesthetic grace merged.

For Mississippians, too, the distance from home to Chicago stayed close. This place they called "the city" had long become the destination for so many of their families. I recall a barbeque hosted by the revered fife player and singer Othar Turner (1907–2003) in the field adjacent to his house in northwestern Mississippi in September 1986. The event was an annual local affair. Old car seats, used as chairs, ringed around it. You could buy a beer or a sandwich. Men carried pint bottles in their pockets, while kids laughed and squealed all around. Flatbed trucks lurched out of the driveway, shooting gravel and dust in every direction.

FIGURE 13. *Sit-In Songs* album cover. The album's singers had participated in the 1962 Freedom Highways project, which sought "to open chain restaurants along major federal highways to all persons."

I met a man there. He asked me my name. I told him, Steve. He said his name was Sam. He said, "See, two S's." He said, "Where you from?" I told him Chicago. So was he, that's where he was born. "What year?" I told him. It was the same for both of us. He said, "See, that's three things right there."

In the field, some people danced in ragged sneakers and others wore hose and high heels. Othar and his three drummers marched loosely around the yard and rocked two steps here, one step back. Folks called it "jump and kick music." He played an old-time reel or a fragment of a blues, while the drummers kept time around it. Sometimes the rhythm sounded like what people up north call the "Hey Bo Diddley" beat. The bass drummer told me that he grew up wanting to play with Othar. They started him on a four-gallon washtub when he was a kid, then graduated him to the side of a panel truck, and finally, when he got good enough, they gave him a regular kettle drum. The music perseveres. Somewhere, someone's whistling a tune and someone else is catching it for keeps.

·3·

The Conduit

The last time I saw my teacher Fleming Brown, he was in a Chicago veterans' hospital. For nearly a year, he had been moved from room to room along a bare fluorescent-lit hallway marked "Oncology" while ardent young doctors administered ever-intensifying treatments. Now at the far end of the khaki-colored wing, Fleming occupied a ward whose beds contained new patients every week. Motioning to the gaunt, drained faces lying around him, he would mutter "terminal" as if it were their christened names. This word described his condition, and five days before he would pass away, the word finally seemed to fit him.

That evening, as Fleming (1926–1984) was falling asleep, I picked up his hand to say goodbye. He had been a captivating man, graced with Gary Cooper looks and rugged charm. Now red Mercurochrome squares mapped fields of radiation across the proud but ravaged landscape of his face. His body was shrinking away, and the big silver ring he always wore dangled loosely on his finger. A nurse came in to change the bedding, but he didn't stir as she rolled him from one side to the other. Under morphine sedation, in a wheezing, exhausted sleep, Fleming was far away. But along

FIGURE 14. Fleming Brown demonstrating "Soldier's Joy" for his banjo class at Chicago's Old Town School of Folk Music, ca. 1968. Courtesy of Old Town School of Folk Music Resource Center & Archives.

the tips of his skeletal fingers, a thin black line, the imprint left by metal strings, was still discernible.

As I held his hand in mine, a moment from three months before came to mind. Sitting up in his hospital bed, Fleming put his hands together into the shape of a box. Smiling slyly he said, "I know the secret of banjo playing." I drew in closer and begged him, "Tell me, what is it, please." Dazzling like an ancient god despite his pale hospital gown and his withered frame—he still a flame and I the moth—Fleming said, "It's all in a little box and someday I'll show you what's in that box."[1]

He was teasing me again with his promise of treasure, still in confident possession of a motherlode of understanding, in complete command of his chosen art. For nearly four decades, he had been tendering a cantankerous, recondite instrument, sharing its Orphic mysteries with all who inquired. Acting as a guardian and exemplar, he exacted only sincerity from novitiates.

Although I had grown up in the same northside Wrigley Field neighborhood as Fleming, I had never walked down the twisting one-way street where he lived. Even the cab driver hauling me, my banjo, and a suitcase containing a bulky reel-to-reel tape recorder for my first lesson encircled the block, finding it difficult to decipher the one viable route to his door. Throughout the dozen years I studied with him, I always felt those trips up to his attic apartment—remote as an eagle's nest—meant entering another world.

We would sit on gleaming tubular chairs in a room that was otherwise crammed with Native American artifacts and antique instruments. We sat facing each other in the blue light from his color television and the yellow light from his collection of kerosene lamps. With his banjo in his lap, he'd drink bourbon after bourbon, the amber liquid spinning around the ice cubes in his glass, his long bony fingers reaching always for another unfiltered cigarette. Lyrics surfaced in his mind, from pools of memory many years deep. He would sing:

> Long John said before he died,
> Two more roads I'd like to ride.
> What, oh what can they be,
> The Southern Pacific and the Sanctifeed.[2]

Sanctifeed? Fleming was rolling again. Although the last word in others' versions would be "Santa Fe," he had pronounced it "Santa Fee," and then reconstituted it into "Sanctifeed." He tied a vernacular pronunciation to a liturgical word and locked it onto a rambler's lyric. The song's dimensions enlarged; a gospel railroad lay just ahead. When Fleming found notches like that, I'd be giggling, he'd be cool, and then, with that sly look again on his face, he'd say "Gotcha!"

The tradition had gone so far into his sinews, it came out in curlicues and flourishes that marked the genuine from the reproduction, and the creative from the quotidian. The music he knew had blended into his frame; the two became indivisible, and the eccentricities of the art and the man merged—inseparable, idiomatic, intuitive. His mastery rested on palatial foundations.

Fleming considered traditional Appalachian music an inheritance bequeathed by players from the past. While he characterized the 1920s phonograph records as "just scratches," as he talked about them, their grainy pockmarked surfaces began to seem like the pages of Holy Writ. He would run his fingers over the flowery Victorian type of their labels and point out the names of the prophets of this religion: Uncle Dave Macon, the Bog Trotters, and the Piedmont Log Rollers. Then he'd give me his interpretation of a tune on one of those discs. I'd play the piece back, and he'd listen to it. If he didn't agree with my version, he'd play his over again. But ultimately, he'd say, "Go back to the record. They got it right."

Fleming often cited a musician from western North Carolina, Bascom Lamar Lunsford. A lawyer by profession, but best remembered as a festival organizer, song collector, and performer, Lunsford recorded in 1949 some 350 pieces for the Library of Congress, at that time the largest contribution any one musician had made to its folksong collection.[3] Fleming particularly recalled his first visit to the old man's home near Asheville: "My wife and I drove a 1951 MG roadster straight through to North Carolina. I still remember looking down the sides of those mountain roads. If you fall off in winter, they don't dig you out till spring. When we got there, Lunsford's greeting was to show us how he'd perfected the art of writing his whole name without ever lifting the pencil off the paper. After we'd driven fifteen hours from Chicago, he wrote his name for the first half-hour." Nevertheless, Fleming maintained, this musician called the Minstrel of the Appalachians "sang like he meant it."

Lunsford had recorded an ancient one-chord song called "Darby's Ram"; the tune, one of George Washington's favorites, describes a mythical beast who:

had a horn, sir,
and it reached right to the moon.
and a man went up in January,
didn't get back till June.

Fleming said Bascom sang, "This old ramma had a horn." Fleming wanted me to know this: "Ramma—he didn't sing ram." The lesson was: "You play it like you want it to be played. You make a statement. This is me—you're exposing yourself—this is the way I see it. And that man knew he wanted to sing ramma." Then Fleming picked up his banjo and sang the old song, and all of a sudden, you saw the mighty animal. He inscribed it, depicted it, and captured it.

Fleming approached traditional music as an art form that surpassed its role as social expression or its function as a cultural artifact. He took a brazenly aesthetic stance and often repeated an aphorism about Big Bill Broonzy, the great Chicago blues singer: "It's not the notes Big Bill played; it's the notes he didn't play." Fleming explored a musicality that made use of pauses, surprises, and suspense. To operate at this level meant going beyond imitation: it had to be an interpretation. He said, "We're all trying to get at it. There's no set way of doing it." Then he paused, and flashed that foxy look, "There's a thousand ways to get to St. Louis."

Fleming never chose music as a full-time profession; he cherished his amateur status. He said, "The root word of amateur is love," and love was his driving force: "You take this piece and say, 'Hey, look what I found, this is real.' When I heard this music, I was hearing something that meant something. There was something about the banjo I just had to do. . . . Just getting that son-of-a-gun out of you the way it feels inside. It's a battle. A real battle." That's how Fleming played—like a fighter—his muscles flexing in his jaw, his fingers jabbing out the combinations of the melody.

As the evenings unfolded, we'd play duets, fusing our styles. Fleming would say, "Don't be afraid to play things simply—what you want all the time is contrast. Play it two-finger, now three." We'd drift through tunes, celebrating the players and their styles. "Here's the attack of Roscoe Holcomb—that's east Kentucky, two-finger, thumb lead. . . . Listen to Wade Ward's clean lope—that's Southwestern Virginia clawhammer. . . . Look how Uncle Dave Macon rocked the rhythm—that's the Tennessee Black influence. . . . " We were drawing from a national portrait gallery of performers, eliciting notes and reproducing licks the way a lawyer relies on precedents. Our renderings would be indebted to these masters. We might take a song recorded by two entirely different players and combine parts, or work out a whole repertoire from a single musician's point of view. Either way, the musicians we learned from signified values. There was only one way to thank them: to learn their styles, to publish them to the world, and finally, to go our own way.

Living in the wreckage of three failed marriages, Fleming was driven to sing. He would look around his apartment at the things he'd hung onto after court costs and alimony payments and say, "The banjo has saved me a lot in psychiatrist fees." Then he'd close his eyes, and play his banjo, attaching himself to the music—these players and their songs—locating himself in a delicate balance between a recollection of them and the audiences he faced. He called himself "a conduit."

Fleming made it his business to know and learn from Hobart Smith, Frank Proffitt, George Pegram, Bascom Lunsford, Uncle Alex Turner, and Uncle Jason Ritchie—all of them great traditional banjo players who lived into the second half of the twentieth century. He formed his style by drawing from living musicians and past recordings. He even invented a "Fleming Brown chord." Modal, ambiguously suspended between standard diatonic formations, the chord (in G tuning, Fleming played a first-position C without the higher third, making the notes, fifth string to first, gEGCD) brought mood and complexity to otherwise superficial arrangements. His songs, filtered through his sensibility, painted emotional canvases: "Cuckoo" rang darkly haunted; "Mountain Dew" summoned anarchic jubilation.

He sang with grace and mystery, power and passion, understatement and drama. But it was in the last decades of his life, in his teaching, where he gave of himself most deeply.

His pedagogy required years of preparation. Fleming bought his first banjo in 1947. The jazz era's tenor banjo and the Dixieland revival's longer-necked plectrum were brash cousins of the older, asymmetrical five-string model Fleming had chosen. Not knowing how to tune it, or even which strings to buy, he struggled to play.

In 1948, Pete Seeger stopped in Chicago during the Henry Wallace presidential campaign. Fleming went to Pete's hotel room, asking if he could suggest a tutor. Pete was still formulating his banjo instruction manual, carrying along a typewriter for that purpose. However, he recommended an old-time Kentucky singer and banjo player currently broadcasting on Chicago's WLS *National Barn Dance* radio show. The musician's name was Doc Hopkins, and he had been playing in Chicago since 1930. Warm-hearted and affable, Doc agreed to pass along the music he knew—technique and songs—demonstrating those elements as best he could. They made a plan to meet at the Eighth Street Theater, where Doc performed. Doc told Fleming, "Come by around five."

"No, make it five-thirty," Fleming said, "I get off work at five."

"No, five a.m.," Doc reproved, "That's when I do my wake-up program" (called, appropriately, "The Smile-A-While Show"). Thus, over coffee and breakfast rolls, Fleming would come to Doc for songs and advice, returning only after he had mastered each lesson's hurdle.

Beginning with homemade disc cuttings of Doc, Fleming began to build his repertoire. He added tunes from the early commercial mountain music records and then drew others from the field collections undertaken by the Library of Congress's Archive of Folk Song. Either by slowing down the phonograph or playing the records at speed, he reconstructed melodies from musicians who relied on neither standard pitches nor standard tunings. They pitched their banjos to suit their voices and tuned the strings to accommodate the primary notes of the songs. Through an idiosyncratic combination of virtuosity and personality, Fleming recorded mentors who represented the classic performances. In his words, "a classic is a song whose interpretation cannot be improved upon. Met, maybe, but not improved upon." Fleming collected these resources. He'd learn songs, absorb styles, and target the parts that attracted him. Then he'd codify what he'd learned into written tablature.

Seeger used this form of music writing throughout his banjo book. In tablature, derived from Renaissance lute notation, notes are numbered according to their location on the fretboard, and the picking of the strings is described schematically. For a player, this method simplifies fingering, but it remains difficult to know how a tune sounds without reference to a recording or a performance. Fleming Brown combined his demonstrations with this practical notation. For thirteen years he brought new tablatures each week to perform for his classes at Chicago's Old Town School of Folk Music.

Fleming became the school's primary old-time banjo instructor and thus enjoyed a special stature there. He had recorded long-playing albums, had performed at the debut Newport Folk Festival, and had traveled south to meet firsthand a number of legendary singers and instrumentalists. A commercial graphic artist by profession, his involvement with the school allowed him to stay in weekly practice with his music. Conversely, bringing images of rural music to much of his daily work, Fleming eventually illustrated Pete Seeger's banjo manual. The original edition appeared in

FIGURE 15. One of Fleming Brown's illustrations for Pete Seeger's 1954 manual, *How to Play the 5-String Banjo,* second edition.

forty mimeographed pages, with a staple in the left-hand corner. Fleming's drawings thanked Pete for recommending Doc Hopkins as a teacher. Pete returned the compliment on the credits page of the second and subsequent editions, writing, "special acknowledgment and thanks go to Fleming Brown, artist and banjo picker of Chicago . . . "[4] And that is how I heard of him.

Who is this "artist and banjo picker of Chicago"? I wondered. On a hunch, I walked over to the Old Town School. I asked the lady behind the front desk, "Have you ever heard of a banjo player named Fleming Brown?"

"Yes," she said, "he's teaching here tomorrow night. Would you like to sign up?" "I think so," I said. "Is he any good?"

She nodded slowly, "Oh yes."

As if to confirm his expertise, I asked, "How many banjos does he have?"

She answered, "Fifteen."

I said, "Sign me up."

Our little class felt like an outpost outside the hurly-burly of the early 1970s. We were on our own. Fleming eschewed the Second Half, where the school would assemble for sing-alongs and refreshments. Instead, he'd go around the room, making each of us play solo, and then record for our tape machines, his versions of the tunes. These first public performances were difficult moments for many of his students. Here was a forceful, emphatic man whose cowboy boots stomped the floor and whose baritone voice flooded the bare classroom while he led us in pursuit of a lofty vision of traditional Appalachian song. He said later, "There were those students who could never quite master taking the banjo out of the case, and there were others who expected a diploma at the end of it." Yet he also said, "Those years at the school were all worthwhile."

How I loved that time with him before he got sick. I was his Frankenstein's creation, and I reveled in his attention. I started out utterly captured by his presence and his sound. Old-timers at the school found resemblances in photographs between the young Fleming and me. Almost immediately people called him my mentor. Fleming used to joke about how I'd come to his classes each week and play back his pieces note for note, including his mistakes. I took to dressing like him, and for a short time, even carried a pint of Jim Beam, his favorite, in the compartment of my banjo case.

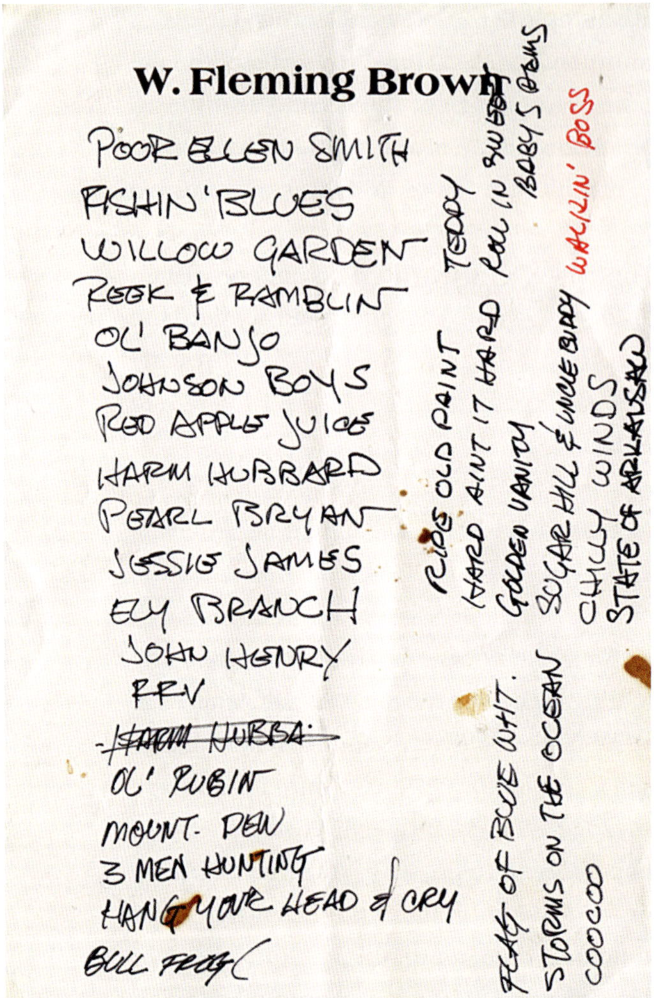

W. Fleming Brown

POOR ELLEN SMITH
FISHIN' BLUES
WILLOW GARDEN
REEK & RAMBLIN
OL' BANJO
JOHNSON BOYS
RED APPLE JUICE
HARM HUBBARD
PEARL BRYAN
JESSIE JAMES
ELY BRANCH
JOHN HENRY
RRV
~~HARM HUBBA~~
OL' RUBIN
MOUNT. DEW
3 MEN HUNTING
HANG YOUR HEAD & CRY
BULL FROG

TEDDY
ROLL IN MY SWEET BABY'S ARMS
WALKIN' BOSS
RIDES OLD PAINT
HARD AINT IT HARD
GOLDEN VANITY
SUGAR HILL & UNCLE BUDDY
CHILLY WINDS
STATE OF ARKANSAW
FLAG OF BLUE WHT.
STORMS ON THE OCEAN
COOCOO

FIGURE 16. A typical Fleming Brown song list, ca. 1976.

Eventually, Fleming told me, I had to go on my own; develop my own repertoire, my own style: "We have to break the umbilical." Soon after, I became a teacher at the Old Town School, and in time, inherited his advanced class. Now a full-time performer, I spent many evenings listening to singers and cadging free cheeseburgers at a local folk music saloon on Chicago's Lincoln Avenue called "Somebody Else's Troubles." It was there I committed my one indiscretion with Fleming. It was a crisis-filled moment during which Fleming taught me—a driven, self-centered twenty-one-year-old—the essence of traditional musicianship.

I was hanging out one night, standing at the end of the bar with Fleming's best friend. He kept asking me to name the best banjo player, and I kept answering Fleming. Perhaps it was the glibness of my reply or the look in my eyes, but he kept pressing the point. I finally allowed, "Well, technically I am." Not long after, maybe a week or so, I called Fleming, urging him to come down to the Old Town School to play at a film screening of *Grand Ole Opry* in honor of the late Uncle Dave Macon. This Republic Pictures B-movie contains the only extant footage of the legendary banjo player who simultaneously sang, danced, twirled, and picked his banjo. Fleming said he wouldn't come. "Furthermore," he told me, "our relationship is marred and endangered." At first, bewildered, and then frantic, I asked, "What is it?" He recounted my indiscretion. Then he said, "There is no best banjo player, there are only different banjo players." Fleming traced in that single statement the separate, yet inviolable paths of all true players. He forgave me, but throughout our remaining years, he never let me forget my lesson.

During that phone call Fleming showed me that we are all players with as many different sounds and tunes and repertoires and skills—as varied as our voices—as are the ways we touch the strings of our banjos. He made clear how the players we studied—persons who made this record or that contribution—offered not obstacles but gifts. These individuals weren't competitors but colleagues. For me to claim I had surpassed him was to lose sight of the fundamental affirmation that safeguards the continuity of traditional music. Here were these old-time musicians—and that includes Fleming himself—all uniquely inimitable; they cannot be bettered, only differentiated, comprehended, and appreciated.

Traditional music is an art form that, like all art forms, depends on subtlety. A tune has recognizable contours, yet becomes most genuinely alive in the personal solutions brought by its practitioners. It is given to us freely and is "published" in the public domain.[5] It persists because of love and respect. It is cherished and remembered by old people, catalogued and conserved by scholars, saved and affirmed by fans. Discs left in a hat box, records found at a yard sale, instruments taken from a closet, recordings made at home—all of these survivals result from an ethic of taking care. The music can be learned, but without commitment, it cannot be played well. It requires devotion and responsibility, wholeheartedness and intelligence.

The lessons my teacher gave me came from another time, almost another world. He also gave me his banjo. It marks a special moment in my life, but Fleming's banjo is merely on loan to me, and someday it must belong to someone else. In that, it is like the music itself. We are fortunate that there is a body of traditional music to inspire us, and that it is capacious enough that we can enter into it and make it our own. But we are all conduits, and at heart, we are all amateurs.

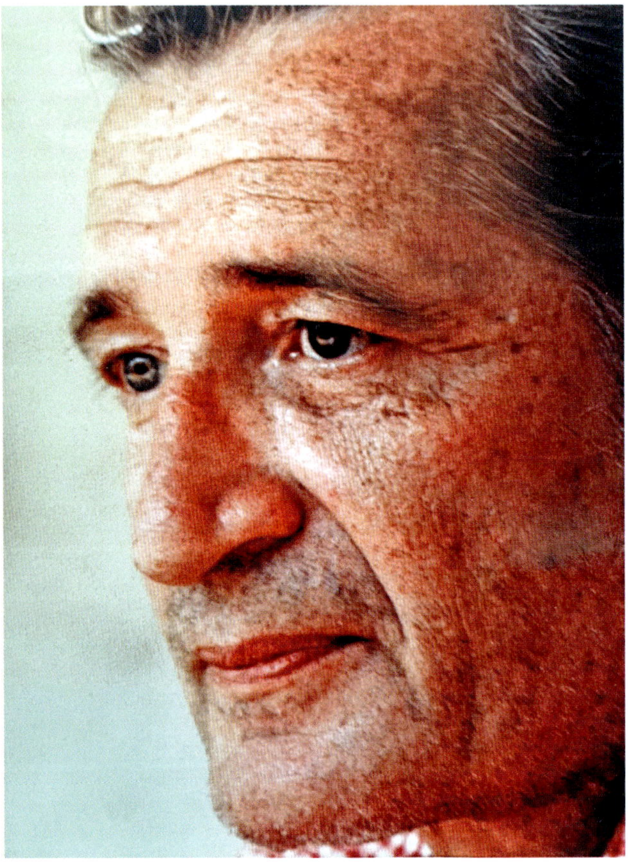

FIGURE 17. Fleming Brown, Chicago, Illinois, ca. 1981. Photo by Frank Brown.

·4·

America's Favorite Folk Singer

Doc Hopkins waited at the Loyola stop on Chicago's elevated line. Born Doctor Howard Hopkins (1900–1988) and raised in rural Kentucky, he headed that evening for the Eighth Street Theatre. There he would appear, as he had many so Saturday nights before, on the WLS *National Barn Dance*, the nation's first major country music radio program. Launched in 1924, the long-running show had found millions of listeners across the Midwest, and when atmospheric conditions permitted, its airwaves reached beyond the prairie states and deep into the Carolinas. Over the years, the *Barn Dance*, which introduced such stars as Gene Autry, Patsy Montana, The Girls of the Golden West, the Hoosier Hot Shots, and Red Foley to the nation, included Doc Hopkins, who first joined the cast in the summer of 1930. While Doc's fame never approached theirs and his commercially recorded output remained slender throughout his professional career, countless devotees welcomed his warm tenor voice and old-time songs into their homes. Here in the late 1940s, he still received monthly sacks of fan mail from thousands of listeners. The station billed him as "America's Favorite Folk Singer."[1]

That night, as Doc waited on the train platform, a tall, elderly Black man approached him. Motioning to his instrument case, the man said:

"What you got there?"

"I've got a guitar."

"Do you play?"

Doc said, "Yeah."

"Do you sing?"

Again, Doc affirmed.

"Where do you play?"

"I'm playing this *National Barn Dance* here in Chicago."

He asked, "Do you broadcast?

"Yeah."

"Do you sing 'Barbara Ellen'?"

"Yeah, I sure do," Doc responded. Then Doc added with a chuckle, "I sing 'John Henry' too."

The man suddenly stopped, as if to say, "whoa." With gathering intensity, he said, "Maybe you won't believe me when I tell you, because John Henry is my father. I'm the son of John Henry."

Doc paused. "Well, I have to believe you because you're the right age. This could be possible. How old are you?"

"I'm 82."

"I sure am glad you let yourself be known," Doc replied. "Because I heard the story about John Henry. He did live and he was a champion steel driver."[2]

No matter how verifiable the older man's claim, to say nothing of the scholarly disputes that have followed this song, that fleeting encounter reflected a constant in Doc Hopkins's life: his abiding interest in the stories that surround folksong, whether factually based or just widely believed. It did not surprise Doc that "John Henry," the single most recorded American traditional ballad, possessed deep personal as well as historical and musical dimensions. Yet his chance meeting on the Loyola platform with John Henry's son exerted a hold on him that did not diminish with the years, and he repeated the story on multiple occasions. Doc's respect for the older man's earnestness, coupled with the possibility of what he professed, only added to the song's significance, its grandeur and wonder.

Since his mid-teens, Doc said, he "made it more or less a practice of picking up true stories behind these songs—as true as I can get."[3] The sheaves of letters he wrote and the scores of tapes we made together, let alone his interviews with earlier researchers, demonstrate his unflagging interest in the music and its background. His fingers stiffened from diabetes, and his hearing got to the point where he said, "Steve, I'm deaf in one ear and I can't hear out of the other."[4] But Doc persisted in his efforts to document this past.

When he could no longer play, he would whistle his songs note by note and if need be, place my fingers along the fretboard if they erred. We talked by telephone until the squeal of his increasingly defective hearing aid finally smothered our voices. Most of all, Doc wrote detailed accounts of his life, historical vignettes, as well as autobiographical ones. Once it became too painful to type, Doc switched to longhand. Finally, when simply holding a pen cut into his fingers, he used a cassette recorder he kept at his bedside. As old stage bits—jokes and sayings and riddles, along with songs and matters of personal advice—came to mind, he recited them into the machine. He wanted all this put to use, not as a memorial, but as a model.

Doc was not nostalgic. He wrote and recorded not to simply reminisce, but to leave a record of experiences that possessed both historical value and immediate utility. Doc hoped that his remembrances of bygone times and entertainments would be not only passed on but transformed into new writing and new performances. Doc believed fervently in creative independence. I painfully remember on more than a few occasions when he pointed out as I played for him, "That note don't belong there." But he also counseled, "If you find some word that don't suit you, change it and put in another word. That's just like putting a new patch on an old pair of britches."[5]

Doc's kindly comparison defines the elasticity in tradition, that freedom, as Benjamin Botkin says of folklore, "to tell it again in your own way, because it is anybody's property."[6] Doc's upbringing, his career, and his music affirm the heritage he received and the autonomy that he encouraged. In recalling scenes of his life, Doc Hopkins told his own history and a nation's too. That history rears up in an old man appearing on an El stop saying, "John Henry is my father."

Doctor Howard Hopkins was the seventh son born to James and Lucinda (Howard) Hopkins. Mountain belief attributed healing powers to that lineal descendant. For this reason, Doc's aunt Elizabeth Howard, childless herself, insisted that the baby receive "Doctor" as his given name.[7] As a boy, Doc lived up to that moniker by practicing imaginary medicine on his grandmother. He rolled pine rosin "pills" that she would feign to swallow.

Beyond this childhood play, however, Doc exhibited therapeutic talents that became apparent early on. He served as a neighborhood healer. Mothers found that he could help their infants afflicted with "thrash" by blowing into their mouths, easing the soreness that teething produced. Doc found that his gift repeatedly brought about desired results, as did his ability to remove people's warts by rubbing them off their arms. Traditional medicine records these practices in both the South and in Southern migrant families.[8] Doc compared his skills, which he considered intuitive, to other poultices and remedies known in his community. Yet he cautioned, when speaking of homemade cures and related lore such as the forecasts found in the *Farmers' Almanac*, "I wouldn't want to depend on that as much as the weather bureau."[9] For Doc, folk knowledge and formal expertise each bore truths.

Fact and belief likewise inhabit accounts of Doc's rearing. He was born in Possum Hollow, Kentucky, a mountain settlement near the village of Wallins Creek in Harlan County. The community credited its first settler for naming the hollow. He had awoken early one morning in his cabin to find a large, reportedly grinning opossum enjoying leftovers on the kitchen stove. As for the standing pail of dishwater nearby, the homesteader had set that refreshment aside for his pigs.

Doc's birth in Possum Hollow occurred on a stormy night in late January 1900. (As a way of measuring his age, he would cheerfully say, "I change with the year.") That evening, Doc's Uncle Lige, unable to contact the family's doctor, called on a neighboring midwife. At a crossing about a mile from home, in the intensifying rain, the two rode double on the Hopkins family's mule. The rising waters came up nearly belly deep on the animal, and coupled with an already slippery rock bottom, the creature stumbled and fell. Uncle Lige and the midwife, now water-soaked, nonetheless reached the home in time to assist with Doc's birth. The village's doctor, who had never gone to medical school but had a license based on his practical experience, soon reached the newborn and his mother. As Doc later recounted, he "finished the job."[10]

FIGURE 18. Doc Hopkins and siblings, Brodhead, Kentucky, 1909. Seated l-r: Doc's brothers Grant, Berry, and Doc. Standing: Doc's sister Lula, and behind her with a banjo, Doc's brother Lige. The family dog, Bob, sleeps on the porch.

In 1904, the family relocated near Renfro Valley, Kentucky, on a farm close to the towns of Mt. Vernon and Brodhead in the foothills of the Cumberland Mountains. The family's move to Rockcastle County stemmed from Jim Hopkins's desire to establish some distance from his in-laws, who hailed, as did his wife, Cindy, from Harlan County. A native of Tazewell, Tennessee, Jim Hopkins worked in timber before the advent of mining and the coming of the railroad to the wider region. "He never tired with an ax," Doc said of his father, whom he described as "a mountain farmer."[11] The Hopkins family, which in addition to Jim and Cindy, numbered eight boys and one girl, worked their new land six days a week. They raised sixty acres of corn plus a hayfield, where they planted wheat or sometimes tobacco.

Jim Hopkins found ease in calculating numbers, a figuring ability as useful in timber management as in crop planning. He gleaned his reading skills from a *Blue Back Speller*. Doc thought that his father possessed an inherently scientific turn of mind, unhampered by a lack of formal education. "The only school he ever went to was held under a big oak tree."[12] He added, "We didn't know addition and subtraction nor division, but we sure did learn how to multiply."[13]

In his younger days, James Arton Hopkins (1861–1933) became known as "Banjo Picking Jim." He established a reputation as a good square dance musician and played the fiddle among his many talents. Jim also read "buckwheat notes" or shape notes, a geometrically shaped form of printed musical notation. This visually ingenious method of sight reading and harmony training played a key role, Doc explained, in fostering that era's singing conventions and development of gospel quartets. For Jim Hopkins, however, his musical activity ceased soon after he and Cindy Howard (1867–1957) wed. Their new church spurned music as personally sinful and socially disruptive. Jim dropped the banjo entirely, while Cindy, as Doc mused, just "played tunes on the pots and pans."[14] Yet at age seven, the first piece Doc learned to play was the banjo song "Free Little Bird." His father had been his primary source.

Doc, like other children living nearby, grew up exploring the saltpeter caves and sinkholes of the Rockcastle County countryside. He made his first earnings by picking blackberries, receiving ten cents a gallon. He brought the fruit to market in buckets and received payment measured by the peck, not weight. For Doc this presented a problem in that the produce inevitably sank en route, requiring him to bring along a second container to repack the contents. In the fall and winter months, with his hunting dog Bob, whom he described as a "bench-legged fice," Doc trapped possums and polecats for their hides, which he prepared by stretching and drying them in the family's smokehouse.[15] These, too, fetched pocket income.

Weather permitting, Doc and his younger sister walked to the Red Bud schoolhouse, a one-room, log-hewed structure set on a wooded hillside near Mt. Vernon. Its rafters gave shelter to the mud dauber wasps that nested there, and its lack of indoor sanitation required boys to go up one lane to relieve themselves while the girls followed down another. Red Bud schoolhouse marked both the beginning and end of Doc Hopkins's formal education.

In childhood, Doc stuttered when he spoke. He found that when the schoolmaster called on him to recite or read aloud, his classmates snickered. "The most embarrassing, miserable thing in the world is to have a whole class of girls laugh at you because you stuttered. I hated every one of them."[16] In the close quarters of the Red Bud schoolhouse, this grieved him so much that he finally refused to attend. Despite his father's misgivings, Doc asserted, "I'll go there no more." The pain he felt over his humiliation even led him to contemplate suicide. Yet during those same challenging years, he discovered that whenever he sang, his impairment, which he called that "stoppage in my speech," entirely disappeared. "You know how I came to sing," he explained. "I couldn't talk."[17] Music gave him his voice.

• • •

At twelve, Doc left school to begin his first formal employment, working at a local stone quarry. Much like a scene from the "John Henry" ballad that he came to know, Doc served as a shaker, assisting two-man, steel-driving teams. These laborers, wielding heavy, limber-handled hammers, took turns pounding drill bits into the shale. Their incisions formed cylindrical holes into which they placed dynamite charges. Before detonation—a daily noontime event at this quarry—Doc, wearing goggles and gloves, would shake the steel bit as the drivers hammered, pour water to cool it off, and then, with a ladle and pail, remove the sand as it accumulated. For these efforts, he received thirty cents a day. To reach the job site he walked four miles there and back.

But it was the Red Bud schoolhouse that served as the originating point for several of Doc's most pivotal and enduring professional relationships. The school's principal, Bill Davis, enrolled his four children there, including his son, Karl, who, in the 1930s, gained lasting fame as composer of the hit song "Kentucky," as well as "I'm Here to Get My Baby Out of Jail." Karl based the latter on Doc's banjo piece "Goin' Down the Creek," itself part of the "Old Reuben" song family. Another of their classmates, Harty Taylor, son of the town's blacksmith and born Hartford Connecticut Taylor, grew close to them both, and in succeeding years collaborated with Karl Davis to establish the long-standing singing duo of Karl and Harty. In the mid-1920s all three—Doc, Karl, Harty, plus accompanist Simmy Purcell—toured the state in a band they called the Kentucky Krazy Kats. The group, with Doc on lead vocals and steel guitar, Karl on mandolin, Harty on second guitar, and Purcell on mandola, performed Hawaiian and related popular music during half-time shows for the Mt. Vernon basketball team, a team for which Karl also played. They also made occasional appearances on Louisville radio station WHAS. In 1930, Karl and Harty again united with Doc as the lead singer for their newly formed Cumberland Ridge Runners, a band that Doc named and which soon became an enduring attraction on the air. All these ventures—the duo, Doc's solo career, and their famed WLS radio ensemble (whose members included, at one point, guitarist Les Paul) were managed by yet another pupil from Red Bud.

Shortly before Doc, Karl Davis, and Harty Taylor enrolled at Red Bud, John Lair (1894–1985), a few years their senior, began attending the school. Lair came to know them all, sharing their passion for traditional music. After coming to Chicago in the mid-1920s to work as an insurance adjuster, he joined the *National Barn Dance* in 1930, following the departure from the program of yet another of their Mt. Vernon friends, the renowned singer Bradley Kincaid. That summer, while on a visit home, Lair invited his old classmates to come to Chicago. "John Lair is the brain and starter and I give him credit for all our radio success," Doc wrote. "He got all our

FIGURE 19. Doc Hopkins with the Cumberland Ridge Runners, Chicago, Illinois, 1942. From *WLS Family Album*.

auditions for us, wrote all the programs, and managed the Cumberland Ridge Runners when we started at WLS."[18]

Early on, Lair featured Red Bud schoolhouse in his radio scripts. The school, as he represented it, epitomized a sentimental past:

> An there's the little ole log school house—Red Bud—where we usta go to school, an all them good old days comes back to us an standin' there lookin' at the ole tumbledown schoolhouse seems like we kin see shadders flittin' around through the moonlight that looks like us when we wuz kids, an all the kids we usta to go to school with. . . . [19]

As Michael Ann Williams points out in her penetrating study aptly titled *Staging Tradition: John Lair and Sarah Gertrude Knott*, Lair "seemed most to want to sell sincerity and authenticity."[20] Lair took that passion one step further when he returned home to establish the *Renfro Valley Barn Dance*, a live radio show and tourist complex, near Mt. Vernon. There he had the schoolhouse physically moved to those grounds, a standing memorial to homespun America.

Six more shadows whose outlines Doc never forgot also numbered among his Red Bud schoolmates. Sometime in 1905 or 1906, four railroad employees, respectively named Weaver, Ponder, Tharp, and Helton boarded the number 24, a daily Louisville-bound passenger train that originated in Corbin. It wrecked on the way, resulting in their deaths. The four victims received a mass funeral in Brodhead, leaving behind their six youngsters, who attended Red Bud with Doc.

The accident soon became the subject of a ballad called the "Wreck of 24." Blind Bill Cox, an itinerant songster who played at the Brodhead Fair, wrote the song and included it in a "ballet book," a ten-cent printed pamphlet that he sold at his performances. In a telling image of Cox as a journeyman, Doc recalled not only the ca. 1909 songbook that included this ballad, which he purchased from Cox, but the blind man's weather-beaten guitar. It had so blackened from wear that Doc found it impossible to determine its original color. He described Cox, who wore dark glasses to conceal his empty eye sockets, as both a beggar and "a troubadour of many songs, many fine, sad songs."[21] Doc learned the "Wreck of 24" from Cox as he did "Wreck on the C&O," and sang both numbers over the years.

Cox's plaintive singing also influenced Doc. While Doc felt that singing lies "all in the individual," and the development of his self-taught skills as "strictly homemade," he freely acknowledged that Cox had affected him. "I kind of latched onto that style of singing."[22] This aesthetic was as steeped in regional tradition as the high, lonesome sound long associated with Doc's Harlan County birthplace. His old friend Merle Travis, from Muhlenberg County in the western part of the state, for instance, sang in a relaxed manner. Likewise, Doc's neighbor and friend from Rockcastle County, Bradley Kincaid (1895–1989), whose role as the *Barn Dance*'s balladeer he took over at WLS, benefited from settlement school training. He, too, cultivated a soft and melodious approach. All this to say that in exercising his style, Doc amplified an established folk precedent. To the end of his life, Doc could recall melodies and texts, and through them all—traditional folksongs from "the old English," his name for the transatlantic ballads and lyric songs of Anglo and Irish ancestry, to latter-day spirituals and blues, from frolic songs to popular numbers—he upheld Bill Cox's singing as an artistic model.

Nor did his embrace of Cox's sound limit his appreciation of other, less traditional music. By the early 1920s, Doc admired the popular guitarist and singer Nick Lucas, "The Crooning Troubadour." Doc mentioned him in relation to Cox, noting a similarly controlled, affective delivery. Doc began performing Lucas's numbers, and by decade's end, his repertory included "Painting the Clouds with Sunshine," "You're a Real Sweetheart," and the most famous of them all, "Tiptoe Through the Tulips." In speaking of them both, Doc mentioned a classically trained opera teacher whom one of his brothers knew. The older singer commented, after listening to one of Doc's early recordings, that Doc possessed "the sympathetic voice."[23] Doc found that description felicitous for himself as well as these others.

Doc's sympathetic singing fit what so many professional performers who shared his background had expressed in country music: "Pervading the entire range is an attitude of seriousness, sincerity, and reality. This attitude survived and palliated the ultimate professionalism of the hillbilly musician. Songs had to be meaningful, in this sense, real."[24] Folklorist D. K. Wilgus, who made this observation, pointedly included Doc Hopkins as an example among these entertainers. Wilgus was the first scholar to write about Doc, whom he remembered from the radio broadcasts of his Midwestern upbringing. Throughout his career, Wilgus explored the realities of musicians like Doc, who performed "folk music for the folk."[25]

Five years after Doc first taped "Wreck of 24" for Wilgus's UCLA colleague Ed Kahn, the professor wrote to the principal Louisville newspaper to ask if any readers knew of this incident or texts of the song.[26] In searching for both its factual and creative history, Wilgus knew that folksongs vary as they move from one person to another. While his 1966 column item, based on Doc's rendition, received no known responses, it calls to mind a distinction Wilgus explored a few years later during his presidential address to the American Folklore Society. There he differentiated "folk history" from "actual practices," pointing out that "folk explanations . . . furnish truths, but not always facts."[27]

Here they form both. Whatever stylistic commonplaces Cox's song might have possessed, the living presence of Doc's fatherless classmates formed an incontestable factuality. Blind Bill Cox had invoked a familiar ballad language, melodic contour, and chord structure to commemorate a local tragedy, and then sung it in a convincingly evocative manner. For Doc Hopkins, the "Wreck of 24," not unlike his meeting John Henry's son at the elevated station in Chicago, epitomized what he meant by "true stories." The sorrow of those youngsters, whom he termed "orphans," touched Doc, and he mentioned them whenever he introduced the song. In those moments his experiences at the Red Bud school came forward. Sadness more than sentimentality filled his memories of that rustic structure and all that it enclosed.

• • •

Doc Hopkins began playing on a fretless five-string banjo that his father and brothers made for him. They carved a plain, red cedar neck that they attached to a square cigar box on which they tacked a possum hide head. It made, Doc said, "kind of a thud-thud" sound. "I was so noisy plunking on it, the rest of the family chased me out of the house, and I went in the chicken house to practice. The chickens also didn't like it, and they went outside."[28] In the same letter, Doc set the banjo across its larger social history. He detailed how the banjo originated in slavery, explaining how Black musicians developed both a body of songs and tunes that fit the instrument and a technique needed to play those pieces. This method bore several names, including "thrashing" and "mountain style." Whatever term one might choose, the right hand plows downward, deploying the thumb to the inside strings for melodic or rhythmic purposes and then returns to chime the drone, the banjo's principal timekeeper. Early on, Doc encountered yet another name for this distinctive maneuver.

When he was twelve or thirteen, Doc received an invitation from a neighboring family with five girls. The sisters, all closely ranging in age, invited Doc to come play for them. He packed his banjo in a tow sack and walked through ankle-deep snow to their home. With a fire warming the hearth and his youthful hosts gathered before it, he began his recital. Soon their father, Jim Smith by name, strode in, bellowing out an indictment:

"Who's that tip-thumbing around in here?" Doc meekly admitted, "Me," and the father rejoined, "I don't allow none of that tip-thumbing, banjo picking around my gals. You can take your tin pan and go home."[29] Doc dutifully returned his banjo to its burlap bag and left, trudging his way back in the cold. He never forgot the unique term, nor, for that matter, his aggravation with Smith, who contacted him years later, having by then become aware of Doc's professional success.

Doc even invoked the memorable term on the air. An April 10, 1942, *National Barn Dance* aircheck reveals Doc making a rare banjo-accompanied appearance:

> ANNOUNCER JACK STILWELL ASKS, "Have you got that educated skillet there?"
> DOC REPLIES: "An old Tennessee tickle box."
> STILWELL: "Are you going to strum or pluck?"
> DOC: "I'm going to tip-thumb."
> STILWELL: "Okay, Doc, you're getting way over my head with these technicalities."[30]

Then Doc sang "How Many Biscuits Can You Eat," a widely known number that originates in Black folksong. Doc noted that at WLS, "the people at the radio station didn't like the five-string banjo, I suppose [because] it came from the black, but I slipped in a tune now and then."[31] This was not the first time Doc mentioned the station's resistance to his playing the banjo with its rootedness in Black culture. Yet African American music formed a cornerstone of Doc's repertory and style and anchored his career at the station. He performed the proto-blues "Sugar Babe" at his audition, the piece itself coming from the same melodic and lyric complex that includes "How Many Biscuits Can You Eat." He called it "the song that got me my job on WLS."[32] Doc originally learned it from a woman banjoist he saw in London, Kentucky, and then sang it on the first Saturday night he appeared as a soloist on the show. Within a year, in 1931, it also became his first commercial recording. There he played it on the guitar.

The station, which presented Doc as an exemplar of traditional song, "America's favorite folk singer," depended on him to invoke history in his presentations as well as his song choices. This culminated in the 1940s with his *Story Behind the Song* series that aired thrice weekly for over three years on WLS. These compact studies that Doc researched and performed framed his songs according to their history and lore. "Many of those songs were written about things that really happened during that time," he said. Speaking of their makers, "They didn't just sit and dream up things. They wrote songs about them. True stories behind them."[33]

Yet in discouraging Doc from playing the banjo in this or any of his programs, WLS kept its distance from the instrument's racial overtones and whatever Doc might communicate about that inheritance. Admittedly, the five-string banjo appeared on the *National Barn Dance*. Early players like Chubby Parker and, later, Scotty Wiseman featured it during their segments that centered on mountain song. In urging Doc to transfer his traditional banjo repertory to the guitar, an instrument less exclusively identified with African American song, the show, which had no Black members among its cast, fortified its neighborly vision of a white, agrarian America.

Musically, neither minor keys nor gapped scales, preacher's growl nor mourner's cry gained purchase at the *National Barn Dance*. Those sounds aired, instead, on stations more closely tied to Southern audiences and their traditions. Many of those listening to WLS's signal, the prairie farmers of Scandinavian and German descent who tuned in during a break from chores, responded to the musical inheritances of their backgrounds. The show accordingly reached out to meet those tastes. These listeners formed a grassroots audience, to be sure, but they had grown up culturally distant from the stridencies of taut mountain singing, the rasp of the Black folk preacher, and the quivering microtones of the down-home bluesman. Doc Hopkins met those predilections with his sweet-voiced singing and major key instrumental settings. He performed old-time breakdowns, newer blues, and imported ballads without calling on the harsher tonalities and textures that thrived elsewhere in American tradition. When he did play banjo, he made no use of its alternative tunings that arose in mountain practice, confining himself solely to the "open G" and "standard C" settings. Doc's accessible style not only fit his sense of the music, which coupled with the expectations of this audience, but it also suited the close microphone technique then ascendant in broadcast technology that would allow a softer voice to project. Doc long remembered how Steve Cisler, program director at WLS, said following his station audition, "I had just the right kind of voice."[34]

Meanwhile, the station transmitted its view of Black culture in its embrace of nostalgic minstrelsy.[35] Doc's performance of "Down on the Old Plantation" suited the mythology of the happy slave that flourished in the popular music of the 1920s. He sang this ode to antebellum life during his first recording session, the same session that yielded "Sugar Babe." Eventually, others at the station, including Red Foley and The Westerners, adopted it, each using "Plantation" as a theme song. Likewise, for "Hush A Bye Baby Don't Cry," his own 1936 song, Doc told me, "I got the picture in my mind of a mammy singing to the baby."[36] During Doc's time on the radio in Kansas City in the early 1930s, and again in the mid-1950s while playing for gospel audiences in California during his post-radio career, he performed Will Carleton's nineteenth-century poem "The Funeral" as a musical recitation. This sentimental vision of Black folklife had long resonated with a national audience, one that appealed to Black readers and listeners as well as white.[37]

Doc's 1936 composition, "The Old Chain Gang," that he wrote with Pat McAdory, is, however, somewhat different than these other racialized songs. An escaped prisoner talks to his sweetheart about the forced labor he recently endured, ending with the fugitive swearing to her, "I would rather hang/Than to go back on the old chain gang."[38] Doc pursued this theme of flight to its grim conclusion in his "Pickin' on the Old Banjo." In this 1945 co-composition with his fellow World War I veteran Jesse Ball, the two crafted a musically upbeat song about a ne'er-do-well, traveling Black minstrel troupe. Its third verse reads: "The leader man tried his best to flee/Pickin' on the old banjo. But he wound up hanging to a tree/ Pickin' on the old banjo."[39] That scene summons realities that have long surrounded the instrument and its past. No wonder Doc's producers at the station steered him away from the banjo.

In our conversations, Doc observed that Brodhead, Kentucky, where he was raised, had no Black population, yet it considered itself "a sundown community." This once-common term dramatized the mortal danger that both Black residents and Black travelers faced at nightfall. As Doc said, "If they stopped in this town, they'd get beat to death."[40] He connected domestic terrorism to the banjo. After crediting its invention to slaves, he added, "white people owned them like horses, like live animals; in bondage until Abraham Lincoln set up the campaign to set them free." Doc's story of Jim Smith, the father vociferously averse to tip-thumbing, goes beyond the term's idiosyncratic charms to invoke the rowdiness associated with banjo-inspired behavior. Jim Smith's dismissal of Doc from the company of his daughters wends back to the instrument's lowly social status, and, by extension, the primitivism ascribed to Black culture.[41] For Doc, who drew upon African American music throughout his life—long into his retirement, he continued learning songs from players as disparate as Charles Brown and the Reverend Gary Davis—this indebtedness that began with his tip-thumbing banjo soon branched out beyond this instrument.

At age ten, Doc's older brother Henry, a three-year military veteran, brought home an item that Doc had never previously seen: a guitar. Doc associated that memory with Henry's playing "Casey Jones," which, in 1909, had made its way onto both sheet music and sound recording. During a bout of typhoid fever that required Doc to stay bedfast, he began to play it on that guitar. Doc's stomach was distended from the illness, and his mother, Cindy Hopkins, wanted to make sure that Doc didn't add any weight to his body. Mother and son found a mutually agreeable solution by having Doc set the guitar on its side as he lay in bed. He tuned it to an open chord like a banjo and reached his fingers over the neck to make one-finger chords.

Soon after Doc's recovery, his father took him to Richmond, Kentucky, where he planned to trade mules. They went during court days, those monthly sessions when the circuit court convened and the surrounding citizenry shopped and marketed. During this visit, in the saddle room of a Richmond livery stable, Doc came face-to-face with a Black groom playing "Joe Turner Blues" on the guitar. That moment marked not only Doc's first contact with a Black musician, but also one whose technique he employed for the rest of his life. "I rather adopted his style and it's stuck to me ever since," he explained in a 1962 interview. Then he added, "I play like old-time colored people play guitar."[42]

Chicago blues veterans and first cousins Moody Jones and Floyd Jones attested to Doc's absorption of Black style. Recalling the richness of the song "John Henry," Moody said of a television performance given by Big Bill Broonzy that he "Come closer to it than anybody I ever heard sing it.

Except Doc Hopkin[s]." To which Floyd affirmed, "Oh yeah, Doc could play it." In this joint 1973/74 interview, Moody then identifies Doc: "he was a white fella with the Prairie Farmers—WLS *years* ago."[43]

• • •

Doc's hometown community resounded with traditional music. "We didn't learn many of the popular songs. It was the old-time ballads, the folksongs, that was brought down mouth-to-ear, and sacred songs."[44] As a boy Doc attended brush arbor meetings, play parties, and shape-note singings. "They were a lively, noisy lot," he recalled of these gatherings, referring specifically to the Holy Rollers, who expressed their fundamentalist belief in energetic ritual and music.[45] During outdoor services filled with congregational singing, he watched various riverbank baptisms with both attraction and amusement. The young women emerged from the water, he said, "looking like September morning," while the drenched preachers in their black frock coats only brought Frankenstein to mind.

Other churches in his community, including the one his parents had joined, considered instrumental music sinful—the banjo and fiddle belonged to the devil—an invitation for unruly behavior. Accordingly, social dances called "frolics" substituted unaccompanied play party songs for their music. The verses sung, for instance, during "Skip to My Lou" guided the participants in their steps. Another of these game songs that Doc later adapted to the banjo expressed similar movement, picturing in its title these old-time frolics: "Swing Your Lady Up and Down."

During the summer months, a local deacon and family neighbor whom Doc remembered as Brother Burke led Thursday night shape-note classes at the Red Bud schoolhouse. Burke, who became influential in training local gospel trios and quartets that competed around the state, stood at the blackboard, teaching vocal parts from paperback songsters such as those published by Stamps-Baxter, Vaughn, and Winsett. Doc recalled learning "There Is a Land of Pure Delight" and "The Hills of Home." While he confined himself to singing the lead parts and not the harmonies, a role he continued to observe into adulthood, in later years, he also used Brother Burke's shape-note training to read melodies. Listeners sent in recommendations for songs he might perform. "I wanted to fly loose and play by ear, but the music reading helped me in getting material for the radio show, looking over whether the song suited the broadcast."[46] But as ever, he learned mostly from personal contact, from older performers like Blind Bill Cox and the Black guitarist he saw at the livery stable in Richmond.

Doc's most sustained exposure to publicly performed music took place at the Brodhead Fair. A three-day event also called the Little World's Fair (a gathering that continues in Brodhead to the present day), it featured balloon ascensions, a horse show, and a small circus with Roman riders where, as Doc remembered, a man dressed in tights and standing up rode six horses at once. (Three horses were bridled on each side.) Locals brought produce and received prizes for their livestock. Events included races, one of which featured, as Doc described it, a little gray mule whose owners reportedly poured coffee and whiskey down her throat before the race. "She always won."[47]

Here Doc met another blind musician, Dick Burnett (1883–1977), who became a pivotal source in his life. A resident of Monticello, Kentucky, some fifty-five miles south, Burnett was a singer, songwriter, banjoist, guitarist, and fiddler. His most renowned influence stems from a song he performed but never recorded, the lament known as "Man of Constant Sorrow." Burnett published the piece in his ca. 1913 songbook as "Farewell Song." This prompted his fellow musician, Kentuckian Emry Arthur, to record it in 1928. In turn, that release inspired the Stanley Brothers in the postwar era. Their interpretation, which they recorded several times, reached still others, the song eventually finding its way into the Grammy-winning soundtrack for *O Brother, Where Art Thou?* as sung by Dan Tyminski, and charmingly lip-synched in the film by actor George Clooney.

Dick Burnett's impact on Doc, let alone so many others, requires a moment's more discussion of Burnett's past. He grew up in Wayne County, Kentucky, and watched that area expand from logging and sawmill operations into petroleum production. In 1901, Burnett became, he said, "the youngest driller in the country," as well as a tool dresser, sharpening the drill bits used in oil excavation.[48] Five years later, at age twenty-three, during a nighttime oil field robbery, he was shot in the face by an assailant and

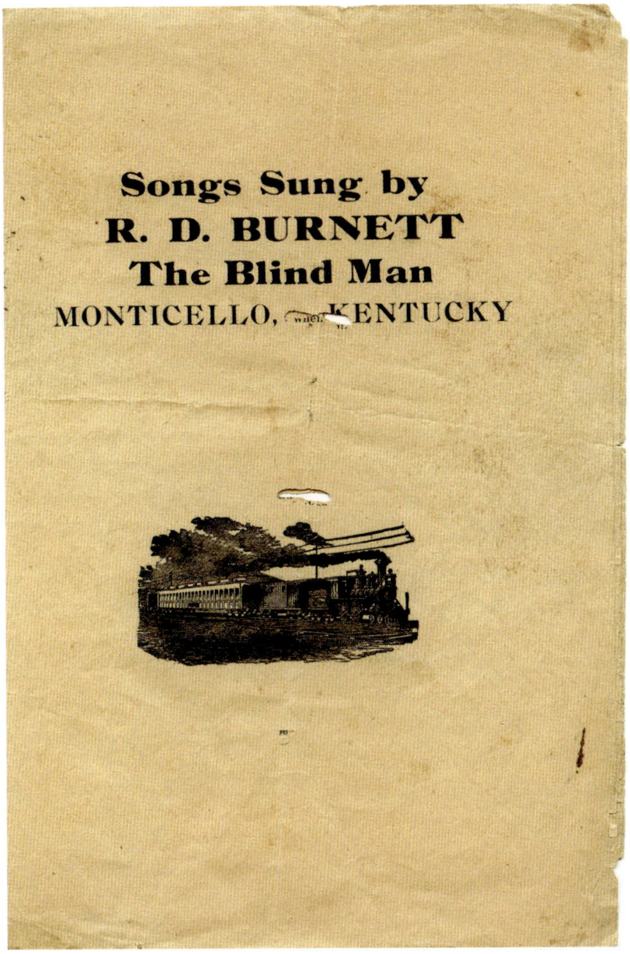

FIGURE 20. Dick Burnett's ca. 1913 songbook.

permanently blinded. Deprived of other sources of support, he began to work as a musician. He traveled first to fairs like Brodhead's and to coal camps around the state. With "nowhere to go," he said, "the miners would pack theaters."[49] To reach those audiences, he initially went by train and horse-driven cab. By 1914, he joined forces with fiddler Leonard Rutherford, a collaboration that lasted thirty-five years. The two musicians journeyed by car "from Cincinnati to Chattanooga, [any town of] . . . any size, [that's] what we been in."[50] At one of those venues, the Bonnie Blue Coal Camp in Kentucky, Burnett met a local merchant who contacted Columbia records on his behalf. Burnett and Rutherford began recording for the label in 1926 and found that selling records at their performances served the same end as did the earlier songbook, but with more profit. Still, Doc remembered the leather cup Burnett strapped to his leg in which listeners would drop their dimes.

Doc's multiple contacts with Burnett began about 1910 at the Brodhead Fair and continued during court days. Doc recalled closely watching Burnett's fingers during, for example, his animated performances of "Coal Creek March," replete with martial drumming and gunshots snapped on the banjo head, along with harmonics that simulated army bugle calls. This marked Doc's first exposure to the banjo instrumental he developed into "Trouble at the Coal Creek Mines."[51]

Over time Doc performed, and in a number of instances, recorded versions of Burnett's "Lost John," "Pearl Bryant," "Going Around the World," "Cumberland Gap," "Ramblin' Reckless Hobo," "Davy, Davy," and the "Death of J. B. Marcum." Sometimes Doc mirthfully quoted a verse from Burnett's unrecorded satiric salute to "The Jolly Butchers": "Come on boys, don't be lazy/The butcher shop is the place to get your pork chops and gravy."[52] Another ballad that Burnett sang but never recorded was "The Lost Ship," which tells of the Titanic's sinking. According to D. K. Wilgus, Doc learned it at the Brodhead Fair from Blind Bill Cox around 1913, but the precise correspondence between Doc's lyrics for "Wreck of the Titanic" and "The Lost Ship" printed in Burnett's songbook makes their textual kinship unmistakable. Doc likely reported one source for the other in error, but either way, Burnett's never-recorded lyrics found embodiment in Doc's recording, issued in 1971.[53]

Another of Burnett's pieces, his autobiographical "Song of the Orphan Boy," had particular significance for Doc. The song appeared in the same eight-page peddled songbook. In this plaintive number—nine verses plus a chorus—Burnett opens with a personal recollection:

> Oh I once was a man who worked hard in the land,
> For support I worked hard every day.
> I worked in the oil green on a seven star machine,
> But now, dear friends, I cannot see my way.[54]

The song sustains this first-person intensity throughout. From the "oil green," a term used to identify a previously untapped field ready for petroleum extraction, to the "seven star machine," a brand of drilling equipment, the verses shift from his description of his work to a lament for the deaths of his parents. Burnett then tells of his assault in the moonless dark by "a railroad tramp." He names the day, month, and year, and describes its aftermath: how "my eyes I tried to gain; Oh, my body how it pained and throbbed." In the next verse:

> Oh, when I was found, my face lying on the ground,
> They picked me up and laid me on a cot;
> Then the robber took his flight, I was carried home that night,
> From the place where I had been shot.

He imagines his eyesight restored in heaven, along with deliverance for others similarly afflicted, be they blind, deaf, or lame. Throughout the song, he reminds us of his plight and, once again, of his financial need. Its chorus ends: "Don't think it any wrong to buy one of my songs/Won't you buy from a blind man like me."

Burnett recorded "Song of the Orphan Boy" in 1927, but it was never released. Consequently, its pleas stayed largely unheard. However, for a few seconds, during a 1962 interview, he sang the opening verse, providing a glimpse of its air.[55]

Doc Hopkins, who saw him perform the number and remembered its words, felt that the piece could be musically improved and its message enlarged. As he put it, "there was not enough of a song to make a ballad." Doc wrote new lyrics set to a new melody. "I didn't use his words and tune but kept the same idea."[56] He recognized that in this idiom, "when you go to writing songs, to ballads, you get parts of other tunes to them. . . . There's

FIGURE 21. Dick Burnett's melody for his "Song of the Orphan Boy."

only eight notes."[57] He also felt free to recompose pieces: "I was always trying to revise songs, fix them up to where they suited me."[58] Doc's composition centers on the plight of blindness and loved ones unseen, which he crystallized in the chorus:

> If there should come a day when you could not see your way.
> And the sun on earth for you would never shine.
> Darkness all your whole life through,
> Oh how sad and lonely too, God have pity on the blind.[59]

Doc's "Song of the Blind" appeared in his first songbook, a 1936 publication titled *Doc Hopkins and Karl and Harty of The Cumberland Ridgerunners, Mountain Ballads and Home Songs.* From that source, the Blue Sky Boys learned it, recording it the following year. This famed North Carolina duo performed several of Doc's compositions on records and over the radio. Bill Bolick, older of the two siblings, praised Doc for "his soft voice," crediting him as "about the best guitar player and singer there was."[60] Though Doc never commercially recorded this song himself, he did more here than create a heartfelt tribute to a musician he much admired. In it, he expressed his creative stance.

For Doc, neither age nor anonymity defined folksong. "To me it's just a song. I've got no preference if it's written yesterday or 100 years ago. Folksongs can be written today."[61] What matters is that "It's a song that can be remembered and sung by the folks in the country."[62] In this thought Doc brought together an audience—country folks—with a style familiar to them, a form both accessible and learnable. Doc felt that even the most venerable songs from "across the waters" took root here to the extent that they reflected "the American style," able "to portray things that was happening in this new country."[63]

In "Song of the Blind," Doc took a lived experience that an individual known to him had achingly endured and translated it into art. Now, in the same idiom, he reshaped that message into a more accessible truth. His version challenges the listener to walk in empathy. Doc often commented that he learned from blind men. Repeatedly, his voice revealed both the care he tendered for these persons and the dignity he ascribed to them.

As a boy still clad in knickers, Doc found a lifetime of resources at the Brodhead Fair. Dick Burnett provided Doc with an inventory of musical material and exemplified an artist whom Doc respected as authentic and accomplished, a musician worthy of tribute and emulation. From Blind Bill Cox he learned still other songs and found precedent for the singing style he adopted throughout his life. Beyond those two, he encountered yet another performer at the fair, one in whom Doc Hopkins found his greatest inspiration.

• • •

At age nine, at the Brodhead Fair, Doc first saw the medicine show doctor known as Dakota Jack. Born John J. Pursley (1879–1943), this former Kentucky schoolteacher began in his early twenties making trips out west to the Dakotas. Known as "a dead shot and a good rider," Jack became one of Teddy Roosevelt's Rough Riders and took part in the charge up San Juan Hill.[64] When American troops left Cuba, Jack went back west to work for thirteen years as a cowpuncher and an immigration ranger on the Canadian border. In 1916 he wrote, "I am nearly 40 years old, weigh 215 pounds. I can ride most any horse. I can rope a cow and tie her down in 30 seconds."[65] He added that he would pay a thousand dollars to "any man who can prove he [Dakota Jack] ever took a dose of medicine from a white man, had a prescription filled out at a drug store, or was ever sick in bed from natural sickness in his life." By then he had met Charlie White Moon, a Cheyenne Indian, who had been selling remedies and herbs in Deadwood, South Dakota. Jack learned about his cures, and the two went into a business partnership. "There ain't an illness," Jack declared, "common to man nor beast that herbs wasn't meant to cure."[66] Their laxatives' active ingredients included bloodroot, sarsaparilla, wild cherry bark, wahoo, and prickly ash.

They came back to Kentucky, where they ran into resistance from the state's medical association. According to Doc, thugs beat up White Moon and, in a 1912 homicide, threw him down a Louisville stairway. Jack, out west at the time, returned to the city. "First thing he did was buckle on his pistol belt and .45, and ride his horse all around town and dare any thugs or anybody to try to run him out of town. And he sold his medicine from a platform right there in Louisville."[67] Jack took over White Moon's remedies and manufactured his own concoctions in his Louisville laboratory, drawn

MORNING, JANUARY 18, 1917.

Victory For Dakota Jack

and COM-CEL-SAR

Read the Startling Testimony of This Estimable Lady, a Resident of Louisville. I Tell You It IS Wonderful What the Blessed Roots & Herbs Are Doing. Don't Wait Too Long, Don't Wait Till Death Has Already Laid Hold Upon You, Till You Have No Vitality Left, But Begin RIGHT NOW to Use the Means God & Nature Intended You to Use to Overcome Disease, & THE VICTORY SHALL BE YOURS.

Louisville, Ky.

Dakota Jack:

Dear Sir—I want to thank you for the good you have done me, as well as the rest of my family, with your God's HERB and ROOT remedy, COM-CEL-SAR.

I have been troubled for about three years with STOMACH trouble and have tried several kinds of medicine for it, but no improvement did I receive until I heard of your almighty remedy, which I gave a trial.

Before I began taking COM-CEL-SAR I could hardly eat anything and only weighed 110 pounds; now I weigh 138 pounds, more than I ever weighed in my life.

I have only been taking COM-CEL-SAR about a year and now I do all my housework and feel as well as when I was 15 years old.

I would be glad to speak to anyone of the good COM-CEL-SAR has done our family. I also owe SCIENCE SOPE a debt of large value. I will never be without either of them in my house.

I remain your most true and grateful FRIEND,

MRS. MARY E. JONES.
1728 W. Market St., Louisville, Ky.

DAKOTA JACK,
The Cowboy Herbalist.

No sane, unprejudiced human CAN POSSIBLY doubt the Samson-like power of Roots & Herbs to overcome disease. If YOU who read this are not perfectly WELL, then something is radically wrong, because health IS natural, disease is UNNATURAL. Let me tell you of the wonders performed RIGHT HERE AT HOME year after year by the blessed Roots & Herbs; if you can't come personally to the office then write for full information regarding the great medicines I represent. It may mean life or death to yourself or some dear one, so don't delay. No matter the disease, I FIRMLY believe that if taken in anything like near time ROOTS & HERBS WILL CURE.

Yours for the blessings of PERFECT health & happiness,
DAKOTA JACK.

COM-CEL-SAR

Only Costs You $1.00 For 3 Quarts—Cowboy Liniment, for all Pains & Soreness, 25c per bottle—SCIENCE SOPE, for Human Skin, 10c bar, 3 bars for 25c—At

SMITH & BATE'S DRUG STORE

Owensboro, Kentucky.

FIGURE 22. Dakota Jack testimonials, *The Owensboro Messenger*, Owensboro, Kentucky, Jan. 18, 1917.

from natural products sent to him from the Dakotas. These resulted in an herbal medicine called Com-Cel-Sar (which Jack sold at three quarts for a dollar), an item called Cowboy Liniment (advertised at 25 cents a bottle), and Science Soap (ten cents each, and three for .25). "That soap," Doc said, "sold like candy bars."

To sell these products, Dakota Jack went on annual tours throughout Kentucky, Tennessee, and Virginia. He and his troupe, which numbered up to four musicians, traveled by train, having shipped their supplies by rail in advance. Typically, they set their appearances on court days or during county fairs. Sometimes local drugstores carried the items, but either way, Jack gave a public lecture. Once in town, they set up a platform, and on two-by-fours around the stage, they attached gasoline torches for nighttime lighting. On the stage they put a card table, two chairs, and a trunk that held Jack's medicines. When Doc first saw Dakota Jack at the Brodhead Fair, the musicians Frank Lewis and Bailey Briscoe introduced the show with their playing. "They were both very good, they had no mics nor amplifiers in those days, and you could hear Bailey Briscoe sing so loud all over the fairground. To me, it was the main attraction of the fair."[68] Doc remembered their tenor voices on "Home Sweet Home," singing as they waltzed with their instruments, holding them close like dance partners.

Doc recalled in particular Bailey Briscoe's version of "Jesse James." Between verses, he and Frank Lewis, the latter appearing in blackface, traded jokes:

> BRISCOE: Did I ever tell you about my farm? The soil is so rich, watermelons grow as big as a barrel.[69]
>
> LEWIS: Oh yeah. My farm has soil so rich that when you plant corn, you better jump back. It will grow up so quick, it will hit you in the face.

Briscoe then sings a verse from "Jesse James":

> Jesse James was a man, kind of heart and quick of hand.
> He would never turn the needy from his door.
> When Bob Ford's pistol ball brought him a-tumbling from the wall,
> And Jesse lay a-dying on the floor.

Then another verbal exchange between them, underscored with music:

BRISCOE: The company I work for builds skyscrapers buildings so high, they have to keep the windows on the upper stories closed to keep the clouds out.

LEWIS: Oh, that's nothin.' The company I work for they build them so high they have to build seventeen stories on hinges.

BRISCOE: Why on hinges?

LEWIS: To let the moon and stars go by.

Sung chorus:

There's no more desperadoes in our land,
There's no more desperadoes in our land.
When Jesse turned his head, Bob Ford shot him dead,
There's no more desperadoes in our land.

With a crowd now assembled, Dakota Jack gave his lecture. He would thunder, "Nine times in the Bible does the Holy word say that roots, herbs, barks, and berries is for the healing of the nation." The program included live demonstrations that usually began with a youngster drawn from the crowd. While holding a pan of water, Jack would give him a shampoo. To the crowd's delight, he built "a great high stack of lather" that would fall from the child's head, the suds all made from Science Soap.[70] He also welcomed stage testimonials about the Cowboy Liniment. After he applied it to sufferers' foreheads and ears, older people afflicted with long-term hearing loss could once again "hear a watch tick." Another customer, in a letter to a local newspaper similarly detailed how, before the cure, "I could not hear a steam whistle, even if I was close to it."[71] Jack responded, attesting to the efficacy of his products, "I, Dakota Jack, the Cowboy Herbalist of Louisville, Kentucky, do hereby solemnly affirm that I believe there is a cure—safe, sure, speedy—in the vegetable kingdom."[72] In another statement, he added, "No sane, unprejudiced human CAN POSSIBLY doubt the Samson-like power of Roots & Herbs to overcome disease."[73] Doc confided that the herb's solution included "ammonia and medicine in it that doctors won't use." No matter the formula, for Dakota Jack and his powers of persuasion, "His spiel would sell anything."[74]

The following year at the Brodhead Fair, Doc approached Dakota Jack and introduced himself. Jack, curious about Doc's name, asked him if he planned to become a doctor. Doc allowed that he might, and then brought up his music-making. Jack handed him Bailey Briscoe's banjo, resting nearby on a chair, and said, "Play me a tune." Doc played "Cripple Creek" and then sang "Free Little Bird," his first song. He also played him "a chording piece," an open-tuned guitar instrumental he had recently learned. Jack asked the boy how he came to sing. Doc said that he stuttered so badly he couldn't talk. Jack looked at him and said, "I'll make a medicine speaker out of you. We'll break that stuttering habit."[75] Then Jack told Doc that maybe he could play on his show when he got to be a grown-up man. Doc said he was "stepping high after that."

• • •

At seventeen, using a fake birth certificate stating he was born in 1899 and thus qualified for service, Doc enlisted in the Army. With World War I underway, Doc trained at the newly built Camp Shelby, located on the outskirts of Hattiesburg, Mississippi. He became a drill instructor, the task requiring him to bellow out stationary rifle drills to his squad. His sergeant, Frank Gregory by name, aware of Doc's stutter and his musical talents as well, told him to "Sing 'em out." In giving commands in his "natural voice," Doc said, "it broke me right there" of his verbal handicap. Necessity (and Sgt. Frank Gregory) required him to "put some force behind it," and to think ahead concerning his uttered speech.[76] "I had to drill my squad. Giving commands: 'Squad right. At ease. Right shoulder arms.'"[77]

With these parade ground directives under his belt, Doc shipped overseas to France in 1918 on the RMS *Aquitania*, sister ship to the ill-fated *Lusitania*. Doc's unit was assigned to the New York 77th Division, their shoulder patch famously emblazoned with the Statue of Liberty. They saw battle under General John "Black Jack" Pershing at Chateau-Thierry. Doc himself was stationed at Pershing's headquarters and escaped personal harm. He returned on the *Aquitania* as a sergeant, recommended by his superiors for reenlistment, and to be elevated to the rank of first sergeant. But Doc had other ideas:

> I went home instead, and all this time I kept plunking on the banjo and guitar, and doing this and that. Just to keep from starving and keep shoes on my feet. Believe me sometimes living was lean. I was a farm hand, a

FIGURE 23. Doc Hopkins in Army uniform, American Expeditionary Forces, ca. 1917.

> pick-and-shovel road worker, a fry cook, an automobile factory worker (Buick), a bootlegger joint bartender, a railroad brakeman, a carpenter's helper, a third-class machinist, a barber, a US Marine for three years, and finally I came to Chicago and auditioned at WLS and got on the Saturday night Barndance.[78]

Doc's brother Elmer got him a job as a railroad brakeman. However, without seniority he could not get a regular run and found himself mostly without work. "Nothing to do, just my room rent going on."[79] One day Doc heard that Dakota Jack was making his annual tour, and so he went from Corbin, Kentucky, to Pineville on his railroad pass. "I made myself known to him." He found Jack in the hotel lobby reading a newspaper when he approached him. Doc asked if he remembered the Brodhead Fair. Jack nodded affirmatively. "Well, do you remember a little guy who sang and played for you on the banjo? I'm the stuttering kid." Jack said he thought he did. Doc said, "I was the guy. I still play, only I play more." Doc played him "Jesse James" on the banjo, then took out his guitar and played "John

Henry" with his jackknife held between his fingers. Jack said, "I like that one." He offered Doc "twenty dollars a week and all expenses, including cigarette money."

Doc went back to Corbin that night, retrieved his suitcase, and joined up with Dakota Jack's 1919 troupe that now featured one-legged fiddler Virgil Lewis and his mandolin-playing wife, along with banjoist Boone Stout. Like Bailey Briscoe and Frank Lewis before him, Stout waltzed with his banjo while singing "The Juice of the Forbidden Fruit." Their trip included stops in Harlan, Kentucky; Appalachia, Virginia; and Bristol, Tennessee. At every town, Jack gave Doc an effusive introduction, paving his way with the audience. Doc performed his knife-style "John Henry" on an "old warped-up guitar," along with "The Wreck of Old 97," and the comical "A Widow and Daughter in Blue," a song in which the protagonist's father becomes his stepson, and his wife his own grandmother. Doc said, "I went over with my singing."[80] But he added that after Dakota Jack's build-up, he could hardly fail. In a typed portrait of his mentor that he wrote in 1986, Doc closed with this handwritten assessment:

> Dakota Jack dressed like a businessman, but he wore a big, fine Western hat. He was a fine speaker and a gentleman in every way. He said he wanted to make an Herb Doctor out of me and I learned a lot about showmanship from him. He was a terrific gunslinger and as fast as lightning, and with his liniment and soap, was a show within himself. Over six feet tall and graceful in everything he did. When he made a speech, he sounded like President F. D. Roosevelt.[81]

Doc saw in Dakota Jack the embodiment of confident showmanship. He told me, "Going over, that's what matters. When they clap their hands, you know they like it. They're swallowing the soup."[82] The individualism and confidence that Dakota Jack radiated applied as much to the shaping of one's music as it did to personal conduct. "Be what you are," Doc learned from Dakota Jack; showmanship in musical performance meant "you just got to be yourself." To the end of his life, Doc felt guided by the showman's example. "He wouldn't brush you off," he said. "That Dakota Jack was one grand feller."[83]

• • •

In 1920, shortly after Doc finished the tour with Dakota Jack that marked his professional entry into "the show business," as he called it, he enlisted for a three-year stint in the Marines. Doc's principal assignment at the Pensacola Naval Air Station, apart from his work in the base's machine shop, lay in providing music for "smokers," recreational gatherings that took place at venues like the officers' club. There, Doc performed nightly on the steel guitar in a trio with ukulele and guitar. He held the instrument horizontally in his lap and used a steel bar to note it, the technique recalling what he had first known as a child playing his brother's guitar sideways. Doc and his band tackled Hawaiian and related popular repertory. All the while, he said, "in back of my head, I knew about these old mountain songs and old folk tunes I used to hear growing up."[84]

Then he went AWOL. For 127 days he hoboed west following the broom-corn harvest. The venture ended when a scab brakeman brandishing a pick handle refused to honor Doc's railroad union card. Summarily removed from the Santa Fe Railroad freight car he had occupied, Doc faced a fourteen-mile trek to the nearest town of El Reno, Oklahoma. Along the way he met "a big Indian boy [who lived] there in Osage country."[85] As the two proceeded in the heat, Doc wondered where they might get water. "There's a river up ahead four or five miles," his companion said. It turned out to be a mostly muddy stream, but Doc had a folding drinking cup and ladled out whatever refreshment he could. Just then he felt his left hand starting to itch, and mentioned that aloud. The Indian replied, "That's a sign you're going to get money." He advised him to "scratch it on wood and rub it." The notion reflected a widely held folk belief. In North Carolina, for instance, one incantation goes, "Rub it on wood, to make it come good; And rub it on brass, to make it come fast."[86] It would seem Doc followed that directive.

Once the two travelers reached town, they parted company. With only a dollar in his pocket, Doc dropped into a barbershop for a 35-cent haircut. Two young women passing by saw him there and pecked on the window. He had recently met them while playing music at an Arkansas hotel where they had worked as waitresses. They asked Doc where he was headed, and he told them, "I'm hoboing my way back east and then going south."[87] He admitted he'd run away, and they felt sorry for him. One of them told Doc that she knew their brother still owed him the sixty dollars he had loaned him back in Arkansas. Then and there she handed him the sum. The Osage's prediction had proved true.

Doc made his way back to the Navy base. At his hearing he "begged on their mercy."[88] His commanding officer, Colonel "Wild Bill" Wallace, who tried him, gave him both a warning and a break: "If you come up before me again, I'll hang you, but you look like you might have intelligence." He promised Doc a clean record if he held to his word, telling him, "I can see in you, honesty." Wallace could read a person, Doc said. He served a month in the brig that began with two days of solitary confinement where he received bread and water (with a pinch of salt for the bread), and at the end of his enlistment, paid a $90.00 fine. He got his honorable discharge.

Once he left the Marines, he traveled again, working his way north to Michigan and then south to the gum tree woods of Lufkin, Texas. He returned home in mid-decade, then went on the road again, touring with the Kentucky Krazy Kats. By early 1927, he came back to Pensacola, where he played steel guitar with harp-guitarist Holland Bobe. The duo regularly performed Saturday night appearances on WCOA radio. But Bobe ran a thriving shoe store business in Pensacola and couldn't tour with Doc. "Feeling restless," Doc went home again and this time learned the barbering trade.[89] His family moved to southern Ohio, and it was here in 1930 that he got word from John Lair to come to Chicago.

• • •

For the next twenty years, Doc worked full time as a performer. Within days of his arrival, WLS offered him a solo, noon-hour show "singing old ballads" five days a week, sponsored by Swift meatpacking, while the Aladdin Lamp Company underwrote the Cumberland Ridge Runners slot.[90] A subsequent contractual dispute with John Lair led him to tell WLS's station manager, Edgar Bill, that "he didn't need to fire me, I quit."[91] The next day, abetted by Bradley Kincaid, Doc began at NBC's *National Farm and Fun Hour*, broadcast over WMAQ, where once a week he was also given a solo show called *Mountain Ministry*. Unable to get his live dates announced on air, he relocated in November 1931 to Kansas City, Missouri, for station WHB. That two-year engagement, sponsored by Georgie Porgie cereal, eventually took him to WOW in Omaha. Crazy Water Crystals became Doc's next sponsor for stints at KDGY in Minneapolis, WXYZ in Detroit, and CKLW in Windsor. For those engagements he teamed up with cowboy fiddler Bunkhouse Bill. Doc had enormous respect for this versatile musician and considered him his "best partner ever . . . and a good gag man."[92] In addition to fiddling behind Doc, he also played mandolin, guitar, steel, mandola, piano, organ, string bass, cello, and handsaw. "Pity we didn't get a chance to record back when we was broadcasting," he noted. Doc then returned to Kansas City on WHB, and in 1936, came back to Chicago. He played six nights a week on the WJJD *Suppertime Frolic* show, both with the Cumberland Ridge Runners and in solo programs, sponsored by Drug Trade. They "pulled tremendous mail," he remembered, receiving up to 160,000 letters a month.[93] Before finally disbanding during the wartime years, the group returned to WLS where Doc appeared with them, and as a soloist on the *National Barn Dance.* By then the station billed him as "America's Favorite Folk Singer," and his daily schedule included work on the *Merry-Go-Round, Dinner Bell Program*, and the *Smile-A-While Show,* while also performing in his *Story Behind the Song* series, sponsored by Polident. Throughout those years Doc made personal appearances, which billed him as a traditional ballad singer, "famous for his true early American folk songs."[94]

Doc's musicological passions never waned. In 1931, while broadcasting in Kansas City, he met Bob James, nephew of Jesse James and the son of bank robber Frank James. Bob had heard Doc sing "Jesse James" on the radio and invited him to visit the family's homeplace in Kearney, Missouri. Bob James helped Doc sort out fact from fancy in the stories that surrounded Jesse and clarified details in the ballad about the outlaw hero, who, in the end, was betrayed by one of his own. He also showed him a pair of Jesse's guns and his handmade leather belt. He took Doc to the old barn behind the family residence that Jesse and Frank had built. By then, falling into disarray, it had sheltered their horses back in the day and afforded them a hiding place when the Pinkertons, in their pursuit, set off a bomb at the house. Doc and his station announcer photographed the barn, and then, with Bob James, visited Jesse's grave in the town's cemetery. They documented how this once sixteen-foot obelisk had, by then, become chipped

FIGURE 24. Doc Hopkins at Jesse James's grave, Kearney, Missouri, 1933.

down to a stump. Over the years, pilgrims had taken pieces of this memorial to America's Robin Hood, until only one letter of his name remained visible.

Doc continued to accumulate still more stories behind the songs. One of these, "In the Baggage Coach Ahead," a hugely popular 1896 song attributed to Gussie L. Davis, describes a coffin in a train's baggage car that holds a dead woman whose child cries for her in the next car. One letter from a downstate Illinoisan in the lumber business informed Doc that he could prove that he had been that weeping youngster. Numerous such claims show the song's emotive appeal.

But no missive matched the one that Doc received at WJJD after performing "The Death of J. B. Marcum." Set to the same tune as "Jesse James," the song originated in a feud between two Kentucky families, its title referring to an attorney who represented one of those clans. The conflict resulted in Marcum's 1903 assassination at the Breathitt County courthouse. Hearing the song prompted this listener's response:

> Dear Doc: I listen to you sing on the Suppertime Frolic and I enjoy all your songs, but the one I like most is the one about J. B. Markham. Will you sing it again and dedicate it to me? I am the man that killed Markham. I got a parole and am out of the pen now living here at Wallins Creek. I am a Baptist preacher and town marshal here in your hometown. I know all of your folks here, and the first time you visit here again be sure to look me up. I'll be glad to see you.
>
> —Curtis Jett[95]

"Funny things happen whenever you get to broadcasting these old-time songs," Doc concluded.[96]

Things happened, too, with Doc's own songs. Beginning in 1930 with his first composition, "The Old Plush Covered Album," Doc explained, "I got so familiar with so many old songs, I'd write similar songs of my own just for my own use."[97] These included "Poor Old Hard Luck Joe," which became his highest-earning number, followed by "The Pal That Is Always True" and "Let's Go Up on the Ferris Wheel." Other musicians also adopted his work. In addition to "Song of the Blind," the Blue Sky Boys recorded his "Asleep in the Briny Deep" and "No Place to Pillow My Head." In 1976, Bill Monroe recorded the latter title, as had Flatt and Scruggs, neither of whom credited Doc as the author. The Delmore Brothers and Wayne Raney sang his "Sinner Man, Where You Gonna Hide," while the Prairie Ramblers featured "Them Ramblin' Blues," and Grandpa Jones sang his "Cabin Just Over the Hill."

Doc also served as a conduit of songs. He rewrote "Little Boy in Colors Green," a traditional song about the death of a young jockey, into "Fatal Derby Day." The song found new life under Doc's title after appearing in one of Bradley Kincaid's bestselling songbooks. Kincaid also published Doc's versions of "Free Little Bird" and "Sugar Babe." Doc's singing of "You Can't Do Wrong and Get By," a song he learned from a Black singer at a tent meeting in Kansas City, so intrigued Uncle Dave Macon that when the two of them worked together during a three-week engagement in Council

Bluffs, Macon asked him for its words. He said he just wanted it for his Sunday school class. Doc obliged, and not long after that, heard Uncle Dave singing it on the *Grand Ole Opry*. Ironically, Macon skipped one other verse Doc remembered: "Read Revelation 21 and 8/Liars burn in the fiery lake."[98]

Doc's recordings appeared on a variety of labels: Paramount, Decca, Broadway, Conqueror, and Radio, as well as subsidiaries of the American Record Company. By far, however, the bulk of his recorded work took place in early 1946 for discs that the public could not purchase. These were 16-inch electrical transcriptions made by Doc's music publisher, M. M. Cole, and sent to radio stations across the country. Doc recorded 204 pieces, fifty-five of which were dance calls. He played them with members of the Prairie Ramblers—Chick Hurt, Alan Crockett, Rusty Gill, and Jack Taylor—identified on those discs only as Doc Hopkins and his Country Boys. After Doc retired from radio, he made two gospel albums of traditional and self-composed songs, plus several audition tapes for proposed radio programs, and a carefully assembled LP of folksongs released in 1971, selected and annotated by Professor D. K. Wilgus, who wrote, "During his years as a professional entertainer, Doc necessarily followed the pattern of the times, singing traditional songs, old favorites, [and] new songs composed in the commercial hillbilly idiom. He got songs from listeners, from acquaintances—and he composed his own."[99] Almost all its contents consisted of pieces Doc learned in Kentucky before 1920. Doc creatively shaped his inheritance, or as Wilgus put it, "He will 'correct' on hearing other versions, and he will 'improve' when a song is not 'right.'"

Near the end of Doc's radio years, he took on a student, a young Navy veteran named Fleming Brown. Fleming called him at the station after hearing him play the five-string banjo. WLS officials, as noted earlier, preferred that Doc play guitar, but Doc kept a banjo stored in his locker. Beginning in 1948, during the half-hour before Doc's morning wake-up show, he and Fleming met over coffee and rolls at the Eighth Street Theatre where the *National Barn Dance* took place. Three times a week, Fleming learned fingerpicking and downpicking and a number of Doc's songs.

In 1950, with the decline of live radio coupled with his meager World War I veteran's benefits, Doc left WLS to find work that guaranteed a pension. He found local employment as a bench lathe machinist, a skill he had acquired earlier in the Marines. In 1956, he transferred to the Los Angeles–based Rocketdyne, where he made drill bushings and dowel pins until his retirement in 1968, when he returned to Chicago.

My association with him began in 1972, when I was still a teenager and a student of Fleming Brown's.[100] Doc and I played as a duo with him on guitar and vocals and me on banjo—up through Doc's last public performance, which took place in December 1982. After that, we continued our visits, letters, tapings, and talks until a few days before he died. Just weeks short of his eighty-eighth birthday, he slumped into his wife Mary's arms at home, passing away on January 3, 1988. The last time we spoke, a few days earlier, on Christmas Eve, Doc said he felt like Joe Louis after a bad fight. "I'm all out of whack," he said.[101]

In December 1982, the celebrated interviewer and author Studs Terkel invited Doc and me to appear on his program, an hour-long show that would mark Doc's final radio broadcast. He introduced Doc as a legendary figure of American folk and country music. With audible delight, Studs recited a litany from Doc's past: his coming to the *National Barn Dance* in 1930, his origins in eastern Kentucky, his service in World War I under General Pershing, his jobs as barber and brakeman, his medicine show travels with Dakota Jack, and his knowledge of hundreds of songs. Studs took note of Doc's nearly century-long life, one that had spanned so much of the American experience.

The show opened with our playing "Free Little Bird," and Doc recalled his first banjo and his rural upbringing. Then he turned to the body of British song that had made its way to the Kentucky countryside. First he offered "The Swapping Song," followed by a verse or two from "Billie Boy." Studs conversed with Doc throughout, prompting him, while taking stock of Doc's breadth. "You reflect so much music," he warmly observed.[102]

Then Studs played Doc's 1965 recording of "Trouble at the Coal Creek Mines," his banjo showpiece of spoken narration, sound effects, and song. Based on historical events that began in this Tennessee community in the

1870s and culminated twenty years later in open warfare, it told a story of the state militia and the free miners, replete with dogs barking, a brass band puffing, a troop train's wheels slipping on the tracks, soldiers marching in formation, and their bugle calls answering back with the miners' own, echoing away off in the mountains. Doc first heard it performed by "Blind Burnett" at the Brodhead Fair, and now on Studs's program, he recounted his times there with Dakota Jack's medicine show. Doc set the scene, promised the cures, and repeated Dakota Jack's spiel. His description of Jack's larger-than-life qualities led to our next song, one that he had also learned at the fair, "Jesse James." Doc then told of meeting Bob James and hearing from him some of the tales about Jesse. In particular, he focused on those about the railroad's mortgage notes, how people would not testify against Jesse when he intercepted the couriers bearing the farm closure notices.

Doc and Studs agreed that people sing from their lives, and the conversation turned to spirituals. In 1964, Doc played with the Reverend Gary Davis at the UCLA Folk Festival that D. K. Wilgus directed. There Doc heard Davis perform "Twelve Gates to the City." He performed it now and told a story of Black people coming into town on market days. They walked in the streets, he said, staying off the sidewalks. This strategy offered a measure of safety during the perils of the Jim Crow years. Mention of that past led Studs to recall the interracial sharing of the song "John Henry," and he played Doc's recording. Then Doc told of meeting John Henry's son on the elevated platform. Like Doc's other stories, Studs observed, "all deal with history, with daily life."

Studs asked Doc about his days of freighthopping, riding the rods. "Money was scarce," Doc explained, and hoboing provided a cheap way to get to a wheat harvest or some other work. Passage only took a dime or whatever a willing brakeman might require. Back then, he hadn't slept in a bed for so long that "all I needed was a newspaper and a brick." While asleep in an empty coal car crossing Kansas, one night, two robbers roused him, one pointing a gun. All Doc had was two dollars and a bag of Bull Durham. They took the money but spurned the tobacco. A few years after that theft occurred, the famed gangster Pretty Boy Floyd met his demise in Ohio. While Doc's holdup had taken place in the moonlight, he managed to catch the thief's profile and fix it into his memory. Now, he said, he couldn't be sure from the pictures running in the newspapers, but the resemblance particularly struck him. His robber may indeed have been Pretty Boy Floyd back when he still worked that territory. For what few funds Doc had in his possession, Studs and Doc agreed that despite the legendry that surrounded him, Floyd didn't just rob the rich. Not like Jesse James, "he'd rob anybody," Doc noted. Then the two of us played Dick Burnett's hobo song.

The conversation turned to the sinking of the *Titanic,* a 1912 event that occurred the year of Studs's birth, but that Doc, then twelve years old, personally remembered. His father brought home the news from the town's telegraph office. Doc sang the ballad solo. Finally, to close the hour, we played "Sourwood Mountain," a lyric song pieced together from his earliest memories in life and music. As it wound to the end, Doc spoke over the banjo and guitar about this mythical place with "all the pretty girls." He "never could find it," for whomever he asked, they always said that place lay "the next one over." In his affectionate search for the elusive Sourwood Mountain, Doc's good-natured warmth and his personalized history filled the airwaves for one last time.

The following day Doc gave his last public performance. Our concert began with a mention of his first name, a name as steeped in folklore as formality. Since birth that name had borne a symbolic as well as literal weight, carrying a traditional interpretation of a professional title. A healer in childhood, and later nurtured by a medicine show doctor, his name forecast his life.

Throughout Doc's years as a performer, radio stations periodically invoked his full name, Doctor Hopkins, as a rustic badge of folk authenticity. Doc's musicianship arose from practices and preferences that flourished outside of schooled methods. As he memorably said to Fleming Brown the first time they spoke, "I can't *teach* you, but I can *show* you."[103] That statement crystallizes the workings of informal tradition. Unconfined by formal pedagogy, Doc could pass on his music in a spirit of freedom, respecting his inheritors' independent choices, mindful of the past, but open to renewal.

·5·

Archie's "Old Man"

In 1942, a young San Francisco shipwright named Archie Green (1917–2009) purchased a newly published 78-rpm phonograph album called *Work Songs of the U.S.A.* Each paycheck he put aside funds to buy single releases or sets like this three-disc, six-song collection. He had previously acquired *Negro Sinful Songs*, a compilation that, as in *Work Songs*, featured Huddie Ledbetter (1888–1949), the singer and guitarist best known as Lead Belly.

On this latest album, the fabled performer closed with a sweetly melodious lyric song of his own that he called "Old Man." It served here as a work song of the roustabouts, those longshoremen charged with manually loading and unloading the sidewheelers and sternwheelers of the packet boat era. "Old Man" incorporates phrases that roustabouts sang at their labors, just as its musical style and melodic shape fit within a larger body of dance reels and songs that emerged in nineteenth-century African American life. Its verses consist of traditional questions and answers, raised here by a stevedore addressing his captain. Within the laborer's playful inquiries, he asks in song what he cannot say in speech.

Previously, Archie had encountered roustabout music only in the swaying balletic procession of Jerome Kern's 1927 musical *Show Boat*. Yet for all the grandeur Archie found in Paul Robeson's rendition of "Ol' Man River" and the musical's plaintive sight of roustabouts rolling cotton bales from gangplank to wharf, Lead Belly's "Old Man" struck Archie differently. Without conscious analysis, he simply felt it closer to his own dockside experience.

In January 1941, following a stint in the Civilian Conservation Corps, where he worked along the Klamath River with Siskiyou Mountain loggers and miners, Archie began his apprenticeship as a skilled manual laborer on the San Francisco waterfront. He learned from older hands the trade that he pursued for the next twenty years. Earlier, buoyed during college by the 1934 longshoremen's strike that Harry Bridges had led, Archie now attended union meetings whose energies reflected the New Deal ardor of that era. After his employment in San Francisco's shipyards, along with a stint in the U.S. Navy, he became a carpenter, working in the city's downtown buildings.

Then, at forty, he entered a second career as an academic librarian, folklore scholar, university professor, and advocate for folk culture. His years of congressional lobbying led to the 1976 establishment of the American Folklife Center at the Library of Congress, while his musical scholarship broadened into a field of vernacular studies he ultimately named *laborlore*. Across his breadth of interests, he applied an etymological method. He might begin, for instance, with a handful of discs, following their dark spiraling trails to their surrounding social, ideological, and historical backdrops. He watched how a given song, like a word in living speech, evolved—how it changed hands and found new meanings. He combined first-person interviews with archival investigation bolstered by a dizzying network of contacts and correspondence, all in addition to his command of earlier research. Throughout these efforts, within both the academy and the world beyond, Archie cited a constant touchstone: that exhilarating period of his life when he was employed in the skilled trades. I used to call him "Socrates in a T-shirt."

As he grew older, he found that "Old Man" had never left his consciousness. In 1996, fifty-four years after first taking this recording up to his studio apartment on Telegraph Hill to play on his phonograph, he began writing a folksong case study of "Old Man." In looking back at his initial contact with the song, along with his youthful impressions of Lead Belly, whom he saw perform in 1944, he whimsically noted time's passage, finding himself now an old man studying "Old Man." He began to contact friends—experts in blues, discographers and collectors, and vernacular music scholars—to assist him in his research.

Among them, he called me, and we began a flurry of conversations about the song. Its verses recalled many old-time pieces I had either played or heard. Archie included these references in the first draft of his study, and a few weeks later as our talks continued, he expanded the draft, adding eight more pages. He completed his last revision in March 1997.[1] Yet he never submitted the piece for publication. His uncertainties about "Old Man's" origins ultimately led him in August 2006 to tell me, "I didn't know enough about the song to complete the case study."[2] Then he added, "I didn't have access to enough songs to prove the point. But you did."

Archie quietly made this comment in a San Francisco radio studio, during a taping break for a piece of mine set to air a few weeks later on NPR's *All Things Considered.* Called "Leadbelly's 'Old Man' and the Work Song Tradition," my story highlighted Archie's experiences with "Old Man" and centered on roustabout song composition.[3]

By then Archie regretted that he had never inquired about the song from those most closely involved with the original recording, all of whom he had known. He framed his paper as a meditation on the "uncertainties in folksong study."[4] "Old Man's" performance that he first heard on *Work Songs of the U.S.A.* led him now to ask a threshold question: "Does the 1941 disc represent an actual work chant by riverboat rousters, or did Lead Belly join stray lines together?"[5] Lead Belly may have suggested "Old Man" in response to the producers' request for a riverboat work song, possibly even crafting it in the flurry of the recording session.

These matters of its origin, of locating earlier models and antecedents, became my assignment. Archie had cast me as his collaborator, viewing this work as a joint effort. Together we sought what he called the song's "hidden life."[6] My task focused on locating the piece in the folk tradition, just as his concentrated on the circumstances around Lead Belly's three recordings of the song, two on issued albums and one captured from a radio broadcast. Now, as he neared ninety, he launched me on my own. He wanted me to complete this study myself, and he wrote a letter to make it official: "You have my blessings and cheers. Go wherever your spirits point."[7] It pleased him when I replied that if I ever were to do so, then I would want it to express what Archie had found in his own working life on San Francisco's wharves: knowledge passed from master to apprentice. When I asked him how his work and work life may have changed from when he first heard the song, Archie welcomed the question:

> Well, I worked at my trade about twenty years. Then I changed my career, I suppose, and became a scholar. Now I'm retired. I've in a sense returned to the waterfront, or to work, in the sense I've abandoned the academy. I try to spend my retirement days writing about, working with, and talking to working people: shipwrights, pile drivers, electricians, tinsmiths. And so my current feeling is that anything I have learned, or anything that I can do to help workers achieve some sense of dignity, some sense of solidarity, some ability to talk back to the boss, or talk back to the system, or talk back to the powers that be, that's wonderful. That's what turns me on. I hope that I can continue to function on this level until I shuffle off this mortal coil.[8]

To the last, Archie worked tirelessly to document working people. He wanted their voices heard. He wanted their resistance heard, their talking back. It turns out that Lead Belly's "Old Man," the song that fascinated Archie for so long, talks back too.

• • •

On December 14, 1941, Lead Belly recorded "Old Man" at Moe Asch's studio in New York. Coupled on the reverse side with "Haul Away Joe," a short-drag shanty long associated with ocean sailing, "Old Man" serves as the closing piece on *Work Songs of the U.S.A.*

Work Songs' eight-page booklet, written and researched by Asch's longtime colleague, Marion Distler (1919–1964), opens cinematically:

> Work gang steel drivin,' plantation Negro, lumberjack, logger and chanty-boys; creaking ox-carts, rattling jallopys, clicking freight wheels. Men on

FIGURE 25. *Work Songs of the U.S.A.* album cover. Photo by Greg Adams.

> the roads, in the fields, of the sea . . . hauling, hammering, planting, splitting the logs, climbing the masts. . . . This is the story of America at work.[9]

Distler's exposition expands on Alan Lomax's notes to Lead Belly's first 78-rpm album, his 1939 *Negro Sinful Songs* (Musicraft 31). There, he located its work songs regionally, for having "helped to build the South."[10] Now with words reminiscent of John Dos Passos's prologue to the 1938 *U.S.A.* trilogy, Distler cast Lead Belly as a gifted musician and poet of the American worker. By age sixteen, Distler writes, Lead Belly knew "hundreds of songs." Over his ensuing travels, he absorbed hundreds more. From this repertory, he gave voice to working Americans. "Old Man," recorded just days after the attack on Pearl Harbor, summons the artistry of laborers past as a shocked nation swerved from the Great Depression into a wartime economy.

Work Songs of the U.S.A. became Lead Belly's second album with the Asch label. It moved beyond his array of field hollers, blues, ballads, spirituals, cowboy numbers, as well as tin pan alley creations and game songs, some of which he had recently recorded for his children's sampler, *Play Parties in Song and Dance*, released in the summer of 1941. While *Play Parties* enjoyed sufficient sales, *Work Songs* fared less well, selling only 304 copies in its first year. Yet it stood out, in the words of jazz critic Charles Edward Smith, who penned its earliest review, as "a carefully selected cross-section of his talent."[11]

The album came with a pocket-sized brochure that included parenthetical tags for five of its six selections:

Asch 101 A "Take This Hammer" (Steel Drivin')
B "Corn Bread Rough" [noted as folk dance within the notes]
102 A "Ol' Riley (Slave Song)
B "Rock Island Line" (Railroad Song)
103 A "Haul Away Joe" (Sea Chanty)
B "Old Man" (Levee Chanty)

These pieces range from songs of the workplace to songs about work to songs that workers enjoyed away from their labors. While "Take This Hammer" functionally coordinated group labor in actual conditions, "Rock Island Line" did so only imaginatively. Lead Belly transformed a quartet number originally designed to commercially promote the railroad into a solo showpiece.[12] "Corn Bread Rough," rooted in the antebellum era, offers a recreational glimpse of those who daily endured involuntary servitude. "Ol' Riley" reworks the tall tale of a fugitive slave eluding his captors and their bloodhounds.

How then to account for the two shanties that close *Work Songs of the U.S.A.*? Perhaps Asch or Distler, as Archie suggested, asked Lead Belly if he knew any sea and levee songs to fill out the album's occupational variety. At that time Lead Belly may have heard "Haul Away Joe" from the Almanac Singers. In July 1941, they included it on *Deep Sea Chanteys and Whaling Ballads* (General G-20). Given Lead Belly's friendship with Woody Guthrie and Pete Seeger, both members of that ensemble, they could have provided him with the song's essential structure. But whoever his source was, he filled "Haul Away Joe" with imagery of the river trade

FIGURE 26. Lead Belly, New York, ca. 1936. Courtesy of Lead Belly Legacy Collection.

rather than the sea. During a subsequent recording of "Haul Away Joe," he made that setting even more specific. On an undated acetate from the 1940s, he sings of going "way down the Missirippi"—a purposeful fusion of Mississippi and river—"when the boats was overflowing."[13]

Lead Belly takes a similar route in "Old Man." Its title incorporates a widely accepted nautical moniker for a steamboat captain.[14] He uses names, too, in "Old Man," as he did in "Haul Away Joe," replacing the *Kate Adams*, another historically recognized steamboat—with the *Belle Lee.* Widespread familiarity coupled with the resources of traditional music amply provided Lead Belly with materials that he could reshape into a new whole.

Lead Belly sings:

Old Man, I'm going up the Mississippi,
Yes I am, yes I am.
Old Man, I'm going up the Mississippi,
Yes I am, buddy, yes I am.
I'm going to sail on that big *Bella Lisa*,
Yes I am, yes I am.
I'm going to sail on that big *Bella Lisa*,
Yes I am, buddy, yes I am,
Yes I am, buddy, yes I am.
Old Man, will your dog catch a rabbit?
Take him and try 'im,
You can take him and try 'im.
Old Man, will your dog catch a rabbit?
Take him and try 'im, buddy,
You can take him and try 'im.
You can take him and try 'im, buddy,
You can take him and try 'im.
Old man, will your horse tote double?
You can take him and try 'im,
You can take him and try 'im.
Old Man, will your horse tote double?
You can take him and try 'im, buddy,
You can take him and try 'im.
Old Man, will your daughter take company?
I don't know, I don't know.
Old Man, will your daughter take company?
I don't know, buddy, I don't know,
I don't know, buddy, I don't know.
I'm going to sail up the Mississippi River,
Yes I am, yes I am.
I'm sailing up the Mississippi River,
Yes I am, buddy, yes I am,
Yes I am, buddy, yes I am.
I'm going to sail on that big *Bella Lisa*,
Yes I am, yes I am.
I'm going to sail on that big *Bella Lisa*,
Yes I am, buddy, yes I am,
Yes I am, buddy, yes I am.[15]

The steamboat loomed larger than we might imagine in the landscape of American life. Lead Belly's "Bella Lisa" is a poeticized rendering of the *Belle Lee*, which plied the Mississippi soon after the Civil War. Two boats bearing the name *Belle Lee*, both of them sidewheelers, operated out of New Orleans. The first *Belle Lee* was built in 1863 in New Albany, Indiana, and served as a ninety-two-ton ferry that operated on the Mississippi. In 1868, a second and much larger *Belle Lee*, weighing 1,284 gross tons, was completed in Louisville, Kentucky. The latter inspired wide notice, favored with numerous reports over the several years of its operation. Early in 1868, the New Orleans *Times-Picayune* wrote of the new steamer that "we heard the remark that she excelled in many respects any boat ever built for the trade and many believe her to be unsurpassed as a passenger packet."[16]

Outfitted to haul 300 tons of freight that included cotton, sugar, hides, oranges, molasses, tin, coffee, and sheeting, while equipped with twelve bridal chambers, "officered by gentlemen in every way," she won the public's heart.[17] Crowds numbering in the hundreds gathered to salute her as she embarked from one riverport to another. During her inaugural voyage from New Orleans in January 1868, a band of musicians "discoursed the airs of 'Dixie' and 'Home Sweet Home' which were doubtless hailed with pleasure by the multitude, who left the landing well satisfied with what they had seen."[18] Similar reports followed, yet all of them ceased by 1875, for by then the *Belle Lee* had been dismantled, her hull converted into a wharf boat, and her cabin and machinery transferred to another boat.

The *Belle Lee* appears in roustabout songs before Lead Belly's recording. During journalist Lafcadio Hearn's forays along the Cincinnati waterfront, his 1876 feature bearing the encompassing title, "Levee Life/Haunts and Pastimes of the Roustabouts/Their Original Songs and Peculiar Dances," quotes two verses he overheard within a longer chant:

Belle-a-Lee's got no time,
    Oh, Belle! oh, Belle!
Robert E. Lee's got railroad time,
    Oh, Belle! oh, Belle!
Wish I was in Mobile Bay,
    Oh, Belle! oh, Belle!
Rollin' cotton by de day,
    Oh, Belle! oh, Belle![19]

Mention of the *Belle Lee* also appears in Mary Wheeler's 1944 *Steamboatin' Days: Folk Songs of the River Packet Era.* Starting in the mid-1930s, Wheeler (1892–1979) began collecting near her home in Paducah, Kentucky, from elderly deckhands, former chambermaids, and others who had worked on steamboats that once plied the Ohio, Tennessee, and Mississippi rivers. Her sources "raised" these songs—their term—at tempos that manual freight handling work required. A trained musician, Wheeler first copied down the words and then mapped out the melodies. Then she notated the rhythms, which matched the singers' remembered movements along a gangway. Whether shouldering 150-pound bags of cottonseed, rolling hogsheads, or hauling lumber, the roustabouts worked at a trotting pace. "The rousters," recalled one to Wheeler, "would be a-runnin' an' a-singin,' a runnin' and an a-singin.'"[20]

Here her source, a woman born in 1854, sang in "Oh Annie, Oh!" which begins, "Hopped upon the *Richmond* an' then upon the *Lee*, . . . I hopped upon the *Belle* an' then she got a-way from me."[21]

In the course of gathering this song, Wheeler mentioned that the pending nightfall required them to stop the day's transcribing. Just then, the singer instructed her grandson to borrow from a neighbor some oil for their coal lamp. When Wheeler returned the next morning to complete their musical work, she saw its still burning flame and offered to blow it out. The woman declined, having kept it lit overnight, lacking matches to otherwise prepare her day's meal. She tended that flickering light as she did her song.

• • •

Bluewater sailors and inland river roustabouts labored under the much quieter conditions of the "pre-propeller age."[22] Without the "rattle of the steam winch" and "clatter of cogwheels" to mute their voices, they could hear one another. Like congregants repeating back Scripture given out by their minister, these work gangs timed their movements to the songs, following the cues and cadences their lead singers provided.

In other accounts, retired roustabouts have described a largely solitary chorale: a fellow crewman, perhaps the first mate or captain of the watch, who, in addition to issuing commands, would position himself on a deck or landing, perched so that all could hear. Either by himself or assisted by another voice to second him, he sang while the rest moved in silence, bearing up their loads. But no matter how many laborers joined in this musical call-and-response, the singing typically ran as long as the task required. Former Ohio River roustabout Sam Hazel, interviewed in Greenville, Mississippi, in 1939 at age eighty-six, recalled the scene. He spoke in graphic terms, dramatically evoking how strenuously he and his companions worked: "Time was not in the wheel of the boat. It was all in the nigger's heel."[23] Their labors, depending on how heavily loaded the cargo, might go on, he recalled, for thirty-four or thirty-five hours.[24]

Lead Belly knew about this work and its demands. In the sole documented instance of him discussing "Old Man," he detailed the rouster's task. On January 13, 1944, Lead Belly performed "Haul Away Joe" and "Old Man," along with "Roberta," a river blues, for a WNYC radio program. From an acetate that Moe Asch dubbed off the air, the announcer begins by stating that Lead Belly "knows hundreds of songs by memory [and] says that he made up these three songs himself; the first and second are about famous steamboats of the Mississippi."[25] Lead Belly then prefaces "Haul Away Joe," saying, "Before you sail on a boat, the big *Kate Adams*, you gotta load it, first; and then you sail. And when you load the boat, then you gonna sail, and they gonna sing." When he introduces "Old Man," Lead Belly says much the same: "Now here come that big *Bella Lee* sailing down Mississippi. You got to load it before you ride and sail, and the boys gonna load that this-a-way." He wanted his listeners to imagine a scene of dockside music and motion. While he took composer credit for these songs, he presented them as part of an occupational practice, as part of a once-thriving employment.

However uniquely Lead Belly crafted "Old Man," tradition informs it. Socially and musically, the song employs structures—lyrics, metrical patterns, and melodic shapes—that he and musicians of his generation repeatedly encountered and reworked to new ends. One time-tested pattern that made its way into "Old Man" may have come to his attention in a setting he knew only too well, a state prison. But rather than arriving as an inmate, this time he came as a musical emissary, and in the case of "Old Man," a musical beneficiary.

On December 12, 1934, at the Bellwood Prison Camp in northwest Atlanta, a penal facility engaged in granite quarrying, four state prisoners sang a piece that the Library of Congress files call "Black Gal."[26] This vocal group, led by singer Jesse Wadley, along with John Wadley, Will Jones, and Felix Davenport, performed a work song that Alan Jabbour, as head of the Library's folk archive, thought misnamed in its card catalog. In a 1969 letter he suggested the song would be more properly titled "Will Your Dog Run Rabbit."[27]

The Bellwood singers approached this piece like others they performed that day, ending their stanzas with a hiccupping vocal flourish that gave them a signature sound.[28] The song, which names the longest river in Florida, centers on the flight of a fugitive. In it, he advises a fellow convict to conceal his escape route from the jailor:

Will your dog run rabbit, [way Dinah?]
Will your dog run rabbit,
Says, I don't know, Lord, Lord, I don't know.

Say you can take him, take him to the woods and try
'em,
Say you can take him, take him to the woods and try
'em,
Well bring him back, Lord, Lord, bring him back.

This old hammer, hammer most too heavy,
This old hammer, hammer most too heavy,
[Well I remain?] Lord, Lord [I remain?]

Take this hammer, carry it to my captain,
Take this hammer, carry it to my captain,
Tell 'em I'm gone, Lord, Lord, tell 'em I'm gone.

If he asks you, ask you was I running,
If he asks you, ask you was I running,
Tell 'em I was flying, Lord, Lord, I was flying.

Tell him I was crossing, crossing St. John's River,
Tell him I was crossing, crossing St. John's River,
County line, Lord, Lord, county line.

If he asks you, asks you any further question,
If he asks you, asks you any further question,
Tell 'em. You don't know, Lord, Lord, you don't
know.

Song collector John A. Lomax made this recording with Lead Belly's assistance. Their collaboration at Bellwood resumed the work they had undertaken two months earlier in Arkansas. There, during visits to various units of that state's penitentiary system, Lead Belly had served as an intermediary for recordist Lomax, demonstrating for the convicts the types of songs the collector desired. In turn, when they performed, Lead Belly heard pieces previously unknown to him. This included "Rock Island Line," which, through Lead Belly's reinterpretation, would later become known across the world.

While we cannot know what tripped Lead Belly's recall when he formulated "Old Man," the lyrical structure of "Black Gal" that he witnessed at Bellwood emerges in his song. He adapted the poetry of the lines that these prisoners sang, beginning with "Old Man, will your dog catch a rabbit/Take him and try 'im/You can take him and try 'im." With this verse, which opens their song and which he includes in his 1941 recording, he also begins his last recording of "Old Man," taped at Frederic Ramsey's home in 1948.[29] Meanwhile, other verses that the Bellwood convicts recorded in "Black Gal" appear in "Take This Hammer," as does the escape theme that underlies "Ol' Riley," both of which appear on the *Work Songs* album. In lyric song, this kind of fluidity repeatedly occurs, as the same verse might move from one number to another. Its meaning shifts according to the dramatic environment it poetically represents.

But do the other stylistic elements of "Old Man" surface in older roustabout songs? The earliest magazine article I've found that uses "roustabout" coupled with a notation of roustabout music appears in the December 1868 issue of *Lippincott's.*[30] This article, titled "Songs of the Slave" by John Mason Brown, came out shortly after the landmark 1867 appearance of *Slave Songs of the United States,* the first book of Black music published in America. Here, Brown disparagingly speaks of the roustabouts' "river songs." He finds their spontaneity—the fact that a song leader might "affect to sing the *solo* part from a scrap of newspaper"—too immediate to be worthy of art.[31] Yet he also writes in detail about the music, apparently

FIGURE 27. Steamboat Song. From *Lippincott's Magazine*, Dec. 1868.

based on personal contact with these songs and their singers. He assays their structural form, observing that "nearly all were constructed of single lines, separated by a barbarous and unmeaning chorus." His transcription of "Steamboat Song" provides a detailed rendering of its wordless chorus, which he terms a "howl." In making this characterization, he echoes his predecessors in *Slave Songs*, William Francis Allen, Charles Pickard Ware, and Lucy McKim Garrison. They admitted that in their representation of the one steamboat song they included, the transcription falls short, "so far as notes can give one, of the strange barbaric songs that one hears upon the Western steamboats."[32] In other words, none of these auditors could effectively capture in print the sliding, blues-like tonalities of these songs. Yet Brown's song, if reimagined with the glissando that marks so much of Black vernacular music, surely anticipates Lead Belly's piece. "Steamboat Song," with its brief but stirring melody, possesses both a lyricism and structure that "Old Man" inherits.

A similar song appears in Mary Wheeler's work. Admittedly, I found that neither her unpublished writings, including her 1937 master's thesis on this music, her correspondence with retired captains as well as journalists assigned to the riverboat beat, nor the clippings she assembled of steamboats and their music, revealed verses that mirror "Old Man." Nor did her niece, singer Bertha Wheeler Wenzel, who had closely studied this music with her, know the song or its larger song cluster.[33] But one number closest to its prosody appears near the end of *Steamboatin' Days*. Called "Woman, Woman, I See Yo' Man," its verses bear syntactic commonalities with "Old Man."[34] Differences lie between them, but both narrators address their listeners, posing questions and portraying everyday dramas. While Lead Belly derived his lyrics and based his melody on sources other than these, the forms he adopted had been long in place.

• • •

Intimations of the song's earlier life emerge on a handful of Library of Congress recordings made during the time that Wheeler conducted her work. Beginning in the mid-1930s through the early war years, Herbert Halpert, as well as John and Alan Lomax, made recordings of surviving roustabouts. Of these, several of Halpert's sources that he recorded in Mississippi in late May and early June 1939 reveal key words and phrases in common with Lead Belly's "Old Man." These usages affirm what Lead Belly had claimed on the WNYC radio show: In some form "Old Man" had walked the gangplanks and docks.

The first usage arose shortly before Halpert recorded James Archer in Vicksburg in May 1939. While seeking potentially recordable informants for Halpert, Miss Jerome Sage, who directed the state's Music Project for the Works Progress Administration, came in contact with Archer, by then about eighty years old.[35] Born in slavery, he remembered the surrender. Sometime around 1881 or 1882, following a stint as a track laborer for the A & V (Alabama and Vicksburg) Railroad, he worked as a steamboat night watchman. While he did not consider himself a singer proper, he summoned a verse from a well-known sea shanty called "Rango," which he initially learned from a captain and also a first-mate, singing to his fellow roustabouts.[36] Despite his modesty, as the subsequent recording shows, he possessed a deep, affecting voice and proved an avid witness to his times. Sage quoted the verse in her report, the same verse he soon sang for Halpert:

> Captain, Captain, Gimme Your Daughter,
> Rango, Rango.
> I'll Treat Her Well and Marry her on the Water,
> Rango, Rango.[37]

Archer had heard the song while shipping on the *Natchez,* and also the *White,* two of the many "coast boats" that traveled from New Orleans

FIGURE 28. James Archer, Vicksburg, Mississippi, May 29, 1939. Photo by Abbott Ferriss. Courtesy of the Archives and Records Services Division, Mississippi Department of Archives and History.

to the Delta. As the vessels neared shore, the hands would form a circle under the boiler deck. Directed there by the mate, and operating with the "sanction" of the captain, Archer explained, "it was the rule of the boat to sing." The gang's best vocalist would "word it," meaning chant "Rango's" verses, lining it out while the rest joined on the refrain. The whole effect, he warmly recounted, sounded "just like a choir."[38] Once the boat reached shore, the music stopped. "After they made fast . . . they didn't do nothing but work." The roustabouts, he pointed out, did not sing from that point on, being simply too encumbered. "If you would see those men how they worked, you wouldn't think that they'd have the spirit enough in them to sing."

Later that day (and the next), Halpert recorded two Vicksburg manual laborers who also had worked on the river: Emmet Jackson, 46, and his longtime singing partner, John Floyd, 39. In the past Jackson had lined track for the Illinois Central Railroad, while Floyd had previously served time at Parchman prison before becoming a steamboat roustabout, an occupation he followed for the next fifteen years. Among their offerings, a verse that appears in two of their roustabout chants echoes in "Old Man": "Old Man, Old Man, you better pray, your head is blooming for the grave."[39] They sang the verse while lifting sacks of seed and cotton onto the backs of their fellow roustabouts, whom they called "toters," assigned to move freight onto the banks.

It appears first in Jackson's own "Steamboat Song." With its stretched-out vowels and wordless humming, it recalls similarly contoured levee camp songs. Time and again pieces like these accompanied the labor born of working from "behind a mule," a task Jackson knew firsthand.[40]

Another of their steamboat pieces, identified only as "Old Steamboat, Roustabout Song," includes the same verse.[41] In this textually longer song, Jackson leads at first and then hands it over to Floyd, who sings the "Old Man" verse. The song's slow pace, stretching out like a long meter hymn, fits the physical labor it is meant to relieve. Floyd termed this a "raise-up song" and used it as part of a four-man team in which two lifters, such as himself and Jackson, would place the loads onto the shoulders of their two fellow carriers. This work, like the singing, might go on all day and into the night, however long the task required. Just before the duo recorded "Old Steamboat," Jackson mentions their having sung it "under those hard mates, the captains on the boats." While the vocal burden transferred from one loader to the other, the roustabouts themselves stayed silent. The weight they bore and the exertion it required left them, much as James Archer earlier observed, with no strength left for singing.

The last of Halpert's field recordings that prefigured the language of "Old Man" took place in Greenville, Mississippi, on June 3, 1939, with Joe Shores. This fifty-two-year-old former steamboat fireman, then working nights as a ferryboat pilot from Greenville to Arkansas City, had begun working on the river thirty-five years earlier at age eighteen. Now, for Halpert's microphone, he demonstrated a set of sounding calls by which steamboat crews measured water depths. The assigned crew member would drop a lead line into a river—a weighted cylinder tied to a rope—with knots tied

FIGURE 29. John Floyd, Vicksburg, Mississippi, May 30, 1939. Photo by Abbott Ferriss. Courtesy of the Archives and Records Services Division, Mississippi Department of Archives and History.

along its length that represented measurements. Depending on which knot surfaced, that marked the deepest fathom below (the sounding call "mark twain," for instance, denotes twelve feet). The leadsman would then sing out that measurement through a megaphone so that the pilot on the upper deck could navigate the boat accordingly.[42]

After the sounding calls, Shores offered an untitled roustabout song, one he termed "just an old make-up song."[43] He mentioned having heard it frequently, and Halpert had him record it twice:

> Say, old man,
> Old man, old man,
> Where you been so long?
> I've been under the boiler sleeping warm.
>
> Old man, old man,
> Won't you tote some seed?
> I can't tote no seed,
> For the boss's too mean.
>
> Oh, I don't raise no seed,
> And I don't roll no cotton.
> I'm go keep off the John [?],
> I'm go' ship on the Georgia Lee.
>
> Oh tell my woman,
> If she want to see me.
> Catch this Stacker Lee [or, in second take, Georgia Lee],
> Come to St. Louis to the Worly Fair.

Shores fixed 1904, the year of the St. Louis World's Fair, as his first exposure to the song. His use of "old man," much like the verse that Jackson and Floyd sang, addresses a fellow roustabout and not a steamboat captain. Realities of this occupation—fatigue, poverty, old age, and uncaring bosses, as well as the attractions of the pending fair and the allure of footloose life—show up in his blues-inflected plaint. Shores's piece also foreshadows the *Belle Lee* in Lead Belly's "Old Man." Over his two takes, Shores names both the *Georgia Lee* and *Stacker Lee*. It hardly matters that the builder of the Lee line that produced those fabled boats differed from the company that constructed the *Belle Lee*. The symbolic surname lies at hand, available for artistic purposes.

FIGURE 30. John Floyd and fellow roustabouts, Vicksburg, Mississippi, May 30, 1939. Photo by Abbott Ferriss. Courtesy of the Archives and Records Services Division, Mississippi Department of Archives and History.

These four recordings—James Archer's, the two from John Floyd and Emmet Jackson, and this last, from Joe Shores—anticipate Lead Belly's "Old Man." The salutation of "old man," the mention of his daughter, and the references to the Lee line show these images in use by veteran longshoremen. Doubtlessly, other singing roustabouts, albeit unrecorded and undocumented, knew this imagery too.

While James Archer's single-stanza performance of "Rango" points to the song's former life as a whaler's shanty, the remaining three recordings call upon the music that arose with the plow and the pickax.[44] Melodically, they resemble, too, what churchgoers have called the "Dr. Watts hymns," the slow, ornamented, long-meter songs named for English hymnodist and divine Isaac Watts (1674–1748). The mournful pace of these unnamed steamboat songs suited the movement of heavy freight borne down gangplanks.

These recorded antecedents of "Old Man," however, musically diverge from the melody that houses Lead Belly's song. While "Steamboat Song" from the 1868 *Lippincott's* article, and "Woman, Woman, I See Yo' Man" that Wheeler collected, bear musical suggestions of it, Lead Belly's piece joins a larger body of African American work songs that had emerged by the late nineteenth century, as well as an inheritance of singing games, banjo songs, fiddle pieces, and pre-blues dance tunes. If one pillar of Lead Belly's "Old Man" stands on the usages embodied by the 1939 Mississippi field recordings, and another extends the verse structure that the prisoners at Bellwood employed in "Black Gal," then a third pillar rises from the social music that Lead Belly came to know in his youth.

Archie noted that "matters of internal meaning parallel those of function."[45] "Old Man's" origins point to a richly colloquial term Lead Belly used in living practice: "sukey jumps." These were the recreational dances that he and his Caddo Lake neighbors enjoyed. On *Work Songs of the U.S.A.*, he performs "Corn Bread Rough," a sukey jump that marked his recording debut with the diatonic accordion, his first instrument.[46] Lead Belly told Charles Edward Smith at the time of *Work Songs* that as a youngster he would tie his accordion, which he otherwise called a "windjammer," to his horse's saddle and ride off to play for these dances. Musician Hally Wood (1922–1989), who knew Lead Belly and who transcribed "Old Man" for his posthumously published songbook, commented on another of his sukey jump songs.[47] Around 1946, she learned "Poor Howard" from him, and she described how he approached it on his twelve-string guitar: "It is surely a banjo melody, lying right under the fingers in G-tuning."[48]

Much the same could be said for "Old Man." Woods's musical transcription shows the opening verse descending the scale, with each word fitting the next successively lower note. Then, in the refrain, beginning with the song's keynote, it completes the phrase set a fourth above the anchoring tone. The second line repeats this pattern with the refrain now doubled in length, sounded an octave below from where the song began. Given this melodic range, a modern interpreter on a guitar or banjo might be tempted to insert the dominant chord (otherwise called the "five-chord") near the end of each verse. But the song, in keeping with its idiom, can be played by holding the "one-chord," the tonic, and working out the notes within that framework.

This harmonic economy places "Old Man" amidst a body of music that arose not only in game songs like Lead Belly's "Red Bird Soon in the Morning" (which mostly stays on the one-chord), but also a number of other stylized work songs like Mississippi John Hurt's 1928 recording of "Spike Driver Blues" (OK 8692), a song that melodically "Old Man" closely resembles.[49] Such pieces emerged in that era's burgeoning railroad construction that required driving spikes for inserting dynamite while tunnel building or rock clearing. Black railroad workers and convict laborers performed hammering songs, as did their fellow white musicians who adopted African American work songs like "Swannanoa Tunnel" into their repertories.[50] Musically, "Spike Driver Blues," and by extension, "Old Man," fits with titles like "Take This Hammer," which appears on *Work Songs of the U.S.A.*, as well as "This Old Hammer" and "I Got a Bulldog."[51] Their compact melodies and major-minor tonalities marked a widespread rural secular music played before the blues arose.

Lead Belly transmitted this older style in "Old Man," both with his guitar on the *Work Songs* album and later as an unaccompanied vocal on his *Last Sessions* album. His approach brings to mind "Green Corn," a boisterous, two-chord, square dance piece that he demonstrated for Alan Lomax during their 1940 discussion of sukey jumps.[52] Lead Belly sings a verse long identified with "Blackeyed Susie," a breakdown widely heard throughout Southern folk tradition, from upland whites to Black Louisianans like himself. He sings, "All I wants in this creation/Little bitty wife and a big plantation." Compare that to an 1882 printed version of "Randso," the sailor song that James Archer knew aboard his steamboats as "Rango": "I've just come down from the wild goose nation/To me way, hay, E-O-yah/I've left my wife on a big plantation/And sing hi-lo, my Rand-so, way."[53]

This interweaving of old-time reels and lyric songs repeatedly ties back to roustabout song. In a 1940 *Harper's* article titled "Mississippi Roustabout," Ben Lucien Burman recalls a Black steamboat night watchman he knew. Assigned to rouse the captain every morning at early light, he quietly step-danced in his cabin, and then sang a familiar old-time ditty:

> The old cow died at the fork of the branch,
> Jaybird died of the measles.
> Here come Mr. Rabbit with a fiddle on his back,
> Going home to Jesus.[54]

In the mid-1980s, while seated in the front room of his home in Monticello, Kentucky, I watched white fiddler Clyde Davenport (1921–2020) sing nearly this same verse, one found in collections from North Carolina to northern Alabama, to his five-string banjo.[55] Both the tune and technique that he used for "The Old Cow Died in the Forks of the Branch"—his title—bring to mind another musically reminiscent piece, a beginner's exercise that reached countless rural homes of the nineteenth century. Called "Old Seventy-Six" in Frank B. Converse's 1865 *Method for the Banjo*, its title varied over its long course, but its substance continually served as a rudimentary introduction to finger-style banjo picking. Its simplicity allowed for the creation of new pieces that elaborated on its melody as well as accommodating the manifold variations that so many musicians have brought to it.[56]

One of Lead Belly's contemporaries who played "Old Seventy-Six" by another name was African American banjoist Clarence Tross (1884–1977). A native of Durgon, West Virginia, he credited his father, Andy Tross, born a slave in 1850, with teaching him both the instrument and this piece. Clarence described his first banjo as one much like his father's: homemade with a possum skin, horsehair strings, and a fretless neck. Both of them played for dances, Black and white. Andy's bandmates included a fiddler, an accordionist, and sometimes a percussionist who rattled beef bones. The instrumentation alone points to the sukey jumps that Lead Belly recalled from his earliest days.

Music they all knew, too, moved among them in ceaseless transit. In about 1892, the first song Andy Tross taught Clarence to play as a boy of eight, the two called "Old Man, May I Have Your Daughter." In a 1974 recording that he made at age ninety, Clarence Tross recalled the principal verse his father sang:

> Old man, may I have your daughter?
> Yes, oh yes, take her if you want her.
> I'm upstairs with a dollar and a quarter,
> Come downstairs with the old man's daughter.[57]

Once again the signal verse appears, transferring from an ex-slave to his son. Within the verse itself, the old man's daughter, pictured as a woman of easy virtue, signifies not only a widely used trope but also the presence of a comic tradition, one that Lead Belly knew well. At the time of *Work Song's* release, during his interview with Charles Edward Smith, Lead Belly sang "Salty Dog," an up-tempo rag that he credited to a barrelhouse pianist named Pine Top. This vigorous player, whom Lead Belly recalled from his early travels with Blind Lemon Jefferson, performed "Salty Dog's" juke joint verses, one of which asks: "Old man, can I marry your daughter, you salty dog."[58] The words carry the same sly suggestiveness and bawdy humor as ever, but are associated here with the leering personage of a salty dog. Musician Tom Paley (1928–2017), who knew Lead Belly and visited him on multiple occasions at his New York City apartment, performed the song too. While his musical precedent more closely approximates the McGee Brothers' 1927 performance (Vocalion 5150), his verses capture the salacious spirit Tom gleaned from Lead Belly: "Come on old man/Go tell your daughter/She better give me back my quarter/You salty dog, mama, you salty dog."[59] The next verse makes the transactional element explicit: "Standing on a corner/With a dollar in my hand/Looking for a woman/That needs a man/You salty dog, mama, you salty dog."

These rhymes, however ribald or rollicking, reach beyond merriment. In the album notes to *Work Songs of the U.S.A.*, Marion Distler writes that slaves communicated protest even in the most playful sukey jump songs like "Corn Bread Rough." Here Lead Belly sings what field hands of that time found repeatedly true: "Corn bread rough and corn bread tough/Ain't got no money, got corn bread tough."[60] Or, as Lead Belly told Charles Edward

Smith, "In slavery times, they had so many ways of sayin' about *the* man, he didn't know what it was all about."[61]

In "Old Man," in a dialogue with the captain, the roustabout asks, "Will your daughter take company," to which the captain replies that he doesn't know. Scholar Norm Cohen compared this verse to the verbal insult traditions documented among state prisoners. He observed how this interchange masked the "thinly disguised insinuation that the daughter of the 'Old Man' (chain gang overseer) is a loose woman."[62] Archie viewed this exchange as fundamental to the song, calling into question both a class system and a racial order, "of the relation of workers to bosses and of Blacks to whites."[63] The rouster's repartee, he felt, crossed significant boundaries. "Who speaks to whom? Does a Black worker challenge a white authority figure?"[64] He thought that consciously or unconsciously, Lead Belly's song raises matters of political, economic, and social identity. Or, as more than one Black preacher has noted: the difference lies between position and power. The city buses of Montgomery, Alabama, had the position, but in the end, Rosa Parks had the power.

In an occupation where men physically lifted staggering loads for hours on end, the idea of their singing among themselves a mockery, an insult, or a sexual innuendo hardly seems surprising. Roustabout chants, unbound to any particular narrative, admitted the bawdy as readily as the satiric and gave vent to the complaints of a fatigued workforce. In terms of song composition, these pieces included phrases long in circulation, and others arising from the moment at hand. "In roustabout songs," Archie said, "the subject matter is as wide as human consciousness, as human nature can be."[65] Within this atmosphere of creative liberty, roustabouts were free to express old ideas anew or to fit new thoughts into long-familiar patterns that reveal rhetorical traditions available to Lead Belly. These ancestries, however widely dispersed, map the genealogies Archie wanted drawn for Leadbelly's "Old Man."

In October 1970, Burl Hammons (1907–1992), a white traditional musician from Pocahontas County, West Virginia, played "Old Man, Can I

Have Your Daughter." He used the same title, tune, and fingering method on his banjo that Clarence Tross had used with his rendition of the song. While the paths of these two West Virginia musicians likely never crossed, the song had moved between them. At the time of Burl's recording, one of his neighbors sang: "Old Man, old man, let me marry your daughter/ She can cook and carry my water/Take her, take her if you want her/She won't work and you can't make her."[66] In the song's ongoing domestic drama, the fallen woman has now become a harridan, the obstinate wife.

Nearly 300 miles away in western North Carolina, Frank Proffitt (1913–1965) sang this same verse but set within a different song, accompanying himself on his fretless banjo. That song was "Sourwood Mountain," a widely known dance piece. Proffitt sings the song in two parts, as a call-and-response not unlike Lead Belly's approach as he slides along his banjo's smooth neck. Speaking, he re-creates a dialogue. He sings, "Old man, old man I want your daughter." Then, in a spoken aside, he says, "What do you want her for?" Now, singing again, he replies: "Bake my bread and carry my water."[67]

The musical antecedent that Lead Belly may have incorporated into "Old Man" parallels the widely known traditional fiddle tune "Granny Will Your Dog Bite." Folklorist David Evans, for instance, found during the field recordings he undertook in Mississippi between 1969 and 1971 that his African American sources performed it as "a banjo piece, a children's rhyme, a fife and drum piece, a piece played on the drums only, and a chant by teenage girl cheerleaders at a community baseball game, accompanied by beating on the grandstand."[68] In 1925, music scholar Dorothy Scarborough, an early folksong authority, considered it one that "every Southerner knows."[69] A particularly colorful version published in 1940 reads:

> Granny, will your dog bite, cow kick, cat scratch?
> Granny, will your hen peck, sow root the corn patch?
> Granny, will your duck quack, old grey goose hatch?
> Granny, will your dog bite? Yes, child, no![70]

One branch of the "Granny Will Your Dog Bite" complex extends to the tune called "Hog Eye." A few days before Herbert Halpert recorded the Vicksburg roustabouts, he called on white fiddler Stephen B. Tucker, a native of Collinsville, near Meridian. Tucker, born in 1859, had learned his music from several older fiddlers who had experienced the Civil War. Among his many tunes, he played "Hog Eye."[71] While Tucker played it as an instrumental, his personal story—his advanced age coupled with his musical past—indicates the tune's long life in tradition. A once regionally popular 1928 recording of Pope's Arkansas Mountaineers presents it as a string band number (Victor 21295). They sing:

> Chicken in the bread pan kicking up dough,
> Sally will your dog bite? No sir no.
> Sally in the garden sifting sand,
> Sally upstairs with a hog-eyed man.[72]

Beyond the fragmentary questions present in the other "Granny" songs, "Hog Eye" carries an additional set of cultural meanings. A hog eye, a term used to denote a ring bolt used on western river barges, applies, as folklorist Gershon Legman has explained, to someone looking for free meals as well as illicit liaisons:

> A Hog Eye man means a wharf roustabout or idler, usually Negro, who is always "just hangin' around" looking for appetizing kitchen hand-outs and especially for sexual opportunities; often called "Jody" (the adulterer) in and since World War II, in Negro "toasts" and brag-songs.[73]

The term, Legman adds, has also been identified as female genitalia, exemplified in song, for instance, in Texas Alexander's "Boe Hog Blues."[74] Just as Norm Cohen connected a jailhouse boast to the proposition in "Old Man," Legman located "Hog Eye" in kindred settings in which competitive, often obscene, humor airs. Together these traditions frame the impudence of a roustabout asking whether his captain's daughter keeps company.

When Archie first introduced me to "Old Man," I responded with a number of these examples, beginning with Frank Proffitt's "Sourwood Mountain," soon followed by "Granny Will Your Dog Bite" and "Hog Eye." Other pieces arose in our conversations, among them a family of contest tunes derived from "Say Old Man, Can You Play the Fiddle." These, too, follow the two-part form present in "Granny Will Your Dog Bite." To this day, live performances of "Say Old Man" frequently open with someone first announcing the title, then leaving the instrumentalist to supply the answer. Recorded versions span Texan Eck Robertson's solo violin to "Georgia Slim" Rutland's limpid virtuosity, from Tennessean David "Stringbean" Akeman's "Say Old Man Can You Play the Banjo," which he answers, "Yes, by Ned, I can play it like a gander," to southern Ohio's Osborne Brothers asking "Say Old Man, Can You Play the Mandolin," to Bob Wills's Western Swing rendition of "Bring It Down to Our House," in which vocalist Tommy Duncan asks, "Say old man, can you play the fiddle?"[75] Through them all runs a challenge posed and then met.

The last of "Old Man's" hypothetical antecedents that I brought to Archie's attention was "The Deaf Woman's Courtship." An old woman is asked to do the washing, then the cooking, then the churning, and then the quilting. To each query she replies that she's hard of hearing and cannot make out the request. Then, when asked if she's fond of courting, her deafness precipitously improves. A full proposal follows, "Old woman, old woman, will you marry me?" She gleefully responds, "O God bless you, O God Bless you! That's the time I heard you."[76] This widely found song, in print by 1826 in *The Popular Rhymes of Scotland,* appears in collections from Arkansas, Missouri, Virginia, Tennessee, and North Carolina.[77] While musically not part of sukey jump, fiddle tune, or pre-blues styles, it, too, anticipates the verbal play that characterizes Lead Belly's "Old Man."

Yet a current deeper still flows within this song. Early on I mentioned to Archie a churning Appalachian banjo piece found among Black as well as white traditional players. Titled "Roustabout," it voices a restless, unmoored individual, a rounder living at the margins. Its troubled message recalls another rhyme of the packet boat era. In the literature of this music, none have been cited more: "Roustabout ain't got no home, makes his living on his shoulder bone."[78] Musically its mood as well as its sense resounds in a banjo song that Uncle Dave Macon recorded in 1926. As a youth in the mid-1880s, Macon listened to the roustabouts docked near his family's residence in downtown Nashville. In "The Cross Eyed Butcher And The Cackling Hen," he sings with blues-like inflection, "Shanghai chicken ain't got no comb/This old roustabout's got no home."[79] Then he repeats the

FIGURE 31. "Old Man" disc in record sleeve. Photo by Greg Adams.

verse. Its mournful lines give aching witness to the lives of these workers, deemed essential in their time, if dispensable in their person.

A cultural mosaic underlies "Old Man." "Lead Belly worked," Archie observed, "with the material that was available to him."[80] The verse form the famed songster witnessed at Bellwood prison; the related sukey jumps, fiddle and banjo pieces, and pre-blues work songs; the older pentatonic roustabout songs found in printed notation; the historical *Belle Lee* depicted in the journalism of its day and the songs that celebrated it; the presence of key words and phrases in recorded steamboat chants; the tradition of jailhouse brags and insults; let alone fellow musicians of Lead

Belly's time—persons like Clarence Tross and his father, keepers of tradition themselves—all collectively meet together in this song. Though Lead Belly's internal deliberations will forever elude us, we can rely on Archie's supposition that Lead Belly, "called on to perform a 'levee shanty' on short notice, would have found it difficult to tell Moe Asch, 'I don't know one.'"[81]

• • •

In February 1997, when Archie sent me the first draft of his case study, he stapled to it a short checklist of items he wanted me to find. These constituted, he wrote, 'missing links,' gaps that ranged from a contemporary review of the Asch album (that the Charles Edward Smith review provides) to the date of the radio broadcast. The weightiest of these assignments consisted of finding "Link to Granny/Old Man fiddle tune," and "Evidence roustabouts sang text similar to 'Old Man.'"[82] For Archie, so many of the song's sources still awaited discovery, sources that might illuminate this song he had found so singularly compelling throughout his working life. He likened "Old Man" to "a sorcerer's clock—texts and tunes perpetually in motion, unending mystery at the core."[83] Near the end of his second draft, he reflected that "tens of thousands of songs move in and out of tradition . . . only a few surrender their secrets."[84] I can only hope that the story told here responds to those mysteries, locating some of those missing links he sought.

Yet even with the joys we shared in pursuing this case study, he also acknowledged that our work, however interesting, "doesn't alter the nature of the song or its function to roustabouts." He went on to say, "Steve, what difference does it make to a roustabout on the river that we have a hypothesis about the origin of a song?"[85] The greater significance, he knew, lay in the realities of their lives, in the experiences of those who had sung these songs as a way of surviving and spiritually overcoming.

I realize now as my years pass and I become an old man too, that Lead Belly's "Old Man" lay at the heart of Archie's aspirations for those workers with whom he felt such camaraderie. Its formal elements—its musical call and response, its verbal questioning and answering—these ricocheting movements tangibly embody challenge. Its poetic traditions culturally express resistance. The role reversal at work here runs through so much of folk narrative and song, sometimes playfully in a schoolyard game, and other times, scathingly when a neighborhood rapper utters a street corner conceit about someone's mother. The brazenness that propels Lead Belly's questioner to ask about the captain's daughter speaks for all who have endured the implacability of formal power, and with it at times, the lash of authority.

"Lead Belly's 'Old Man,'" Archie's title for a case study he never completed, comes down to what he said in 2006 regarding how he felt about this song. He expressed then what he still hoped to accomplish in the time left him: to abet the ways workers might talk back. He devoted his final years to those who, in myriad ways, had built this country. By then he no longer wrote for academic presses, placing his final three books with unions or organizations allied with them. He published in union magazines and led the Fund for Labor Culture and History that he established in 2000, which promoted conversations between workers and academics and supported labor research. The Archie Green Fellowship that bears his name today at the Library of Congress and the more than 1,200 interviews undertaken there by the Occupational Folklife Project (OFP) extend his pursuit of laborlore into contemporary life.[86]

One example can suffice: A 2011 OFP interview with Timothy Charles Harris, a Houston longshoreman and union business agent, followed his family's tradition of dockside labor. At sixteen he felt that "legacy behind me," finding himself drawn to the older longshoremen "chasing the work," watching them go from one port to the next to operate the RTGs, the giant rubber-tired gantry cranes that move freight into a ship's hold. He talked about "containerization," and marveled over the skill his fellow heavy machine operators displayed in loading anything from Black Hawk helicopters en route to Afghanistan and Iraq, to receiving cattle from Brazil, to securing locomotives headed for Russia. "To watch these guys move cargo is art. Definitely an art," he notes.[87]

Harris acknowledged that the work that he, his father, and their companions did reached back to the roustabouts of the past. The principal difference lay in today's mechanization of physical brawn. Harris's ardor for this work and his admiration for those who came before him brings to mind another term applied to the old longshoreman's task: *coonjine.* A racially burdened word, *coonjine* represents the gyroscopic adjustments that roustabouts physically made as they negotiated a wavering gangplank under a heavy load. It names, too, a cluster of vernacular dance numbers that arose to celebrate the motions and music that purportedly accompanied this labor.[88] But by then, these freight handlers of an earlier time had already in song and step transformed their toil into art. Regardless of their station in life, as Archie said, "The mind of the shantyman is free."[89]

6

The Sound Wagon

The sound wagon made its way down a Mississippi highway. With its windowless panels and rectangular body, it resembled a Black Maria in profile, the muddied dust raised from its backroad travels streaking the van's dark exterior. Here in June 1939, this reconditioned Army ambulance, a ca. 1930 Ford Carryall fortified with dual rear wheels, had until recently hauled stage flats and scenery around New York City for the Federal Theatre Project, a relief-era undertaking of the Works Progress Administration (WPA). The vehicle, now repurposed into a mobile recording laboratory, was transporting a Presto Model 12-E disc cutter designed to make on-site phonograph records. WPA carpenters had also installed storage cabinets to hold several hundred aluminum and acetate recording blanks, camera equipment, cutting and playback needles, some canned food items, and a shelf for the song collector's books, along with a small cot. Extra lead-acid batteries and a converter to power the disc machine allowed recording when the truck ventured beyond the limits of the commercial power grid. Rural electrification remained a work in progress.

At the wheel of the sound wagon—so named by the director of the Mississippi unit of the Federal Writers' Project—sat Herbert Halpert

FIGURE 32. Eri Douglass and the recording truck that she christened the "Sound Wagon." Guntown, Mississippi, May 10, 1939. Photo by Abbott Ferriss. Courtesy of the Archives and Records Services Division, Mississippi Department of Archives and History.

(1911–2000), a twenty-seven-year-old folklorist from New York. Beside him rode his state-appointed assistant, Mississippi native Abbott Ferriss (1915–2014), at twenty-four, a recent journalism graduate and member of the Federal Writers' Project's unit headquartered in Jackson.

They were in the last days of Halpert's three-month-long, multi-state Southern Recording Expedition sponsored by a consortium of WPA arts

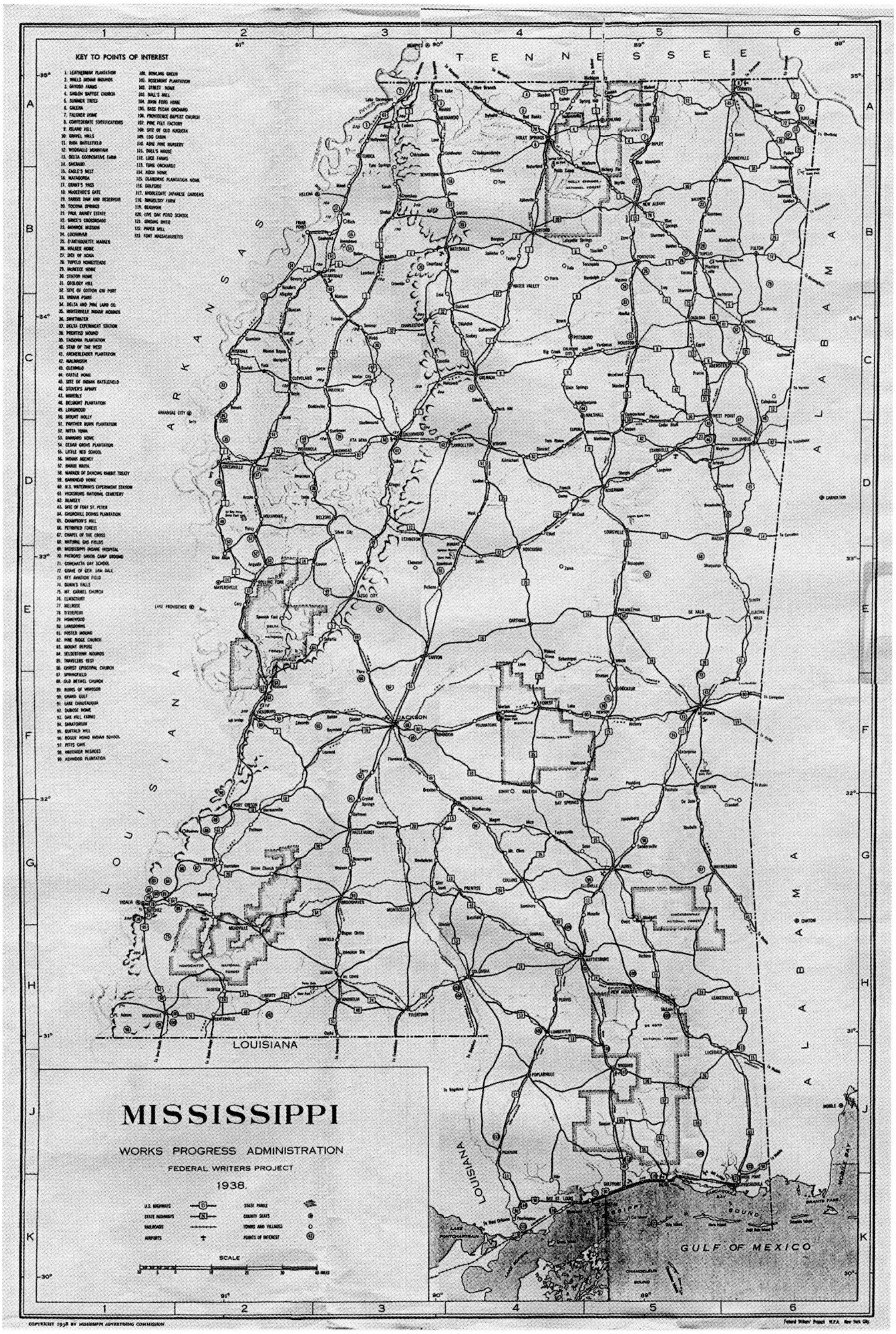

FIGURE 33. The map that Herbert Halpert and Abbott Ferriss used on their 1939 expedition. Courtesy of Abbott Ferriss.

agencies and the Library of Congress. Despite a month of "bad roads, hot weather, and greasy food," Ferriss and Halpert had ventured during this four-week assignment into numerous towns and cities, where they documented songs, ballads, and tunes that ranged from the sales pitch of a neighborhood tamale vendor to the sounding calls of a former steamboat deckhand.[1]

Throughout their Mississippi travels, Halpert made 169 records with some seven hundred tracks that yielded over 300 songs and tunes. Ferriss transcribed lyrics, photographed the singers and instrumentalists, and took copious notes. Now they headed towards their last recording session with a fifty-five-year-old banjoist named Thaddeus Willingham. Two months earlier, a member of the Writers' Project living in Gulfport had informed the state office about him, leading to this final stop on Halpert's and Ferriss's itinerary.

The first of the numbers Willingham played for them, "Roll on the Ground," a lyric piece long wedded to the banjo, bears outlines of his own life. His experiences, like the song's lineage, reached from the antebellum South to the postwar twentieth century. Though the collectors would soon fix this piece in the waveform of an instantaneous acetate, Willingham's performance embodies how a folksong changes, transfers, and lives. What the two researchers could not know as their sound wagon sped south was just how much this tall, gentle-voiced musician would capture the spirit of the entire trip.

Thaddeus Constantine Willingham Jr. (1884–1947) grew up near Tuscaloosa, Alabama, on a plantation called Sylvan Glen. Both his grandfathers had migrated from South Carolina around 1840 to become slaveholders, each of them the owner of large plantations in Tuscaloosa County. Willingham's father, born at Sylvan Glen, served in the Confederate army, accompanied by his slave, Henry. Afterward, during Reconstruction, Henry wed Dixie, also an ex-slave, who served as a maid for Willingham's mother after her own plantation upbringing. In turn, Henry and Dixie remained with the Willinghams long after Emancipation. A similar closeness in matters of race took place in Thaddeus Willingham's life. Black influence ran through the music he knew and loved.

Thaddeus Willingham began playing the banjo at fifteen, having learned from "the boys around the neighborhood."[2] By this, his children and others understood that he meant his Black neighbors. He watched them make music and dance, he told Halpert and Ferriss. According to Willingham's third-oldest daughter, Jeana, "He taught himself from listening to the other young men around there, the other boys." She added that "a lot of the songs were sung by field hands or chain gangs" and said that he attended "visiting minstrel shows and fairs," where he heard Black troupes and tent show performers.[3]

All eighteen of the songs Willingham recorded in Gulfport on the morning of June 11, 1939, reflect music shared across the racial divide, and all of them reach deep into the nineteenth century. Only once during the session, which took place at the Gulfport Women's Clubhouse, did he mention a piece that he drew from mass media, a radio performance of "Charming Betsy." While that number did not get recorded, it too had long circulated among Black and white interpreters, the song itself voiced with familiar racial hierarchies from Reconstruction on. Before playing each item, Willingham reiterated the same answer to Halpert's questioning as to when he learned this or that piece. He had heard these songs all his life.

That April, Clarence Kerns, a local writer who lived in Gulfport and served on the state's Federal Writers' Project, first alerted the state office about Willingham:

> Mr. Willingham . . . plays a wide number of the old tunes—with harmony accompaniment—on his banjo (5-string) in a very pleasing manner and with unusual fidelity. He readily 'sits in' with other country musicians (fiddlers) and adds a great deal with his correct harmonies. He has played . . . over our local radio station (WGCM) on a regular feature. I would like to see him employed to assist in all our recordings where needed. He is a very poor man but has the finest personality, character and intelligence, though is rather unschooled.[4]

Kerns would soon learn that Willingham had graduated from high school in Alabama. Either way, Kerns never wavered in his view of Willingham as an exceptional artist, a point he made in subsequent memos.

FIGURE 34. Thaddeus Willingham on the day of his recordings, Gulfport, Mississippi, June 10, 1939. Photo by Abbott Ferriss. Courtesy of the Archives and Records Services Division, Mississippi Department of Archives and History.

More extensive knowledge about Thaddeus Willingham's background comes, naturally enough, from his family. Three of his daughters, two of whom I came to know, and another whose self-penned history the family shared with me, remembered him as both a thoughtful person and an avid reader, sitting out nightly on the porch with either a book or his banjo. In the words of his daughter Mary, "Some people called him 'Professor.' He was a walking bureau of information. Lots of people came to him for legal advice, and he wrote business letters for people who couldn't afford legal counsel."[5] He also taught adults, possibly at the business school in Jackson, where his older sister worked before his move to Gulfport.[6] While Willingham's ensuing poverty in the Depression years kept him from purchasing more than a handful of books and magazines, his daughter Carolyn remembered one that he did keep on the shelf: *Of Mice and Men*, John Steinbeck's 1937 novella of that era.

Music filled their home. He owned only one instrument, his banjo, which he kept on the wall, although he sometimes played mandolin, guitar, and fiddle. "He played banjo all the time. Night, daytime, anytime we wanted him to do it," Jeana recalled.[7] She also observed how he maintained his instrument, preparing a new banjo head to replace a broken one. "He made his own skins, calf skin. Take it, completely clean it; get it real thin, translucent. Then he would stretch it on a table. Nail it. And then cut it to fit."

Mary's younger sister, Carolyn, also remembered the music he played back then. "His fingers seemed like lightning. He'd play the tunes on the strings," adding that "he played the notes rather than just the chords." She detailed a typical scene: "Daddy had a chair. We'd hang our feet off the porch. And he'd play and we'd sing. We were all bashful, not wanting to sing alone." On some numbers he soloed, while for most others they all joined in. "Mother would sing along, and the sisters would harmonize."[8] These songs included popular pieces like "Red Sails in the Sunset" and the old standard, "Clementine." Jeana added, "We had fun singing on all of them [such as] 'Shake your little foot, Sally Ann.' It had a good melody you could understand. It sounded like it said." Then she quoted another: "'Old Dan Tucker was a mean old man.' He could almost make it talk."[9] In both instances, the rhythm of the song corresponded to the rhythm of the spoken phrase.

Throughout his 1939 recordings, Willingham holds to this model, performing on a low-toned banjo (set one step below standard pitch) that he couples with his lilting voice.[10] The loosened strings accentuate his loping rhythm. At the outset he explains to Halpert that the five-string banjo allows him to play melody and accompaniment, "either one." This differs from the then more modern tenor model with its strummed chords, which he calls "seconding." With the five-string, he says, "You can just get more music out of it."[11]

Apart from a waltz, in which he employed three fingers to produce an arpeggiated accompaniment, he played everything that day by up-picking. This dexterous approach allowed him to produce a stream of decorative elaborations, pauses, and beat anticipations around the melody. Based on a photograph that Jeana kept, it appears that he also knew the down-picking style. This circa 1940 image of him with his string band shows his right hand clamped in the tell-tale pose, his thumb extended forward like a handsaw or clawhammer, the latter name commonly used to denote this style.[12] However, for the 1939 recording session, he did not use clawhammer style. Halpert pressed him about the technique he employed. Willingham initially says, "You just pick it." Then he elaborates, "It depends entirely on how the tune runs. Sometimes you need two or three [fingers], sometimes one."[13] With that comment, the last disc ends, but by then Willingham had given a masterful exposition of solo banjo performance and also of the banjo song genre.

Robert Winslow Gordon, first head of the Library of Congress's Archive of American Folk-Song, characterized banjo songs as possessing a lyrical rather than a narrative coherence. He observed how they form composites, built of related imagery and tied together by the accompaniment. "The whole will have a basic unity that comes from the sustained mood or tone of the dialogue and is heightened in effect by frequent repetitions and something approaching a refrain. He [the banjoist] sings as he picks."[14] That is, the lyrics entwine with the playing, each element augmenting the other, gathering in intensity as the songs proceed.

Thaddeus Willingham's performance of "Roll on the Ground" encapsulates the genre Gordon described:

Roll on the ground, boys,
Roll on the ground.
Roll on the ground, boys,
Roll on the ground.

Work on the railroad,
Sleep on the ground.
Eat soda crackers,
And the wind blow 'em around.

Roll on the ground, boys,
Roll on the ground.
Roll on the ground, boys,
Roll on the ground.

Work on the railroad,
Work all the day.
Eat soda crackers,
And the wind blow 'em away.

Roll on the ground, boys,
Roll on the ground.
Roll on the ground, boys,
Roll on the ground.

Work on the railroad,
Sleep on the ground.
Eat soda crackers,
And the wind blow 'em around.

Roll on the ground, boys,
Roll on the ground.
Roll on the ground, boys,
Roll on the ground.

Work on the railroad,
Work all the day.
Eat soda crackers,
And the wind blow 'em away.

Roll on the ground, boys,
Roll on the ground.
Roll on the ground, boys,
Roll on the ground.[15]

Thaddeus Willingham applied this practice even beyond his vocal numbers. While he identifies several of his tunes as "breakdowns," meaning dance pieces on the banjo to accompany the fiddle, the 1939 recordings show him performing them as he would a song, as stand-alone solos. His approach to these pieces draws out the banjo's inherent qualities—its stridencies and subtleties—to form a self-enclosed work.

Thaddeus Willingham's choice of songs recalls another banjoist, one whom he outwardly admired, who also knew how to "just get more music out of it." About a year after he had made his recordings, Willingham moved his family once again. They resettled a block away in the last home they would share before his death. By 1941, that street as yet unpaved, they had received electrical service, and the Willinghams purchased a radio. All three of his daughters recall his listening to Saturday night broadcasts of the *Grand Ole Opry.* Foremost among its varied cast, Uncle Dave Macon numbered as his favorite. Macon, born in 1870, became the show's first star and that era's preeminent banjo songster. Willingham marveled over his performances: "No one could play *that* unless they're on a banjo!" he exclaimed.[16]

Little surprise that Willingham cherished Macon. Most of the pieces that Willingham recorded consisted of titles that Macon also performed. Yet Willingham owed no discernible debt to Macon as a source. Rather, these two gifted banjoists, only twelve years apart in age, shared a common fund of material known to their generation. They separately drew upon them to build their banjo song repertories. Likewise, both players benefited from the Black banjoists they had encountered as firsthand sources of material and style.

In his *New York Times* article, Robert Winslow Gordon concludes with an idea that stresses the cross-cultural inheritance in banjo songs and suggests that they likely formed a significant antecedent to the blues. Macon's repertory reveals an enormous body of material filled with blues-like qualities that circulated before the newer idiom fully emerged. Likewise, the banjo songs that Willingham performed, his formative contact with his young Black neighbors, his sinewy timing and the artful way he phrased this music—using elements and inflections that Macon also employed—fit with Gordon's insight: "Whatever their [banjo songs] origin," Gordon writes, "the folk are certainly making them over, and they are now 'folk-songs in the making.'"[17] The banjo, brought to America via slavery, became shared with whites, whether urban or rural, upland or lowland, and now engendered new creations. Willingham's syncopated up-picking on slackened strings provides an ongoing example of the remaking of African musical ideas in American musical tradition.

Thaddeus Willingham's banjo also spoke to the life that he and his family found at home. A number of the selections Willingham recorded bore slave-era lyrics that employed racial tropes. The most explicit of these, "Run Nigger Run," centers on a fleeing bondsman and the "pateroller," a slave catcher. In this song, common among both Black and white musicians, Willingham details its background to Halpert by referring to his grandfather's plantation. As he explained how slaves needed passes, and if lacking them, found themselves pursued and punished by these overseers, he facilely employed the racial epithet. In other songs, too, it arises, and again it flows unapologetically in his performances.

Yet race, as Willingham impressed upon his daughters, did not justify personal scorn or social prejudice. Neither Willingham nor his wife would permit the word "nigger" to be spoken aloud at home or to be used by their children in any way. They also encouraged them to play with the neighboring Black children. As his daughter Jeana remembered, on multiple occasions he would say, "If you have a Black friend, you have a real friend."[18] For him this axiom expressed esteem, and he meant it as a salute. She added that "he thought the world of his Black neighbors."

Still, Willingham was a man of his time and place. He and his wife, Larlie Warden Willingham (1898–1950), lived their entire lives in the Jim Crow era of the Deep South. While they observed racial norms of the day—telling their girls that they could play outside all they wanted but not to enter the homes of their Black playmates, nor to bring their Black friends into their own home—they transmitted to them a message to respect Black people in a separate and unequal society. Mary, Jeana, and Carolyn's adult recollections reflect this ethos of acceptance they received from their parents. Racism, they all agreed, made no sense.

Despite imposed segregation, both cultural and legal, Black and white interaction was a constant. Jeana remarked how much her father loved oysters, and when he had some money to spare, or when she could afford to give him something from her earnings, she and her siblings would wait for a certain peddler, a fishmonger, who visited their block with oysters aboard his truck. In musical rhyme, this African American merchant would call out, "Oyster man from Pass Chris tee-ann; fifty cents for a hundred." The fishmonger, who lived the next community over, kept the oysters in a galvanized washtub, cooled under the back roof of his old Ford pickup. Here along the gulf, Jeana explained, oysters were harvested "in any month with an 'R' in the name," meaning from September to April. During those months, the Oysterman from Pass Christian's street cry brought a palpable pleasure to this family long weighted with poverty and illness.

• • •

Clarence Kerns noted at the time of the recordings that Willingham and his family lived perilously. "He is a squatter, living in a house on the edge of town constructed principally of tin."[19] Indeed, Willingham had built this makeshift home, two rooms under one roof. "One room where everyone slept"—six children (with two more yet to be born) plus Willingham and his wife, and the other, their kitchen, heated with its wood stove. The toilet was located outside, as was the water pump.

Yet Jeana added, "There were lots of trees on the lot, and we were happy playing Cowboys and Indians, swinging on a tire swing, climbing trees, playing jump rope and marbles, hop scotch, jacks, mumblety-peg, and hide and seek." Another time she summed up this home, "It wasn't much but we didn't know it."[20] Her older sister Mary remembered it too: "All of us had a lot of fun playing in the woods, climbing trees, picking blueberries, smoking rabbit tobacco, and building playhouses."[21] Jeana continued, "We always had music at our house. Daddy would play the banjo, and sing. We kids would sometimes sing and sometimes dance . . . Mother sang too, especially when she rocked a baby."[22]

Even as their financial circumstances worsened, with a move from their previous home out in the country on Landon Road, located a few miles north of town, to west Gulfport, the family stayed united. They lived there at the outset of the Depression. Jeana recalled:

> There were no street lights, of course, since there were no electric wires there then. When night came, if the moon wasn't up, it was totally dark. Stars were vivid and bright moonlight made the nights beautiful. Lots of times we could burn leaves and pine straw. Daddy would play the banjo;

> we'd sing or talk, then catch fire flies (or lightning bugs, as we called them). The night noises were varied—a chorus of crickets, frogs, cicadas. Rain, thunder, and lightning seemed so loud and close. I still like the smell of burning leaves and straw.

From time to time, she added, "a hobo would come by. Daddy would always give him a meal and let him sleep in the barn. Times were very hard and there were millions of people out of work."[23]

Willingham's fortunes had declined with the years. When he first came to Mississippi as a young man, his family's estate in Alabama had, for reasons lost to time, largely dissipated. While mentioning his status as the sole male heir, surviving accounts agree that he had relocated to begin anew. Once he reached Gulfport, he found initial success in local truck farming—this area once held the title of radish capital of the world—as well as obtaining work with local logging operations. But his health diminished in his mid-thirties with the first of several heart attacks. After that, Jeana said, "He was never completely well."[24] He lost his teeth, and standing at six feet two inches in height, he weighed but 170 pounds. Jobless by 1930, he sold newspapers and pencils on Gulfport's street corners. By the time of the recordings nine years later, unable to handle any heavier physical tasks, he periodically worked for twelve dollars a month for the WPA as a waterboy for construction workers.

Willingham also served as the principal parental figure in the home. Shortly before the 1939 recordings, his wife, Larlie, underwent hospitalization for mental illness. Following the birth of their sixth child two years earlier, her health precipitously declined. In his profile about Willingham that appears in the field notes, Kerns also took note of Larlie's condition, but without specifying it. All three daughters, too, attested to their mother's infirmity. "Her mental condition was not sound. The Lord gives you as much as you can put up with. No house, no money."[25] Larlie took occasional employment at a sewing factory, and for a time at another company, washing out oil lamp globes, a task that fit her small hands. But apart from nursing her babies, which became increasingly difficult in her illness and affected them to the point of malnourishment, she became increasingly distant from the family. Willingham found it necessary to stay home to care for their youngsters. Schools did not provide lunches, and by day

Willingham prepared biscuits and gravy as their daytime meal. "Life was hard, no money," Jeana said. "If you had beans and rice for supper you were lucky."[26] The older siblings, once out on their own, contributed earnings for the family's upkeep too. "We had enough to stay alive," she continued. "Just not as much as we needed."[27] That said, she noted that many others underwent the same leanness in the impoverishment of those years.

Yet for all these hardships, the Willinghams remained close-knit. Repeatedly, the sisters cited the unifying role their father's banjo played in the home. His playing, Jeana said, "brought us together, made us want to be there."[28] Observer Clarence Kerns, too, recognized the well-being they found in his music: "Harassed by ill health and the collapse of the trucking industry, logging and other available sources of income, they have become very poor." Then he ends his profile of Thaddeus Willingham with the sounds he made. "But the old plantation melodies still live in this man's memory and skilled fingers and the magic of his banjo playing and singing has helped to keep him and his family more cheerful in the face of disheartening circumstances."[29]

A few days before Halpert and Ferriss reached Gulfport, they documented an eighty-six-year-old African American singer named Sam Hazel who lived in Greenville. Born in Kentucky, Hazel had worked as a roustabout on the Ohio River during the steamboat era, toting cargo by shoulder and heel, as he said, onto vessels and wharves. Song accompanied this labor, and Hazel recalled for the documentarians some of the chants he and his coworkers heard back then. Along with recording several riverboat depth-sounding calls, Hazel sang a British broadside ballad called "The Golden Willow Tree." Hazel performed it, Halpert felt, "in a true mountain style."[30] The song, accorded an entry in Francis James Child's landmark study, is number 286 of *The English and Scottish Popular Ballads* and bears a centuries-old pedigree. Its earliest imprint references seafarer Sir Walter Raleigh. Sam Hazel remembered not only from whom he learned the song, but where: "on a boat running from Louisville, Ky. to Evansville, Ind."[31]

As they drove along, Ferriss scribbled down Halpert's thoughts on Mis-

FIGURE 35. Sam Hazel, Greenville, Mississippi, June 2, 1939. Photo by Abbott Ferriss. Courtesy of the Archives and Records Services Division, Mississippi Department of Archives and History.

sissippi folk music. The folklorist's comments about Sam Hazel amplified something he had written the year before: "Since folksong, when truly living, is in a constant process of change and re-creation, not the origin of the song but what has happened to it and what it means now . . . is significant to us. Scholars do not reject old English songs when sung by Negroes or descendants of non-English stocks; they find them an interesting proof that culture is based on environment rather than on racial descent."[32]

Decades later, in 1978, Halpert reiterated this idea while listening to another recording he had made in Mississippi during the folksong trip, this time with a group of five-year-old Black children performing a singing game. He contrasted their performance with similar songs he had collected from their white counterparts. The two yielded altogether different results. In the first, the Black children received encouragement from their older companions, while the white children played more or less on their own. Different traditions shaped these performances, but what ensued in either case reflected nothing predisposed in the children themselves. "All this business about inherited Negro talent for singing and so on." He paused, as if to say "no," and then explained, "It's culturally inspired."[33]

Just as Sam Hazel's performance of a British sea ballad demonstrated this understanding of cultural inspiration rather than blood inheritance, so, too, do the songs that Thaddeus Willingham performed.

"Roll on the Ground," the piece with which Willingham began his 1939 recording session, exemplifies the tensile nature of folksong. Though Willingham's lyrics pertain to railroad labor, "Work on the railroad/Sleep on the ground/Eat sody crackers/And the wind blow 'em around," the words recall similar phrases used in the earlier work of the roustabouts—comparable labor that Sam Hazel had experienced aboard steamboats. Related texts found among ocean-going sailors suggest a transfer of verses from the river trades to hoisted sail.[34] Those verses, in turn, draw on an inventory of comic images and similes taken from stage minstrelsy that once again reaches back to the banjo. In yet another transfer, Charley Goff, a white Mississippi fiddler from Lucedale, seventy-five miles northeast of Gulfport, offered an instrumental rendition of the song in 1936 for a local collector/transcriber. He called it "Big Bill's in Jail, Boys."[35]

These associations surface in the earliest recordings of "Roll on the Ground," made by blackface-era comedian Billy Golden (1858–1926). The song is listed in a circa 1903 Victor record catalog with other "original Negro songs and shouts" he had made.[36] Golden recorded the song at least sixteen times between 1896 and 1909. His accompaniment ranged from solo piano to horns. Throughout these performances, he enacts minstrel laughter, an exaggerated vocal technique that he couples with a stage patter story about a craps game that centers on dice rolling and depicts gambling in an overtly racialized manner.[37]

Within twenty years, beginning in 1927, the song made its way onto recordings by rural artists, the first of these by Al Hopkins & His Buckle Busters. Hopkins's version recalled melodic and verse elements present in Golden's rendition. Soon other hillbilly artists issued recordings, each bearing their individuality. The Skillet Lickers' rendition, sung by Riley Puckett, kept a measured pace, while Warren Caplinger's 1928 version included a simultaneous commentary. That same year Taylor-Griggs Louisiana Melody Makers used a bowed bass to frame the piece. The Georgia Yellow Hammers, meanwhile, invoked a melody associated with "Do Lord, Remember Me." In 1929 Fate Norris, a member of the Skillet Lickers, strung together minstrel verses for a craps game with a chorus of "Roll 'em boys, roll 'em." By the 1930s, the Prairie Ramblers and the Delmore Brothers introduced melodic materials redolent of the "Do Lord" melody and "Nobody's Business." Stringbean's 1971 recording includes his signature tag to end each phrase, coupled with canned applause, while the Stoneman Family, seeking to attract the commercial folk music market in 1964, spliced "Oleanna" into the song. Bluegrass musician Bill Clifton recorded it as early as 1952. Before the decade ended, a Galax, Virginia-based group, the Mountain Ramblers, led here by singer Thurman Pugh, followed with "Big Ball in Boston." Both Bill Clifton and the Ramblers treated it as a high-velocity banjo showpiece. Bill Monroe recorded it in 1962, and Flatt and Scruggs played it at Carnegie Hall.

The song's title migrated too, from "Roll on the Ground" to "Big Ball in Town," as well as versions that include "Big Ball in Memphis," "Big Ball in Brooklyn," "Big Ball in Nashville," "Big Ball in Monterey," and "Big Ball in Texas." An August 1876 newspaper sketch by Lafcadio Hearn about Black levee life in Cincinnati cites "Big Ball Up Town," accompanied by banjo and bass violin to the "wild thunder of the dancers' feet."[38] Its earliest known musical notation, identified as "Big Ball Down Town" appears in Fisk University folklorist Thomas Talley's collection. Derived from Black folk sources, this version combines a minstrel-era verse with a quartet-friendly refrain.[39] Recordings made in the Mississippi Delta in 1937 and 1941 reveal some of the song's most telltale lyrics, albeit set to a different melody, and applied to levee camps and their construction.[40] "Rolling on the ground" becomes the motion of a wheelbarrow. For hillbilly recording artist,

FIGURE 36. Tex Logan, dressed as a member of the Confederate Mountaineers band. Boston, Massachusetts, 1953. Courtesy of Tex Logan.

Wade Mainer (1907–2011), a native of western North Carolina, that picture corresponded with his own sense of the song. He thought it stemmed from railroad work or prison labor. In our discussion, he spoke at length about this piece he had known throughout his life, one that both he and his brother, J. E. Mainer, recorded. Wade saw it as something that prisoners might sing after work, a lyric song that reflected their living conditions—sleeping on the ground—but also their wish to carouse, to attend some big ball in town. He commented, "Now that's back in hard times, when I was a kid."[41]

Meanwhile, the song continued to renew itself. West Texas fiddler Benjamin "Tex" Logan had learned the song from J. E. Mainer's 1947 recording and then played it himself for his lifelong friend, the bandleader Hoyle Nix. "He'd get me to play it in every show," Tex remembered. "I used to do it as a showtune." Tex noted that "He liked it a lot. . . . He took my version."[42]

Hoyle then crafted his version from Tex's. Tex had earlier changed Mainer's lyrics to re-create the song as "Big Ball in Boston." This change, in turn, influenced other bluegrass musicians to do the same. In 1949, Hoyle Nix took Tex Logan's song and renamed it "A Big Ball's in Cowtown." Its success inspired Nix to re-record it ten years later as "Big Balls in Cowtown." Under that title, it has become a classic of Western swing. As Tex Logan said, "It got real popular." Subsequent recordings by artists from Merle Haggard to George Strait prove his point.

One last example of this regeneration, albeit bearing a personal dimension. Not long after Willingham recorded "Roll on the Ground," the song made its way into the folk music revival. It appeared on the second full album issued by the Library of Congress in 1942, which concentrated on notable performances of dance tunes and lyric songs. In 1948, *People's Songs* published Willingham's tune and lyrics. While not citing him personally on a page with other dance breakdown tunes, the editor called it "a humdinger."[43] By then banjoist Tom Paley had learned it as had Fleming Brown, both of them drawing from Willingham's published recording. Years later, this became the first song Fleming taught me, one that he brought to his intermediate banjo class at Chicago's Old Town School of Folk Music. To this day I continue to perform it.

In thinking about Thaddeus Willingham, I remember dearly my visits with Jeana Willingham Dodge. Visibly moved at the cemetery where her father and mother lie, her spirits brightened when we went to the city park where Willingham and his bandmates performed during the Second World War. Under the same roof, still over the bandstand, we talked about songs like "Roll on the Ground" that he played at those weekly government square dances for the servicemen soon shipping out. Jeana's older sister,

FIGURE 37. Jeana Willingham Dodge at her parents' graves, Gulfport, Mississippi, Feb. 1997. Photo by Stephen Wade.

Mary Willingham, recalled those evenings too, attending them with Jeana and their older brother, Willis, where they danced the Virginia reel and other hoedowns to their father's music. "We had loads and loads of fun," she wrote, "from meeting so many good-looking soldiers, sailors, and Army Air Force guys. We made fun of the way the Yankees talked and they made fun of our Southern drawl."[44]

That friendly banter resounds like this song. Over its 125 years of sound recordings, "Roll on the Ground" has shifted between rural and urban milieus, moved across race and genre, varied its instrumentation and style, and reset its name according to its locale. One year before Halpert began his long drive south in the sound wagon, Benjamin Botkin, who directed the various federal folklore collecting endeavors that would sponsor this trip, spoke of creative products like this song and its proliferation: "The restriction of immigration, the depression, and the breakdown of the older isolation and individualism had something to do with the new feeling for cultural diversity and roots which succeeded the abortive 'melting pot' myth."[45] That new feeling for diversity helped fuel the 1939 folksong expedition. Halpert and Ferriss soon found those varied realities fully alive in Mississippi and crystallized in the multiple traditions they discussed on their way into Gulfport.

Years later, Ferriss said that this trip that reached from the "cool hills of Tishomingo County to the sands of Harrison" had been "a revelation" about his home state. It allowed him "to see the variety of cultural streams that one encountered going from one house to another." What he found in those homes was that music offered "a tonic for the soul."[46] Certainly, the memories of Thaddeus Willingham's children prove that true.

Herbert Halpert expressed similar thoughts. Speaking first of the performers, he noted that they were terrific and charmingly described his role as recordist: "I was just the man winding up the old hand organ."[47] He remembered the trip as both "exhilarating and exhausting." Halpert concluded that "it was a wonderful trip for a 'damYankee' to make."[48] He, along with Ferriss, had witnessed over four weeks how one state's homemade music traditions were flourishing. The two had uncovered a cultural reservoir worthy of preservation, a depth that Thaddeus Willingham epitomized. They found in him an unassuming man, gifted with a graceful musicality. He possessed an ingrained sense of the banjo's rhythmic potential. In turn, the supple ricochet of his strings would propel "Roll on the Ground" across the years and along the byways of American music.

Like "Roll on the Ground" and the routes it has taken, the sound wagon that Halpert and Ferriss piloted plots a course still worth following, one that encompasses and cherishes the different and the strange along with the familiar and the shared. In our own fractured time, our country struggles with disparity and difference, with a contested history and a threatened social compact. That well-traveled vehicle carries the voices from a past unedited by the future, here for us, now.

FIGURE 38. Thaddeus Willingham at home on 43rd Avenue, Gulfport, Mississippi, ca. 1940. Courtesy of Jeana Willingham Dodge.

·7·

Any Way You Can

Between the United States Capitol and the Washington Monument lies the mile-long greensward of the National Mall. There, on July 4, 2003, under the white, windless sky of a D.C. summer's afternoon, the Smithsonian Folklife Festival neared the end of its annual ten-day program. That year, the festival highlighted Scotland, Mali, and Southern Appalachia. Traditional performers hailing from these storied places concertized, danced, and crafted, explaining their arts and interpreting their heritage for an estimated one million spectators.

Beginning at 3 p.m. on this holiday afternoon, just a few hours before the nighttime fireworks, a mountain banjo workshop was taking place on a small stage whose painted backdrop memorialized the landmark country music recordings that occurred in 1927 in Bristol, Tennessee. In keeping with the celebrated innovators and traditionalists who performed at those long-ago sessions, attention here focused on personal style. Lee Sexton, who appeared as the begrimed East Kentucky banjoist in *Coal Miner's Daughter,* portraying on film what he had done for thirty-four years as a working coal miner, described his own playing: "I just sit down and put me a pattern together. I don't try to copy nobody. If I heard a tune that I

FIGURE 39. Will Keys, likely Norris, Tennessee, late 1980s. Courtesy of Bill Keys.

like, I'll change it some way. I don't like to play this exactly like somebody else now."[1]

Then Will Keys (1923–2005) took his turn. A former factory shift worker who lived his entire life in rural eastern Tennessee, he had grown up in the shadow of the Bristol recordings. Will had played with extended members of the Carter family, who, along with Jimmie Rodgers, emerged as the star performers from those famed sessions. But now, as the workshop neared its close, Will didn't select any melodies from that mythic past. Nor did he draw from the nineteenth-century repertory that his older sisters had shown him years before on the parlor piano at home. Instead, in his rippling banjo style, one that defies imitation, he played the theme from *Hello, Dolly!* He had created a down-home rendition of a Broadway show tune.

In that moment of delighted recognition running through all of us who witnessed it, he implicitly pointed to an idea at the heart of American folklife. He had a name for it too, one he previously confided as an acronym and then spelled out in block letters, a phrase that the old timers around him had used to describe their musical individualism: "A.W.Y.C. style. That amounts to ANY WAY YOU CAN."[2] Another letter, written ten years after the first, extended his thought. "Old time music," he wrote, "is whatever you figured out on your own, or Any One Old Way You Can See Fit to Do It (AOOWYCSFTDI)."[3] In that spirit, Will Keys's independence epitomized Independence Day in America.

• • •

Will Allison Keys grew up in the Blackley Creek settlement of northeastern Tennessee's Washington County. This farmland of rolling hillsides and private homes lies near the Tri-Cities region of Johnson City, Kingsport, and Bristol. In Will's youth, most of his neighbors lived a mile or two from one another, those distances lessened only by taking a shortcut across a field. Locals cultivated tobacco in addition to raising corn. Will's family principally grew vegetables on their acreage. To the end of his life, he continued this practice, as did his mother. "I make garden," Will said, as he cut open and then tasted a homegrown melon, "because I like to see things grow."[4]

Blackley Creek flowed across the Keys's property. Further downstream, a small waterfall offered a shower the family used for bathing in summertime. Nearby roads remained largely unpaved, requiring the postman coming some ten or twelve miles from Limestone, Tennessee, to make deliveries either with his Model-T pickup in dry weather, or else, as Will recalled, his "big red horse" when the lanes turned muddy from the rains.[5] On visits back to the homeplace—the house itself, a two-story, eight-room structure that no longer stands—Will's son, Bill, remembered his father's acuity in spotting both arrowheads and four-leaf clovers, which he found, seemingly, wherever he went.[6]

Will's father, William Aaron Keys (1870–1930), who operated a country store, supplemented his merchant's income with stints of teaching school. He also served as county magistrate, conducting outdoor court sessions on his store's front porch. By then the Keys family had lived in this community since 1800, and the churchyard of the Pleasant Grove Methodist Church, standing two miles from Will's childhood home, harbors many of his ancestors. Joe Keys Road and Jimmy Keys Road nearby commemorate still more members of Will's family.

In the opposite direction, also a two-mile walk from Will's home, stands the former Glendale School that Will attended for the first six years of his formal education. Dilapidated now and used as a barn for storing hay, in those years, the newly built schoolhouse counted among its faculty Will's older sister, Nelle, who became his first teacher there. He recalled how classroom misbehavior resulted in a disciplinary paddling, bemusedly noting that when Nelle found Will and his brother, Howard, getting into mischief, she had to give them extra licks to avert any hint of favoritism. Or, as he said, of "petting us."[7] Then Nelle would go home and weep.

At that age, Will confessed he thought the whole world his kin. "Almost everybody in the neighborhood were cousins, at least."[8] He was the second youngest of twelve—six boys and six girls—and part of an even larger family. His father had previously married, and with his first wife, Laura Baskett, had five children. When Laura took ill, Will's father hired Amy Elizabeth Taylor (1886–1971), a trained nurse from the community, to help care for her. In 1905, following Laura's death, Amy became his second wife. Barely five feet tall, this self-determined woman, widowed by age forty-four, oversaw a family of seventeen. Her siblings, numerous themselves, enlarged the filial circle. Bill Keys remembers his father identifying "Grandmom Keys's brothers" as they drove around the community: "This was Uncle Bill's farm, or this was Uncle Bob's farm."[9]

Music repeatedly echoed in the lives of Amy Taylor Keys's ancestors. Brigadier General Nathaniel Greene Taylor (1771–1816) fought alongside Andrew Jackson at the Battle of New Orleans, remembered in the "Eighth of January" fiddle tune. In turn, his grandson, also named Nathaniel Green Taylor (1819–1887), lived in Elizabethton, Tennessee, by Sycamore Shoals, a rocky length of rapids in the Watauga River. This spot marked a staging area for the Overmountain Men, a battery of backwoods militias that participated in the 1780 Battle of Kings Mountain, a turning point in the Revolutionary War. That drama became commemorated in "Sycamore Shoals," an instrumental that Will and his neighbors played. Will learned this frequently requested piece from Bob Clark, "who ran cattle in our neighborhood," and was a half-brother to Will's future sister-in-law.[10]

Elizabethton's Nathaniel Green Taylor, himself a member of the United States Congress, and subsequently Commissioner of Indian Affairs, counted among his children two sons—Amy's great-uncles—who each became governors of Tennessee: Alfred Alexander Taylor (1848–1931), a Republican, and Robert Love Taylor (1850–1912), a Democrat. (The latter served multiple terms as governor and also as a U.S. senator.) Music, too, prominently figured in their renown. They both fiddled, most notably during their 1886 gubernatorial campaign when they ran against one another. Popular journalism depicted this amiable sibling rivalry in illustrations that showed them side by side, holding forth on their violins while competing for votes in what the press gleefully dubbed the "War of the Roses." Robert Taylor, alert to the appeal traditional music held within the body politic, created an artful series of written anecdotes that he punctuated with song in his widely shared 1896 lecture called "The Fiddle and the Bow." He extended its themes in a 1899 public letter titled "To the Fiddlers." Defending his fiddling, he says, "Politicians sneered at me as a fiddler; but the girls said it was no harm, and the boys voted while I fiddled, and the fiddle won."[11] It follows, too, in keeping with family tradition, that in 1924, his older brother, appearing as "Ex-Governor Alf. Taylor's Old Limber Quartet," led a singing group in a recording studio. The Victor company ledger shows him, along with his sons, singing spirituals as well as performing two unissued fiddle tunes.[12]

Closer to home, Amy's father, Allison Wagner Taylor (1855–1940), carried a walking stick that had a removable flute. "Grandfather Taylor," Will remembered, "would walk around his farm, and when he got tired, he would sit on a rock or log and play that flute."[13] Amy herself did not play, but often sang hymns to her children, several of which surface in Will's recordings. "I don't know if she actively encouraged her kids to play music," her grandson Bill reflected, "or if it was just the thing to do for poor kids who had no other entertainment."[14]

A year after Amy's husband, William Aaron Keys, died, Will, now eight years old and fatherless, began playing the banjo under a directive given to him by his older brother, Jay Keys (1916–1975). "He appointed him," said Jay's son, Jerry, to take up the instrument.[15] "Most people get a chord or two from somebody else, like I did," Will explained.[16] In his case, Jay showed him the chords to "Little Brown Jug" on an old banjo found at the house. The instrument, Will recalled, possibly left there by one of Amy's brothers, sported numerous metal brackets around its drum head, a widely admired feature of manufactured banjos from the late nineteenth century. Jay restrung it with some screen door wire to make it playable. "From there I was on my own," Will said. "Just work out your own thing." He would apply that lesson for the rest of his life.

• • •

Though Will lost his father at seven, his family, which Amy led, remained close-knit. The senior Keys's death occurred early in the Depression, but both Will's siblings and their older half-siblings helped one another during that time, and, for the most part, remained emotionally connected in the years that followed. "We were poor, but we didn't really know it," Will recalled. "Everyone was in the same boat."[17]

Nearly all of Will's brothers and sisters achieved domestic stability over the course of their lives. The boys worked, Bill Keys notes, as "general labor types."[18] One ran a large farm, while another maintained shop tools used at the nearby Holston Ordnance Works. Will's brother Jay gained local repute as a carpenter, while the brood's youngest, Howard, took a job in Oak Ridge at the Y-12 Plant, which built the atomic bomb. Will's school-teaching sister, Nelle (1910–1999), became the first in the family to receive a college degree, and during World War II, earned the rank of Navy lieutenant. She served under James Forrestal during his tenure as Secretary of the Navy. Her writing skills, which included authoring public statements for him at the Pentagon, led to her assuming an editorial role on the *Ladies Home Journal*, and eventually she became the senior editor of *Jack & Jill* magazine.

Music, too, continued to exert its hold among them. Will's brother Charlie played both harmonica and guitar, while Howard concentrated on singing, including an early stint with the Oak Ridge Boys. He performed gospel material with the nascent group, then known as the Oak Ridge Quartet, while also accompanying himself on guitar. The musical relationship between Will and Jay remained especially close throughout their lives, and Jay distinguished himself as an amateur guitarist, who in later years overcame the challenges of Merle Travis's virtuosic thumb-picking and used it on his electric guitar, in addition to acoustically performing the fiddle tunes and mountain songs popular among string players in East Tennessee.

Will's oldest sister, Ruth Keys Kennerly (1905–1999), pursued music with an avidity that matched her brothers, playing piano both by note and by ear. Lorenz Publishing Company, a long-standing Southern gospel music publisher established in 1890, disseminated her compositions. Her best-known work, the 1952 "Blow Ye Winds Softly," became a favorite of school choirs. Set to a plaintive, waltz-time melody she composed, her verses celebrate the Christ child in his manger and the promise he brings to the world. She did not, however, limit herself to sacred music, and Ruth's nephew, Bill, a musician himself, recalled, "she could play like nobody's business."[19] She not only knew the keyboard, she could swing too with "Chattanooga Choo-Choo."

Ruth's and Will's older half-sister, Mame Ellis, also played piano. She focused on both ragtime and stride styles, and over the years Will warmly spoke of their jam sessions. Her upbeat music, redolent, as Bill Keys recalled, of Fats Waller, furnished technique and repertory that Will absorbed. In addition, he drew from yet another pianist and organist in the Keys family: his sister Lucy's piano-playing repertory. He chose pieces that included rags, marches, big band numbers, and gospel hymns.

His siblings also inspired his note-rich arrangements that spanned the banjo's neck. This pianistic method he devised pivots from his right thumb and forefinger plucking the strings. He overcame pauses that other players typically covered with a brush stroke by continually playing single, separated notes. He described this brushing motion as a "kick back."[20] In place of that recoiling movement, his thumb might play the first string, while sounding the fifth string with his index. Will crossed his fingers, forming an X-shape, a technical maneuver unique to him.

Will couldn't explain the method. "Steve, it's a mystery to me. . . . I have a way of coming down with the thumb and then coming up with the finger," he offered. "It works for me."[21] No matter which picking finger he used to sound the strings, he executed a stream of melody-centered notes. At times this also required his fretting the fifth string along the fretboard, another move rarely ventured in old-time banjo. Once, when I asked him whether his unorthodox techniques possibly owed any debt to his sisters' playing, he concurred. Likewise, when he played on their keyboards, he applied a similar patterning with his fingers, moving across the keys with a spidery right-hand roll. As Bill Keys said when he watched his father sit at Aunt Ruth's piano: "He played it like a banjo."[22] From a boyhood beginning on a leftover instrument restrung with screen door wire, Will Keys found his way.

• • •

In 1942, at age eighteen, following his graduation from Sulphur Springs High School, a community near Blackley Creek, Will enlisted in the United States Marine Corps. Despite his slim frame and five-foot-six-inch height—his reserves of wiry strength and physical balance had allowed him to become a running back for his six-member high school football team—he served as an infantryman in the Pacific theater. Like so many who have waged hand-to-hand combat, Will rarely discussed his wartime experiences. But he did share three stories that illuminate his determination as they do the workings of chance.

Soon after boot camp, Will numbered among the first Marines to land at Guadalcanal. From the lowered bow ramp of a Higgins boat, he moved with his platoon towards shore, holding his weapon above him and weighted down by a backpack bearing radio supplies in addition to personal gear. He found himself caught in the coral beneath his boot. Though previously warned about these formations and the danger they presented, he knew that his slight stature added to his peril. In describing this scene at the beachhead, in what he considered possibly his life's single most frightening moment—his lucid brown eyes looking steadfastly into mine—he called himself "a runt."[23] Beyond whatever gunfire he faced, he feared even more drowning in those waters that arose chin-deep on him. He ultimately extracted his foot, but when he recounted the same experience to fellow banjoist Jim Lloyd, he told him, "I *knew* I was going to step into one of them holes, and it'd be 'goodbye, Will.'"[24]

As the battle for Guadalcanal continued, Will received word from a forward unit to report to the radio tent. On reaching it, he learned that his predecessor, who operated this equipment, had, shortly before, lost his life. In the sole military story he shared with his son, Bill recounts: "Dad was in the tent and he dropped something and bent down to pick it up. And a shot went over his head and through the side of the tent. There was a Japanese sniper. Dad said, 'I guess I was at death's door, but didn't even realize it.' He just bent over to pick something up."[25] The missed shot revealed the shooter's location, and the other Marines then killed him.

The jeopardy Will faced in Guadalcanal found a more peaceful counterpart in his remaining war story. As the theater moved closer to Japan—he was initially scheduled for deployment at Iwo Jima, but that island had been taken by fellow Marines—his unit skipped ahead to Okinawa. Along the way, he acquired a guitar from a Dutch Marine but could not find a banjo among his fellow troops. While in Okinawa, however, he came across a *shamisen*, a three-stringed traditional Japanese instrument with a small, square, hide-covered drumhead, tonally and physically akin to its five-string American cousin. "I tuned that as a banjo and we played up a storm with it."[26] Not long after, Will and his captain entered a village where they came upon a pump organ. "We loaded it up and brought it back to the CP [command post], and he and I gave a concert that night. Snakeskin banjo and an old organ."

Discharged in late 1945 as a corporal, Will returned to the family farm at Blackley Creek. By then he was engaged to Lola Vale Hobbs (1922–2010), whom he met during basic training at Camp Lejeune in North Carolina. The two wed the following year, and they lived at the Keys's home place. In 1948, Will's sister, Nelle, purchased some land for their mother in nearby Gray, Tennessee. Will and Lola, along with Amy, moved into the small two-bedroom house that stood on the property. Then in 1951, following their daughter's first birthday, Will and Lola built their own house in sight of Amy's home. They allowed no structure that could obstruct their view across the two-tenths of a mile that separated them. To the end of Amy's life, her home filling with the canvases she began painting in her sixties, Will's family visited her daily.

Throughout those years, Will worked at Tennessee Eastman, a chemical operation locally established in 1920 and occupying more than three hundred acres in Kingsport. As a division of the Eastman Kodak Corporation, the plant produced materials used in photographic film manufacture and acetate textiles. Before his Marine Corps enlistment, Will had briefly worked there, and on discharge, he found a job still awaited him. The company credited Will's wartime service towards his pension, and his tenure with them eventually numbered forty-two years. Tennessee Eastman was Will's sole employer throughout his working life. He retired in 1984.

Will's assignments at Eastman spanned his initial job as an electrician's helper to his working at the company's synthetic yarn plant, and ultimately, in the Tenite plastics division, where he spent thirty-five years as a machine operator. Assigned to the swing shift, he followed a schedule that repeated in three-week cycles: the first week he worked from 7 a.m. to 3 p.m.; the next rotation required him on site from 3 to 11 p.m.; and in the final third, his duties ran from 11 p.m. to 7 a.m. Given these uneven hours, Will repeatedly found himself going home and falling asleep in his chair, banjo in hand.

Two years after his retirement, he still felt this schedule's impact. In 1986 he wrote me, "Sorry I fell asleep in my chair at your apartment, but after forty-one years of shift work I find that I'm cursed with that habit (the beer probably helped too)."[27]

• • •

In 1970, while on annual leave from Eastman, Will and Lola visited their daughter in southern California. At a Long Beach music store, he came across a mid-1920s, Paramount style-A plectrum banjo. Attracted by its decorations and design, Will purchased it. To keep the instrument undamaged during shipment in those pre–bubble wrap days, the shop swaddled it in Pampers. Once the instrument reached Will in Tennessee, he bored a hole on one side of its neck and added a tuning peg, converting this ornately inlaid, blonde-colored, jazz-age resonator banjo into a rural five-string. Will's old friend Carl McConnell, himself a close relation of the singing Carter family and a longtime hillbilly radio performer, had earlier done the same with a Paramount plectrum banjo.

The original instrument, designed for chord-melody jazz, allowed for easy fingering high up the neck. This freed Will to play in upper positions with accurate intonation, otherwise lacking in many manufactured five-string banjos that he had previously encountered, let alone the homemade fretless models some of his older neighbors had played. For many of them, he observed, saddled with those instruments, any venturing above the fifth fret, and "you couldn't play the dang thing."[28]

He found, however, that customary five-string banjo bridges, as his son explained, "didn't sit correctly for him due to the unusual spacing between the strings."[29] Plectrum banjos, requiring only four strings, have a narrower neck than five-string models, and Will needed to make an accommodation for his reconstituted Paramount to work.

At that time, Will operated a large, high-temperature extruder. This machine took plastic sheets and chopped them into small pellets of varying colors. These heated pellets were then molded into products. As Bill Keys elaborated:

> Once the plastic was melted and cut into pellets, the pellets were dumped into a bin. However, some of the melted plastic remained, so the operators (Dad and others) would have to scrape it out of the machine before the next batch was run. Some of the plastic would harden in the machines, so the company supplied the operators with the putty knives and some hammers to scrape the plastic out. Dad said that it worked well, but the putty knives would blow off the handles when you smacked them with a hammer. The company told Dad to take all the handles he wanted, because they just tossed them into the incinerator.[30]

Those Red Devil brand putty knife handles, Will recognized, invited possible reuse. Made of pressed rosewood and internally reinforced with epoxy, they offered both the shape and density needed for an effective banjo bridge. With his Case pocketknife he shaved these wooden handles razor thin, finding them hardy enough to maintain form under full string pressure. This item, essential in the transmission of banjo sound, helped Will find the tone he wanted from his converted Paramount.

In repurposing this otherwise expendable resource for his music, Will Keys attested to a reality of his upbringing when he stated, "we made do with what we had."[31] He applied the dictum broadly: from restoring a short-length 1959 Chevrolet school bus that he turned into a fully equipped vacation camper (a vehicle that he painted in bright green house paint, and which unmistakably marked his campsite for so many at Southern fiddlers' conventions) to the circa-1800 Virginia log cabin he reconstructed piece by numbered piece on his property in Tennessee. (He also fashioned a large hoist that he attached to his bus's front bumper to move those logs into place.) He carved a pair of intricately detailed miniature work boots from discarded plastic molding while at work, and he reassigned the 18-inch-wide opening in his cement mixer to become a bulls-eye for his young son's football practice.

Will focused this homegrown inventiveness toward non-utilitarian ends too. He would sit down to read an unabridged dictionary page by page, an effort inspired by his mother, who wanted to compete better at Scrabble. He overheard his teenager listening to "Snowblind Friend," a Hoyt Axton song recorded by the rock band Steppenwolf, and then the next morning, standing at the doorway of his son's room, played it back note for note on the banjo to the surprised but delighted youngster. For his sister, Nelle, Will carved a richly burnished wooden chess set, creating a cast of figures and geometric shapes utterly unique for a game that he himself had never played. For his friend, musician Tom Mindte, who inadvertently crumpled one of Will's kitchen chairs at his festival campsite in his rush to join a tune already in progress, Will found a creative way to ameliorate an embarrassing moment.

"I made a dash," Tom recalled, "for the empty chair and quickly brought the jam session to a halt as both the chair and I became victims of Newton's second law—'Force equals mass times acceleration.'"[32] The following year, Will arrived as usual at his Galax campsite via his bus, but now bearing a chair weighing two-hundred pounds that he had carved by means of a chain saw from a tree trunk for "Big Tom," his nickname for him. He cut the stump three feet high and two feet in diameter so that it included a back, and he upholstered the seat in Naugahyde. "Now there's a chair, you can't break," Will told him. Well-designed for Tom's girth, it resides today on his porch, an affectionate reminder of past friendship.

Will's capacity to re-envision available resources never lessened. Since his youth he had witnessed members of his community practice an ethic of self-reliance when faced with scarcity. He recalled, for instance, how his older brother fashioned a guitar capo from a wood dowel, using a piece of inner tubing to form the rubber band that held it to the neck. As he explained, "The thing about it, Steve, people back then figured out what would work best for them."[33]

In his music Will applied that principle by taking a traditional, two-finger banjo technique that local players had long employed, adding, "I hadn't heard of clawhammer until I got older"—that is, the popular banjo downpicking style often associated with this genre of music—and forging his approach.[34] "He could just go where he needed to go and do what he needed to do with his thumb and first finger," said his nephew, banjoist Jerry Keys.[35] "His picking was very intelligent. . . . He had no boundaries." Though Will worked within a traditional framework, he developed a flexible technique that allowed him to play anything from Glenn Miller's big band rendition of "American Patrol" (which itself reaches back to an 1891 march) that his oldest sister played on the piano, to "Sweet Marie," featured in the film *Life with Father* and sung by Irene Dunne. He continued to learn from younger players, too, who visited his campsite at fiddling conventions, bearing more recently crafted melodies. He carried this curiosity to the end of his life. "I try anything I like the sound of, not just the old tunes," he told the *Boston Globe* in 1993. "And I'll be playing as long as I'm able to, until nature and arthritis catch up with me."[36] Will's musical breadth—from movie scores to the hit parade to airs drawn from the Methodist hymnal to contemporary fiddle tunes—succeeded, as Jerry Keys explained, "because he understood how things work."[37]

His resourcefulness bears wider significance. "If you needed something," Will said, "you either did without, or you'd build it yourself."[38] In devising his putty knife bridges, let alone so much else he fashioned from discards, he followed his elders' counsel to find practicable solutions, however unconventional. An aphorism long uttered among Black Americans speaks to that tenacity: "hitting a straight lick with a crooked stick."[39] It tells of achieving a desired end with few resources, undeterred by scarcity and despite racial adversity. In the countless works that have followed from individuals acting according to their creative self-determination, this proverbial phrase echoes in the spiritual that speaks of "making a way out of no way." For all these persons, Will included, stands the notion of *mother wit*, a term reaching back to the mid-1400s, merging inherited knowledge and common sense, permitting custom and wisdom to adapt to changing circumstances, not through formal means, by rule and regulation, but through observing and doing and responding and venturing.[40]

• • •

On September 28, 1996, Will recorded several tunes in our home. He played them in the hushed space of my wife's sewing room, surrounded by the acoustic baffling afforded by Michaelle's supplies of fabric, and supported by his longtime accompanists, Barb Kuhns on fiddle and Doug Smith on guitar. By the following year, those performances made their way onto Will's first solo compact disc, *A Banjo Original*.[41] I suggested that title for the album, hardly a stretch given his distinctive musicality.

The night before the trio made those recordings, Will and his musical partners performed for some 1,500 listeners who had filled George Washington University's Lisner Auditorium. The event celebrated the thirteen recipients of the 1996 National Heritage Fellowship Award, the highest honor the United States government annually gives its traditional artists. Identified in the program book as an "Appalachian banjo player [of], Gray, Tennessee," Will numbered among this group of honorees. At the time of his induction, which took place two days earlier at the State Department, Jane Alexander, chair of the National Endowment for the Arts, called attention to his creativity, emphasizing both his inimitable playing method and his unique musical renditions that together made him a "creative traditionalist."[42] Will's senator, Fred Thompson of Tennessee, present at the ceremony, concurred. Through it all, Will maintained his mirthful independence, mentioning on stage that J.C. Penney Company served as one of the event's sponsors, and he was wearing a new suit he had recently purchased off their racks.

Jane Alexander's remarks drew from the nominating letters sent on his behalf for the prize. On the same day that Will recorded in our home, I had the good fortune to talk that morning with Will's primary nominator, Bobby Fulcher, who would himself become a National Heritage Fellow in 2019. A naturalist, documentarian, and folklorist employed by the Tennessee state park system, Bobby felt that Will "managed to add detail to a tune that many banjoists do, and yet his notion of what that tune is, is always surprising."[43] Bobby viewed traditional tunes not as finite works but as pliable entities, so that "there can be enough contours that you don't know it all. . . . It has something in it that defies perfect replication." He contrasted the social creativity of folk tradition against the fixity of popular music. "For stamping out little replicas . . . the industrial world is completely consistent. But in the non-industrial world, you don't have the means to do it. Each person is their own factory, each product goes through that person, through their own vision . . . that leaves room that you'll see in individual variation." Bobby pondered how grassroots musicians like Will, whom he considered this genre's most outstanding practitioner, fashioned settings for the melodies they played. "They all thought they were playing with the same basic thought. Then Will comes up with new variations. Why would he do that? Was he more isolated? More adventurous?"

Bobby's ruminations about Will and his fellow players raise both questions and answers. An abbreviated response to the question of Will's possible isolation can be dispatched with a simple "no." He lived observant of wider society, attuned to both modernity and its media, whether transmitted via radio, records, or television, let alone his continual contact with fellow musicians. At the same time, his musical adventurousness exceeded that of his companions. Not always comfortably either.

In the early 1970s, Will visited many regional mountain music contests that annually convened in Virginia and North Carolina. He often encountered resistance, if not bafflement about his style. Organizers, confounded by his playing and uninformed about the two-finger banjo as a long-standing traditional method, repeatedly prevented him from competing. Their guidelines recognized only the downstroked, clawhammer approach, or else the more recently developed Scruggs-style banjo technique as legitimate, admissible forms. One competition insisted that because he fingerpicked, he needed to enter the bluegrass category, even though he neither played bluegrass music nor echoed its style. Several of his fellow players, who themselves notably employed old-time picking—Carroll Best, Marvin Gaster, and Bill Birchfield—urged judges throughout this circuit to allow him to compete, "even if they didn't know what he was doing with the banjo."[44] Eventually, Will found both acceptance and accolades, receiving the first-place banjo prize in 1978 at the grandest event of them all, the Galax Old Fiddlers' Convention.[45] Undeterred by these earlier experiences, Will repeatedly advised others to follow their leadings. When southwest Virginia banjoist and barber Jim Lloyd marveled over Will's style that he began trying to master in the mid-1980s, Will told him, "You don't need to sound like me, Jim. You need to sound like you."[46]

Once again, Will Keys voiced the idea inherent in "any way you can." A living tradition operates in a dual state of flux and continuity, of people creating from materials sourced in the past. In an essay defining this supple, tenacious quality, folklorist Henry Glassie writes of tradition that "Its opposite is not change but oppression. . . . Acting traditionally, by contrast, they [practitioners] use their own resources . . . to create their own future."[47] The contest judges Will encountered insisted on an orthodoxy that didn't recognize the rootedness of his style, nor did they perceive how animate traditions move along the stream of time. At best, they saw his approach as idiosyncratic, but seemingly, they did not listen to what he played. If they had, they would have heard music, paraphrasing Glassie, which kept faith with the past.

When players and singers venture a melody learned by ear and expressed by word of mouth, variations naturally arise. Early in the twentieth century, Harvard-trained ballad scholar Phillips Barry observed this reality firsthand by watching unaccompanied traditional singers in the Northeast. Their performances revealed a fundamental paradox of folksong that equally applies to instrumental music: "There are texts, but no *text*; tunes but no *tune*."[48] From this artistic malleability, he concluded in 1936, "the folk singer, however much he be keeper of a tradition, is never for a single moment dominated by it."[49] Several years earlier, Fisk University music professor John W. Work III likewise studied the effects of contemporary media on folklore. He observed how a distinctive performance—perhaps a gospel quartet's arrangement or a blues guitarist's phrase—subsequently issued on a sound recording or broadcast over the radio, moves from being "originally the property of one player."[50] Once this happens, he continued, the idea can "become the property of all." Media-generated products surely impose uniformity, but in Work's view, they also stimulate reinterpretation. These resources are adapted, and new ideas change old idioms, just as time-tested notions come to serve emerging styles. In the end, folk musicians and singers, like artists anywhere, exert their creativity on inherited forms. This impulse surely echoes in Will Keys's encouragement to Jim Lloyd.

To return to Will's 1996 letter: "Old time music is whatever you figured out on your own."[51] Around home, some of Will's friends knew only a handful of pieces, like fiddler Little Earl Nelson, whom he recalled, "when he'd played his six tunes, he'd lay his fiddle down."[52] But within that compass, he imprinted them with the force of his personality. Unlike other jam sessions where a greater emphasis on recordings by prominent musicians like Flatt and Scruggs as bluegrass avatars provided stricter models for emulation (or elsewhere, for those active in Irish music circles where similar authority long surrounded Michael Coleman's body of work, elevating it above all others), Will and his neighbors observed in their practice of old-time music a more fluid ideal. Several versions, rather than one defining source, might equally lay claim to the essence of a tune and communicate its originality. "On Saturday night we'd gather at somebody's house or on the store porch," Will told his nephew, "and everybody just jumped up and did their thing."[53]

In this unfettered environment, Will Keys learned the banjo. Early on he cited banjoist Clyde Dykes (1903–1956) as a primary influence. Of looming size—over six feet tall and more than 275 pounds—Dykes worked as a tenant farmer in Washington County, Tennessee. Raised in a family of musicians, he played in two- and three-finger style, occasionally strumming with his remaining fingers to create added texture. Dykes smoothly shifted through all these techniques during the house parties and country store sessions that Will, along with his guitarist brothers, Jay and Howard, attended. Will approached his songs and tunes differently from Dykes by sticking closely to the melody's notes rather than outlining them. However, they were both rhythmically centered on the forward part of the beat and picked the strings with comparable authority. In short, they played differently but sounded alike.

On the six acetate recordings that Dykes made for an amateur recording engineer at the Limestone, Tennessee, hotel between the late 1930s and 1951, he plays melodiously: sometimes up-picking, pinching, sometimes brushing, making bass runs to set off chords, plucking out rolls reminiscent of the early ragtime banjoists, and employing these accompaniments all within the same song. Dykes's recording of "Coal Creek March," one of his self-professed favorites, bears out Will's recollections of his index-led fingering style. In it, Dykes plays a fully realized solo during which he brushes in two directions while working his way up the neck. In "Please Mama Please," a 1944 Eddy Arnold hit with a nineteenth-century sound, Dykes crafts an entirely different background that quietly complements the lyrics. In "Plant Some Flowers by My Graveside," a song that soon became a bluegrass cover, his playing anticipates an emerging three-finger style. Given this breadth and repeatedly amplified by local musicians who attested to his influence, the late folklorist and fiddler Richard Blaustein, who unearthed these recordings, understandably called Clyde Dykes "a banjo player who inspired a generation of East Tennessee pickers."[54]

The example set by Dykes and his musical partners, which included fiddler Gib Broyles and guitarist Tom Slagle, inspired Will and his contemporaries to continue these informal music gatherings. "Anybody in the community that attempted to play at all," Will said, "I've played with."[55] These included multi-instrumentalist Bob Crawford, fiddler Ergie Light, guitarist Vestal Jackson, and country singer Vernon Fillers with whom Will performed on radio station WETB in Johnson City in the early 1950s. By 1974, Will moved beyond these neighborhood networks to help form the Home Folks, a group centered in Scott County, Virginia, with lead guitarist Paul Davis, rhythm guitarist and vocalist Tom Bledsoe, and fiddler Beachard Smith. On their 1980 album, *Last Chance,* Smith described their music: "It ain't exactly bluegrass and it ain't exactly old time. It's that old mountain sound."[56] They had, by then, become the house band at the

Carter Family Fold, organized by Jeanette Carter, daughter of A. P. and Sara Carter. (Jeanette herself became a National Heritage Fellow in 2005.) Saturday night audiences danced to Will's popular group, one evening counting among them the Carter family's most famous in-laws, June Carter Cash and her husband, Johnny Cash. Will played the 1982 Knoxville World's Fair with the Ottway Four, named after an unincorporated community near Greeneville, Tennessee. The group, which included fiddler Walt Harmon and his guitarist brother, Gube, began from sessions held at a local store. Eight years later Will completed his first solo album, a cassette that he co-produced with musician and recordist Doug Dorschug. A testament to Will's musical curiosity, *Evergreen* takes its title from one of his most requested numbers: his instrumental rendition of Grandpa Jones's 1952 recording of "Mountain Laurel," written by Chilton Price.[57] In the mid-1980s he formed his longtime trio with Ohioans Barb Kuhns and Doug Smith, whom he met at a Kentucky fiddler's festival. Playing together to the end of his life, they unceasingly kept Will at the center of their appearances and recordings, the couple viewing their role to support his singular musicianship. Will affirmed that care: "I don't do any covering for them. They do covering for me."[58]

• • •

Will's statement that "Old time music is whatever you figured out on your own," is not only autobiographical, but emblematic of folk tradition. Will's self-reliance, from the beachhead at Guadalcanal to how he reconstructed a log cabin back home, speaks to an essential feature of the music he played. A living tradition thrives by its mutability, becoming the way, as Henry Glassie writes, "people convert the old into the new."[59] The musical freedom that Will exercised, both in what he chose to play and the means he devised to do so, drew inspiration from other, equally independently minded stylists.

In the liner notes to *Down Around Bowmantown,* a 1989 phonograph album that explores the informal music making of his northeastern Tennessee community, Will mentions three fellow Tennesseans whose broadcasts in the late 1930s particularly touched him. He cites fiddler Arthur

Smith and the multi-instrumental singing duo of Sam and Kirk McGee. In 1931, Smith and the McGees (older brother Sam McGee, 1894–1975, and his youngest sibling, Kirk, 1899–1983) joined forces as a trio that for the next seven years reached listeners across the nation. When Will referred to the McGees, he added, "They were my notion of high-class musicians back then."[60] As exemplars that Will admired in his teenage years, their instrumental expertise and prodigious repertory portended his own creative traditionalism, attesting to his adage of "any one old way you can see fit to do it." Or, as Kirk McGee, who played everything from Sousa marches to barn dance hoedowns to commercial blues to early ragtime on his banjo, told me in July 1981, "You just find more and more on it all the time."[61]

Earlier that day, I had called on Kirk's neighbor, banjoist Eugene Benjamin Bagsby (1893–1983). Mr. Bagsby, then eighty-eight, had played

FIGURE 40. Eugene Bagsby, Franklin, Tennessee, July 9, 1981. Photo by Stephen Wade.

the instrument for over seventy-five years. A Franklin, Tennessee, native who had known the McGees all his life, he noted that "I was raised up with them."[62] Mr. Bagsby mentioned his six-year seniority to Kirk, and then added that when Kirk first began the fiddle (Kirk also played guitar and mandolin), Mr. Bagsby served as his practice partner. Now, on his gold-plated, Gibson resonator banjo that he stored in a red cedar chest, he favored, as did Kirk, chord-centered arrangements that went up the neck. All the while he picked with a muscularity that defied his age.

His tunes ranged from "Twinkle, Twinkle" to "Over the Waves" to "Red Wing," the last of which he had learned decades earlier from a woman who had played it on the piano. His repertory, while less diverse than Kirk's and absent of vocals, touched vernacular favorites of the countryside, many of them waltzes, polkas, and a "Spanish Fandango"-like two-step that he had composed. Or, as he said, "A little old tune we made ourselves." His pieces frequently followed the circle of fifths, the basic pattern of early rural ragtime. Over the years he had played for dances, performed at fiddling contests, and in 1945, broadcast with a string band over a Clarksville, Tennessee, radio station. He mentioned that he continued to play with others, tackling material that encompassed everything from Hank Williams's "Your Cheating Heart," to a nineteenth-century set piece he called "Sweet Plants and Daisies." He ended our visit with a rendition of "Leather Britches."

Between tunes, Mr. Bagsby relayed his perspective on music. It all began for him at age six when he went to Nashville with his father, also a banjo player. The two spotted a red banjo in a shop window and brought the instrument home. Mr. Bagsby recalled how his father had been a "knocker," meaning he played the banjo in the frailing style. But for himself, "I never could slap a banjo." He was also referring to Uncle Dave Macon, the *Grand Ole Opry* star responsible for bringing the McGee Brothers to the stage. He had seen Macon "when he first come around here," and remembered his earliest records as he did his personality. "Funny old fellow, curious old fellow . . . sour old fellow. Good showman, good singer . . . and could knock the banjo any kind of way." He conceded that Uncle Dave's fingerpicking "on the first bunch of records, he played well." This changed, however, as Uncle Dave came to increasingly rely on the knocking method.

FIGURE 41. Eugene and Lula Bagsby, Franklin, Tennessee, July 9, 1981. Photo by Stephen Wade.

Eugene Bagsby viewed two-finger banjo style as musically more evolved than the older, knocking/slapping style. Born in the last decade of the nineteenth century, he used his preferred technique not only for traditional waltzes and breakdowns, but in service of more recent repertory sourced in blues, ragtime, and white gospel. His precision-engineered banjo, itself a product of those years, gave him the facility to do so. Like Will's reconditioned Paramount banjo, these instruments allowed them both, as with Sam and Kirk McGee who used similarly high-quality tools, to express their creative traditionalism. Equipped with this latest technology and committed to a technique they could deploy across the fingerboard, they possessed the means to make new statements of old ideas. Country music historian Charles K. Wolfe's assertion about the McGee Brothers and Arthur Smith speaks to this venturesome spirit. "All three had come from venerable folk traditions, and had the creativity and ambition to parlay these traditions into music of great commercial appeal."[63] Much the same could be said of Eugene Bagsby.

Before I left, Mr. Bagsby placed his instrument back into its cedar box. I took out my camera, and Mr. Bagsby and his wife, Lula Marlin Bagsby (1897–1986), a singer of hymns that she self-accompanied on piano, sat in front of their Victrola, their hands entwined. Like the figures in Grant Woods's 1930 painting, "American Gothic," they looked straight into the lens, a scene from another time that once, too, had been modern.

• • •

Creative traditionalism also marks the other musician that Will Keys remembered from the radio: Arthur Smith. A native of Dickson County and a former railroader, Smith (1898–1971) became in the 1930s the most admired country fiddler on the air. Apart from being an effective vocalist, his long-bow violin technique, which emphasized flowing melody lines, multiple notes fitted to a single stroke, and blues-inflected slides, inspired countless players to follow his example and learn his songs. While Will heard Arthur Smith's fiddling with the McGees on *Grand Ole Opry* broadcasts, he would have heard him perform on the banjo far less often, if at all. A prolifically recorded fiddler, he left only a handful of banjo recordings, consigning this task instead to accompanists like Kirk McGee.[64] However, before the McGees joined his Dixieliners band, Smith's original 1927 broadcast ensemble included banjoist Omer Forster of McEwen, Tennessee, a community near where Smith resided and lies buried today.

A year after I first met Kirk McGee and Mr. Bagsby, I visited Omer Forster (1901–1990) at his home in McEwen. In July 1982, he lived in the same small house where he had grown up. Like his walls adorned with family pictures and his kitchen table filled with homemade pickles, jams, and jellies, his musical lineaments proved equally detailed and intricate. He played the banjo bare-fingered and with quiet detail, his strings set low to the fingerboard to ease movements up the neck. For hours, Omer worked through an array of reels and hornpipes, schottisches and songs, including "It Wasn't God Who Made Honky Tonk Angels," popularized by his wife's cousin, singer Kitty Wells.

"I can't tell you how I learned to play," he explained, "because I don't know. It's just always natural."[65] His musical influences began with family

FIGURE 42. Omer Forster, McEwen, Tennessee, July 9, 1982. Photo by Stephen Wade.

members that included fiddler Floyd Ethridge, who also influenced Arthur Smith in his early years, and later played on the *Grand Ole Opry* himself. Another local figure who affected Smith, as he did Omer, was fiddler Walter Warden. Omer credited Warden as the source of his banjo masterpiece, "Flowery Girls," a softly sounded, gracefully complex instrumental that reaches from its lowest note on the bass string to the seventeenth fret on the banjo's outside string.

We took breaks for midday dinner, prepared by his wife, Inez, and later for her country supper that meanwhile waited, sheltered beneath a cloth on the table. Omer preferred to make music rather than conversation. "I used to sit and play all day and never play the same piece," he quietly noted, as he turned to the next tune.[66] I could only feel wonder and admiration when he said, "I wish I hadn't forgotten a lot of my pieces." Other banjoists before me who had made this pilgrimage to his home had likely felt the same. They included Grandpa Jones, Earl Scruggs, and Stringbean, who said about Omer, "He makes more notes with his little finger than I knew was on a banjo."[67]

Of the Tennessee banjoists mentioned here—Sam and Kirk McGee, Eugene Bagsby, and Arthur Smith—Omer Forster most closely anticipated Will's style. With his thumb and forefinger working in constant rotation, Omer traced elegant musical lines that spanned the fingerboard. Like Will, he did not punctuate with brush strokes nor depend on chords to focus his playing, but instead orchestrated an uninterrupted melodic flow. Though Will would neither hear nor meet Omer Forster until 1986, at the Smithsonian's Festival of American Folklife (the first of the two in which he participated), their musical courses had traveled along kindred routes. They developed independently of one another, but each had fused parlor music structures with fiddle tunes. An observation that Will's former bandmate, Tommy Bledsoe, made about him, that "You get melody the whole time," equally applies to Omer Forster.[68]

In contrast, the McGee brothers and Mr. Bagsby worked with melodies framed within chords that they filled out with right-hand pinches and arpeggios to complete the phrases. Arthur Smith used yet another approach. He hewed to an old mountain style, emphasizing the banjo's propulsive qualities. He played it in a spirited, first-position, two- and sometimes three-finger method, staying within the first few frets and outlining his melodies with an appealing simplicity.

Not surprisingly, Will, being some twenty years younger than all these players, ventured into a newer musical territory than had occupied their attention at a comparable age. In the late 1940s, the team of Flatt and Scruggs broadcast live on WCYB, Will's nearby Bristol station, and he began to explore bluegrass banjo. Will purchased a Gibson RB-100, a serviceable if unadorned resonator model, and began studying Earl Scruggs's method. Despite his brother Jay's admonitions during their get-togethers back then, saying "you're not playing that like Earl Scruggs," Will resisted and replied, "Well, I'm not Earl Scruggs!"[69] Ultimately, Will recognized that despite his wearing picks and playing with three fingers, he never fundamentally mastered the style, despite the extra digit he put to use. By 1972, he told his son that he would return to the music he knew best and focus on two-finger banjo as he had always done. When Will's nephew subsequently asked him about his Scruggs period, Will replied, "Well, I played three-finger style, but it was not Earl's style. It was an old-fashioned style, and my main claim to fame was that I would pick out the old fiddle tunes, you know, with the three-finger roll."[70] Will's "note-for-note" playing—his term—points to his musical sensibility: playing notes in time with the tune.[71] For him, it began when Jay showed him his first chords on the family banjo with the screen door strings, and it echoed his sisters' piano playing at home.

Earl Scruggs established a different model. With the fiddle and mandolin by turns communicating the full melody, he outlined a given tune via a series of right-hand rolls and left-hand phrases that coordinated with the changing chords.[72] In essence, he played melody by playing around it, highlighting its principal contours within a rhythmic matrix. He typically worked in an eight-note sequence, playing the keynote with his thumb, leaving his fingers to fill out the accompaniment that, in ever-shifting emphases, propelled the tune forward. He also developed a vocabulary of reusable tags and licks, applicable across the fingerboard that marked refrains, beginnings, and endings. Unlike old-time music, where the banjo characteristically highlights the main melody notes in step with the fiddle, Scruggs, playing in a similar duet, fashioned a pulsating amphitheater that housed the lead instrument without using melody or harmony. Likewise, the chord accompaniments that he played behind a vocalist or between instrumental breaks proved repeatedly adaptable from one song to the next. In short, Earl Scruggs created a comprehensive method, a grammar for the instrument that became a folk tradition all its own.

No wonder, then, that Will, during his Scruggs-style years, so deeply admired the melody-centered approach of Don Reno. A contemporary of Scruggs, Reno created in the 1950s a distinctly different style that he brought to bluegrass. It centered around a single-string technique he devised, in which he set his thumb and index alternating like a guitarist with his flat pick, to play note-for-note melody lines. "Don Reno," Will said, "really set me on fire."[73] Reno's method reconstituted for Will the approach he had always known.

By the early 1960s, this idea developed even further with the melodic banjo players that included Carroll Best, Bobby Thompson, and Bill Keith.

These musicians played, as Carroll Best called it, "fiddle style" banjo, making detailed melodies on alternating strings.[74] Their scalar method viewed every note as part of the melody, unlike Scruggs's style, based on chords and roll patterns that presented a tune, as banjo expert Tony Trischka has written, "in a sort of chordal wash."[75] Another feature developed by the melodic players entailed their noting the fifth string. Instead of its customary role as a rhythmic marker played as a ringing, open note, it became in this style an equal partner with the other four strings in tracing out a melody. Some of Will's movements when he fretted the fifth string sound like passages found in these melodic stylings. Attuned to this similarity, Richard Blaustein, who produced and annotated *Down Around Bowmantown*, the record that documented home musicians who had nurtured Will, deemed him "amazingly melodic, almost the Bill Keith of old-time banjo playing."[76]

The time Will spent by the radio, both as a youth in the late 1930s and later as an adult in the postwar years, underlines these contrasting approaches to the five-string banjo. One branch purposefully traces out melody as it unfolds, while the other houses the music within an oscillating harmonic structure. For countless countryside pickers, the artful timing of Earl Scruggs's style stands apart from the inventiveness of his melodic-style inheritors, let alone the antecedents that Will's note-for-note playing represents. Each requires, as Jerry Keys explained, "a different thought process" on the banjo.[77]

Both currents converged in Will's family. They appear side by side on a posthumous album issued in 2013, which Will made with Jerry Keys, himself an accomplished Scruggs-style banjoist. Years earlier, beginning in the 1950s when Will dropped by to play music with his brother, Jay, Jerry, then a child, found himself drawn to his Uncle Will's banjo playing. Will became his first teacher as well as his earliest model. In time, Jerry's banjo interests shifted to Earl Scruggs, who became his close friend as well as musical paragon. In late 2004, Jerry began this recording project with Will. They structured the album around their two styles, each taking turns. The two finished the recording early the following year, just months before Will died in November 2005. Jerry recalled how Will, by then self-conscious about his skills as his health worsened, "told me I had waited too long to do the CD."[78] Called *Sycamore Shoals* after the opening tune, it reiterates a piece of Keys's family history and geography, expressive of Jerry and Will's personal bond.[79] In 1988, while returning from the first Tennessee Banjo Institute, an event directed by Bobby Fulcher that took place at Cedars of Lebanon State Park, Jerry learned the tune. He adapted Will's two-finger rendition into his three-finger style. "I tried to keep the melody of the song using different roll patterns."[80] Jerry added, "He drove home while I worked out my break and it got his approval." On this track, and those that follow it, Will's misgivings aside, these two players, celebrating their differences and united by blood, reveal the varied tributaries that course through tradition and the resourcefulness of their carriers to navigate those routes.

To the end of his life, Will attended fiddlers' conventions. Friends congregated by his landmark green bus and tirelessly played tunes throughout those events. His intrepid musical companions, Doug Smith and Barb Kuhns, had obtained a "no smoking" sign from which they scratched out the word "no," in honor of his unremitting tobacco habit. Will proudly displayed it on his bus's route sign window. Its affectionate rebelliousness captures the tenor of these gatherings and the sociability of the man behind them.

Though Will could not slow down his hands to teach others his playing method, he continually encouraged those most hesitant at his campsite to play however they might. He once told a nervous accompanist about to perform with Will's group for the first time at the Carter Family Fold, "We've got all the confidence in the world for you, son."[81] Likewise, at these festivals, he continued to warmly welcome all players.

Music offered Will what he termed "a meeting place . . . an opening."[82] His campsite jam sessions might seat a doctor beside a lawyer, and next to them, "a rogue or a thief. It doesn't matter," he asserted. They shared a common purpose—to make music. In the end, he said he could "get together with people from all walks of life," adding that "most of them become friends." Will's son, Bill Keys, paraphrasing his father's point of view, explained, "If you were different from him, there was a reason for that." Then, quoting his father on the matter, "'If you want to be different, you be different.'"[83] It fit Will Keys, this banjo original, who freely admitted strangers in fellowship. From this pluralistic openness, his life and his art merged. An appraisal, long repeated by others, sticks with him yet: "There are 10,000 banjo players and then there's Will."[84]

Once, when Jerry Keys was remodeling the house that Will's mother, Amy, had lived in, Jerry had taken down both the interior bathroom and the rear porch. This temporarily left the back door opening five feet off the ground. Will dropped by to visit, and suddenly needing to step outside, he exited by that door. It happened so quickly that Jerry didn't have time to tell him about the missing porch. As a result, Will walked out only to dance on air. Fortunately, he landed on his feet. "The fall didn't bother me," he told his nephew. "What I was worried about was the landing."[85] Meeting this life situation, he somehow made it work in spirit and humor, just as he had in music—any way you can.

·8·

Equipment for Living

The second-best question I ever asked—the first being when I proposed marriage to my wife—arose one evening in Okolona, Mississippi. In March 1999, I came to this community in Chickasaw County hoping to find the closest surviving kin to Wash Dennis, a musically agile, baritone-voiced, Black singer who had left behind one published song that he recorded while imprisoned at Mississippi State Penitentiary at Parchman. His descendant turned out to be his niece, Helen Marie Rowe (1936–2006). Moments after we met and I handed her the sole image of Wash Dennis known to exist—his prison mug shot—she grabbed it eagerly. Holding his picture closely in her hand, she radiated joy. Then, as I played a compact disc on which her uncle was singing, she listened intently to that voice, silent for her since his death decades before. In a twisting route somehow characteristic of American life and its capacity to reinvent, Wash's 1936 recording with fellow inmate Charlie Sims, of "Lead Me to the Rock," a two-man, unaccompanied tour de force, was now scheduled to appear, if only for a few seconds, in a mainstream Hollywood movie, *The General's Daughter*, then in its final stages of production. On behalf of the motion picture company, I sought her permission to include Wash's piece in the film's soundtrack, in addition to passing along an escrowed royalty for its appearance two years earlier on *A Treasury of Library of Congress Field Recordings.*[1]

My arrival that evening took Helen and her daughter, who shared the same first name, by surprise. The older Helen lacked a telephone, which made my showing up at her door the only possible way to address the matters of her rights. The *Treasury,* it turns out, had served as the source for four pieces intended for the movie. These songs, all originally performed a cappella, were subsequently remixed with added instrumentation, including the film company's full studio orchestra recorded on a soundstage. As that work took final form, I received a call from the Library of Congress, the staffer wondering if I had current addresses for the scheduled performers or their families. Given the array of titles, I suspected that this selection did not result from someone surveying the library's published holdings, but more likely stemmed from a single point. After talking with the record label that issued the *Treasury,* the film company's legal department, and most of all, via correspondence and conversations with the composer, who had chosen these numbers from the album and then restructured them, I soon found myself engaged by Paramount Pictures to obtain release rights for these usages.[2]

From my earlier work, I had come to know families of three of these sources, and I welcomed this opportunity to visit them again. One had even appeared on these recordings, a centuries-old tale that she and her sisters sang at their Louisiana home in June 1934.[3] But the fourth selection, "Lead Me to the Rock," presented difficulties. I had not succeeded in locating Wash Dennis or his family, nor that of his singing partner, despite having previously gone to Parchman to research their incarceration. Now, in 1999, after starting in Jackson, Mississippi, and exploring various state and county records housed there, I made my way to Aberdeen, then Okolona, and finally to Helen Marie Rowe. On those days when I wasn't seeking out Charlie Sims's relatives, Helen welcomed me into her small, single-family, public housing residence set along a street of other identical houses.

I arrived that evening with someone from the community whom Helen Marie knew and who had known of Wash Dennis and his connection to

FIGURE 43. Helen Marie Rowe, Okolona, Mississippi, Mar. 3, 1999. Photo by Stephen Wade.

her. But soon the police, summoned there via a neighbor's phone, pulled up. In a sense, we became bit players in an old and ongoing story of race in America, even though in this effort we upturned the usual order. At first, my presence, quite naturally, sparked incredulity. After checking me out, however, the officer explained, "Helen, he's trying to *give* you a check."

In truth, Helen felt more at ease about the check than her daughter, Helen Bell Rowe Ware (b. 1960) did, as she was, understandably, protective on her mother's behalf. She was the one who would need to receive the payment and pass it on to her mother so that this unanticipated revenue would not interfere with the elder Helen's state and federal benefits. Until that evening, too, the younger Helen had never heard of this long-deceased great-uncle Wash Dennis, let alone his music. It didn't help that the next day one of her coworkers examined the check and noticed that some of the printed numbers weren't in perfect alignment. As the week progressed, however, we worked through these matters.

Now, near the week's close, the three of us sat together in the front room. My question on this evening pertained to the elder Helen. A few days earlier, she had mentioned that she had given birth to sixteen children, of whom twelve had survived. It suddenly occurred to me to ask if she had ever told any stories to ease her brood to sleep. Though she did not read or write, when she spoke that evening, calling on resources that oral tradition provides, it seemed as if every folklore book that I'd ever read came alive. She regaled us with tall tales, proverbial sayings, bawdy stories, and folk beliefs. A steadfast raconteur, she required both her daughter and me to *work* the riddles she told. In my case, that proved a fruitless exercise with only one exception: "What's round as a biscuit/Busy as a bee/Prettiest little thing in Tennessee: A watch."

Repeatedly, Helen would not give up the answers, making that night both hilarious and agonizing. Sometimes both mother and daughter just waited me out with quiet bemusement, listening to my stumbling analyses. From each side, they faced me, the older Helen situated on her sofa, the younger Helen poised in a kitchen chair, while I decamped between them, cross-legged on the floor with my files, camera, CD player, and tape recorder. Mercifully, the elder Helen turned these puzzles into solutions when, after I'd exhausted either their possibilities or her patience, she at last unlocked their secrets. Happily, what we pursued over those hours did not end there.

Part of the movie's recompense allowed Helen to get a telephone, and for the next four years, when she would call, sometimes on New Year's Day and sometimes on July 4th, she would say, "Steve, I've got another joke to tell you." Other times, she detailed the preparation of old-time foods or recalled long-held omens. Some of that knowledge, both of rural culinary practices and of the social life she had enjoyed in years past, appears in *The Beautiful Music All Around Us*.[4] In a July 2001 call, she explained how to make shortening bread and how its namesake song and those like it found a hearing in the juke joints of her community. Three years later, as illness progressively engulfed her—her voice weary, her teeth gone, and both her legs soon to be amputated due to diabetes—she phoned one last time. She spoke with characteristic kindness, leaving a message on the answering machine with an offer to call her back collect. She said that she was "ready to go through with it," willing for her story and those stories she knew to be recorded in a book.[5] Her earlier hopes to have her own book, a wish she expressed on the first anniversary of our meeting, had not borne out.

Fortunately, in 2024, Helen Bell made herself available despite the passage of twenty-five years since that memorable night when her mother challenged the two of us with her riddles, sayings, and folktales. Throughout numerous telephone conversations, several lasting more than two hours in length, Helen Bell filled in myriad gaps. We read aloud to one another, taking turns with Zora Neale Hurston's *Mules and Men* and its folktales, as well as drawing from Harold Courlander's *Terrapin's Pot of Sense*.[6] I sent her photocopies from each, and eventually, the books themselves. Anthologies proved useful, too, including ones by J. Mason Brewer, Langston Hughes and Arna Bontemps, Thomas W. Talley, Newbell Niles Puckett, Roger Abrahams, Leonard Roberts, Harry Oster, Richard Dorson, Vance Randolph, and Bessie Washington Jones.[7] The encyclopedic efforts of these folklorists included materials drawn from the same generation as those who had raised Helen Marie Rowe. These resources helped frame the elder Helen's repertory. For Helen Bell, even single words spotted on a page, reproduced from one or another of these works, recalled stories her mother had told. These traces summoned childhood memories that, she noted, were "allowing me to feel the presence of my mom."[8]

Helen Marie Rowe's spoken-word pieces operated in her family's life much as did the music her uncle Wash Dennis and his singing partner Charlie Sims (whose immediate descendants I never located) made in prison. Both mediums attest to a principle that Hurston's near-contemporary, literary scholar Kenneth Burke, found in the relationship of art and life "outside of art."[9] In a celebrated essay titled "Literature as an Equipment for Living," he addressed a basic but prevalent form: proverbs.[10] He found that these verbal constructs operate no differently than more extended creative writing. All these forms, from an aphorism to a novel, navigate life situations. Their fundamental objective, he added, arises as much in Aesop's fables as it figures in Shakespeare's plays or laces Dashiell Hammett's detective stories. No more or less than these formal and popular modes, folklore—traditional cultural practice arising from everyday life—inherently offers a critique of experience. Burke's sociological approach to literature extends to what Wash and Helen transmitted, from spirituals to bedtime stories. As he observed, "Every document bequeathed to us by history, must be treated as a *strategy for encompassing a situation*."[11]

Much has been written about the Mississippi State Penitentiary at Parchman. Numerous histories recount its origins in plantation-era slavery that resulted in a profit-making enterprise for the state. Its court-ordered reorganization, mandated in 1972, established more modern and ostensibly more humane practices. The sixteen separated work camps that once housed inmates like Wash Dennis and Charlie Sims consisted of barracks, typically of 120 men, divided by a wall. This barrier separated prisoners from the trusties, who, by day, guarded their fellow convicts with live weapons. At the time of my visit in January 1997, relatively few physical vestiges of that past remained, beyond the facility's flat expanse occupying some 22,000 acres. With the judicial ruling, living quarters separated over the grounds came to be replaced by cell blocks, arc lights, and razor wire. Convicts became classified by the severity of their crimes, with their striped uniforms—from green on white, to black on white, to red on white—representing an ascending scale of danger, and their housing was accordingly assigned from general population to solitary confinement.

Housed within the older camps, with the trusty system still in place, and administered without the kind of convict classification protocols that later arose, Wash Dennis and Charlie Sims arrived at Parchman on November 14, 1934. A fortnight earlier, they had been separately tried in the Chickasaw County circuit courthouse, with their hearings occurring two days apart. When I located their trial records in 1999, these documents had remained at that same courthouse despite the passage of years. Barely yellowed by time, these pages had, by all appearances, neither been examined nor opened since the hearings. Stored upright in a large drawer, and rolled into tubes, each was tied with identical ribbons and knots along with scores of others. The lives of both these men likewise entwined. Following their convictions, they were transported together to the penitentiary and processed sequentially. As their mug shots reveal, only one digit, presumably

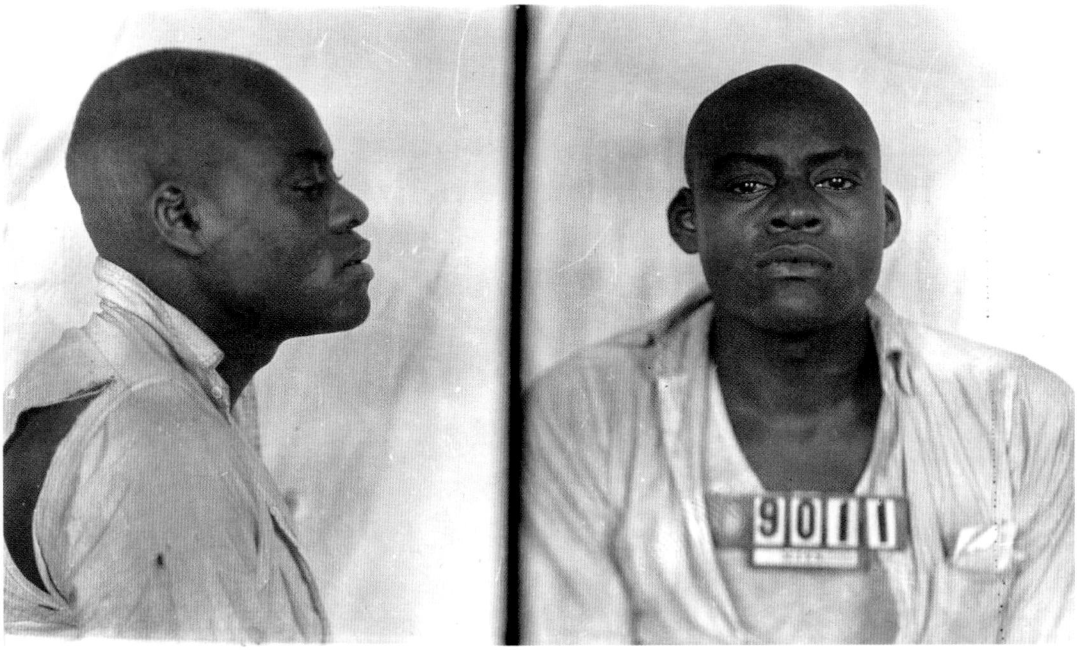

FIGURE 44. Wash Dennis, Parchman, Mississippi, Nov. 1934. Author's collection, courtesy of the Mississippi Department of Corrections.

assigned to another inmate photographed between them, separated their respective convict identification numbers. Moreover, they were assigned to the same barracks, where they made their recordings two years later.

According to Wash Dennis's Parchman files, he had been convicted of "highway robbery."[12] His earlier trial records add more specificity:

> Wash Dennis . . . willfully, forcibly, feloniously, and against the will of Sam Burdine [Wash's victim], did take, steal, rob, and carry away . . . one certain suit case filled with men's clothes . . . of the money value of thirty-five dollars . . . by exhibition of a deadly weapon, to wit a pistol.[13]

At the hearing, Wash had no attorney and lacked the means to employ one. Following a conference with an appointed representative, he pled guilty in open court. At that point, he received a seven-year sentence at Parchman. He was not paroled, and he served out his entire term, discharged in 1940, after which the state reported his whereabouts as unknown.[14]

However, that imprisonment was not Wash's first time at the penitentiary. In October 1927, he had been convicted of robbery in Monroe County, which neighbors Chickasaw to the east. At the residence of one Jimmie Green Sykes, Wash "feloniously and burglariously did break and enter . . . to take, steal and carry away; and twenty five cents, in money, the property of said Jimmie Green Sykes."[15] For this "burglary and larceny," terms used in his commitment papers, he received a two-year term and did not receive a pardon or early release.[16] Neither the court nor prison documents of that time report his age, but if his 1934 intake form reported correctly, listing his birth there as 1913, then he would have been fourteen years old at the time of his first imprisonment. However, the rolls of educable children for the town of Prairie, where he grew up, and compiled in 1923, indicate that at that time his age was thirteen.[17] That would mean he was born in 1910, and consequently first sentenced to Parchman at seventeen. Either way, for the theft of one quarter in change and some unspecified property, Wash was an adolescent when first imprisoned at the state's principal correctional facility.

His 1934 report further identifies him as a farmer; his residence in Prairie, Mississippi, and living with his mother, Emma Walker; his education completed through the fifth grade; his faith Baptist; and his ability to read and write. His bodily examination revealed five scars, with most of those wounds centered around his neck. Described as "stout," he weighed 165 pounds and stood five feet, nine inches tall. He signed his name on the form.

Charlie Sims's records at Parchman bear more detail than Wash's, understandable given the severity of his crime and length of his imprisonment. His conviction reveals that he "unlawfully, willfully, feloniously and of his malice aforethought kill[ed] and murder[ed] Lewis Henderson, a human being."[18] Seven people testified at Charlie's trial. A handwritten entry in the state docket explains that Charlie (like Wash) was unable to hire counsel. Following a conference in the courtroom, he admitted guilt, for which he received a twenty-year sentence for manslaughter. His prison folder also includes tickets that note his receiving corporal punishment for "impudence" in January 1942, and another specifying that he underwent eleven lashes in July 1947 for "carelessness."[19] Conversely, he merited six suspen-

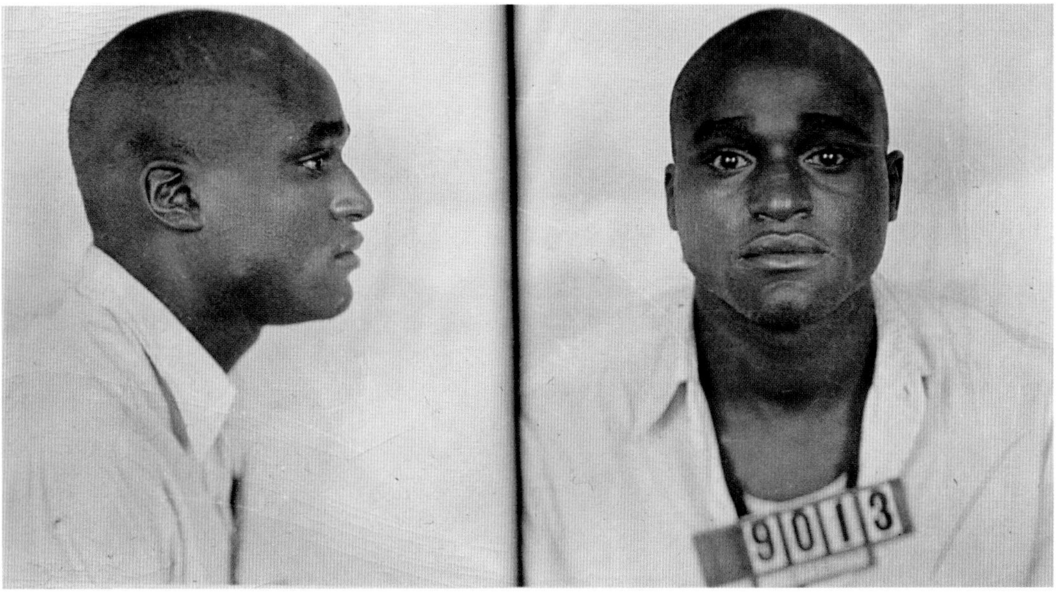

FIGURE 45. Charlie Sims, Parchman, Mississippi, Nov. 1934. Author's collection, courtesy of the Mississippi Department of Corrections.

sions of his sentence for limited periods, and four ten-day-long furloughs, credited in his prison report as "good time." These began in 1945, giving him Christmas holidays, during the last of which he wed Thelma Davis of Indianola, Mississippi. Initially paroled in January 1947, he found this freedom revoked six months later. Yet that July, soon upon his return, he became elevated to trusty guard status. Then, in short order, he was "lined upon suspicion of passing uncensored mail out of the Penitentiary."[20] This violation meant he was no longer a trusty, but put to stringent manual labor and monitored at gunpoint. That status again changed, and by January the following year, he returned to his post as a trusty. His last release began in August 1948, and he received his final discharge in January 1950, at which point the Mississippi prison system lost track of him. His file includes letters from several outside employers willing to engage him following his parole board hearings.

According to the penitentiary's file, Charlie Sims was born in 1909 and lived in Egypt, Mississippi. He had worked as a farmer and could read and write, having received a seventh-grade education. He, too, had been previously imprisoned at Parchman, although this document says nothing more about what precipitated the earlier confinement. Charlie reported his having no religion. The form describes him as of slender frame, and standing five feet, eleven inches tall at 161 pounds. The papers specify his assignment beginning in 1934 to Camp 8, which remained his quarters throughout his time there. On his physical examination sheet, a handwritten notation speaks not only for Charlie, but captures in prison lingo the omnipresent reality of Parchman: "In case of accident: Notify: Boss Man."[21]

John A. Lomax's recording of Wash Dennis and Charlie Sims singing "Lead Me to the Rock" took place on April 13, 1936.[22] It occurred at the outset of the folklorist's five-day visit to the penitentiary, marking his second trip there. Lomax identifies Wash and Charlie on the disc just after they sing, giving the recording's date and locale within the prison. Wash also appears with Charlie as they accompany fellow convict D. B. Prowell on "There Was a Man," a children's song. Wash provides the trio's low voice as each verse playfully lengthens with its expanding inventory of barnyard cries. Charlie, a fluid, sometimes piercingly high tenor singer, participated in two more selections that day: a gospel number called "Do You Know Him" (this, too, includes D. B. Prowell as one of its four named singers), and the work song "She's Gonna Write Him." At the close of the two numbers that both Wash and Charlie performed, Lomax refers to them as "boys." That convention becomes all the more pointed when, after they sing "Lead Me to the Rock," he thanks the officials present at the recording, beginning with Camp 8's sergeant and the prison's commissioner. In making these acknowledgements, Lomax navigated an institution essentially skeptical of his work. He recorded those whom it confined, individuals that his efforts implicitly prized. Small wonder he confers a mantle of high purpose and solemnity on the disc when he adds, as he did so on many of his recordings, "for the benefit of the Library of Congress in Washington, D.C."

Scattered across the ninety-some tracks Lomax documented that week at Parchman, Wash's and Charlie's fellow performers also comment on the powers, pressures, anxieties, and grief they face, as well as hopes they harbor. Their songs range from veiled sarcasm about their keepers to suggestive expressions of desire. Convicts "chipping mortar from old bricks" coordinate vocalized rhythms with the repeated motions of their tools, while others voice Biblical deliverance in call-and-response cadences, allowing the numbers to expand for however long their tasks require.[23] In these musical forms that preceded mechanical farming and the tractor's roar, their performances include a prisoner intoning a field holler, while his partner contributes a series of mule commands, simulating an individual guiding his work animal plowing furrows. Labor squads musically synchronized their movements with their hand tools, helping to ensure individual safety, let alone relieve monotony. Across Parchman's thousands of tillable acres, songs like these served as a functional mechanism in outdoor labor much as religious pieces stirred comparable passion in chapel or at the "cages," the prisoners' name for the housing units.

The same day that Lomax recorded Wash and Charlie, he also called on singers domiciled in the women's unit as well as inmates housed at the tuberculosis and disability camp. Both as soloists and in groups, they offered a mixture of slow blues, more recent juke joint numbers, and field hollers. One even unspooled a narrative toast. "This is the alphabet of the Parchman Penitentiary," the unidentified performer begins, and goes from comic to earnest effect in a verbally dazzling commentary that elaborates on all twenty-six letters. After coming to L for "Lincoln," "who freed the Negro," the narrator goes on to M for "McKinley," who "was also a great President, but unfortunately he was assassinated by a man called Zolgotz."[24] Later that week, Jim Taylor, the energetic song leader known by his prison companions as Dobie Red, leads his fellows in both work songs and sacred numbers. "His voice," Lomax recalled years later, "carried the shock of a bugle call."[25] Luther Boyd, identified in the Library of Congress card catalog only as "Old Train Caller From New Orleans," names each stop made by the Illinois Central's *Panama Limited* traveling from New Orleans to Chicago. At the close of both takes, he notes, it was a "white folks' train."[26] In "Lord, I'm in Trouble," a song paced to accompany outdoor tasks such as chopping weeds, Joe Miller and Jim Henry reprise an image that arises in other Parchman-based numbers too, calling it "the murderer's home."[27]

Its closing verse speaks for the perils of this benighted place: "Oh, I don't want to be here when trouble rise, I want to be gone."

"These songs," writes David Evans,

> tell of the realities of everyday life in rural Mississippi early in the twentieth century . . . of hard work, poverty, violence, imprisonment, hunting, dancing, love and lust, prayer, and a strong desire to leave one's troubles behind . . . all associated with ideas of freedom, escape, and the overcoming of insurmountable obstacles.[28]

Evans's annotations to the 1999 collection called *Mississippi: Saints & Sinners*, an anthology selected by Alan Lomax with Peter B. Lowry, include five tracks that John Lomax recorded on this 1936 Parchman trip. The relief

FIGURE 46. Crosses left in Parchman prison's graveyard, Parchman, Mississippi, Jan. 27, 1997. Photo by Stephen Wade.

that song provided there, whether among laborers engaged in team effort or the plaint of a solitary field hand, points to a reality that folklorist Roger Abrahams found true of vernacular practice elsewhere: "In ghettos and other zones of containment, such as prisons, concentration camps, and refugee camps, the rehearsal and replay of tradition may be all-important for the maintenance of sanity."[29]

"Lead Me to the Rock" offers a case in point. Its title originates in Psalm 61, in which David addresses "the chief musician" with the first two plaintive verses: "Hear my cry, O God; attend unto my prayer. From the end of the earth will I cry unto thee, when my heart is overwhelmed: lead me to the rock that is higher than I."[30]

A nineteenth-century printing bearing the signature phrase appears in Chicago music publisher E. O. Excell's 1896 songster, while the same refrain appears in John W. Work III's 1940 collection of Black songs and spirituals.[31] The image echoes elsewhere as in Psalm 89, verse 26: "He shall cry unto me, Thou art my father, my God, and the rock of my salvation." Later, in 1 Corinthians, a communion image amplifies this belief: "And did all drink the same spiritual drink: for they drank of that spiritual Rock that followed them: and that Rock was Christ."

Howard Odum's 1909 doctoral dissertation, "Religious Folk-Songs of the Southern Negroes," includes the song's lyrics, finding its lines structured like a "riddle."[32] He reported how one singer would pose the question, "Who is the Rock?" with another musically replying, "King Jesus is the Rock." A 1949 shape-note version appears in the Stamps-Baxter series of paperback songsters that made their way into rural singing schools and religious meetings, both Black and white. Here it reiterates the song's promise of spiritual safety that will "lead me to the solid Rock."[33] In 1951, famed sacred music composer Thomas A. Dorsey copyrighted an arrangement of the song that combines the title with its most commonly heard refrain, "Lead Me to the Rock That's Higher Than I."[34]

By the time Wash Dennis and Charlie Sims recorded at Parchman, John Lomax had previously encountered the song. It appears among the earliest Library of Congress discs he made. Shortly before his first trip to Parchman in 1933, and accompanied by his son, Alan, the two folklorists reached the Tennessee State Prison in Nashville. There, a group of unnamed prisoners performed “Lead Me to the Rock” (AFS 180-A3) in a closely matched quartet performance. Everything about their energetic recording, despite the disc’s cutting it off before they ended, especially their high tenor’s lead and the disciplined harmony support his companions lend him, suggests the group’s familiarity with commercial stylists of that time. While this truncated performance marks the song’s earliest recording, it was followed two years later by commercial releases of the Mound City Jubilee Singers (Decca 7134), made in March 1935, and the Heavenly Gospel Singers with their August recording (Bluebird 6094).

These field recordings and commercial counterparts, particularly the latter, invite questions of influence.[35] The Heavenly Gospel Singers present a contrapuntal arrangement that prefigures the one Wash and Charlie subsequently crafted. Gospel music scholar Doug Seroff explained to me that in the mid-1930s, this popular group broadcast over WBT, a 50,000-watt radio station in Charlotte, North Carolina. There, the Heavenly Gospel Singers may have performed “Lead Me to the Rock” and reached listeners, including Wash and Charlie. More likely for them, however, Seroff added, “they might have heard the song performed by a local group at a gospel music program. That was the most common way songs spread in the gospel music community.”[36]

Seroff also noted that quartet singers of that time generally reserved the terms “jubilee” and “rhythmic spiritual” for songs that bear a celebratory quality and function as entertainment, in contrast to “gospel,” which emphasizes more somber emotion and subjectivity.[37] By that light, “Lead Me to the Rock” occupies a middle ground, being an example of “rhythmic country gospel,” a mix of jubilee style with rural gospel. Seroff notes that some of “Rock’s” lyrics consist of floating verses drawn from an older body of nineteenth-century, post-Emancipation, Negro spirituals.[38] Given Wash’s upbringing in the Baptist church, he might have heard the song there, if not over the air, by printed medium, or on recordings. Wash and Charlie had grown up within ten miles of one another and under similar circumstances. Now, in the confines of Parchman’s Camp 8, they came together in this song.

In their performance, which runs less than three minutes, Wash and Charlie take turns during the verses and overlap their voices. When Alan

Lomax prepared the brochure notes for the song's first release in 1942 on a Library of Congress album, he admitted that their complementary singing, each with different lyrics simultaneously performed, made it "impossible to do more than approximately transcribe."[39] More than eighty years later, even with twenty-first-century sound studio processing and an artificial intelligence program to help sort out their voices, these gaps remain:[40]

> [Charley Sims, high voice]: Mmmm . . . Lead me, my Lord.
> [Wash Dennis, low voice]: Why don't you lead me to that raising [seemingly pronounced "racial"] rock that's higher and higher?
>
> 1. [High voice]: I wonder what my mother want to stay here for?
> [Low voice]: Why don't you lead me to that raising rock that's higher and higher?
> [High voice]: Well, this old world ain't no friend to her.
> [Low voice]: Why don't you lead me to that raising rock that's higher and higher?
>
> [Together, but with independent verses]:
> [High voice]: Well, you can dig my grave about . . . ten feet deep . . .
> [Low voice]: . . . I tell you . . . you can't go round it . . .
> [High voice]: You can bury my body . . .
> [Low voice]: You can't go round it . . . I tell you . . .
> [Together]: Lead me to that raising rock that's higher and higher.
>
> 2. [High voice]: I wonder what old Satan keeps a-grumblin' about?
> [Low voice]: Why don't you lead me to that raising rock that's higher and higher?
> [High voice]: Well, he's chained in hell and he can't come out.
> [Low voice]: Why don't you lead me to that raising rock that's higher and higher?
>
> [Together, but with independent verses]:
> [High voice]: Well, you can make my grave . . . four feet wide . . .
> [Low voice]: Can't go round it rock . . .
> . . .
> [Together]: Lead me to that raising rock that's higher and higher.
>
> 3. [High voice]: Well, some come crippled and some come lame,
> [Low voice]: Why don't you lead me to that raising rock that's higher and higher?

[High voice]: Well, some come limping in my Jesus's name.
[Low voice]: Why don't you lead me to that raising rock that's higher and higher?

[Together, but with independent verses]:
[High voice]: You can make grave . . . four feet wide
. . . You can dig my grave . . .
You can bury my body . . .
[Low voice] Can't go around the rock . . . can't go round it . . . I tell you . . .
. . .
[Together]: Lead me to that raising rock that's higher and higher.

The recording's refrain departs from most versions of the song. Alan Lomax concluded that the lower-voiced performer (Helen Marie Rowe immediately recognized this as Wash) sings "Why don't you lead me to that racial rock." Four-time Grammy-winning sound engineer Pete Reiniger, with whom I worked in preparing the tracks for *A Treasury of Library of Congress Field Recordings*, thought that Wash instead sings "righteous rock." But he pronounces it as "RAY-tious." Similarly, Memphis quartet singer Opal Broadway suggested it might be "why don't you lead me to that raising rock."[41] It was that, she said, or else "raging rock." But she added, Wash might indeed have sung "racial rock," not because it was the "correct" word, but just that it made metrical sense. "The words that *really* go there," she explained, "had to do with raising oneself above a desperate situation." Opal spoke from twenty-five years of performing in the Memphis-based groups Moments of Joy, Holy Spiritual Travelers, and Travellers Unlimited, all gospel quartets. In addition, she was the daughter of Katherine Shipp, who, in May 1939, recorded "Sea Lion Woman" along with her sister (and Opal's aunt), Christine, for the Library of Congress in Byhalia, Mississippi.[42] While that children's song found new life in both popular music and mass culture, including a prominent role in *The General's Daughter*, the still unsettled refrain to "Lead Me to the Rock" found new interpretation, too, in the movie. Cast within a blues-rock framework of cymbals, drums, and electric bass, the recording appears there rebranded as "Rachel Rocket."[43]

Yet for Opal Broadway, the song's message brooked no ambiguity, no matter its diction. "We always know how to get through," Opal said, likening this piece to other spirituals about overcoming hardship.[44] Opal's grandfather, Walter Shipp, had been a Colored Methodist Episcopal (CME) preacher as well as a sharecropper in Byhalia, Mississippi, and the music that his congregants knew and that his wife, Mary, led within the family's ensemble centered on expressions of faith akin to this song.[45] Accordingly, Opal explained, "Lead Me to the Rock" tells its listeners that "the only way out is through Jesus . . . capable of lifting me, bringing me from this pitiful condition." Opal's aunt, Luella Shipp, who attended the 1939 recording session that yielded "Sea Lion Woman," listened twice to the Parchman recording and concluded that Wash sings the word "region," as in "lead me to the region that goes higher and higher."[46] Again, however it sounded, it served an unmistakable purpose. "This music," said Opal, "has been a survival weapon. It protected their minds . . . kept them hopeful. . . . There's not a lot of 'don't' in this music. It's a freedom music."[47]

On listening to Wash Dennis and Charlie Sims sing "Lead Me to the Rock," Appolonia Cotton, a longtime pianist at the Silent Grove Baptist Church in Clarksdale, Mississippi, and community historian immersed in sacred music styles of that era, independently agreed with Opal Broadway. Ms. Cotton heard something autobiographical in their arrangement, a message that went beyond its customary theme. "They're trying to tell a story about the treatment that they're getting."[48] Acknowledging Biblical precedent for some of the song's images, she viewed the performance as principally a statement about the singers' own condition. "They're having," she concluded, "a hard time." Similarly, Helen Marie Rowe likened the recording to a prayer. Speaking of her uncle Wash, "He wants to be led to the promised rock," which is Jesus.[49] The next day, she added, "It was just him, getting his life back on the road again. I believe that's what it was. . . . He had strayed away from what he was raised to do. He's trying to make it in with the Lord."[50]

• • •

From the scattered memories of Wash Dennis, an image emerges. "He would steal sugar from a tea cake," said Willie "Tough" Jones, who had known Wash from the time of his Parchman release to his death decades later.[51] He called him "a roguish man," a reputation that followed him for the rest of his years. "That name," he said, and that criminality associated with him, would "go forever forward." But along with his roguishness, Wash's singing, too, stayed in his neighbor's memory. Back at Parchman, Wash had served as a lead man, where his singing coordinated his work gang's hoe strokes down the turnrows. Jones, who also sang quartet music in Prairie, recalled Wash's mentioning the 1936 recordings he had made in prison. For Ernest "Pappy" Broyles, whose father knew Wash and who mentioned him on multiple occasions, Wash Dennis had achieved notoriety in the community. Broyles called him "a hero's man," respected as much for his physical strength as his publicly known criminal past.[52]

When Broyles and I called on Helen Marie Rowe—both Broyles and Jones had accurately identified her as Wash's closest kin—the first words Helen uttered about Wash was, "He was good."[53] She continued, "He was not what you call a mean person," but then quietly acknowledged, "He was light-handed." She explained this as "putting his hands on stuff. That was his only problem." She went on to describe a solitariness about him. "He would take up with a stranger before he would with his own family." Wash found it more comfortable to stay on his own than consort with his kin. "He was a kind of loner . . . mostly by hisself. That's just the way he were. He didn't believe in running with nobody." Just the same, his family's affection for him didn't waver. Whenever he worked outside, his older sister, Bessie, would call out to him, "dear brother."

Wash moved between homes in his youth, homes that included that of his paternal grandmother, Bessie Dennis. "Different people raised him," said Helen. His mother, Emily Walker, was, she explained, "a wild lady," which necessitated this transience.[54] Helen recalled Wash's mother, "always be giving them the father's name, but she'd end up putting them in her name." At times, Wash went by Wash Walker, as he did Wash Dennis. Ultimately, he chose his paternal identity in keeping his father's name, a man also called Wash Dennis.

Wash Jr. did not lack determination. "He was not afraid of nothing," Helen mentioned more than once. "They [people] was afraid of him."[55] Even though he did not carry a razor blade or knife, "He just didn't fear. . . . You didn't bluff him out of anything." Helen remembered her dismay when he stole some of her school clothes and Sunday church wear, along with a quilt, items she kept in boxes under her bed. He also stole items left in cars, sometimes guns, and even stores of meat from people's larders. Meanwhile, he warned her, "Don't be so quick to accuse people for taking stuff unless you know for certain."[56] Despite that admonishment, and recognizing his impatience, Helen insisted that Wash loved his family. Though he never hugged her, he addressed her with affection, repeatedly calling her "baby girl." Of his darker forces, she said "something was in him." When Wash did follow conventional employment, it was, she said, "farming work, hayfields, cotton fields." Otherwise, his thefts continued. Helen remembered how in 1948, while working for Bus Miller, a white landowner in Prairie, Wash was again caught stealing. The two had a long, if intermittent employer/employee history, and for this latest encroachment, Miller did not fire Wash, even though he had committed the crime on his property. It appears, from Helen's account, that Miller required him only to work off the theft, or else, she thought, Wash went back to jail, although his sentence did not lead him back to Parchman. Either way, Helen admitted, "I worried about my uncle, and I used to cry about him. But I was still scared of him."[57]

As for music, Wash sang throughout the years of Helen's childhood. "He wasn't much of a round-home person. But most time when he was home, he was always singing, humming something, mumbling something."[58] She knew, too, that he strummed the guitar, playing blues with his sister, Bessie, herself a guitarist. Helen remembered her having "a real box guitar," ordered from the Sears catalog.[59] Bessie and Wash's brother, Buddy Austin, also built a reputation as a bass singer in the locally based Crowns of Harmony, a gospel quartet formed in nearby Shannon, Mississippi. While the family did not own a phonograph, the music that Helen came to know from jukebox recordings of Howlin' Wolf and Muddy Waters, and songs like Big Joe Williams's "Baby, Please Don't Go" that she heard at nightclubs, were all pieces her aunt played. Wash, she said, had known them too. The siblings performed at Saturday night parties, where she remembered the adults dancing to steps such as the jitterbug swing.[60] Ernest Broyles said, "Wash played at house parties with guitar after Parchman."[61]

Helen mentioned, too, the presence of homemade instruments both at these gatherings and in the household. These included what she called a "guitar played on a broom wire."[62] The instrument consists of a metal string held taut between two protruding wedges, "upside the wall." The musician plucks it with a finger, a stick, or a metal object (possibly a nail or a can opener), while with the other hand notes it with a smooth item such as a small drinking glass or snuff bottle. Helen called it "playing the house." Another improvised instrument she mentioned was a kazoo fashioned out of a comb and paper. Describing her Uncle Wash's technique, she said, "You blow a tune like a harp."

At home, within his community, or while in prison, Wash's music, like that of his siblings, touched multiple realms: from blues and gospel to field chants and improvised instruments. Persons close to "Lead Me to the Rock" and its liturgy, individuals that included Opal Broadway, Appolonia Cotton, Louella Shipp, along with Helen, all detected in his recorded performance a personal yearning, while recognizing the song as an inherited product. We know this too: "Parchman was the second thing to hell," said Ernest Broyles. "There was no mercy there."[63] Small wonder Wash Dennis and Charlie Sims crafted their piece so artfully. It framed a way out, even when they could go nowhere.

This bridging of "the art itself and outer reality" speaks, in turn, to Wash himself and the conduct of his life.[64] His criminality, Helen Marie Rowe observed, was a trait that he unapologetically possessed. "It was just something, I guess, that he was just capable of doing."[65] Yet beyond his forbidding demeanor and unlawful behavior, he exhibited a solitude, a separateness that hovered, Helen Marie said, "on the edge of being scared."[66] She noted that whenever he entered homes, both those he burgled and those where he resided, he used the rear entrance. That hiddenness, that guardedness, did not lessen with the years. Even when he sat outside with his family, he would stay out back. He never married, nor did he drink or smoke. Late in his life, Willie Jones recalled, Wash sought to get away from those who trafficked in crime. He "rehabilitated himself."[67]

Wash's death in West Point, Mississippi, occurred around the time of President Kennedy's assassination in late 1963. At the Ebenezer Missionary Baptist cemetery in Aberdeen, not far from other members of his family, they buried him in an unmarked grave. All that remains is his recording.

On June 4, 1936, the same year that Wash recorded "Lead Me to the Rock," Helen Marie Haynes was born in Memphis. Early in Helen's childhood, her family moved to Shuqualak, Mississippi, a largely Black agricultural and lumber settlement in Noxubee County. Back then, locals called it by its "country name . . . 'Sugar Lock,'" a name still in usage.[68] From there, Helen, along with her two brothers—one younger and one older—and their mother, relocated to Monroe County, sixty miles north of Sugar Lock. They came to Prairie, an unincorporated community where Wash and his mother lived, and also to Aberdeen, the largest town nearby, both places being close to other family members. Much as Wash had moved among relatives during his youth, sleeping under different roofs due to domestic unrest, Helen Marie shuttled between residences, sheltering with various kin for similar reasons.

Friction existed early on between Helen and her mother, Willie Mae Dennis Haynes, one of Wash's sisters. Described by Helen Bell as "a huge, tall woman, a lot of Indian in her," Willie Mae was a victim of incest.[69] Abuse patterns continued, and early in Helen Marie's life, Willie Mae began inviting older men to sleep with her daughter. She prostituted her for income. Clients included strangers and family members. In Helen Bell's words, Willie Mae "used her to bring money into the home."[70]

This led to trauma that governed Helen Marie for much of her life. At thirteen she wed Henry James Carr, with whom she began to have children. At age fifteen, she then married John Rowe, a man some six years her senior. Though her marriage to Rowe was not legally recognized by the state, as she lacked a legal divorce from Carr, she soon gave birth again. She had six children bearing his name who lived to adulthood, some having different fathers. During these years, she also had the first of four births that did not survive early infancy. Of her twelve children that did thrive, her last delivered at age thirty-two, Helen Bell said they had "seven different daddies."[71] In 1969, Helen Marie lost physical custody of her five youngest (with one more to follow), having previously faced a series of temporary placements for her first six. The state's interventions stemmed from Helen

Marie's absences from the home. "She lost all her kids to foster care because she was a street woman," Helen Bell recounted. "She lived the streets."[72]

"My mom lived a very strange life. Beginning of every month, she would get things together. Then somewhere between there [and her coming back], she would go."[73] Helen Marie would stay away from home for a week, sometimes two, often in the company of older men and fueled by drink. Alcoholism afflicted Helen, who kept a pint under her pillow well into her later years. Many of her inebriated forays in Okolona took place at a nearby tavern called Lou Dunkin's.[74] Set in a shack, with a hardwood floor for dancing, along with chairs and tables, leaving space for the live musicians to play, it became a haven for Helen Marie. Helen Bell recalled her mother walking to the club under the lone street light at the end of the alley. The air carried the smell of the fish and chicken prepared there, and the breeze tinkled with the music. With her hair fixed in a French roll, wearing red lipstick, a red dress, and red high-heeled shoes, she would spend her evenings drinking whiskey and dancing to the blues. Sometimes Helen Marie would come home with companions and wake up one or another of the children. Helen Bell said, "They get drunk. Wake us up to dance. Show her friends that I sucked my fingers."[75] Behind all this partying, Helen Bell observed, was the reality that her mother "never got to be a child . . . and that's what took her so long to come in. She started just running the streets."[76]

On the eve of these bouts, Helen Bell added that "when she got ready to be in the streets, she would bring us to Big Mama," Helen Marie's mother.[77] Despite tensions never reconciled between the two, Helen took pains to live near her. When Big Mama could not oversee Helen's brood, Helen enlisted one of her eldest children, Millie V. Carr, whom the younger ones called "Dot" or "Mama," to take over mothering responsibilities. Helen's cousins also brought them in, but at times vented their anger with her for this imposition that, in turn, fell upon the children. "We lived," said Helen Bell, "from house to house."[78] At other times, the youngsters stayed on their own. More than once food ran out. Water, heat, and electrical service ceased, although Helen Marie sometimes jury-rigged the meters to keep the utilities working. They tore up the furnishings and were truant from school. As a result, whether the welfare office relocated them or by Helen

Marie's initiative, the family repeatedly moved. Between 1964 and 1972, the period when they lived in St. Louis, they changed addresses twelve times. Helen Bell, who acknowledged the hardships that she and her siblings faced throughout those displacements, of that period "when things started getting really bad for us," still spoke compassionately about her mother's behavior: "The life how she was brought up, given to older men sexually, I guess that was just something she became accustomed to. She was just having kids, one, two, three, and putting them on to my grandmother. She just basically lived how she was taught to live."[79]

Violence and imprisonment also played a role in Helen Marie's life. Not only did her husband John Rowe serve time at Parchman, but Helen Marie "even had to fight him off."[80] During a domestic dispute, she shot and wounded him, grazing his shoulder. Both John Rowe and his brother, Tater, went to prison for the murder of a local policeman. However, neither of them committed the crime. It was their younger brother who did, and they covered for him. Helen Bell likened the Rowes to the James gang, the fabled bank robbers whose ranks similarly consisted of members bound by bloodlines. Meanwhile, Helen's younger brother, Tommy Lee Haynes, echoed Wash's patterns. He, too, like Wash, was a thief and served time at Parchman, first imprisoned there at age fourteen. "He carried," Helen Marie told me, "a whole lot of Uncle Wash in him."[81] Released in his early twenties to Helen's care during the years she resided in St. Louis, he again got into trouble. Helen Bell remembered him committing burglaries that included "breaking into places, robbing prostitutes," and so on.[82] He also molested some of her brothers. This led Helen Marie to banish him from their home. Tommy Lee soon found himself locked up again, where he was killed, stabbed eighty-four times by a disgruntled lover in a Missouri lock-up.

Yet for all that turmoil, when Helen Marie returned from her binges, she proved herself an able, loving mother. She brought a warmth and engagement that her children basked in. "Our house was everybody's home," said Helen Bell.[83] "All kids flocked to us. Everywhere we moved, we always had a friend that just didn't want to go home. My mom always had an extra child." This openness extended across race. In St. Louis, white children of a neighboring family stayed over, as welcomed there as any Black child. No matter her forays away from home, Helen kept a job to support her family, whether employed as a field hand in Mississippi (where she was working when she got word of Wash Dennis's death) or picking produce outside St. Louis. She worked as a seamstress (also making most of her children's clothes), as a caregiver for the elderly (both Black and white) in nursing homes and private residences, as a popular cook at a nearby truck stop, and finally at a furniture plant, her last placement before retiring.

"My mom done a lot. Got off factory work, and then go take care of sick family members. Going from one job to another in the same day."[84] Capable as an improviser, Helen Marie, using fabric she obtained from secondhand stores, made corn shuck dolls for her daughters and fashioned rubber band guns for her boys. She washed all their clothes by hand, organized a family baseball team, made up yard games to play, and caught fireflies alongside them. Holidays typically kept her at home. "My mom would not go anywhere on New Year's Eve. She wanted to be with us."[85] What she gave her children reflected not only the deprivations she had suffered and the dissolution that followed, but a richness of countryside knowledge that she brought home to them.

Helen Marie's cooking expressed that legacy. She had butchered hogs in her youth and knew how to wring a chicken's neck. Out in Prairie during her childhood years, her family raised sorghum and cultivated peanuts, along, as she said, with attending to "lard, ham, and jowl meat."[86] By adulthood, she added to this cookery by preparing turtles, making fish head soup, and, to her children's dismay, sometimes meals involving snake. Although she never let them eat any such reptiles, she admitted that she had done so herself. She gutted those that she caught and hung up the carcasses by the head. Helen Bell recalled her mother and neighbors going to a nearby creek to fish on Saturday mornings: "When we lived in St. Louis, they didn't carry poles, they carried baseball bats. They would catch some of the biggest fish with that bat. They would hit the fish. Big catfish, garfish, and buffalo fish. . . . We never saw her kill a hog, [but] we saw her kill a coon here in Mississippi."[87] One of Helen Bell's brothers once pushed away the table when she served them a meal made from raccoon or possum. "You just feed us anything," he groused.[88] But, as Helen Bell explained, "If it was to be cooked, she'd cook it."[89]

"Whenever you came to her house," Helen Bell continued, "she had fatback on the stove. It would be fatback on the stove. And every day she cooked greens." This included greens with dumplings, plus garden beans, sweet potatoes with onions, boiled hash from a hog's head, head cheese, and crackling bread. Sometimes for breakfast she prepared cush, or else hoecake—bread crumbled up in a cast iron skillet—that she served with salmon croquettes dunked in sorghum. Her sweets included two favorites: "We loved her molasses cake and her jelly cake."[90] She soaked the first of these in Brer Rabbit brand syrup, and for the other, she made grape jelly icing, preparing as many as fifteen cakes at a time, twelve for the children and a few extras. During the holidays, she typically took three days to fix all the items. (On a personal note, Helen Marie invited me to one such gathering, promising, as she said, "soul food" of every description.[91] She listed a menu that included sweet potatoes, peas, okra, crackling and shortening breads, and tea cakes.)

In Mississippi, the family had no electricity or indoor plumbing, necessitating both the use of well water and cooking either on a pot belly stove or else the fireplace. Nor did they have refrigeration, so Helen stored her prepared foods in a cooling closet. Not until they got to St. Louis in the mid-sixties did they have electric and gas appliances. Welfare gave the family "surplus," canned commodities stripped of their labels, and Helen Marie did the rest. Her daughter said, "She always had supper ready for us."[92] But as Helen Marie cautioned, a full table for them was neither automatic nor assured: "I would feed my children what I had."[93]

This scarcity extended into matters of decorum. Whenever Helen's youngsters visited others, she insisted they decline any edibles that might be offered. "That food was bought for *them*," Helen Marie explained, referring to the hosts and their families.[94] Not only that, had Helen's children partaken, it would have communicated that they did not receive enough at home. Moreover, as guests during mealtimes, they must stay quiet. "You do there what you do here, which is to mind me," she instructed. Beyond this etiquette, she knew they faced a difficult situation. "A lot of times my children be wanting, they couldn't get." Those straitened circumstances affected Helen Marie too, within her social circle. "On Sundays," when she went out in public, her daughter said, "she smoked Salems [a store-bought brand of cigarettes], which came in a pack."[95] Meanwhile, at home, she rolled the more cost-efficient Prince Albert brand. This type of loose tobacco can produce a trail of sparks and ashes, and Helen Bell observed that "Almost every piece of clothing she had, had holes in it because the Prince Albert popped. Or Bugle Boy, that came in a little flat can." For both her children and herself, Helen Marie faced down poverty by upholding their dignity amid the tattered clothes and averted treats.

In her last years, she returned to the Baptist church. "She had come out of the world," Helen Bell said.[96] Her warmth towards others, her extroversion, did not dim with her turn towards faith. Like Wash before her, Helen Marie could hold a tune, and she joined her church's choir. "She loved gospel music," Helen Bell explained, much as she had enjoyed the blues and dancing in years past.[97] She served on the usher board during services, and through the week with her church sisters, she called on neighbors as part of their proselytizing mission. "Her whole life changed. . . . By 1999 [when you visited us], she was in the house, but she was still drinking. But she wasn't living that fast life. The calmness was coming, coming to her. She gave her life back to the Lord." Helen Marie Rowe became well-known in her community, and when she died, "everyone stood on every corner. Police saluted her. The day they buried her, they really gave her a farewell goodbye. My mom was really loved."

In his 1977 study, *Black Culture and Black Consciousness: Afro-American Folk Thought from Slavery to Freedom,* historian Lawrence W. Levine writes, "slave tales functioned . . . as the bondsman's books."[98] For Helen Marie Rowe, born seventy-three years after the Emancipation Proclamation, that aspect of enslaved life had not substantially changed. She grew up in a largely bookless environment, except for a family Bible at home. Like her mother, Helen was illiterate. Although she lamented this gap in her learning, she explained her lack of formal education in relation to the social forces she faced: the limited hours of schooling allotted Black children like herself, combined with the necessity that they either work in the fields or tend to babies at home while older family members labored. Accordingly, she found mechanisms apart from print to receive accumulated knowledge. She absorbed the Bible from others, noting, "I can't read . . . [but] I can keep up with it, chapter and verse."[99] Helen came to know Scripture well enough to recognize the assigned passages for Sunday School lessons, no matter how indecipherable the printed words. By this same gift of memory and discernment, she became conversant with a body of traditional tales, folk beliefs, and songs: all by hearing them.

Helen credited Emily Walker, her grandmother (and Wash's mother), as her principal source for this material. Walker grew up in the Jim Crow era, dying sometime around 1948, having lived well into her sixties. Based on Helen's informal chronology, this places Walker's birth in the late 1880s, squarely within segregation-era decades. For Emily Walker's contemporaries, slavery lay in the immediate memory of many, and the stories she transmitted to Helen were repeatedly tied to that experience. Along with the slave-era menagerie of Brer Rabbit and Buh Alligator fables, she regaled her granddaughter with characters like the "old marster" or "captain," interchangeable names for the slaveholder and the bossman. John, the wily protagonist and sympathetic hero, often showed up in those myriad tales as well.

As a child, Helen viewed her grandmother as someone "mean" for confining her inside when the weather was either too hot or too cold.[100] Yet it was during those times that the storytelling took place. Helen eventually recognized that with these stories, Emily Walker "was trying to teach me and tell me right from wrong." Historian Lawrence Levine, surveying this body of oral literature, concurs with what Helen said. "[W]hile the slaves' didactic tales attempted to inculcate elements of proper conduct and righteous living, they were also filled with strategies for survival."[101]

The example Levine chose to illustrate how these works offer strategies for survival was a tale that Helen also told. In it, a talking skull amazes a slave who wants to tell the master about this miracle. The skull warns him, "Mouth brought me here. Mouth's goin' to bring *you* here."[102] Undeterred, the slave goes back and implores the master to come along and witness this phenomenon for himself. He consents to see the head but warns the slave that he does so under threat of mortal punishment if he does not live up to expectation. When they do venture back, the skull stays mute,

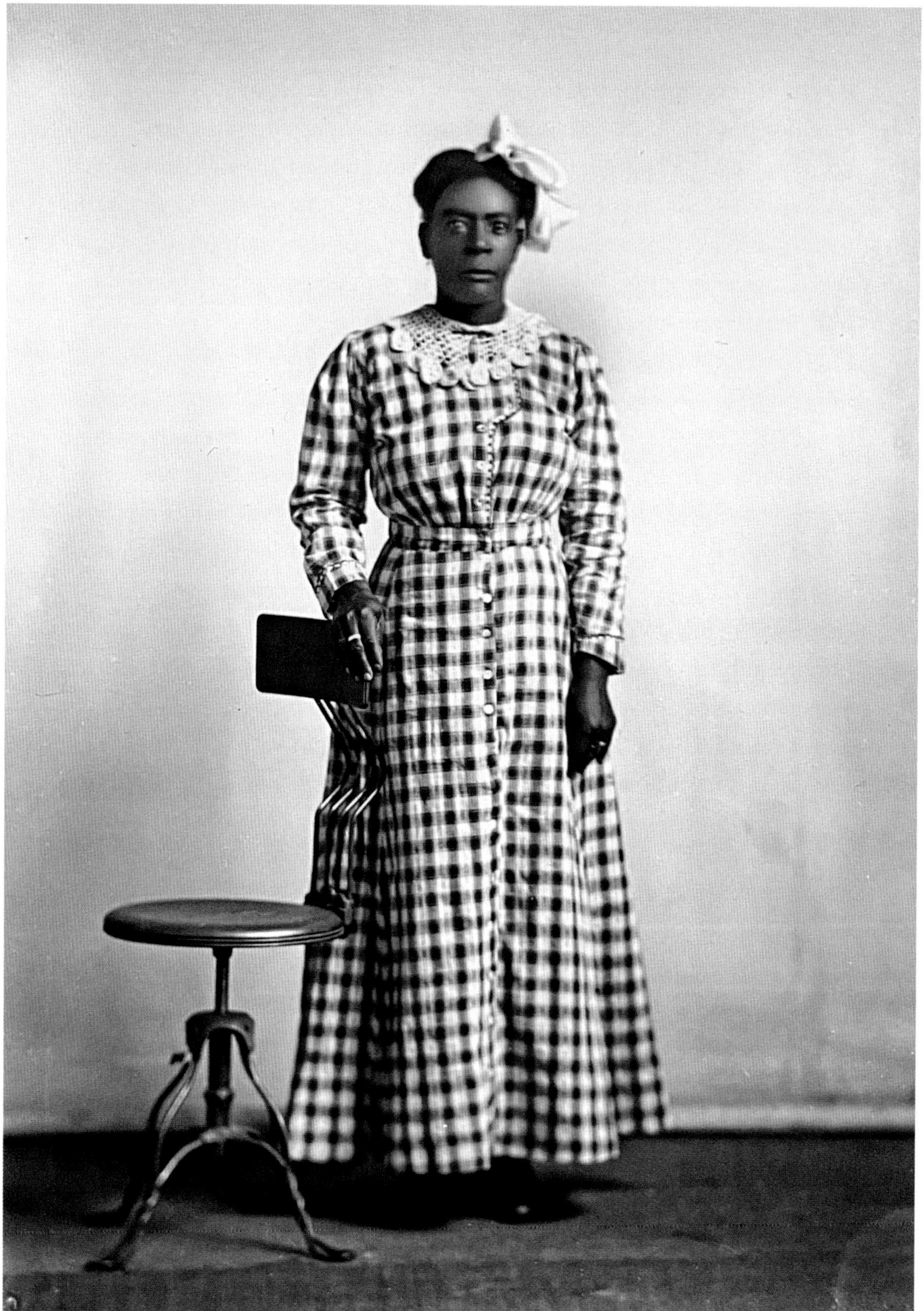

FIGURE 47. Emily Walker, Prairie, Mississippi, May 1915. Courtesy of Evans Memorial Library, Aberdeen, Mississippi.

and the slave is killed. Afterward, the skull tells the slave, "Didn't I tell you Mouth was goin' to bring you here?" Within the bondsman's community, Levine noted, the lesson of this much-repeated story lay in its warning not to share too much.

Zora Neale Hurston recounted this tale as "High Walker and Bloody Bones," which she collected among her Florida townsmen in the late 1920s. While Helen Marie stumbled at first reciting the unprompted version that she summoned in 1999, having not told it in years, the story remained imprinted in her daughter's memory. A quarter century later, when the two of us read the Hurston version from *Mules and Men* aloud, it all came back. Helen Bell said about her mother's rendition, "She used that. The skull head. She used to tell us."[103] Moreover, her mother had invoked the name High Walker in her telling.

The traditional stories that Helen Marie learned from her grandmother and other family members, including Wash Dennis, served instructional, entertainment, and disciplinary purposes, and she, in turn, shared them with her children. Throughout the forty-five items I recorded from her, and adding at least that many more from Helen Bell's recollections, a quality of playfulness springs out. Helen Marie's pieces, apart from the folk beliefs she shared about death and its omens, fit within a category she labeled "old time tales," or more often, "old fashioned jokes."[104] These tiny dramas, repeated over the generations, communicated hypocrisies and resolutions, foibles and victories. In Helen's telling, they presented ways of taking control of a given situation. As Brer Rabbit merrily told the wolf whom he tricked down into the well, while he rode the bucket up: "This am life; some go up and some go down."[105]

Helen extended this pedagogy to riddles, challenging her children as she did me to solve these mental puzzles. Her riddles depicted common items: shoes kept beneath a bed, a bar set across a door, a couple making their bed, the steps in front of a house, a wasp flying indoors, a ticking watch, a kitchen sifter, a sewing needle, and a river's name. She provoked her youngsters to think through the riddles, to follow their poetic misdirection and comically suggestive imagery, and by doing so, translate them into practical strategies. The task required that they pay attention as they exercised their imaginations. One of Helen's favorites was: "What goes in and out the woods, but you can't catch a thimbleful?"[106] The answer is "smoke." Poetically, it operates much like her stovepipe riddle, which seeks the proper name for the metal conduit fixed atop a round stove, itself mounted a few inches above the floor: "A big fat mama, four bowlegged children, and a long tall skinny dad." Repeatedly, she stressed the need to "listen to what I'm saying": "Eleven pears hanging high/Eleven men come riding by/Each man picks a pear/And leave Eleven hanging there." This riddle that Helen learned from "older people" creates an aural deception, as its answer lies in "Eleven" being the man's name.[107] Riddles, paraphrasing Roger Abrahams, pose enigmas that are answered.[108] Citing Kenneth Burke's connection of expressive art and the surrounding society, Abrahams explains how this verbal form, along with related "vernacular cultural practices can provide insight into the ways others, and we ourselves, operate on a daily basis and amid the most profound disruptions of social life."[109] Or, as Helen Bell characterized her mother's bedtime plots and paradoxes, they communicated "what she wanted us to know."[110]

Helen Marie's store of lore included folk beliefs such as "you don't sweep dirt outside the door after sundown" (which Helen Bell explained as "sweeping out the life of a loved one") nor "clean out ashes out of the fireplace and throw them outside," or for a living person to bathe after midnight, a time reserved to cleanse the deceased.[111] Back when Helen Marie and her children had a cat in the early 1970s, she took pains to make sure it didn't get near her newborn. In feeding the child some milk, Helen told her daughter, "Get the cat out of there. That cat will suck the baby's breath. And would kill the baby."[112] This widely spread idea echoes in Hurston's *Mules and Men* when one of her sources told her that a cat belonging to his female companion jumped on him one too many times while he lay abed. "One night Ah woke up and he was on my chest wid his nose right to mine, suckin' my breath."[113] In Hurston's telling, the man then kills the cat, thereby inviting a spate of bad luck, but in Helen's telling, she expresses a lifesaving strategy, designed to protect her child.

From the folklore Helen Marie absorbed as a youngster to a bowdlerized version she told of "The Signifying Monkey," a rhymed poem often reported in barrooms, jailhouses, and street corners, comes a cultural history, borne by oral tradition. In one telling (that Helen Bell remembered), it begins:

The Monkey and the Lion
Got to talking one day.
Monkey looked down and said, Lion,
I hear you's king in every way.
But I know somebody
Who do not think that is true—
He told me he could whip
The living daylights out of you.[114]

"We always figured," Helen Bell said, contemplating her mother's stories, "it was just something that was made up . . . her parents making it up, and then she holding on to it, remembering it, and telling it to us. We never thought it would be put in a book." Helen Marie's storytelling preceded their acquiring a television in the early 1970s. Its capacity to tell dramatized stories soon displaced her nighttime narratives, much as steam heat supplanted their fireplace. Before those appliances came into their lives, however, Helen Bell recalled when she and her siblings gathered around their mother for her storytelling. The wood burning in the fire with its popping sparks inspired Helen Marie to create an imaginative battlefield: "Look at them, how they fight," she said. "Like cowboys and Indians."[115] With as many as nine of her children, each having had their washbasin baths, followed by a bowl of popcorn to share, wearing long tee-shirts as their pajamas, and all of them looking up at her, Helen Marie, seated in her chair, would tell stories and call up riddles in rapid succession. She held her infant in her arms, with her "knee baby," that is, her second youngest, standing close by. Eventually the children would fall asleep during these sessions.

One of the stories she told them, and the first that came to Helen Bell's mind when we reconnected in 2024, was intended to maintain the family's safety. "She would tell us about the hair that could walk."[116] In Okolona, as she headed down the alleyway, Helen Marie would pass a corn field that bordered her juke joint. Once the season changed, and the crop turned brown, fibers otherwise known as corn silk would settle along the row's edge. This was what Helen Marie called "the hair." She told her children that if caught there, "Don't ever look behind you. Keep on walking because that hair is going to run behind you 'til you fall out and you will die. . . . That hair can come alive." Helen Marie, like parents immemorial, and conscious of her extended absences, used this device of a scary story to enforce discipline and discourage her youngsters from venturing out at night.

For that matter, the first tales that she told me, all from her uncle Wash, also dwelled in the mysterious, if essentially comical. Among them: After visiting with some friends and on his way back home one evening, while going through a churchyard, Wash saw two shadows, his own and one other. The second shadow, sometimes pictured as hiding behind a door, signals the nearness of death.[117] But until that night Wash "didn't ever notice he had two shadows."[118] He came around a curve, where "he looked on this side and sees one shadow over here, and he looked and sees another shadow over there." He says, "I don't know what I'm going to do." Helen Marie continued, "But Lord help me, he struck out and went to running." About that time the second shadow got close, and Wash tackled the figure. Holding it down, he said, "Mister, I don't mean no harm, but goddamn it, you're going to leave me alone." The second shadow turned out to be Wash's brother, Willie B., who had been trying to keep up with him and who now implored, "It's me, Wash, turn me loose. Turn me loose." With laughter, Helen reported that Wash replied, "he wouldn't turn him loose for nothing in the world."

Helen began recounting another of Wash's exploits. On the way to the Baptist Grove Missionary Baptist church in Prairie, Mississippi, Wash and a fellow churchgoer called Sister Brown saw its lights and heard the singing, foot patting, and hand clapping of the congregants. Suddenly, as they got close, the sanctuary went dark, the singing stopped, and they both heard something stir near them. Brown grabbed him by his sleeve, and Wash said, as he extracted his arm and readied to flee, "Sister, you can have the coat, but you can't have me."[119]

These stories led to others, some factual and others fanciful. One real-life experience occurred in West Point, Mississippi, in early 1964, before Helen Marie's move to St. Louis. Helen's husband was in prison at that time, and his brother was staying with the family. They rented a house that had no lights. That night, two of her children heard someone in the house and then saw a man downstairs sitting and playing the piano. The next morning Helen got up and found the lights on and the stove red hot.

They moved out immediately. This was a family, she added, whose members, her sons included, did not easily rattle. "My boys, they never been scared of nothing."

On a less unsettling note, Helen Marie recalled cleaning up another house where they had lately moved. That morning she had mopped the floors and cleaned thoroughly, including the commode. Needing to use it herself, she looked down, and something caught her eye. She saw "something green." She looked again, and it peeked out from a "nation bag" lying there. (These were tiny fabric bags adopted from Native American practice, with the name stemming from "Indian Nation." Women wore "nation sacks" around their waists, which they kept under their skirts. These typically contained charms or valuables.) Helen reached down and found the sack held forty-some dollars, an unanticipated bounty on a day when they had run out of groceries. Another time, soon after her mother died, a day when "we didn't have no food to eat," and wondering what they were going to do about it, they came into the kitchen. There, sitting on her mother's table, were two cans of meat and a bag of flour that Helen's mother had kept in reserve. "Things work," Helen noted, "in mysterious ways."

Two of her stories had ribald content, which she relayed with quiet bemusement: The first, which Wash told her, involved a man looking for his missing dog. He had gone under a house to find him. Overhead, he could see some women working together, making an old-time quilt, all of them "sitting up high," and none of them wearing underclothes. His dog had white fur, but now all he found was black. Then Helen told of a girl sitting over a hole in the floor, "twisting and laughing and grinning." Her mother takes an interest and sits there next, and "mama got to grinning, enjoying it too." A young fellow had also crept under the cabin's floorboards, and as Helen Bell explained, with his "manhood coming up through the hole."[120]

Principally, Helen told folktales that had wide currency. Among them were the story of the missing golden arm (which she transformed into a missing head) and a version of "Raw Head and Bloody Bones." During another visit (this by telephone, two months later), she told the one that scholars call "Dividing Souls."[121] She both sang and recited a tale identified as "My mother slew me, my father ate me."[122] In her version, a sharecropper's child at the table asks where the baby is, and is told, "She over to my momma's home." Later, the child raises a question, "Is she going to stay all night?" Outside the window, a bird sings, "My mama killed me/ My papa ate me/Brother buried my bones in the old ellum tree." Later, the sharecropper goes to the tree where the bird nests and digs up the missing baby's remains.

Still another story Helen told that memorable night in March 1999 was called "Ask John." In it, a slave who eavesdrops on the master is continually able to both dazzle and outwit him. Astonished by this capacity and unaware of John's wiliness, the slave owner sets up a situation that requires John to guess what he placed under an iron pot. In Helen's words, he says, "'John, you know everything that goes on. You tell me what's under that tub and I gonna give you ten dollars. But if you don't tell what's under that tub, I'm gonna shoot you.' John sweated and sweated. 'Captain, you got the old coon at last.'"[123] Not knowing that the plantation owner has placed a raccoon there, and to the delight of the master, John guesses right and thus prevails. Usually, at that point in the piece, Helen Bell remembered, "When Mama would say it, she would say it real loud, like she really meant to say it, like it was happening to her."[124]

Helen Bell called this tale her favorite. "These stories back then is what they listened to for entertainment, and really, deep down, it [this story] had a meaning to a better life."[125] She related it to her mother's experience. That folktale "is how she came up. It's what she had to endure coming up." A couple of days earlier, while discussing this same story, Helen mentioned a distant family gathering. As the youngsters ran around, involved in yard games, playing tag and catching lightning bugs, while "we shucking this corn, sitting on this porch, breaking these string beans," Helen Marie sang "She'll Be Comin' Round the Mountain" with Helen Bell's cousin.[126] Helen Bell savored that moment. "We made these songs up for a family get-together. Those were good times, a song we sang as a family and as a race of people." It echoed her reaction to *Mules and Men*. By then we had been on the phone for hours, going through the book day after day, locating single words, sometimes sentence fragments, and often finding whole pieces, stories that her mother had once told. The book contained, Helen Bell said, "my childhood memories." Then she added, "This is part of our history."[127] Zora Neale Hurston knew that too. In an essay titled "High John

De Conquer" that celebrates the spirit he embodied, she found a "hope-bringer," one who both laughed and sang, a force that speaks equally as much for Helen Marie Rowe and Wash Dennis. He brought to others, as did they, "an inside thing to live by."[128]

That inside thing that Helen and Wash possessed, and which they transmitted in their music and words, repeatedly points to emancipation. Wash Dennis communicated in "Lead Me to the Rock" a message of spiritual release so persuasively that others familiar with the song and its foundations detected in his Parchman performance an unmistakable personal urgency. This drive towards liberation appears, too, in the famous tale of the upturned washpot that Helen told. As she spoke, this often wayward but intensely loving mother, closely gathered in her brood. Wash's music and Helen's stories offer resilient testimonies, widely shared African American expressions of insight and control, survival and triumph, folly and hope, limits and possibilities. In the compass of their lives, Wash and Helen faced adversity born of larger circumstances that coupled with their frailties. Through the practice of their arts, they not only coped but also transcended those boundaries. In doing so, they touched not only themselves and their loved ones but all of us.

Soon after I met Helen, she told me something I will cherish to my end. She said it, in fact, on the same night I had asked her if she knew any stories. As I headed out the door to leave, with a first glimpse of that bounty thankfully preserved on tape, she remarked, "Whenever we think of something good, we'll think of you."[129] I mention this remarkably generous statement for how it reflects upon her. This idea, in its capaciousness, tells us who she was. She brought that same warmth to her stories, folk beliefs, and riddles, much as her uncle brought his muscular intensity to "Lead Me to the Rock." Their repertories of speech and song, in Roger Abrahams's characterization of folk tradition, add to "the common currency of collective experience."[130] It strikes me now that whenever I think of something good, I'll remember that thought, and then I'll think of Helen Marie Rowe.

·9·

Hands on the Tune

In April 2023, I finished a new compact disc called *Hands on the Tune*.[1] This phrase addresses the workings of folk tradition, of what happens when a piece of music becomes common property. Songs and tunes, unmoored from formal commercial and legal mechanisms, give succeeding singers and players the freedom to reshape those pieces. One person transmits it to another. Each makes changes. Some of the changes are accidental, some are deliberate, but all occur in an atmosphere of artistic liberty. Without copyright laws, ASCAP representatives lurking nearby, or karaoke bars playing the "correct" instrumental accompaniment, nothing hampers the revision of words or melody.

At bluegrass festivals of the late 1960s and early 1970s, parking lot picking sessions repeatedly brought together rednecks and hippies who found common ground in the music of Earl Scruggs and Bill Monroe. By the first quarter of the twenty-first century, that cultural scene had broadened, the participants having become more multiracial and less male-dominated than before. The same creative process continues to hold. Attendees at the Appalachian String Band Music Festival at Clifftop, West Virginia, huddle by a campfire, playing an extended version of "Sugar Hill." In its repetition they find new ripples within the old song, a song that many of them learned, if not from one another, then perhaps from a YouTube channel. For all the newer grooves they've found and trance beats they propel, they call on verses that reach back to nineteenth-century minstrelsy and uphold a melody that has remained intact since before the advent of recorded sound. They, too, have gotten their hands on a tune. Eventually, one or another of them will take that piece to the next step, performing it in a way utterly unique. Some already have.[2]

Yet with this freedom to re-create the song or tune in an infinity of different forms, oral tradition also appears to impose a discipline that crosses all lines of development. Unless "conscious re-composition by individual ballad makers" arises, writes G. Malcolm Laws Jr. in his definitive study, *American Balladry from British Broadsides,* "the essential character of the text" will remain, passing along from singer to singer. "The repetition of familiar patterns is the essence of traditional art."[3]

Consider how the ballad "Pretty Polly" might have made its debut in the world. Picture a typical market day in the little English town of Gosport, circa 1727.[4] The body of a young girl, murdered by her ship's carpenter lover, has recently been found and reburied in the churchyard. Everyone is talking about the tragedy. When the local printer wends his way through the crowd announcing a broadside on the subject, sales are brisk: 213 copies in one afternoon. Over the next year, half a dozen women purchasers memorize the poem and sing it as they go about their daily work at home. Two or three young men also take the trouble to learn it. One of them goes to sea and sings it during leisure hours on board ship. Eventually, he takes a job in the lumber woods of Nova Scotia and sings it there during long winter evenings in camp. Another of the young men who bought the broadside and learned the melody steals a ham from a neighbor's meat house, is caught red-handed, and transported to Australia. "Pretty Polly" is transported with him.

Meanwhile, for several of Gosport's children, "Pretty Polly" has become household background music. As they grow to adulthood, they hear their mothers sing it repeatedly. The words stick in the minds of one or two in each family, but being children, they find some of the phrases hard to understand. They forget those phrases, or they change them, so they "make sense."

A young woman who has grown up in such a singing household marries a young man of the village, and together they indenture themselves to a German farmer in southeastern Pennsylvania. Later, they move to Virginia. The woman loves to sing "Pretty Polly;" it reminds her of her girlhood and her home far away. However, some of the verses seem a bit too explicit for her own children's ears. She retouches the words to fudge the matter of Polly's pre-marital pregnancy.

As the years pass, the song passes with them. One can only wonder at how many have contributed to the song. In this parable, local printers, street hawkers, Grub Street poets, hard-working mothers, small children, deep water sailors, convicted prisoners, American emigrants, indentured servants, and Blue Ridge farmers have all become a part of "Pretty Polly."[5] Each singer will have their own variant of the song, but each of these will fit into one or the other of just two general versions: an elaborate text in which Willie (the murderer) runs away to sea, his ship is visited by Polly's ghost, and Willie goes mad and dies. The other takes a more streamlined form.

In 1927, this leaner version of the ballad did, in fact, reach B. F. Shelton (1902–1963), an eastern Kentucky barber and banjo player who sang it that July for the Victor label, the company then on a field expedition in Bristol, Tennessee. A new market had arisen with the sale of home phonographs, and Victor, like other labels of that time, recognized that regional consumers welcomed music familiar to them. In this part of the Southeast, Shelton's record added to that supply and helped meet this demand. Not long after its release, Estil C. Ball (1913–1978), a singer and musician from the tiny mountain community of Rugby, Virginia, a place he liked to describe as "a wide place in the road," purchased this record.[6] He shortened its text, but kept the tune, resetting the song's cruel story and mournful tone to the sonorities of his guitar. In September 1941, at the only house in town wired for electricity, he recorded it for the Library of Congress. Years later he described this musical transfer as putting "a banjo lick on the guitar."[7] Then Ball added, "I don't like to copy anybody. I mean I like to do what I do as best I can, in my own way. Don't you think that's best?"

Ball posed a question central to musicians of comparable artistry. His desire to follow his own invention recalls a lesson that my teacher, Fleming Brown, repeatedly expressed. It is this: to explore these widely shared songs and tunes for performances, to seek out a prized interpretation. Elsewhere in this book, I have mentioned the lessons I received from Fleming up in his attic apartment in Chicago, where we listened to his records and tapes. During one of those evenings, he told me to sing a song "like it was attached to you."[8] By this, he meant "a welding of the instrument to the performer, to the man, to the subject. They all become a unit and you can't separate one from the other."[9] The banjo forms a natural extension of the song, and in that indivisibility, it becomes "not a song with banjo accompaniment, [but] a performance, a musical performance." Then he added, "This is true of the great country artists I have fallen in love with or fallen under the spell of."

This chapter centers on Uncle Dave Macon, the country artist Fleming prized above all others. A grandfatherly figure, Uncle Dave (1870–1952) became the first star of the *Grand Ole Opry,* performing there from its earliest days in 1925 until three weeks before his death in 1952. Instilled with rural values of the non-industrial South, he nevertheless projected the image, not of a hayseed, but of a man about town.[10] Within the realm of old-time music, he achieved a stature akin to Louis Armstrong, leaving behind an enormous body of recordings of historical importance and aesthetic value. These spanned melodically descriptive chases to parlor instrumentals, social commentaries to comical patter, all of them invested with his expansive personality. He incorporated reels and rhymes that reached across the racial divide, preserved stage numbers that antedated the phonograph, and composed an array of songs based on older models. Over the years, a handful of younger players based in Middle Tennessee accompanied Uncle Dave on the radio and in performances. They toured with him, sometimes appeared on his recordings, and invariably drove him to the next engagement. While of another generation that steered automobiles rather than mules, these musicians, some of whom appear in this chapter's latter half, bear witness to a process that ceaselessly pivots, in Ruth Crawford Seeger's words, between common possession and individual contribution.[11] In her painstaking transcriptions of folksong performances, she sought to capture the particularities of a singer's approach, what she called "the breath of the singer."[12] Crawford expressed that ideal in connection to what collectors John and Alan Lomax found in

FIGURE 48. Uncle Dave Macon, Nashville, Tennessee, ca. 1940. Hand-colored image, courtesy of Sol Korine.

"the song-makers and the song-rememberers" they recorded: "Singing in their homes, in their churches, at their dances, they leave on these records imperishable spirals of their personalities, their singing styles, and their cultural heritage."[13]

• • •

On November 26, 1947, while in Miami performing with Ernest Tubb, Curly Fox, and Texas Ruby under the auspices of a *Grand Ole Opry* tour,

Uncle Dave Macon wrote a letter to Alan Lomax. He penned it during a four-day tent show engagement, after which he and his fellow players would travel up to Boston before returning to Nashville. In this handwritten note set on hotel stationery he had saved from an earlier *Opry* tour, Uncle Dave affectionately addresses the folklorist as "My Dear Beloved Sir & Friend."[14] Earlier that year, Lomax reissued two of Uncle Dave's out-of-print Brunswick/Vocalion recordings on the label's *Listen to Our Story* anthology.[15] One was Uncle Dave's 1926 rendition of "Death of John Henry (Steel Driving Man)," an unusual version of the song that he had learned from Tom Davis, a Black grist mill worker from near his home in Readyville, Tennessee. The other, a 1927 performance of "Rock About My Saro Jane," was also a Black song. In a separate note, Uncle Dave informed Lomax that he first heard it during his youth from steamboat roustabouts unloading cargo on the Nashville waterfront.[16]

At the time of the Miami letter, Lomax had just completed a companion collection for Brunswick called *Mountain Frolic.* He included among its tracks Uncle Dave's "Sail Away Ladies," an ebullient string band–accompanied dance number, drawn from the same 1927 recording session as "Saro Jane." The thrust of Uncle Dave's message to Lomax centered on recovering such older recordings. Uncle Dave and his friends, he wrote, would pay premium prices to acquire those titles as keepsakes. He singled out one song, "Arcade Blues," a moody solo performance that he recorded in September 1926. In this note, Uncle Dave names a friend, "Mr. Chas Keys," who, in past years, had sold that disc at the Nashville Arcade, and whom he had just seen the week prior in Nashville. "He told me he would freely give $5.00 for just one record of the Arcade Blues if it could be found."[17]

On the recording, Uncle Dave first plays through the melody, then follows with a spoken declaration: "Hot dog! Sung especially for Mr. Charlie Keys and Mr. Hyde in the Arcade, who will play your records on both sides."[18] The Arcade, a designated landmark, was built in 1902 and is still in use more than a century later. It was the city's first shopping mall, a graceful, two-story bazaar set under a steel-latticed glass roof. Its architect designed the interior to hold forty retail businesses on the main floor, with second-floor offices set around its upstairs balcony. According to the narrative that accompanied the building's National Register of Historic Places application, "one could buy anything from a twelve-cent hamburger to a $5,000 diamond."[19] By the mid-1920s, one of its tenants included Hyde's Phonograph Shoppe, which sold Brunswick phonographs, radios, and records. It was there that Charlie Keys worked on commission selling Uncle Dave's music. "If it's one thing the people in Nashville want, it's the latest records," said proprietor Erle Hyde in 1924. "We get them just as soon as possible, and no sooner are they received, someone wants them. I don't know how the folks in Nashville get the names so quick, but the new records just literally walk out."[20] The "Arcade Blues" was numbered among those items that customers bore away from Hyde's store.

In January 1925, fully a year before Uncle Dave recorded the song, he performed its antecedent during an engagement at Lowe's Bijou Theater in Birmingham. To attract continued attendance at this appearance, then entering its fourth week, he announced some added titles, along with a new performer for the held-over show. Along with his fiddler, Sid Harkreader, and step dancer, Bob Bradford, the guitarist Sam McGee now joined Uncle Dave's performing ensemble. In Birmingham, "Guitarin' Sam," as he was billed, performed what has since become the most celebrated of his traditionally based tunes, "Buck Dancer's Choice." As Sam played each of its stop-time sections, "Dancin' Bob" punctuated them with percussive steps. Uncle Dave also included among the new numbers he promised his Alabama audience a piece called "The Nigger Blues."[21] This benighted title was the same song that Uncle Dave transformed into the "Arcade Blues."

The piece had, by then, a long commercial history. In November 1912, Dallas-based blackface performer Leroy "Lasses" White (1888–1949) submitted a fifteen-verse song for copyright called "The Negro Blues." For him, its appearance came early in a show business career that began in his teens with a Texas minstrel troupe. Within two years of publishing the song, White became a headline entertainer. He subsequently founded several minstrel companies of his own, some quite sizable, as well as recording both sketches and songs. When the audience for full-scale stage minstrelsy narrowed, he abridged these routines for the radio. As leader of the two-man team of "Lasses and Honey," he reached a national audience through his network broadcasts, and his music became known to President Franklin Roosevelt (and his Texas-born vice president, John Nance

Garner), for whom he had written a song soon after their first election. His souvenir books, which combined lyrics and comic bits, furthered his success. He spent the last decade of his life in Hollywood, where he found steady employment working as a character actor, largely in a sidekick's role, making more than seventy appearances on film.[22]

"The Negro Blues" was White's earliest registered song, and it stands out as one of the first twelve-bar blues in print. This telltale pattern, despite its presence in folk use, was then just coming into the mainstream. Similarly, White's lyrics had had prior life in Black usage. The song's litany of trains, its imagery of Noah's dove, its protagonist's farewell in which he lies down on a railroad track, and its characterization of blues as a type of heartache all had precedent in oral renditions. White's second verse might speak for the whole: "The blues ain't nothing but a good man feeling bad."[23] Scholars Lynn Abbott and Doug Seroff write, "Obviously, Lasses White did not *compose* these floating verses; for the most part, at least, he had to have *overheard* them, 'collected' them in the streets and vaudeville theaters of Dallas's emerging entertainment community."[24]

One possibility that researchers David Evans and Luigi Monge subsequently uncovered stems from the location that White affixed to his copyright submission, that being Dallas's Happy Hour Theater. In 1912, it stood in the theatrical district near "the corner of Elm and Central," where bluesman Blind Lemon Jefferson often performed.[25] Lasses White may have witnessed Jefferson's street singing since he used some of these same verses in his own songs. The location where the legendary musician operated at that time was also near the central train depot that White frequented as an itinerant performer. But whether contact between the two of them occurred, the song, by its words and music, shows that a transfer from Black sources to Lasses White had taken place.

White's 1934 songbook demonstrates how extensively he based his work on preexisting folksongs and sayings. These include his adaptations of "Casey Jones," "Frankie and Johnny" (depicting FDR and VP Garner), "Old Spinning Wheel," and "After the Ball."[26] In this collection of "songs, parodies, jokes, poems," he even prints in amended form a verse that Uncle Dave used in one of his comic talking songs, "Uncle Dave's Travels, Part 4

(Visit at the Old Maid's)." By the time his songbook was published, White had become a *Grand Ole Opry* cast member, performing on the broadcast just minutes apart from Uncle Dave's assigned segments. Earlier, at the start of White's tenure at the station, *The Nashville Banner* documented their making at least one joint live appearance in the community.[27] The two knew one another, but the song they shared preceded their time in Nashville.

Earlier, in 1913, a Dallas-based publisher issued "The Negro Blues" in sheet music, having retitled it as the "Nigger Blues." Its cover featured Lasses White dressed in full blackface with white gloves, glistening lips, tilted hat, and ill-fitted trousers. With his verses pared down by more than half, it was this text that George O'Connor (1874–1946), a Washington, D.C., lawyer and businessman who specialized in dialect material, recorded in 1916. As someone who performed for nine presidents, from McKinley to Truman, and who made thirty-five recordings between 1914 and 1918, O'Connor's "Nigger Blues," issued on the Columbia label, stood out as his biggest-selling release:

> Oh, the blues ain't nothing, oh, the blues ain't nothing
> but a good man feeling bad.
> Oh, the blues ain't nothing but a good man feeling bad.
> Oh, that's a feeling that I've often had.
>
> You can call the blues, you can call the blues
> any old thing you please.
> You can call the blues any old thing you please.
> But the blues ain't nothing but the doggone heart disease.
>
> When a man gets blue, when a man gets blue,
> he takes a train and rides.
> When a man gets blue, he takes a train and rides.
> When a woman gets blue, she hangs her little head and cries.
>
> Oh, yonder comes, oh, yonder comes the train
> coming down the track.
> Oh, yonder comes the train coming down the track.
> To take me away, but it ain't gwine to bring me back.

Oh, when I die, oh, when I die, honey, honey,
don't you wear no black.
Oh, when I die, honey, don't you wear no black,
'Cause if you do, my ghost will come sneaking back.

I'm gwine to lay my head, I'm gwine to lay my head
down on some railroad line.
I'm gwine to lay my head down on some railroad line.
Let the Santa Fe try to pacify my mind.[28]

O'Connor's version reveals an essentially white reading of a Black music form. His arrangement, supported by a small studio band with trumpet, trombone, tuba, and clarinet, couples with simulated train effects. O'Connor's vibrato-infused singing style, wrote Robert Palmer, finds expression in its "perfectly articulated major thirds, without a hint of 'blue' pitch treatment" (microtonally lowering or raising pitch).[29] By 1919, the song had appeared on three more commercial recordings as well as four player-piano rolls. In succeeding years, it made its way onto both race and hillbilly discs, where it received Black interpretations from such artists as Ida Cox on her 1924 "Blues Ain't Nothin' Else But!" followed by Georgia White's 1938 remake. Its white vernacular music performances include Jess Young's "Old Weary Blues" (1929), the Brock Sisters' "Broadway Blues" (1929), and Milton Brown's "Texas Hambone Blues" (1936).

Unlike these other renditions, Uncle Dave offers a blues in structure but not in sound. In "Arcade Blues," he neither sings in a stage voice associated with popular music of the sort audible on its earlier recordings, nor with flattened, diminished, or augmented notes, the pitch contours that identify blues performance. His verses also call on earlier tropes. Here, the twined image of the rabbit and the hound, a widely known figure of countryside speech, appears in a stanza that focuses on the sexual trade that he ascribed to the Arcade. Not until late in the piece, not before his penultimate verse, does he sample the wider cache of folk blues that Lasses White and the others had employed. Uncle Dave sings:

They got the Arcade blues, got the Arcade blues
Got the Arcade blues so bad.
Got the Arcade blues, got the Arcade blues
That's a trouble I never had,
That's a trouble I never had.

These silk-dressed women, these silk-dressed women,
This Arcade's always had.
These silk-dressed women, these silk-dressed women,
Make a married man feel sad,
Make a married man feel sad.

If you've got a good woman, if you've got a good woman,
I'd advise you to leave her at home.
These Arcade boys, these Arcade boys,
Won't let a good woman alone,
Won't let a good woman alone.

If you've got a good woman, if you've got a good woman,
Don't never bring her to town.
But a red-headed woman, yes, a red-headed woman,
Make a grey rabbit love a hound,
Make a grey rabbit love a hound.

Gonna lay my head, gonna lay my head,
Upon some railroad track.
It'll carry me way, it'll carry me away,
But it will not bring me back,
Oh, it will not bring me back.

Said a rubber-tired hearse, yes, a rubber-tired hearse,
Like a great big Cadillac.
Carry you over to the graveyard boys,
That man won't bring you back,
That man won't bring you back.

[coda]:
That man won't bring you back.[30]

The assertiveness of Uncle Dave's banjo immediately sets "Arcade Blues" apart from all others, and with it, he makes this song his own. He plays throughout the piece a flurry of right-hand triplets to fill the musical spaces. This three-finger method recalls the professional banjoists of the minstrel and vaudeville stage, as it does the parlor players of the late Victorian period when the five-string banjo enjoyed its greatest popularity and Uncle Dave first began to play. The instrument's most technically able proponents, and who made the preponderance of cylinder and disc recordings from the earliest years of phonographic reproduction, deployed this technique in their marches, popular favorites, and display pieces, including patriotic fanfares, Beethoven minuets, Stephen Foster arrangements, Dixie medleys, reconstructions of Berlioz and Liszt compositions, and any number of cakewalks, tickles, and rags. Unlike these consciously virtuosic works that spanned the banjo's fingerboard and which used this triplet to power those settings, however, Uncle Dave limits his playing in "Arcade Blues" to the open strings and the first few frets. He makes no use of closed chords, fifth-string fretting, chromatic passages, key changes, or up-the-neck elaborations favored in sophisticated arrangements of that era. His plucked triplet (which has its counterpart within the banjo's downstroke style, also found in method books and collections from the mid-nineteenth century on) points to the folk influence that Uncle Dave had absorbed since his youth, the traditional styles that had flourished among Black and white rural players. He then applied this bicultural technique to make an unadorned statement of the melody. The song's poetic economy contrasts with his high-spirited instrumental accompaniment.

"Arcade Blues" reflects an earlier music that Uncle Dave knew, a music from before the blues. In a preliminary survey of Uncle Dave Macon's recorded work, Norm Cohen identifies the divers genres that he encompassed: pre–Civil War sacred songs, British ballads and imported dance tunes, native American ballads (which denote not tribal, but English language songs that arose on this soil), minstrel songs, rewritten plantation folksongs, late-nineteenth-century pop songs from Tin Pan Alley, and Southern fiddling breakdowns, in addition to his own topical compositions, variations of pre-existing works, as well as original melodies.[31] Cohen also notes that a number of his recordings combined songs, in which Uncle Dave merges multiple pieces on a single side. His miscellaneous grouping includes Black-originated songs, beginning with "Keep My Skillet

Good and Greasy," the first song Uncle Dave recorded and one of the last he performed. His source, according to fiddler Sid Harkreader, who accompanied him at his maiden recording session, was the same Tom Davis mentioned in connection with the musically similar "Death of John Henry." Like "Arcade Blues," Uncle Dave's three-finger triplet animates them all.

Blues, a largely twentieth-century development, arise rarely in his body of work. Between Uncle Dave's first studio session held in July 1924 and his last, which took place in January 1938, he made 167 published recordings. These do not include dozens more of unreleased masters, pieces recorded by his accompanists at these sessions (where Uncle Dave serves, at times, as interlocutor), air checks, home recordings, and his appearances in the 1940 *Grand Ole Opry* film. "Blues" appears by name on only seven of his published recordings. Beyond these items, record collector Robert Hyland compiled, over twenty-three years, a checklist of 218 titles that Uncle Dave performed but never recorded.[32] Hyland's list of radio appearances names ten more bearing "blues" in their titles, with at least half of these denoting recent hillbilly favorites, and many separately recorded in cover versions by Uncle Dave's younger accompanists. One surviving air check from a 1945 *Grand Ole Opry* broadcast in which he sang "Laugh Your Blues Away" bears no blues qualities at all, but it is a comic song with nineteenth-century analogues set to a hoedown tune. Of his recorded blues, only one, his "Heartaching Blues," which he performed as a solo in May 1927, fully reflects the twelve-bar structure that became such an ascendant pattern in American music. His other blues, like so much else of his repertory, looked further back.

Scholarship about Uncle Dave Macon has richly explored this past. Notable accounts include George D. Hay's 1945 written portrait of Uncle Dave; Ralph Rinzler's 1966 liner notes for a Decca reissue LP that he produced, as well as his work with Norm Cohen on a 1970 bio-discography published by the John Edwards Memorial Foundation; and Charles K. Wolfe, who, by 1972, had begun conducting interviews with musicians, family, and community members who had known Uncle Dave. Wolfe soon authored numerous pieces about him and became his leading chronicler, as well as producing the definitive corpus of his recordings. More recently, Uncle Dave's great-grandson, Michael Doubler, wrote with insider's detail the first book-length biography, *Dixie Dewdrop: The Uncle Dave Macon Story*; and younger scholars, including Eric Hermann and Corbin Hayslett, have sensitively probed both his musicianship and his sources.[33] Collectively, this body of work goes a long way towards fulfilling Archie Green's invitation to Macon devotees made more than a half-century ago: "Particularly welcome would be an analysis of his total recorded repertoire with attention paid to the degree to which he altered traditional materials."[34] In other words, how did Uncle Dave put his hands on the tunes?

"Arcade Blues" exemplifies what Green termed Uncle Dave's "recompositional skill."[35] Musically, he both repurposed extant melodies and crafted new ones based on folk and popular models. By no means a rural isolate, Uncle Dave stayed attuned to contemporary events to create his own populist-infused, Southern agrarian musical commentaries. Not unlike the scene he evokes in "Arcade Blues," in which he contrasts illicit desire with the stabilities of married life, before drawing on older verses that broaden its mournful atmosphere, his song topics included the Scopes monkey trial, Henry Ford cars, Tennessee highway scandals, Al Smith's presidential ambitions, resistance to Prohibition, farm relief measures, and the human toll of the Great Depression.

Knowledgeable on guitar and piano, he refined his compositions, learned sheet music renditions of hearth-and-home songs, and stabilized his arrangements in collaborations with his sight-reading older sister, Annie (1868–1960), herself a music teacher. Admittedly, a paucity of primary documents veils their interactions. Materials left in Annie's care were consumed in a 1952 house fire that she survived.[36] But other resources, such as Uncle Dave's letters and his self-published songbook, along with his family's, neighbors', and colleagues' memories, and a comparison of his recordings with those of similar traditional and commercial provenance, lend insight into his compositional choices. Committed to his Methodist faith, he paid special attention to Black and white religious practices, where he absorbed pulpit oratory and revival songs that he added to his repertory. His work as an entertainer, in particular his banjo acrobatics and spoken-word preludes, attests to his inventiveness, his sources, and his self-reliance. He said so himself: "Now people when it comes to the scientifical parts of music I know nothing about it, but I can play."[37]

• • •

David Harrison Macon began playing the five-string banjo in his early teens at the Broadway House, a residential hotel in Nashville that catered to the theatrical trade. During the four years between 1883 and 1887 that his parents owned and operated this lodging (which stood only doors away from the Merchant's Hotel, where Uncle Dave lived at the time he wrote to Alan Lomax from Florida), he met a clientele of circus, minstrel show, and vaudeville performers. He absorbed not only songs and methods for his chosen instrument, but stagecraft that became a signature of his performances. One of these routines later formed a slogan touted beneath his picture on a printed showcard: "Uncle Dave handles a banjo like a monkey handles a peanut."[38] The bit began, recalled Robert Hyland, with a few chords on the banjo. Then:

> the feet would start, and he would say "Clean gone now, ah," spinning it in position held, the banjo leaves his hands up in the air, back to his hands as he says "got to get behind the plow," then in a clock like motion the banjo, still plunking all the while went under one leg, under the other, then behind him, back to the front, up in the air again, with more verses and stomping which by then had brought the house down. He had knocked them cold: he knew and the audience knew there were no toppers.[39]

I know, too, from my visits with Cordell Kemp (1909–2005) of Defeated, Tennessee, the accuracy of this description. Cordell learned these moves as a youngster from watching Uncle Dave's schoolhouse appearances as well as having received personal lessons from him. In Cordell's hands, they became a balletic coordination, a maneuvering between banjo and banjoist. Cordell's rendition of "Hear Jerusalem Moan," which Uncle Dave showed him, operates in a call-and-response with its lyrics. He timed his movements according to the song's vocal parts, making the performance as much a work of mime as music. Cordell, like Uncle Dave before him, switched the banjo from one hand to the other, turning, sliding, and spinning the instrument, all the while tapping the fingerboard and sustaining an underlying chord. Even within the smallest of these gestures, he kept momentum, shuffling the banjo like a deck of cards, riffling it from side to side. Cordell likened these sweeping movements, as well as the space they required, to “making molasses.”[40] Repeatedly, he’d coax the banjo, saying, “Come here, five-string.” Earlier printed music, such as S. S. Stewart’s 1885 “Church Bell Chimes,” and Frank B. Converse’s “Imitation of the Bell Chimes, Hand Organ and Bag-Pipes,” from 1871, also physically required moving the banjo with simultaneous playing from pendulum swinging to hand cranking. Previously, the “Sangalli Dance,” another so-called “trick tune” of the sort Uncle Dave and Cordell Kemp had mastered, appeared in newspaper reports of 1850s banjo performances. According to banjoist and historian Joel Hooks, this widely seen maneuver had become “old-fashioned by the 1880s.”[41]

Cordell likened one of Uncle Dave’s routines to “sawing wood.”[42] Uncle Dave typically carried three banjos to his shows, each set in a different key, and each tied with a differently colored ribbon. Under the pressures of stage performance, he found that this visual cue allowed him to readily identify them by their tunings. The act that Cordell now described required two of these banjos set in complementary open chords. Uncle Dave stood the banjos up like ski poles and levered them back and forth, alternately striking them with a finger across the top of each neck. Uncle Dave moved the banjos like “a crosscut saw,” that Cordell characterized as sounding something akin to “Yink-Yawnk, Yink-Yawnk.” All the while, Uncle Dave’s accompanists, Sam McGee and Sid Harkreader, “kept time with him.”

Cordell could not only recount and replicate Uncle Dave’s banjo feats, but he could also musically reproduce Uncle Dave’s style. Before he met Uncle Dave in 1923, Cordell’s father and two of his uncles all played the banjo, and they had taught him his first picking techniques: thumb lead, two-finger style, and a brush pattern with the forefinger. Then, at age fourteen, Cordell’s musical imagination forever broadened when Uncle Dave performed near his home. The morning after that appearance, Cordell ventured over to the house where Uncle Dave had stayed the night. Before traveling to his next engagement, he responded to the youngster’s inquisitiveness. He demonstrated his three-finger triplet and his downpicking method, which Cordell called “knocking.”[43] Cordell absorbed both, putting special focus on Uncle Dave’s right-hand triplet.

At the time of our taping, Cordell was then in his early seventies, his playing filled with vigor. He performed entire songs not only with the

FIGURE 49. Cordell Kemp, Defeated, Tennessee, July 8, 1981. Photo by Stephen Wade.

right-hand styles his family had initially given him, but supercharged with Uncle Dave's rhythmic fulcrum. The triplet lent so much to his songs that it required Cordell to play only the barest of melodic outlines along the fingerboard to fully execute these pieces. He employed it in nearly everything we recorded, from Uncle Dave's "Chewing Gum" and "Death of John Henry" to Johnny Horton's 1959 hit, "When It's Springtime in Alaska

(It's Forty Below)." Cordell typically presented a limited number of Uncle Dave's songs in his public performances, amounting to some thirty minutes of material. As we worked through his favorites, he felt, at one point, a stiffening in his hands. We stopped the machine, and he ran his fingers through the sand outside his house. This loosened him up, he said, "just like grease." Then he launched into still other pieces from Uncle Dave. "He's my choice," Cordell said more than once that day. To the end of his life at ninety-six, that allegiance never wavered.

Cordell's wife, Olean Canter Kemp (1916–1999), who sang in a nearby Missionary Baptist church, followed a different model. Olean had absorbed a traditional style that was evident in her lyrics and through her singing. She had written "I'm Getting Ready to Leave This World," about the stillborn birth of one of their children. "It's a true story," she said, recalling the sorrow she felt for this infant boy.[44] Though this loss had taken place decades before, she had written the song only six years earlier. "It just come out," Olean explained, her singing epitomizing the strident nuances of her faith's gospel laments.

FIGURE 50. Olean Kemp, Defeated, Tennessee, July 8, 1981. Photo by Stephen Wade.

The difference between Olean's contained emotionality and Cordell's ebullience contrasts how an inherited idiom stands apart from a stylist working within it. A question that researchers Paul Oliver and Mack McCormick posed in their multi-decade study of the Texas blues ends with this distinction between tradition and the individual talent. Oliver called on modern linguistics with its terminology of *parole* and *langue* to identify the music and the players. "The *langue* tends to determine the appropriate structure for the particular idiom, the singer exercising his creativity through the *parole* of his own interpretation."[45] Olean Kemp communicated her song in keeping with the performance practice of her church, its *langue*. In a sense, she anonymously told her child's story. Focus more properly belonged on the message than calling attention to herself via *parole* with individual flourishes. Even as Cordell cheered her on, his praise chattering away as she sang other hymns that day, their contrasting musical personalities recall the question Archie Green had posed: How did Uncle Dave Macon receive tradition, and how did he personally transform it?

A clue lies in his spoken-word commentaries. Uncle Dave approached his recordings as multilayered performances. Instrumental overtures followed verbal set pieces that, in turn, preceded songs accompanied by percussive dance—all framed within a single side of a 78-rpm disc. He speaks, if only for a moment, on over 40 percent of his published releases, his remarks appearing on some sixty-seven sides. Many last only the length of a phrase, with Uncle Dave, like a conductor setting time with his baton, calling out a metronomic string of words that rhythmically fit the music that follows. On others, he offers personal salutes as in "Arcade Blues," or his dedicating "Put Me in My Little Bed" to his ten-year-old son, Paul.

Most notably, his extended anecdotes draw from printed and oral sources found in popular discourse. His invocation for "Death of John Henry," for instance, anticipates the song's lessons of courage and fortitude: "Listen, in every heart there burns a flame/For the love of glory or the dread of shame/But oh happy we would be if we understood/There's no safety but in doing good." This aphorism repeats a widely reprinted eighteenth-century couplet attributed to Alexander Pope. The quotation, subsequently expanded to four lines, found a far-flung life, appearing in a 1915 Winston-Salem, North Carolina, newspaper, much as it did three years later in a Winnipeg daily, submitted by a reader there as simply "some poetry."[46] Uncle Dave's son, Esten (1913–1993), a Church of Christ minister, writing a column in the Murfreesboro, Tennessee, newspaper in 1942, attributes the quatrain to Thomas A. Jackson, the humorist best known for *On a Slow Train through Arkansas*. Jackson collated from oral and newsprint sources to create his published collections, and his multiple volumes found a place in Uncle Dave's library at home. Like a freely floating lyric in folksong, these words circulated in the public domain.

Similarly, Uncle Dave's 1928 recording of "Worthy of Estimation," with its Gilbert and Sullivan-esque refrain—"Worthy of estimation/After long consideration/Of a great reputation/I'm presented to the nation"—reaches back to a long-standing comic conceit. An 1890 letter found among Uncle

FIGURE 51. Esten Macon, Murfreesboro, Tennessee, July 11, 1981. Photo by Stephen Wade.

Dave's papers, one that he wrote to a young woman during his courtship years, concludes with nearly identical words. This passage, as Paul F. Wells's research has shown, employs an epistolatory rhyme in print by 1800, called "A Curious Love Letter."[47] Wells found this humorous curiosity expanded and elaborated over the years—including a salacious version—appearing in English and American publications as late as 1880. I might add one more sighting to Wells's already rewarding checklist, this penned by English poet and wit, Thomas Love Peacock (1785–1866). Peacock embellished the conceit, which a twentieth-century observer then appropriated to describe Chicago's open-air speaker's forum known as Bughouse Square.[48] Between 1910 and 1940, the forum's heyday, soapboxers proclaimed their individuality to all within earshot. Peacock's verse captures the Bughouse ambiance with its leather-lunged personages competing for their listeners' coin:

After careful meditation,
And profound deliberation,
Of the various pretty projects
which have just been shown.
Not a scheme in agitation,
For the world's amelioration,
Has a grain of common sense in it,
except my own.[49]

These reworkings of "A Curious Love Letter" speak to Uncle Dave's creative handling of traditional material. As a young man he encountered the piece very likely through reading or possibly recitation. Then he incorporated it into his 1890 epistle to his sweetheart, and subsequently adapted it into "Worthy of Estimation," the song he recorded in 1928. By then he had created a melody to communicate the rhyme and heightened its effect by pairing his banjo with Sam McGee's banjo-guitar. Their closely meshed ascending and descending runs bind the whole into a tight melodic package. The chorus's wordplay offsets the five verses that Uncle Dave penned. In them, he preaches a pulpit message of earthly snares, the tree of life, and the lure of mass media. Among these warnings, he mentions a nonbeliever's susceptibility to suicide.

This juxtaposition of righteous behavior leavened by comic wordplay plays out repeatedly in Uncle Dave's performances. Throughout his career, both on stage and in the recording studio, he melded piety with earthiness. Stories abound of how Uncle Dave could shift registers in a single moment, going from moral allegory to unrestrained ribaldry. "He'd just come out there," his longtime accompanist Kirk McGee affectionately recalled, and at the start of a typical show:

> He'd sit there. Of course, he'd tell a story or two, you know. And I'd called it "selling hisself." The first thing he'd do was sell hisself to the audience, you know. Then anything he did was alright. He would talk some religion. That was the reason he got by with a lot of his stuff. They'd say, "He's a religious old man. It don't make no difference what he says."[50]

Kirk chuckled about this person he so dearly admired. "I thought he was the greatest man in the world, and I always did—as long as he was living. To me, he was the greatest entertainer."

As with his recomposition of "Arcade Blues," Uncle Dave repeatedly applied his capacity to personalize received material, spanning everything from biblical quotation to printed trifles to minstrel show banter. Another example of this creative process, let alone his reprising a whole strain of American frontier humor, precedes the ugly man joke he tells at the outset of "Sourwood Mountain Medley":

> Hello folks. I was walking down the street with one of the ugliest men I ever saw in my life. We passed a real pretty girl, and the ugly fellow said, "You see that girl smile at me?" "Well," I said, "Good Lord man, that's nothing. First time I saw you I laughed out right."[51]

Other familiar motifs abound in his recordings. Vexatious mothers-in-law appear in "More Like Your Dad Every Day" and "I'll Never Go There Any More." In the latter, he quietly puns that an overly talkative matron set on purchasing some fabric at a dry goods store needs "muzzling"—instead of muslin. He invokes the widely adopted boast about the "land of hog and hominy" to preface "Rise When the Rooster Crows," and reprises the archetypal conflict of country rubes and city slickers in "Rooster Crow Medley" and "All-Go-Hungry Hash House." "The Cross-Eyed Butcher And The Cackling Hen" draws not only from an existing popular song and a newspaper cartoon but a widespread comic anecdote. The butcher's assistant, variously cast as a Black character or else an Irishman, flees his post for safety's sake, strenuously avoiding a cleaver-bearing boss whose aim cannot be assured. In "Poor Sinners Fare You Well," Uncle Dave tells of a minister who announces from the pulpit that he has personal knowledge of a wayward husband seated among the congregants whom he would publicly expose if he fails to make a fit offering for the collection box. In classic joke lore form, the receptacle comes back brimming with multiple contributions, including one partial payment affixed to an IOU.

More serious contemplations also occupy Uncle Dave's preambles. He introduces the hymn "Walking in the Sunlight" by saying, "A man comes to this world naked and bare/He goes through life with troubles and care/He departs this life and goes we don't know where/But he'll be alright there, if he lives alright here." Although this quotation does not itself appear in Scripture, it serves, as one Vermont newspaper commented in 1902, as "a practical religion, a working religion, which applies to every day needs."[52] Similarly, his instinct to comment on daily conduct reaches from the sacred to secular and back again in "Comin' Round The Mountain" and "Whoop 'Em Up Cindy," both string band breakdowns. Here he summons his listeners and accompanists alike with "If you ain't right, get right." He launches both numbers with this axiom, while the directive itself stems from a motto that evangelist Sam Jones (1847–1906) famously delivered early in his ministry.

In May 1885, Uncle Dave, not yet fifteen, numbered among the thousands who attended the first of Jones's revivals in downtown Nashville. The excitement that Jones generated among his followers, documented in the city's papers and which included this quote, reached local steamboat magnate Tom Ryman. At first a disbeliever, his conversion at this multi-day tent meeting led to his underwriting the construction of the Union Gospel Tabernacle. Soon after his decease, the 1891 building became, at Jones's instigation, renamed the Ryman Auditorium. In 1943 the *Grand Ole Opry* took possession of the sanctuary, and from there Uncle Dave broadcast until his death nine years later.

He sometimes called one of the songs he performed on that stage "Tom Ryman," the piece better known as "Rock About My Saro Jane."[53] The laborers that Uncle Dave heard sing it—themselves former slaves or their immediate descendants—worked for Ryman's steamboat line only blocks away from the spot where he heard the preacher's call to get right. He became exposed to this musical evocation of steamboat life during the years Sam Jones first evangelized in Nashville.[54]

Lived experience likewise surrounds "Arcade Blues." The song's evolution from a commercially published work by a minstrel show performer that, in turn, derived its lyrics from Black folk culture points to racial attitudes that Uncle Dave both absorbed and transmitted. The son of a Confederate army officer, he lived in the segregation era, a period when popular music resounded with racial derogation. His discography includes numbers such as "Pickaninny Lullaby Song" and "The Coon That Had the Razor," just as others, like "Mourning Blues," bear verses equally heavy with race caricature. Songs like "Them Two Gals of Mine" (which he recorded at the same session as "Arcade Blues") and "Sassy Sam" emerge from blackface minstrelsy in all its vehemence. In "Bile Them Cabbage Down," however, he goes another step, at first using the racial epithet, but then performing unaccompanied in a Black vocal style. After commenting on his sense of displacement in an overwhelmingly urban landscape, specifically referring to New York's elevated trains, Uncle Dave likens himself to a solitary Black man bereft and alone: "He begin to sing: 'Lord, I wonder when will I ever get back home, get back home.'" "Got No Silver Nor Gold Blues," also a non-blues lyric song that he recorded within a year of "Arcade Blues," ends with Uncle Dave *eephing*, a form of mouth music associated with hambone percussion. His breathless vocalization, audible in his inflections when he chants "oph, eph, ekaph eith," captures another instance of his indebtedness to Black folk style.[55]

Even in that most burdened of his titles, "Run Nigger Run," Uncle Dave acknowledges the racial proximity that marked rural life below the Mason-Dixon line. He begins by saying, "Hello folks. Raised in the South among the colored folks and worked in the fields of toil with them all the days of my life, I will sing them good old Southern songs." This number, widely collected from traditional singers, both Black and white, tells of a fleeing slave. Uncle Dave's rhythmically compelling refrain, recalling the fluent motion of other chase songs he performed, whether human, animal, or locomotive-powered, counterbalances the lighthearted verses and his musicalized laughter. The song frames an escape from chattel slavery with merriment and mayhem. Uncle Dave's fleet banjo picking intensifies its ironic message, particularly during his movement down the fingerboard in which he jarringly implants a major chord redolent of minstrel practice, let alone Southern folk tradition, that employs this deliberate dissonance.[56] Yet behind the precedents that have shaped this piece—in print since 1851—lies the interracial music that Uncle Dave embraced.

At the same Birmingham, Alabama, venue where he performed the prototype to "Arcade Blues," Uncle Dave also played "Run Nigger Run." In announcing the addition of both titles to the show, he told a local journalist, "I picked up my banjo playing from the darkies who used to work for my father."[57] Here he referred to his childhood years when his family still lived in the countryside and before they moved to Nashville as hoteliers. Similarly, in a June 1928 article, titled "My Life and Experience" that he penned for Brunswick Records, he mused how one listener, thinking him a Black musician, wrote, "'You must be one of the most wonderful old negroes in the South.'"[58] Years later, in what has become a widely cited remark, Virginia blues guitarist and singer John Jackson, himself African American, thought Uncle Dave to be a Black performer. "But what about Uncle Dave Macon?" he asked in 1965.[59] Uncle Dave drew from a folk storehouse that John Jackson associated with an earlier style.[60] DeFord Bailey, Uncle Dave's longtime friend, radio colleague, and the *Grand Ole Opry*'s first Black performer, had a name for that repository: "black hillbilly music."[61]

This body of music—cross-culturally shared dance reels, ballads, and lyric songs—comprised "a common stock."[62] In a slim, insightful 1970 volume titled *Blacks, Whites and Blues*, which highlights Uncle Dave Macon, along with his contemporaries who recorded in the race and country music categories that record manufacturers began marketing in the 1920s, music scholar and discographer Tony Russell identifies the Black hillbilly music that preceded those commercially motivated divisions. "The bearers of tradition are not purists, but eclectics," writes Russell. DeFord Bailey (1899–1982) gleaned from his grandfather, Lewis Bailey, an ex-slave fiddler from Smith County, Tennessee, a repertory that included "Fox Chase," "Old

FIGURE 52. Joe Thompson, Mebane, North Carolina, Nov. 3, 1987. Photo by Stephen Wade.

Joe Clark," "Old Hen Cackle," and "Lost John." All of them identify widely known numbers that he passed on to his grandson, and all of which predate the blues. Of this admixture of dance breakdowns, fiddle tunes, ditties, badman ballads, display pieces, chants, lonesome songs, and hollers, "Everybody around me grew up playin' that," DeFord recalled.[63] "They weren't playin' no blues then."

Sometimes called "regular old-time country music," or else simply, "old-time country music," terms used by Black rural musicians Turner Foddrell and Joe Thompson well into the 1970s, this legacy permeates Uncle Dave's recorded work.[64] The tradition informs his plaintive "Oh Lovin' Babe," no less than his exuberant "Railroadin' And Gamblin,'" whose melody suggests a variation of "Shortenin' Bread" and whose content touches on the administration of justice in the post-Reconstruction years. The pre-blues style, with its seemingly asymmetrical timing that creates its rhythmic feel, animates Uncle Dave's handling of breakdowns such as the "Rooster Crow Medley" and "Wouldn't Give Me Sugar in My Coffee," as it does his reworking of the blackface minstrel song "When Reubin Comes To Town." The Black-originated "Over the Road I'm Bound To Go," which tells of a prisoner's escape in the Jim Crow era, is another pre-blues, contemporaneously recorded by Cannon's Jug Stompers as "Feather Bed," and subsequently adopted into bluegrass by Flatt and Scruggs.[65] Their titles notwithstanding, neither Uncle Dave's "Backwater Blues" nor his "Got No Silver Nor Gold Blues" has the conventional twelve-bar blues pattern.[66] Instead, their melodic contour reflects the older corpus, each invoking a chase motif. "The great quality of the common stock," Tony Russell writes, "was adaptability; its great power, assimilation; it was neither black nor white, but a hundred shades of grey."[67]

Uncle Dave's Black-influenced banjo playing dates back to the beginning of his recording career. As mentioned earlier, "Skillet Good and Greasy" was the first song he recorded (he also re-recorded it in 1935), let alone the first he reportedly played on the *Opry*, and one that he continued to perform to the end of his life. The piece is a one-part reel, a structure not uncommon in Black folk practice, and particularly apparent in banjo songs from the Jim Crow era. Its lyrics, too, align with other chase motif songs, just as its deliberately flattened notes carry a blues tonality common to them all. When Uncle Dave slides along the banjo's third string and then drops away vocally to let his playing complete the line, his instrument at that point mimics his lyrics.[68]

This practice reiterates an African American and ultimately African folk aesthetic. A fellow Tennessean and near-contemporary of Uncle Dave's was Black banjoist Will Slayden (1878–1965), who lived near Memphis in the western part of the state. Independent of one another, the two not only employed the intonational effect like that heard in "Skillet," but performed at least several songs in common. Uncle Dave's playing technique resonates with Slayden's throbbing right-hand rhythm, which one of his neighbors perceptively called the "drag-thumb" style. They further shared the call-and-response merging of banjo and vocal, and what David Evans identified as Slayden's "overall percussive quality."[69] Recordings of other

Black, Tennessee-based banjoists from Uncle Dave's time—Nathan Frazier, Murph Gribble, and Gus Cannon (particularly in the latter's demonstrations of his earliest playing)—fit here too. All these musicians drew from a collective fund of songs and tunes, an older repertory of reels and proto-blues, and performed them in ways not interchangeable but stylistically conjoint. As DeFord Bailey said, "The Black and the white all wanted to hear the same tune."[70]

Like "Arcade Blues," "Skillet Good and Greasy" appears in print and on recordings that also point to that era's Black/white musical interchange. In 1909, folklorist E. C. Perrow published a version of "Skillet" called "With a Chicken on My Back," that he remembered from the singing of mountain whites in East Tennessee. In 1913, he printed it alongside of two Black versions from Mississippi, also documented in 1909.[71] Perrow's student Arthur Palmer Hudson, who became a major collector himself, published in the same journal in 1926, "I'm Going to Make It to My Shanty Ef I Can," a version that a schoolchild in Panola County, Mississippi, sang.[72] John W. Work III included "Goin' Keep My Skillet Greasy" in his 1940 collection of Black music largely gathered in Nashville.[73] The first Black recording of the song appeared in 1927 as "Shanty Blues" by Uncle Dave's label mate, the songster Henry Thomas, otherwise known on his records as "Ragtime Texas."[74] In 1930, the Mississippi Sheiks contributed their "Bootleggers' Blues." A 1942 field recording of Sid Hemphill, made near Sledge, Mississippi, has him playing it on the fiddle and singing, while accompanied by his Mississippi-born banjoist Lucius Smith, drummer Will Head, and guitarist Alex Askew. Hemphill performed a text that echoed the one that Arthur Palmer Hudson's source, who had lived in that same area, had earlier provided.[75] John Lee Hooker's riff-centered 1949 performance of "Rabbit on the Log," with its slowly building drone and gradually unfolding variations, unmistakably locates the piece within this body of old-time country music played in Black style.

Meanwhile, white Ozark singer Almeda Riddle (1898–1986) sang "Mandy," contributing new lyrics that she wrote with her nephew, a professional hillbilly musician, fiddler, and banjo player based in California. He sang it over the air, she estimated, between 1935 and 1950. Riddle pointed out that in this song, "You can make up all the verses you want to. Uncle

Dave Macon used to sing that 'Grease Your Skillet.'"[76] Just as Uncle Dave's version included "Mandy" as the name of the narrator's girl, Riddle's rewrite underlines her sense of the song's malleability. Implicitly, she is also saying that vernacular Black social music possesses this versified freedom.[77]

Uncle Dave himself wrote a variant of "Skillet" that he titled "My Money Matters Easy." He printed it alongside the earlier song in his 1938 songbook. Unlike the original, which addresses food, its scarcity, and its theft, the newer song advises thrift. After the narrator touts his railroad stocks and bonds, a meal of sirloin steak, and the choice of owning a Buick and a Cadillac 8, he asserts, "If you 'spect to live on honey/Then you'd better save some money."[78] This rewrite offers not just a one-to-one comparison but a case in point of the recompositional impulse that Archie Green perceived throughout Uncle Dave's work. In turn, Uncle Dave proceeded from traditions and forms that invited creative license.

• • •

In July 1924, when Uncle Dave first recorded "Skillet Good and Greasy" in New York, he brought with him the fiddler, guitarist, and singer Sid Harkreader (1898–1988). Sid recorded four pieces with Uncle Dave during that four-day session, either as a singer or as an instrumentalist. "Fiddlin' Sid," like Uncle Dave, came from Middle Tennessee. He had been raised in the Cedar Glades community between Murfreesboro and Lebanon, an area dotted with farms and cabins amidst the cedar thickets. In the years of Sid's youth, a sizable Black population had settled there along with white, and a shared body of banjo and fiddle music had arisen. Drawn to play since childhood, Sid began learning old-time fiddle at age fifteen under Robert Knox, a Black laborer who worked on his family's farm. In his autobiography, Sid remarked on his feelings back then, "If I could just play like him, I would be the happiest boy in the world."[79]

Sid's passion increased with his skills, and he "left the farm at twenty and never went back to farming."[80] He arrived in Nashville at a time when live radio was becoming established. Stations naturally wanted to broadcast music of interest to their listeners. On WDAD, that included the barn dance sounds of the Tennessee countryside. Sid played on this station, which preceded WSM and its establishment of the *Grand Ole Opry*, and soon numbered among the first of Nashville's musicians to quit his day job and pursue country music professionally.[81] In 1923, Sid met Uncle Dave at a downtown barber shop, where they began playing together. By the following year, the two began an association that reached from schoolhouse

FIGURE 53. Sid Harkreader at his apartment. Nashville, Tennessee, ca. 1971. From *Fiddlin' Sid's Memoirs: The Autobiography of Sidney J. Harkreader*, JEMF Special Series No. 9, 1976.

performances throughout the countryside (one of which Cordell Kemp attended) to making extended forays on the Southern vaudeville circuit. Those early audiences heard Uncle Dave Macon introduce "Fiddlin' Sid" as his son.

In August 1979, I visited Sid Harkreader. With wiry energy that coursed through his thin, stooped frame, Sid Harkreader belied his eighty-one years. For nearly an hour, Sid stood up and played a seemingly free association of tunes and key changes that summoned his stage-lit nights as a performer. Starting with "John Henry," he sailed through "Alabama Jubilee," commenting just after it, "A good one, ain't it?"[82] His numbers went from "Tip-Toe through the Tulips" to "I'm Looking over a Four-Leaf Clover" to "Amazing Grace" to "Red River Valley." Sid, whom Charles Wolfe characterized as more an interpreter than a creator (and also as a self-styled crooner), began his career on the *Grand Ole Opry* as a featured "display fiddler."[83] He specialized in audience-pleasing numbers arranged for listening rather than dancing, a talent he thoroughly demonstrated now. He moved quickly through his tunes, sometimes singing a verse, his foot tapping on the linoleum of his East Nashville senior citizens' apartment. He played with a reedy tone, sprinting from waltzes to sentimental songs, rags to minstrel numbers, popular hymns to blues.

His seamlessness carried its own musicality, suggestive of his stage performances from years past. Apart from his appearances as Uncle Dave's sideman and the many recordings they came to make, Sid developed his shows, putting together, he said, "a 25-minute act," featuring his fiddle and guitar while he sang and told jokes.[84] In addition to his solo work in which he might play two different theaters in a single day, he led various bands, beginning with organizing a group in 1927. The troupe, billed as "Fiddlin' Sid and his Arkansas Charleston Dancers," consisted of six boys, including one female impersonator, all garbed, he said, in "overalls, red socks, checkered shirts, and patent leather shoes." The curtain would draw back to reveal Sid stationed on a tree stump playing the fiddle, before he switched to guitar to accompany his ensemble. In 1928, he toured with Oddie McWinders (1887–1933), a banjoist who later accompanied Jimmie Rodgers. McWinders would challenge their vaudeville house audiences. "Name your number," he'd call out, and he and Fiddlin' Sid would rise to the occasion. From scenes of bravado like that to this moment in his home, Sid Harkreader joyfully put his hands on all the tunes he could.

Of all the pieces Sid played in his apartment that day, he reserved his dance breakdowns for the longest treatment and none more so than his rendition of "Old Joe." In June 1927, he made the tune's first recording, a piece locally executed by Black performers that included fiddler Frank Patterson (who subsequently recorded it with Nashville street banjoist Nathan Frazier) as well as the Nashville Washboard Band. Harmonica player and band leader, Dr. Humphrey Bate (1875–1936), another *Opry* stalwart of Uncle Dave's generation, recorded the tune within a year. He credited his exposure to it, and others of its sort, to a former slave employed on his father's farm in Castalian Springs. The tune's melody, moving with gathered intensity from major to minor, reappears in "Whoa Mule," a Texas rendition as played by the oldest fiddler known to have recorded, Elijah Cox, an African American born in 1842. Apart from the recordings he made with Uncle Dave, "Old Joe" became Sid's most famous piece.[85] Perhaps he had this tune in mind when he ruminated, "Some of the people got my numbers." Though that influence yielded him no compensation, he added, "But I don't care. My material is known all over the world."[86]

Near the end of our visit, musician John Hartford, who took me there that day and backed Sid on banjo, asked him about the most recent song he had composed.[87] Sid quietly replied that he had written one about the *Opry* titled "It Seems Like Yesterday." Sid, who had appeared on the air playing his old-time fiddle even before the *Opry* began, had witnessed "the first country music was ever thought of. I was right there." Of the *Grand Ole Opry*, "It'll go down in history, I guess, as long as the world stands."

It made sense, too, that Sid sent us away to carry on a historical expedition. We asked him about the Broadway House hotel where Uncle Dave reported his first learning the banjo. Sid replied:

> Broadway hotel is where Sterchi Brothers is. That's where Uncle Dave learned to play the banjo, in the basement of Sterchi Brothers. Circuses put up at Broadway House, and had the basement to rehearse in. That's a true story, and he told it about a thousand times. See, I traveled with him for about twenty years.

While we weren't certain if the present-day building that housed Sterchi's furniture store had been rebuilt, including its basement, we did venture there that afternoon. We implored the manager to let us go down into the basement on our subterranean quest. If surprised, he graciously granted us access for our musical archeology. Sure enough, the basement offered a large, square rehearsal space worthy of a full-scale theatrical production. Just the place, too, for a fifteen-year-old boy to learn the banjo in 1885.

In a 1962 phonographic study titled *Traditional Music from Grayson and Carroll Counties,* annotator Eric Davidson detailed a marked change in that region's fiddle and banjo music.[88] Within the first years of the twentieth century, this area, which lies in southwest Virginia, began shifting from its former self-sufficiency as a farming community to a cash economy. Newly built mills, coupled with the arrival of the railroad, spurred the establishment of the factory towns of Fries and Galax. One musical outcropping of that development arrived in the form of the guitar. The instrument, previously not part of local tradition, introduced new styles and repertory among its community-based players. According to banjoist Wade Ward (1892–1971), who grew up in Independence, Virginia, nearby, neither he nor his fellow players chorded or finger-picked the banjo before the guitar's introduction. Not until 1906, when Wade was fourteen, on a trip to Tennessee (a memory reiterated to me by his nephew, Sam Ward) did he witness up-the-neck banjo playing, another byproduct of the guitar and the music it invited. The adoption of the new styles, Davidson writes in a subsequent study, brought about "complete alterations of the melody, and the old harmonies, often based exclusively on intervals of fourths and fifths, were replaced by the I, IV, V7 chord structure the guitar is so well adapted to play."[89]

In Middle Tennessee, siblings Sam and Kirk McGee, who succeeded Sid Harkreader as Uncle Dave's accompanists, underwent a similar experience. Sam McGee, born in 1894 and initially a banjoist, reported not seeing a guitar before 1910. Kirk, born in 1899 and equally unfamiliar with the guitar in those years, initially credited his start in music to the repertory of fiddle tunes and ballads that their parents had shared. These handed-down materials coupled with his exposure to singing schools that he attended as a teenager. Sacred music publishers, many of them located in Tennessee, found a means to sell their paperback songsters by conducting summertime sessions devoted to harmony singing. Kirk later credited his interest in sentimental and religious songs to this early chord-centered, formalized training. But what struck the two brothers most profoundly came from their youthful exposure to a new Black music played on the guitar, this period when the blues emerged. This music stood apart from the earlier shared banjo songs, fiddle tunes, and dance breakdowns—themselves Black inflected and inspired—let alone the British-American ballads that together comprised the old-time country music that the McGees already knew.

In 1965, Jon Pankake, the Minneapolis-based co-editor of *The Little Sandy Review* and old-time music aficionado, talked with Kirk about this gulf that he and his brother felt when they first witnessed the songs and techniques of Black guitar-playing section hands and travelers passing through Williamson County, Tennessee. These men, who gathered at lunchtime at the country store run by Sam and Kirk's father, played music that stymied Kirk, oriented to a different musical grammar. "They didn't play much of anything, just fooled around," Kirk told Pankake. "You had to take it and make something of it."[90] Drawing on a McLuhanesque dichotomy, Pankake essayed that the McGees stressed the eye over the ear, themselves more accustomed to literate organization than aural improvisation. He notes: "In re-creating Negro music in terms they could understand, the McGees seem to have imposed their logical musical **forms** on the rhythmic and melodic **content** of the Negro music."[91]

Consequently, the McGees made sense of the new material by arranging it into movements drawn according to their own cultural maps. As far back as Sam's earliest solo recordings, made during an April 1926 session with Uncle Dave, both his "Buck Dancer's Choice" and "Franklin Blues" (followed several days later by his performance of "Knoxville Blues"), employ modular sections. "Franklin Blues," which bears no blues qualities in its structure or its sound, reflects "the genteel, cultivated urban guitar tradition" translated into a folk sensibility.[92] Sam runs through its sections with assertion and speed, leaving behind any trace of a delicate parlor style, much as he navigates "Buck Dancer's Choice," which, as his subsequent recordings have shown, includes added sequences that he could introduce or substitute at will. I know that when I played the tune for Kirk, he corrected one such passage, saying: "You do it. But it is."[93] For him, this was a set piece, and all the parts had to fit in a repeatable, orderly way. "Buck Dancer's Choice," like all their instrumental showpieces, reached Sam and Kirk via oral tradition, and their sound forever reflected that vitality.[94] At the same time, they reinterpreted these pieces in ways so woven together that the two brothers often sounded indivisible.

To the end of his life, Kirk upheld this structural ideal. His blues, paraphrasing David Evans, lacked the strident vocal qualities, repeated riffs, non-patterned picking, and improvisations that characterize Black folk tradition.[95] The McGees re-created newer blues and ragtime pieces in ways that they could memorize and repeat. Kirk bore out Jon Pankake's observation that of the Library of Congress's holdings of comparable white Southern folk musicians, the McGees stood apart from the guitar and banjo players it had documented before 1940. As professional musicians, whose talents combined with the influence of mass communications, the McGees went "beyond the borders of their inherited cultural environment."[96] They not only incorporated the Black influences they found in their youth but translated the broadcast sources increasingly available to them into a uniquely identifiable sound.

In July 1981, two days before serving as judge for the fourth annual "Uncle Dave Macon Banjo Picking Contest," a task that Uncle Dave's family asked me to undertake, I visited Kirk McGee twice.[97] Only months earlier, at age eighty, Kirk had completed a new album. For this 1980 record, *Mister Kirk, 54 Years of Country Pickin',* the title's number marked his tenure to date on the *Opry.* It featured his melodious voice and guitar.[98] While not an old-time music album per se, it consistently reflects Kirk's older orientation. With the help of his supporting musicians, he foregrounds his finger-picked guitar playing, a hallmark of the McGee Brothers, on nearly every track. He covered pieces like "Gulf Coast Blues" that Bob Wills, the Light Crust Doughboys, and Riley Puckett had previously recorded (and before that, Clarence Williams, Bessie Smith, and Fletcher Henderson).

Along with a waltz Kirk composed, and a remake of "Wheels" that he and his brother had previously done, he offers a version of "House of the Rising Sun," cast entirely in major chords, and revisits "The Tramp," a sentimental song published in the 1870s, that he and Sam McGee first waxed in May 1927 during a celebrated, four-day session with Uncle Dave. He reprises in "Mabel Clare," a love song in print by 1859, that he doubtlessly had performed with fiddler Arthur Smith in the 1930s. He plays a rag of his own called "Blues Come On In," and along with a country plaint that his eldest daughter wrote, he vigorously frails the banjo for his remake of Uncle Dave Macon's 1928 "Over the Road I'm Bound to Go." Amidst such variety, this all-acoustic album, which would be his last, might speak for Kirk's lifetime of musical expression.

During our concluding visit, as the telephone rang unanswered, Kirk demonstrated some of that individuality on his 1950s-era Gibson resonator banjo. Using a two-finger technique, wearing metal picks, and using heavy-gauge strings that could support his raising them a whole tone, Kirk elaborated melodies within and around chords. By this chord-melody approach, he played nearly everything in standard-C tuning, which, at pitch or tightened up a full step, gave him a bass note to make connective runs, a wide harmonic range, and melodic options that an open tuning, typical of older-style folk playing, might otherwise restrict. Like the ragtime banjoists on the Edison cylinder recordings (which he physically likened to "a cone") and to whom he listened as a youngster, he favored the diatonic, pianistic music they played, more than the pentatonic modes prominent in pre-blues and old-time banjo repertories. Those melodies he saved, instead, for his fiddle, which he approached with scraping, high-density velocity. But on the banjo, Kirk had even altered his instrument to reflect its connection to more emergent music. He had recut his banjo's bridge, widening its grooves to mirror the width between the strings of his guitar. This not only eased his fingering when he went from one to the other, but also reinforced his connection to the guitar's claim on modernity.

I remember, too, being struck by how Kirk sometimes played in flat keys on the banjo in his favored C-tuning. Earlier stylists like Uncle Dave would retune the entire instrument and ring out the open strings to match the needed intervals. Such players might also use a capo to suit their voices.

FIGURE 54. Kirk McGee and Stephen Wade, Franklin, Tennessee, July 9, 1981. Photo by Dianne Couves.

Kirk, however, didn't use a capo, but instead held down full chords to fit the key. Nor did he necessarily reset the drone string. Instead, he simply did not sound it, giving the effect of his playing a tenor banjo. When I asked if he had previously used that or a plectrum banjo, which arose in the Jazz Age, he replied, "I never had my hands on one. They're tuned like a mandolin though." Like Uncle Dave, he kept to the older five-string design for all his banjo needs. (In a January 1926 interview in Birmingham,

Uncle Dave wryly said, "Once a fellow asked me to play a tune on these here tenor banjos as he called it and I told him it would be like spooning with a gal with short hair—there wasn't no place to ketch hold."[99]) As a result, Kirk utilized a more modern, chordal vocabulary to perform most of his pieces and employed a more modern strategy to play them. He kept in reserve older banjo practices and repertory, employing the banjo's traditional downpicking technique for his Uncle Dave Macon numbers and those akin to it. He noted that this was not his primary style. In his words, "I never did a lot of rapping."[100] Even on "Old Joe Clark," the first breakdown he learned and one that his father had shown him in boyhood, Kirk performed it in his arpeggiated, chord-conscious, guitar-based fingerstyle.

Though only one generation separated them, with Kirk just thirty years shy of Uncle Dave's age, the two approached their music from different eras. Uncle Dave focused on single-line melodies that his three-finger playing ornamented, or else, with his propulsive rapping (that he accented with rolls dragged down across the strings), to create essentially solo performances that supported his singing. Through it all, he emphasized, much as Cordell Kemp demonstrated, his right hand in preference to his left. In Uncle Dave's older stratum of music, referring here to his pre-blues repertory, chords played a lesser role, unlike his newer pieces, many of which came from the religious revival hymns of that time. With them, he reverted to a chord-based approach. But as Glenn Stagner, his last accompanist in the recording studio, compounded by their four years of touring together, noted:

> He was at his best when plunking out tunes on his banjo and singing songs of his own composition. When he did venture a current-day hit, it was generally butchered, both in tune and words, until any similarity to the original was pure coincidence, but he suited it to his style and the audiences loved it.[101]

Kirk McGee took another route. He explained that his noting along the neck rather than his picking over the drumhead predominated. "This hand [the right] follows this hand [the left]."[102] He soon clarified the idea. Just after we played two duets—with him on fiddle and me on banjo, beginning first with the breakdown "Sail Away Ladies," followed by "Blackberry Blossom"—he suggested we try "Danny Boy." I followed the melody as best I could, but several measures into it, he stopped us short. Instead of just playing the tune, he suggested, "You could chord that." For Kirk, playing this music most effectively meant introducing chords and adding harmony. By doing so, he added, "You can work out a lot of stuff." This venturesome spirit, no matter the song, captured his eclecticism and his expertise. He added, "Now that would work on anything." Kirk's openness fit the changing music of his time. He was, in his heyday, a modern traditionalist, leaving the breakaway solos of the younger *Opry* musicians to their generation.

Near the end of our visit, Kirk asked me how I had learned. I mentioned my teacher and how, in part, he had learned from records, much as Kirk had done himself. I asked him, "Who were you mostly listening to?" He replied:

> Nobody. Back then, I just played the guitar after him [Uncle Dave]. I didn't pay a lot of attention to what he'd done. In that day and time, we didn't play with Uncle Dave much. All we did was rehearse the records before we went to New York and made them. After we got back, we didn't work with Uncle Dave too much.[103]

Evening coming on, Kirk played one more of Uncle Dave's numbers, a piece he knew that could no longer be performed, however fetching its melody. He didn't sing it, though its title, reaching back to blackface minstrelsy, said enough. His last words on the tape, quietly observant of the complexities that surround music in American life, equally conveyed his warmth: "I hope I hadn't done you any harm."

We walked to our cars—we had met over those two days at the Franklin, Tennessee, real estate office where Kirk worked as the face of his community's past—and he mentioned past road trips with Uncle Dave. He recalled long, frigid drives towards the next engagement, with curtains draped down the sides to keep out the cold. As Kirk spoke of bygone travels, we stood next to his late-model Cadillac where we stowed his banjo, fiddle, and guitar in the car's trunk. He watched with bemusement as the lid slid into place and electronically locked. In that moment, memory and modernity coalesced.

• • •

Throughout her life, Jewell Fagan Haynes (1914–2005) kept her hands on the tunes. A musician since childhood, for twenty years, beginning in

1932, she played as one of Uncle Dave's occasional accompanists, as well as spent, as she said, "five solid years" working with Sid Harkreader.[104] Now in July 1982, in her Murfreesboro home, she sat at her piano. Above her on the wall hung a picture of herself as a young woman standing between Uncle Dave and his son, Dorris. Beneath this fifty-year-old portrait taken in front of her parents' home, she began playing a dazzling array of pieces that Uncle Dave, Fiddlin' Sid, and Kirk McGee all knew. Looking back, she told one journalist, "I don't expect that old-time music will ever be played again like it was then. It was mostly music that folks could dance to."[105]

It seems stunning, though not surprising given who she was, that the day I taped her, she played continuously for two-and-a-quarter hours, going through each tune twice, each running slightly over one minute in duration. This enormous repertory she summoned fit her musical capaciousness. Shortly after, she wrote, "Hope you can make another visit in the near future, and we will make it an *All Night* Jam Session. Ha." A couple of paragraphs further down, she mentioned more tunes still: "Stephen, did we tape '8th of Jan.' or 'Soldier's Joy,' 'Chinese Breakdown?' I don't believe we did. They are all good numbers."[106]

Jewell Fagan Haynes grew up in a spot called Holt's Corner, a community near Chapel Hill, a small town in Marshall County, Tennessee. She was raised in a musical family, and in what amounts to a perfect encapsulation of the common stock inventory, Jewell said, "I was playing all types of music. My daddy played old-time fiddle and my mother played accordion. She played 'Casey Jones' and all those old pieces."[107] Her ten siblings all played, most of them favoring harmonica and guitar, and one, still alive at the time of our taping, steel guitar. "I've always loved music from a tiny little girl," Jewell said, having started on the family's pump organ.[108] Her father's fiddling was notable enough that their home became a way station for traveling *Grand Ole Opry* performers. In 1931, Jewell first met Uncle Dave Macon and Sid Harkreader playing at a nearby schoolhouse. They stayed overnight with others, but on the return trip, which Jewell marked down as May 7, 1932, Uncle Dave and Dorris Macon headquartered at the Fagan home, this time for a week. "Of course, he was playing schools at night, but we would play during the day."[109] When her family, led by her father's fiddling, joined in, she added, "We'd just have a roundup."

FIGURE 55. Jewell Fagan Haynes with Uncle Dave Macon and Dorris Macon, Murfreesboro, Tennessee, 1931. Courtesy of Jewell Haynes.

Two months later, at age eighteen and wearing a new dress her mother bought her for the occasion, Jewell appeared on the *Grand Ole Opry* with Uncle Dave and Dorris. The three of them subsequently appeared multiple times on the show. Once, she recalled during a performance they played "Bully of the Town," one of Uncle Dave's favorites, and he "rode" three times around the piano, strumming the song on his banjo as she played it on the keyboard.[110] She commented on how much he and Dorris embraced the piano with the old-time breakdowns. The joyfulness of their collective music making extended to others of his favorites: "She'll Be Comin' Round the Mountain," "Turkey in the Straw," and "Golden Slippers." Later numbers also figured in their performances, like the 1929 march "Down Yonder" (which later became a *Grand Ole Opry* standard for Jewell's friend and fellow pianist, Del Wood), and Dorris, she remembered, especially liked her rendition of "Dill Pickles Rag." As a trio, they took repeated requests for "Skillet Good and Greasy," "Late Last Night When Willie Came Home," and "Shall We Gather at the River," all Uncle Dave hits. In her journal, she identified fifty-three school auditorium programs they played, in addition to doing multi-day runs for a Tennessee-based theater circuit.

She described a similar pattern during her stint with Sid Harkreader, with whom she worked both as a duo and as a member of his larger band: "We played at a hundred schools, courthouses, theaters, and two-week square dances."[111] Along with Jewell and sometimes a second fiddler, the "Fiddlin' Sid Harkreader Band" included his brother, the one-armed banjo player Emory Martin, and Robert Lunn, "The Talking Blues Man."[112] As Jewell put it, Lunn, nationally known for his spoken-word performances set to his guitar, "would talk his pieces off." Audiences frequently requested "Soldier's Joy," "Sail Away Ladies," and "Bill Cheatum," all country classics. She left no question either about how closely she knew Sid Harkreader's music. Her spirited rendition of "Old Joe" perfectly matched his fiddling. Afterwards she said, "Learned it note by note from Sid."

Before raising her family, Jewell made her living as a musician, her repertory solely focused on playing old-time reels, rural ragtime, and favored hymns. Her style, like other pianists working in this idiom, derived from a pianistic adaptation to the fiddle. Jewell initially learned from her father's playing, and accordingly, emphasized her right hand, picking out the tunes much as he had done on his violin. Often during our taping, she would start with the melody, and then a few moments later, introduce her left hand, adding a chorded, rhythmic drive. She uniformly kept a bright pace, and during her second pass through the tunes, might add a trill or triplet. She always kept the melody foremost. In "Alabama Jubilee," for instance, one that I was then just learning, she said, "Just listen and pick it out. [It has] just so many crooks and turns. [Go] down half a note. Same notes, then it goes back." Next, she played "St. Louis Blues" and "Memphis

Blues," followed by "Music Box Dancer" and "Maiden's Dream." I mentioned "Fisher's Hornpipe." She stopped and said, "My daddy used to play it, years and years ago." I started it, and for a few bars, Jewell stayed entirely silent. Then she dropped into it, in complete possession of the tune. In her own "Jewell's Blues," she described her high octave triplet as playing the "small notes," those she afterward explained as written above the staff. An inventory of her titles reads like the scrapbook she kept of *Opry* musicians, a photographic roll call of persons she had known, all of whom have made an enduring mark. These included DeFord Bailey, Arthur Smith, Ernest Tubb, Minnie Pearl, Del Wood, Earl Scruggs, Lester Flatt, Red Foley, and Charlie Louvin. Much as their names have stayed in public memory, Jewell's seemingly fathomless songbag of tunes and rags has largely stayed in tradition. This continuity reflects a choice that players and listeners have freely made, or as Charles Seeger has written, "by currency among the people, and by a process of aging and adoption."[113]

From the pump organ of her childhood to the microphones of the nation's premier country music broadcast, Jewell Fagan Haynes transmitted a body of breakdowns and show pieces passed from her parents, minstrel numbers and frolic songs adopted by Uncle Dave, and rags and blues that flourished in her youth. She numbered among the few instrumentalists of similar background versed in these styles, despite the widespread presence of pianos and organs in Southern homes and churches due to the rise of mail-order houses and rural free delivery in the early twentieth century. Just as record producers in the 1920s abjured Black country music and the shared repertory it represented, wanting instead to promote the newer, proliferating (and racially targeted) blues, they similarly consigned the piano to cosmopolitan salons and jazz emporiums. The idea of regular old-time country music played on pianos, with sparse recorded exceptions, veered away from the conventional imagery for this idiom, even if it conflicted with the record buyers' own experiences. For Jewell, those marketing assumptions played no role at all. She remained unstoppable, devout in her music. For her, it was personal. When she went on engagements with Fiddlin' Sid and Uncle Dave, sometimes the venues they booked had no piano, and in those instances, undeterred, she substituted on guitar. Though she never recorded with either of them, she kept to her pursuit, harboring nothing but praise for them both. As she told one reporter years later, "the Macon family was like [my] own family."[114]

• • •

In August 1979, during the same week I saw Sid Harkreader, I went to the Nashville Arcade, a visit prompted by my interest in Uncle Dave's "Arcade Blues." After nearly sixty years since Charlie Keys first sold Uncle Dave's record within its ornate gallery of shopfronts and store windows, it seemed that wherever I looked, individuals lingering there met my gaze, each with something forbidden for sale. Informal signals designed to veil prohibited activity passed between buyers and sellers in a sad and gritty rough trade. In the quiet bustle of this downtown landmark, the tacit knowledge and unceremonious communication that Uncle Dave had once discerned, continued. This Edwardian-era place of business, of merchants and retailers, was also a center for trafficking. In "Arcade Blues," with its sorrowful theme, Uncle Dave created a work that reflected the experience of the Arcade. So little had changed. The song felt timeless.

Two days before meeting Fiddlin' Sid, I drove out to Uncle Dave's closest and longest accompanist, Dorris Macon (1910–1982), at his home in Woodbury, Tennessee. With companions John Hartford, his fiancée Marie Barrett, and Dave Macon III, Dorris's grand-nephew (and a terrific banjo player), we spent the afternoon with this fifth of Uncle Dave's seven boys. Dorris made no secret as to why his father had enlisted him as his musical companion. With an initial offer of five dollars a day and all expenses, Dorris served as their driver. Uncle Dave, he explained, would otherwise turn the wheel in the wrong direction, as if pulling the reins of his mules. As for his dearth of musicianship—his skills limited to uncomplicated guitar and secondary vocals—when Dorris said to him, "Pap, I ain't good enough," Uncle Dave countered, "I'll get you by."[115]

They started in a 1928 Ford Model A, but soon acquired a 1929 design, thankfully equipped with a manifold heater to warm themselves across the miles. In the years that followed, Dorris drove continuously, managing essentially everything on their road trips but the music and the bookings. He described their going, for instance, immediately after the Prince Albert Show, a late-hour Saturday night *Opry* segment sponsored by the tobacco company, and then driving through to Atlanta to make a Sunday matinee. The day after that, they performed in a town four miles outside Fort Bragg, North Carolina. They did all this, he said, traveling the "old winding roads" of that pre-interstate era. Long into the Depression, they went on tours where they worked every day, playing shows for an hour and fifteen minutes each, without public address systems or air conditioning. "Rough times then," Dorris said, speaking more of the communities they played, than of themselves. He mentioned how in Eastern Kentucky, the two would draw crowds by "selling lots." By that he meant they performed in towns where people's homes were being sold off due to bank foreclosures. The lots marked where the houses stood. He remembered the crying of the women and the fact that "there wasn't no money." He also told of theater shows held in gilded vaudeville houses, featuring four acts nightly with the Macons as the headliners, and Uncle Dave doing his "trick tunes" on his banjos. Dorris recounted someone once calling out, "Uncle Dave, you're the first monkey ever I saw play the banjo." Uncle Dave laid his instrument down and replied, "Brother, I want to thank you. That's the first compliment ever I received from an ape before in my life." Dorris concluded that "you strike all types in this work."

That led to the last of his stories. He mentioned matters of dressing room security. Dorris recalled the theft of Sam McGee's famous Martin D-28 guitar. He said that Sam "got to inquiring around," and called one or another of the shops at the Nashville Arcade, leaving its serial number, just in case. The following week someone came in with the guitar. The clerk recognized it as bearing Sam's number and got it returned to him. Dorris shook his head in disgust, speaking of the thief. "Wanted $25.00 for it, that's all he wanted. They'll do anything. You can't tell me nothing. I learnt the hard way."

Words of blues researcher Robert "Mack" McCormick come to mind. During a 1994 visit at his home in Houston, we were talking about Uncle Dave Macon and the pre-blues tradition, when he said, "Folklore is facts floating anonymously, reflecting social attitudes."[116] Mack's observations spoke to the disquieting realities of the Nashville Arcade. Folklore took place there in the unspoken signs sent between dealers and users, pimps and johns, and back again. In contemplating Uncle Dave, Mack pointed out the difference between the best versus the representative. Now he asked: "Which really tells about the culture?" Then he said, "Macon reflects, but does not represent the culture." Uncle Dave's exceptionality set him artistically apart. Mack had found over the course of his musicology, first in one of Houston's wards, and then in counties across the state, the need to "find the predominances," to pay attention to average players as much as to the music's most notable exponents. He made another equivalency of an amateur high school play set alongside a professional Hollywood movie. Some of American culture, he explained, is "represented by Duke Ellington, some by Ernest Hemingway, and some by street singers." Just as recipes shift and language works when "everyone is a participant," Mack viewed culture as a map of "all the things that tie human beings to a landscape."

Tunes work this way too. Jewell Fagan Haynes and Sid Harkreader joyfully drew from their boundless stores to play and perform. Cordell Kemp took what he learned from Uncle Dave and passed it along to all who visited. Olean Kemp would sing in her church as she would for those who sat with her on her porch. Others have taken these materials to share among themselves, and sometimes to enter contests. A few, like the McGee Brothers, crafted a singular body of work transmitted on broadcasts and recordings, while some just stayed home, like Blue Ridge banjoist Wesley Sharp, who chose, he said, to "play only for his own amazement."[117] All have put their hands on the tunes. In "Arcade Blues," Uncle Dave revisited that process anew. He drew from tradition, his playing an amalgam of stage entertainment with home-learned music. There, as in his other songs, he took from pre-existing forms, his words and melody fitting these precedents, as he built upon them. Patterns within this song were familiar to his listeners. Perhaps the uniqueness of his performance, the song's starkness or the specificity of his banjo playing kept it from wider adoption. Yet with other songs of his making, listeners rewarded his creations in the way of folklore. They added his titles to those they already knew, and in turn, those performances found new life. A tune has so many people in it.

·10·

Folksong Street

Shortly before America entered the Second World War, a 1941 phonograph album titled *Smoky Mountain Ballads* went into print and helped shape a new audience for folksong. This compilation, edited by folklorist John A. Lomax, consisted of ten previously issued titles drawn from Southern string band and song traditions. Recorded between 1930 and 1938, these selections had earlier appeared on Victor records, primarily on its Bluebird label, whose "Old Familiar Tunes" series specialized in white rural music. In keeping with the recording industry's emphasis on the music's domestic roots, this anthology included three songs from siblings Wade and J. E. Mainer, two from the Carter Family (husband, wife, and sister-in-law), and one each from the Monroe Brothers and the Dixon Brothers. The remainder came from the regionally popular Skillet Lickers of north Georgia, as well as *Grand Ole Opry* stars Uncle Dave Macon and Arthur Smith, the latter two hailing from middle Tennessee. Lomax had chosen these songs with the assistance of his son, Alan, who, the year before, had completed a State Department survey of 3,000 commercially issued discs of American folksongs, identifying 350 among them as most "representative."[1] In spring 1939, the younger Lomax, then employed at the Archive of American Folk Song at the Library of Congress, concluded:

> My opinion is that the commercial recording companies have done a broader and more interesting job of recording American folk music than the folklorists and that every single item of recorded American rural, race, and popular material that they have in their current lists and plan to release in the future should be in our files.[2]

This statement marked a changed consideration of folksong. Since 1923, rural American music had systematically begun appearing on phonograph recordings, yet many professional folklorists, including the Lomaxes, had not initially recognized the documentary value of what the commercial enterprises had created. These records, produced for monetary ends rather than scholarly ones, could not possibly be sources for true folksongs, they believed.

Smoky Mountain Ballads was designed to reach an audience that Victor executives now sought to attract: urban, educated, and interested in but not largely familiar with grassroots material.[3] John Lomax's liner notes bear the kind of effusive prose that commonly framed folk materials for consumers more accustomed to *belles-lettres*. Lomax speaks of his 300,000 miles of hunting for folksongs "in their native lair . . . I have wandered for days 'Way out West where the antelopes roam.'"[4] Touched by the "freedom and abounding life" that he found in mountain hollows as well as the prairies and lowlands, he summons the poem "Invictus" to characterize the mountaineers and their songs: "Here is the master of his own soul, the captain of his fate no matter what ills betide. . . . His songs reflect . . . the environment of freedom—far removed from the sordid . . . crowd." Howard Taubman, reviewing the album that August in the *New York Times*, saluted Lomax, calling his notes eloquent, and observed how these performers happily lacked the sophisticate's inhibitions of "self-conscious or pious restraint." The album "brings us folksongs of our Southern mountain people with unquestionable authenticity."[5]

Not long after, Woody Guthrie wrote a review of *Smoky Mountain Ballads*. His single-spaced, five-page response, partly handwritten and partly typed, begins with a cheerfully self-deprecating comparison.[6] He observes John Lomax's role as the album's editor, and as such, his picking out of particular songs primarily for having liked them. Guthrie opines that he might be called an editor too, for the same reason, admitting that he just would have taken longer if given such a task, as he liked so very many records. He had heard all these recordings when they first appeared on disc, and now he poetically recalled his contact with them. In Wade Mainer's "Riding On That Train Forty-Five," for instance, he said it possessed "something rock bottom about it." During its fiddle break, Guthrie hears the instrument "squall off like a lost engine on a blizzardy rail," adding, "You'll feel in your bones the spirit of the men that build, run, and ride the railroads, from cushion to the reefer hole." He expresses reservations about only one selection, Arthur Smith's "Chitlin' Cookin' Time in Cheatham County." Although based on "When It's Peach Pickin' Time in Georgia," Guthrie identifies it as a version of "Old Joe's Barroom," splicing the old melody to new words. While he praises the recent lyrics, he criticizes its style, feeling it sounded labored, "like a good guitar player and singer taking his first nine steps toward Hollywood or Broadway." But Guthrie ultimately applauds the piece, adding, "It shows you, too, that the rural people have got a pretty good knack of taking citified music and overhauling it to suit their selves. (Lots of times it needs it)."

In 1964, RCA Victor reissued *Smoky Mountain Ballads* with six additional selections and notes by scholar Ed Kahn. With a clarity that long marked his work, Kahn called attention to previously neglected questions neither asked nor possibly even pondered when the musicians first made those recordings. For example, no one had seemingly queried the musicians on the origin of their songs or how these artists had learned them. But Kahn, while teaching at UCLA, wrote that he and his students "are actually trying to see how this music is a reflection of society."[7] Kahn pondered how "the musical culture, which apparently had been relatively stable for a generation or more, respond[ed] to . . . alien ideas and different forms of musical expression" that arose with the new media of phonographic recording.

Collections like *Smoky Mountain Ballads,* and those that followed its precedent, would in time find new admirers and acolytes not just for the music but the musicians themselves. For now, the music would appear, as Woody Guthrie wrote, among "people that work in the crowded towns, live in the nickel bus lines, thunder along with the street cars—and wish for a taste of the clodded dirt."[8] Ed Kahn's queries can be extended into questions about how urbanites, bearing divergent traditions, translated folk values according to their experiences and institutions. A case in point arose in the salon of journalist Lloyd Lewis (1891–1949), a nascent record collector in Chicago, and his companions. What happened there, years before *Smoky Mountain Ballads* emerged, represents a movement of folk expression, in Archie Green's words, "from its base in enclaved societies to acceptance within mainstream culture."[9] With *Smoky Mountain Ballads* as a harbinger of so much that followed, folklore and folk music reached from the front porch to the concert hall and back again in new ways.

In 1917, journalist, editor, and historian Lloyd Downs Lewis began hosting folksong gatherings at his home. During his boyhood in Pendleton, Indiana, he had experienced occasional contact with traditional music. Raised as a Quaker in advantageous circumstances, Lewis encountered several "North Carolina uplanders" who worked as farmhands for his family.[10] He recalled how those outdoor laborers "had sung many ballads, most of them westerns, 'Jesse James,' 'Poor Dying Cowboy,' etc., etc." Lewis then wrote that he had also begun making summer trips to northwest Colorado, where he "learned a lot of cowboy songs from sheep-herders and wild-horse wranglers." The first of those visits began around the time of his 1917 music sessions. While these contacts launched his exposure to folksong, other intimations of this interest had surfaced early in his life.

Among the items housed in the Newberry Library's collection of Modern Manuscripts and Archives are some books Lewis assembled during his schoolboy years. In what appears to be a common practice of the time, he took previously existing volumes and cut and pasted new pictures onto the old and now bulging pages. His chosen illustrations range from his cartoons to newspaper photographs of some recently widowed first ladies to an illustration he found in an issue of *Popular Song Illustrated*. The latter shows the figure of Uncle Sam, the outlines of his face conforming to the shape of the United States, looking sadly down on the Southern Hemisphere, personified there in a female shape. Her hands clasped, she looks sadly up at him. Meanwhile, a gnarled figure identified as "Congress" stands in a boat heading menacingly towards Panama, demarking the thinnest point between the two land masses. Congress clutches a handsaw, poised to sever the continents. Uncle Sam, meanwhile, sings to his Southern counterpart, "Good-bye Darling, I must leave thee." If the child is the father to the man, Lloyd Lewis's magazine clipping not only foreshadows his interest in popular song but also anticipates his later retellings of history. Repeatedly, Lewis's mature body of work—his books, essays, and newspaper articles—shows a love of the idiomatic and idiosyncratic. As his friend Carl Sandburg said at Lewis's funeral, if his writing could be criticized, it would lie in the complaint that "he overcolors." However, Sandburg added that that capacity allowed Lewis to "take an ordinary or drab affair and give it the colors to make it interesting or memorable."[11] One might say the same for folksong in its portrayal of social events as human drama, admitting different literary standards at play.[12]

Following adolescence in Indiana, Lewis attended Swarthmore College, where he served as editor of the school's newspaper. In 1913, he graduated and became a reporter for two years at the *North American* newspaper in Philadelphia, before coming to work at the *Chicago Herald*. After a year's service in the Navy, chiefly in the Philippines, he returned to Chicago. Lewis worked as a publicist for the Balaban and Katz movie chain and, in 1930, moved from drama critic to sports writer, and eventually to his final post as managing editor of the *Chicago Daily News*. Over those years, Lewis, an outgoing man remembered for his warmth and catholicity of interests, became a confidant of an array of leading writers, artists, politicians, and sports figures. A number of his closest friends, like Carl Sandburg, were associated with the Chicago Literary Renaissance. From these contacts he established the Newberry Library's collection of modern manuscripts now named in his honor—a rich panorama of the local luminaries of his time and place, the preponderance of them representing, as did he, Midwestern life at that time. In 1945, he retired from his editorial post at the *Daily News* to concentrate on historical writing, which by then included his 1929 *Myths After Lincoln*, as well as his 1932 biography of General William Tecumseh Sherman and his posthumously published study of Ulysses S. Grant.

His work also included the 1929 *Chicago: The History of Its Reputation,* with Henry Justin Smith, and *Jayhawkers*, a three-act Broadway play he completed with Sinclair Lewis in 1935. He died of a heart attack in April 1949.

Lewis confined his singing to his informal gatherings. Early on, poet Carl Sandburg and song collector John A. Lomax numbered among his guests, both of whom first met at Lewis's Dorchester Avenue apartment. Other invitees included John T. McCutcheon, the renowned cartoonist/illustrator; Alfred George Wathall, arranger and composer for the WGN radio orchestra; Elizabeth Carpenter Marshall, niece of composer John Alden Carpenter, who was a composer herself as well as contralto singer; and Charles Farwell Edson, an opera-trained bass vocalist, song composer, and actor. Together they played shaping roles in the first major popular collection of the nation's traditional music. That is to say, using their written arrangements, or through songs they shared, they variously contributed to Carl Sandburg's 1927 landmark publication of *The American Songbag.*

A year before the book appeared, John T. McCutcheon passed along a song he had learned from locals during a visit to his Nassau vacation home. Called "The John B. Sails," it subsequently became known to millions as "Sloop John B." "Time and usage," the cartoonist presciently wrote, "have given this song almost the dignity of a national anthem."[13] In an undated but contemporaneous reply, Sandburg, having integrated his thoughts into the song's headnote for the forthcoming volume, told McCutcheon, "I think you know every last one of my intentions about it [the song]. Your eloquent and whimsical note about The John B. Sails watches [over] that strange song."[14]

Sandburg's collection of 280 songs, reaching from early colonial settlement to the twentieth century, possessed what the poet called "strips, stripes and streaks of color . . . rich with the human diversity of the United States."[15] Well-received in its day, and still in print, it became a truly popular collection, its settings meant for singing more than scholarship. Sandburg's musical sources included not only fellow visitors to Lloyd Lewis's home but literary colleagues, including Robert Frost and H. L. Mencken. He used other sources as well. These included his days of boxcar travels and IWW labor organizers, as well as a prolific, Brooklyn-based publisher of nineteenth-century paperback songsters and the enormous collection of

FIGURE 56. Lloyd Lewis and Carl Sandburg, Chicago, ca. 1952. From *A Tribute to Carl Sandburg at Seventy-five.* Ed. by Harry E. Pratt, special edition of the *Journal of the Illinois State Historical Society,* Jan. 6, 1953.

"Old Songs That Men Have Sung," assembled by Robert Winslow Gordon, who was soon to become the first head of the Archive of American Folk-Song at the Library of Congress. Sandburg celebrated each of the entries with affectionate synopses about his sources and the songs, so many of which, like "The John B. Sails," have since become standards. As Sandburg wrote with characteristic charm in its Apologia, "It is a book for sinners, and for lovers of humanity."[16]

Lewis, described by Sandburg in those pages as "a man of sterling integrity and many devices," contributed both entire songs and stray verses to the collection.[17] John Lomax introduced other favorites, such as "Frankie and Albert," "The Boll Weevil," and "The Buffalo Skinners" from Lewis's singing sessions. Sandburg's assessment of Alfred Wathall, an English-born musician and Northwestern University faculty member who wrote many of Sandburg's songbook's harmonizations, might speak for all these friends of the folksong: "He knows what is verandah and what is ashcan in the realm of music and can mingle them with effective contrast."[18] Privileged culture and grassroots expression came together in Sandburg's book, as they did among these visitors to Lloyd Lewis's.

From among Lewis's guests a core group emerged, convening both at his home and at his weekend retreat in the Indiana dunes. It consisted of Lomax, Lewis, and Sandburg, along with two others: Tom Peete Cross and Alfred MacArthur. Cross (1879–1951) was an expert in early Irish folklore who initially brought Lomax into this fold. He worked as a humanities professor at the University of Chicago. Earlier, Cross, along with his then-classmate Lomax, studied Shakespeare at Harvard under George Lyman Kittredge's direction. Kittredge had recently completed the final volume of Francis James Child's renowned ballad study. Lewis described Cross in his June 1940 letter to Lomax as "the most interesting talker about folklore I ever knew; has more information about legends, myths and folk sayings."[19] Lewis similarly characterized publisher Alfred MacArthur, brother of philanthropist John D. MacArthur, as "a hard-fisted Scot," adding that like the rest of them, he "couldn't sing a note in the conventional way." Furthermore, Lewis noted, "MacArthur was, and is, as you know, one of the best of all tellers of stories that have a native tang."[20] Lewis also mentioned Sandburg's song gathering "from all the sources that the cultivated musicians scorned," in addition to his collection of legends about Abraham Lincoln.[21]

In 1940, Carl Sandburg separately addressed Lewis's interest in folklore. For the second edition of Lewis's *Myths After Lincoln*, Sandburg recounted in its introduction those years in the 1920s when they both first labored on their respective Lincoln-era studies: "Friend Lewis found himself nourished and rested by reading hundreds of books about the War of the 1860s and its leading characters, following at the same time a parallel course of reading in folklore, mythology, and myth making."[22] Lewis viewed Lincoln as a living individual who came to fit long-standing traditional patterns, demonstrating how he became America's first "folk-god," surpassing Washington, Jefferson, and Jackson in the national imagination.[23] Comparisons to Buffalo Bill and Jesse James (whose reputation as an American Robin Hood Lewis had learned of in song) arise here, too, in " the working of the old folk-fancy," as does the ignominy of John Wilkes Booth as "an American Judas."[24] Lewis credited Sir James George Frazer's *The Golden Bough* as inspiration for his understanding of these motifs. Lewis originally named his book *The Dying God*, after Frazer's fourth volume in the series, though ultimately he just used the title for the book's first section. Lewis also listed among his acknowledgments his friend Tom Peete Cross, "for the use of his immense and scholarly information on folk-lore and its examination."[25]

Thus Lewis spoke faithfully for this quartet of friends—Lewis, Sandburg, Cross, and MacArthur—when he told Lomax, "You met a set of men who were ready to recognize the authentic collector, the artistic characterizer when he came along."[26] They, in turn, all embraced Lomax as an emissary of folk expression. "Here we were," continued Lewis, "in a modern metropolis, all farm boys or small-town boys, and all getting a little sick of the efficiency, the mechanism, the culture of the big industrial cities of the 1920s." Lomax was valued as someone whose extended contact with native sources enabled him to knowingly reach "the sharp, often piercingly right note that gave the song character, made it descriptive, made it a picture of somebody."[27] Lewis amplified this enthusiasm by calling attention to a vocal turn Lomax yodeled at the close of "Git Along Little Dogies." Lewis recalled, "It was one of the damnedest pieces of transporting the imagination I ever experienced." He saw Carl Sandburg react similarly when Lomax sang "The Buffalo Skinners." A mesmerized Sandburg, reported Lewis, commented at its close, "'That's a novel—a whole novel—a big novel—it's more than a song.'"[28] Folk music, as Lomax represented it, brought Lewis and his friends a sweat-stained realism they both admired and idealized. Lomax, in turn, found their encouragement inspiring, and in his autobiography wholly credited this quartet for the undertaking of his second book, the 1919 *Songs of Cattle Trail and Cow Camp*.

By the mid-1920s, this down-to-earth aesthetic also led Lloyd Lewis and

Alfred MacArthur to begin collecting commercially issued phonograph records that featured folksong. Even though these recordings initially targeted the communities from which those artists originated, for Lewis and MacArthur, these "cowboy songs, rural songs, mountain music, hill-billy ballads" provided an antidote to the urbane arts and artists favored in elite society.[29] Lewis noted Lomax's support for their collecting efforts, adding, "you set us off hunting more." Nor did the significance of their record buying escape scholar Archie Green, who found in their efforts the earliest known report of "sophisticated disc collectors," outsiders appreciating and purchasing traditional music on recordings coincident with their release.[30] Others in those years who focused on recorded Black folk music included Abbe Niles, Guy Johnson, and Sterling Brown.

Some sophisticates of that time like Lewis and MacArthur were also encountering newly recorded, commercially issued, grassroots music. During an August 1923 camping trip with his friends Thomas Edison and Harvey Firestone, Henry Ford called on Jasper "Jep" Bisbee, a traditional Michigan fiddler related to one of the auto maker's in-laws. The visit shortly led to a recording session for the musician at Edison's laboratory in New Jersey.[31] Ford revered the social dancing of his youth and, in particular, the square dance fiddling that accompanied it, as epitomized by Jep Bisbee. As a result, the company sponsored a widespread series of fiddle contests in 1925 and 1926 that briefly became a national fad.

Another conduit from country music makers to cosmopolitan listeners arose in Washington, D.C., with the Hopkins brothers from rural North Carolina. Their father joined the Census Bureau in 1904 and moved his family to the Federal City. The Hopkins siblings were, by 1910, performing at a prominent downtown theater and subsequently broadcasting over Washington's radio station WRC. In 1925 they "gave hillbilly music its name," when they formed The Hill Billies, recording for the OKeh, Vocalion, and Brunswick labels.[32] Their listeners included President Calvin Coolidge.

For Lewis, contact with the folk went beyond just the music. The annual trips that he and his wife, journalist Kathryn Dougherty, took to northwest Colorado introduced them to working cowboys and herders. On the back of one photograph showing Kathryn with a lamb in her arms, Lloyd Lewis wrote, "150 miles from a railroad, 70 from a hotel, and had ridden mountain trails 12 miles on horseback to reach the sheep far up on the Rockies where they summer."[33] One of the herders at that encampment that the Lewises particularly admired was Oscar Collett, who, Lewis observed, despite being "withered and feeble, he survives because he uses his head incomparably. . . . Life in the wilds is simple and not difficult for him, one of the smartest men I ever knew anywhere."[34] Glossing another photograph, Lewis noted that Collett, who left the Mormon orthodoxies of his upbringing, had forged for himself a spiritual independence better suited to his circumstances. "He had asked the elders so many puzzling questions that the church was glad to see him leave it. There is in him the rationalizing humor of Benj. Franklin, Voltaire and Anatole France." In placing him in this august company, Lewis not only expressed his admiration of Collett, whom he termed "one of a vanishing type," but he revealed deeply held values of his own.

Among the photographs taken of Lloyd and Kathryn Lewis at that time, roughly between 1925 and 1930, two images show them outdoors in riding clothes, each of them, in turn, leaning back on a rocker set outside a rough-hewn, chinked log cabin. Theodore Roosevelt had sat in this very chair. In 1901, during the brief period of his vice-presidency for William McKinley, Roosevelt went on a hunting trip and visited this camp, the White River Ranch near Meeker, Colorado. Lewis, bearing that history in mind, modestly noted on the reverse side of his portrait that sitting there he felt like "a sparrow in an eagle's nest."[35] Roosevelt stood out for so many of Lewis's generation as a model of an educated adventurer, let alone a folksong appreciator—he famously penned the endorsement that opens John A. Lomax's 1910 *Cowboy Songs,* a book which Lomax dedicated to him. Though Roosevelt, like Lewis, lived distant from the world of Oscar Collett, he, too, admired individuals like this sheep herder, who exhibited skill and courage in the course of his daily work. This attitude anticipates, as well, John Lomax's invocation of "Invictus" in *Smoky Mountain Ballads.* There he connected the mountaineer's autonomy with the music he made, how, as captain of his fate, his songs possess "this feeling of freedom of independence" that "catch the spirit of Henley's poem."[36]

In 1947, Lewis assembled some of his past writings in *It Takes All Kinds,* a title he adopted from a weekly column he had penned in the *Chicago Sun*'s

FIGURE 57. Lloyd Lewis, White River Ranch near Meeker, Colorado, ca. 1925. Lloyd Lewis Papers, The Newberry Library, Chicago.

book section. Lewis received the name as a suggestion from his friend, the playwright Marc Connelly, who wrote *Green Pastures*, the Pulitzer Prize–winning 1930 dramatic work based on Black church life. Following Lewis's salute to Connelly on the book's dedication page, the entries, nearly all of them portraits of individuals, repeatedly cite folk experience as a key to personal character. He describes, for instance, Cordell Hull, who served as Secretary of State during the Roosevelt administration. Some years later, called to testify before a crowded congressional hearing, Hull stirs Lewis not only by his patrician bearing, but as a native son of Tennessee:

> On that . . . serene old face was the story of the Republic, a particular blend of idealism and backwoods cunning—the aquiline nose of Uncle Sam himself, the wide mobile mouth of the frontiersman, the heavy eyelid of the dreamer half hiding the steady eye which could look through a foreign aristocrat or drop a squirrel at 200 paces—either one.[37]

Lewis's approach brings to mind the words of Benjamin Botkin, writing in the introduction to his 1944 bestseller, *A Treasury of American Folklore*: "I have sought to give not only an American view of folklore but a folks-eye view of America."[38]

Elsewhere in *It Takes All Kinds,* Lewis includes his most extended writing on folk music, a profile of Carl Sandburg titled "Last of the Troubadours." Lewis had previously written an undated draft citing Sandburg's 1928 Phi Beta Kappa address at Harvard.[39] Lewis first develops a comparison between the poet's hopes during his college days to become a baseball outfielder and his subsequent guitar-accompanied poetry recitals. Lewis parallels Sandburg's musicianship to pitcher Grover Cleveland Alexander's control, noting their mutual deliberateness and wily precision: "Both men are grey and cunning, working with a minimum of effort and a rich economy of style."[40] He locates Sandburg's music at the core of his artistry, his guitar providing an even more profound means for its realization than his typewriter. Sandburg himself characterizes folksongs as "things that are authentic," having told his listeners that "these songs tie into the folk-quality that I have tried to get into my verse."[41] The musical half-hour with which he typically closed his lectures allowed Sandburg to share that undiluted quality with audiences. Sandburg added that whether he went on stage or not, he would sing these songs as a daily habit. For him they served a need that went beyond his public obligations. Driven by this commitment to his art, Sandburg stood out to Lewis as one who "wanders over the Republic spading out the people's songs and singing them back to them like revelations." Just as John Lomax had appeared in 1917 to Sandburg and Lewis as an "artistic characterizer," Sandburg brought his folksong portraiture to urban listeners outside folk society.

All the while, Sandburg sang idiosyncratically. Traditional singing practices did not guide his vocal style, as his phonograph recordings, beginning in 1926, show. His deliberative pace, instead, suited the individualistic persona and stagecraft he devised for his performances. He acknowledged gleaning his method largely from popular and classical singers. "'A song is a role,' Sandburg told Lewis, 'it must be sung with the whole body.'"[42] Both men enjoyed vaudevillians Bert Williams, the Leighton Brothers, and the team of Moss and Frye. Lewis elsewhere cites opera star Mary Garden as another model of the artistry they admired, while Sandburg noted Lewis's affection for Eddie Leonard's "Roll Them Roly Boly Eyes."[43] The two sang this stage number during their "sessions of song follies," mixing folksongs with show songs.

That Sandburg also received late-in-life personal guitar instruction from Andrés Segovia further reflected his non-traditional handling of traditional music. The two had met before in Chicago, but as Segovia wrote about his student, "His fingers labor heavily on the strings and he asked for my help in disciplining them. I found this precocious, grown-up boy of 74 deserved to be taught."[44] Sandburg reconnected with the maestro in 1950 during the time he worked on *New American Songbag*, which formed a counterpart to his 1927 tome. In the same passage in which Sandburg's friend, Harry Golden, cites Segovia's words, he also recalls how a photographer from New York's *Herald Tribune* sought a picture of Sandburg playing the guitar. On this particular visit, Sandburg lacked one and suggested they find a substitute, as he put it, "one battered and worn, such as might be found in a pawnshop." They made their way to Sixth Avenue and the shop owner suggested one he kept displayed behind glass. However, "the poet eyed this somewhat distastefully. 'Kalamazoo guitars,' he said, 'used by radio hillbilly singers.'"[45] Instead, Sandburg chose "a plain guitar with no fancy polish." In making this choice and in expressing scorn about hillbilly singers and their chosen instruments, he reprised an old notion about the purported purities of folk music. Ironically, at least one of those hillbilly singers, WLS *National Barn Dance* performer and eastern Kentucky native, Doc Hopkins, used to telephone Sandburg to gather additional historical information about various songs he performed on his broadcasts.[46] The role reversal implicit in those exchanges reveals the difficulty in the classifications of folk versus elite. Sandburg poses with a threadbare guitar, a sophisticate attempting to appear as one of the folk. On the other hand, Doc Hopkins breaks the stereotype, consulting one of the elite for information that sources like himself typically provided collectors like Sandburg. In the end, they both met their respective needs. Concerning Sandburg's style, his solo music remained unmistakably his own.

In the printed edition of "Last of the Troubadours," Lewis bears down on this singularity. While his earlier, unpublished draft explores Sandburg's repertory and how it changed, the final version centers on a 1925 dinner honoring author Sinclair Lewis. That evening, while performing for his fellow Chicago litterateurs, Sandburg sang "The Buffalo Skinners," which, as noted before, he had learned from John Lomax. Lewis describes the scene: "It was like a funeral song to the pioneer America that has gone, and when Carl was done, Sinclair Lewis spoke up, his face streaked with tears, 'That's the America I came home to. That's it.'"[47] Lewis praised the artfulness of Sandburg's singing: "You should have heard him sing the night he made Sinclair Lewis cry."[48]

Two years later Sandburg completed *The American Songbag.* In "The Buffalo Skinner's" headnote, he observes that "the words are blunt, direct, odorous, plain, and made-to-hand."[49] They fit, he explains, a distinctly American idiom. For him, "The Buffalo Skinners" evoked a disappearing national past.

Both Lewis and Sandburg were haunted by this consciousness of earlier times. In a 1936 letter to Gertrude Stein, Lewis mentions the current presidential campaign. He admiringly refers to Franklin Roosevelt's radio orations, "speaking via the air machinery."[50] Then Lewis observes, "New Dealism seems worldwide. . . . I'm too steeped in American pasts to understand Communism, but as a Jeffersonian, I feel Roosevelt is restoring the old agrarian civilization in so far it can be restored in the age of automobiles." Two years earlier, Lewis similarly explored this contrast between the industrial present and the rural past to characterize his Chicago friends and fellow singers: "John T. McCutcheon and Carl Sandburg have thrived by keeping their viewpoint essentially agrarian [rather] than Chicagoan."[51] In "Chicago and the Midlands," a 1934 magazine article he penned at the outset of the city's second century, Lewis focuses on the cultural divide between the abilities of downstate farmers and the ambitions of Chicago's go-getters, acknowledging the isolation resulting from mechanical farming versus the sociability of horse-drawn times, when "the miles between cabins were shorter than the inches between apartments."[52] With the passing of the "old, gone agrarian civilization," he noted, an alienated yeoman of the present day, "this scion . . . of the agrarians," will, at times, disdain an increasingly composite nation. "Its concentration of middle European races prompts him to salve his wounds with rumbled imprecations against Poles and Jews and Wops and Catholics and Hunyocks."[53] Without dismissing the achievements of modernity or the virtues of Chicago, Lewis's awareness of this cultural strife, of this divide between countryside and metropolis, brings to mind his far more benign letter to John Lomax in which he acknowledged his small-town beginnings and that of his friends, who had also come to the city: "We were ready . . . for the genuine folk music, and it seemed important, seemed nostalgic and natural when you sang it."[54]

At a May 1950 memorial luncheon, where some 800 assembled to honor Lloyd Lewis, Adlai Stevenson, then governor of Illinois and himself a habitue of Lewis's folksong gatherings, spoke effusively about his friend. He characterized Lewis as "American as apple pie and as midwestern as green corn. . . . When he talked . . . the past arose from a thousand graves."[55] Carl Sandburg's tribute, read by another on his behalf, closed the event. Not only did Lewis, he noted, stand out as the sole person in his life who could sing duets with him, but he was "many men in one and lived a life that comprised and encircled many lives."[56] For Lloyd Lewis, folksong provided a channel—genuine, natural, and nostalgic—to those lives.

His folk music gatherings lingered, too, in public memory. In 1951, *Chicago Tribune* columnist Will Leonard mentioned Lewis's evenings from a quarter century before when spreading word of banjo-picker Fleming Brown's newly organized Mid-West Folk Tune Society, and Leonard referred to the new gathering as an offshoot of Lewis's, "a similar attempt to revive the art of folk tune singing in Chicago."[57] Without mentioning Lloyd Lewis by name, but including a picture of Carl Sandburg and citing John Lomax and John McCutcheon among its participants, Leonard questioned whether Brown's new initiative would continue. He noted the passing of the earlier gathering, that "when the club dissolved so did Chicago's interest in the American ballad."

Will Leonard invoked a scholarly term, "the narrative ballad," to differentiate it from the "hillbilly lament or the cow country wail that clutters the air lanes today."[58] His attitude reiterated the undying trope that *real* folk music couldn't be commercial. This idea is reflected in John Lomax's praise for Sandburg's *American Songbag*, for its having "so few cheap tin-pan-alley maunderings. He [Sandburg] loves simple folk, and his instinct for their real product is uncanny."[59] Both commentators—Leonard and Lomax—failed to recognize in making these statements a deeper complexity about persons coming from within traditional culture. Leonard likened the narrative ballads, which he described as a form of public editorializing from a hundred years before, to modern calypso songs commenting on current events, including the daily gossip. But he did not connect this pattern to similar editorializing in American hillbilly songs that included decided opinions on everything from prohibition to the Scopes trial, from new Ford cars to presidential candidates Al Smith and William Jennings Bryan. Instead, he raised the specter of commercialism. Superior artistry belonged, instead, to canonically approved works of the past, in this case, various antiquities identified in Francis James Child's collection. Yet the capacity to absorb and reshape materials, whatever their age and origin, is a constant of folk creativity. John Lomax's *Smoky Mountain Ballads* collection proves that point. Innovation, as much as inheritance, generated its 1930s recordings and inspired its musicians.

Earlier, in the collegial gatherings that took place in the comfort of Lloyd Lewis's home, his guests, if born of the verandah, still valued the ashcan. As they offered their contributions to Carl Sandburg's *American Songbag*, they could also enjoy the phonograph records of cowboy songs and hillbilly ballads that Lewis had recently acquired. In the years to come, urban social progressives would discover similar homegrown sounds among rural tradition bearers, but with more clang, out on the streets of Chicago.

• • •

One Sunday afternoon in the fall of 1946, until rain followed by a chilly dusk sent him resignedly home, Raeburn Flerlage, director of Chicago's recently established chapter of People's Songs Inc., a socially progressive musical organization, visited the Maxwell Street market on the city's Near West Side.[60] Untouched by the Great Fire of 1871, this mile-square tenement district had long served the city's poorest emigrés. It began as an enclave of German immigrants, followed by Irish, Bohemian, and Italian arrivals, who, in a similar pattern, moved beyond its confines as their circumstances improved. Likewise, Greek and Romani communities followed their example, as did Southern Black, Mexican, and eventually Korean residents, each settling there for a time. Beginning in 1880, and for the next forty-five years, Eastern European Jewish immigrants, largely from Russia and Poland, formed the neighborhood's largest population. Early observers identified the community as the "Poor Jews Quarter," a name more widely translated in later years as "Jewtown."[61] Musician Benny Goodman, Admiral Hyman Rickover, CBS chief William Paley, and Justice Arthur Goldberg, as well as Lee Harvey Oswald's executioner, Jack Ruby, and con-man Joseph "Yellow Kid" Weil, all spent their childhood here. For their families and fellow residents, sweatshops serving the garment industry initially provided principal employment.

Despite the slum conditions of its workplaces, housing, and streets, Maxwell Street's central concourse, its open-air bazaar, thrived for 120 years. At its peak, it counted some "2000 vendors selling from stores, pushcarts, wagons and boxes," and by 1920, it had become one of the city's three principal shopping districts.[62] Even when its expanse shrank in the post–World War II decades—the community subsequently severed by expressway construction and its dilapidated buildings flattened by the bulldozers that City Hall and urban renewal commanded—street life buzzed with hawkers stationed on sidewalks, spieling like carnival barkers. "Pullers" collared passersby into their stores for fittings, while outside, shoppers found a profusion of tastes spilling from its food stands and butcher shops. A 1954 study estimated typical weekend crowds of 70,000 patrons seeking out bargains.[63] Until local ordinances permanently shut down the market following Labor Day weekend 1994, its legacy of Old World haggling long coexisted with New World hustling. At the time of Ray Flerlage's visit, he found an admixture of vendors, selling "everything from rusty nuts and bolts, alarm clocks and auto wrenches to Hershey bars and 51-gauge Nylons."[64] Amidst this bustling, makeshift scene, Flerlage came

FIGURE 58. Maxwell Street market, Chicago, Illinois, 1955. Photo by Mildred Mead. Hanna Holborn Gray Special Collections Research Center. University of Chicago Library.

upon something else too: a musical landscape that he called "Folksong Street."

On Saturdays and Sundays on Maxwell Street, from before noon to sunset, "you could make more money," remembered Muddy Waters's long-time guitarist Jimmy Rogers (1924–1997), "with three or four guys than you could make in a club for the whole week. Man, there'd be hundreds of peoples around . . . like Mardi Gras."[65] For scores of musicians like Rogers, Maxwell Street served as a hub for the city's blues scene. Rogers also lived in the immediate neighborhood, following the Chicago-bound route taken by members of his family who had journeyed there from Mississippi in the Great Migration. The skilled instrumentalist Flerlage identified in his "Folksong Street" article as "Jimmy Lane"—playing expert harmonica and guitar—was Rogers himself. He had yet to adopt the surname by which most came to know him. Moreover, the same "John Henry" whom Flerlage heard playing with Jimmy Lane that day was his bandmate John Henry Barbee (1905–1964), who, in 1938, had already made four sides for the Vocalion label in Chicago. Now, as they performed a jukebox number previously recorded by Big Bill Broonzy, someone in the crowd held aloft an amplifier, powered by a cord that stretched from the second-story window of an overlooking apartment. The listener, bearing the loudspeaker, turned around like a compass needle so listeners in all directions could hear Barbee and Lane.

Others whom Flerlage glimpsed that day included a blind couple who sang in a Southern twang, "struggling through the crowd, tin cup strapped to chest, banjo in playing position, yellow matted hair falling over shoulders."[66] Earlier still, he spotted an old man, "an ancient bard sitting on the curb . . . blowing into a battered harmonica, beating his own guitar accompaniment." As he played some Tin Pan Alley numbers, "an elderly midget, wrapped in a much worn Army coat," joined him for a Louis Armstrong solo that he rendered on a battered coronet. Then the bard grabbed a kazoo for "Easy Rider," followed by the duo combining choruses on "Sunny Road." Across all these moments, Flerlage witnessed music that appealed to the "well-dressed, poorly-dressed, dark-skinned, light skinned, in between skinned . . . light hair, dark hair, white hair, no hair at all . . . they stand and listen."[67] Only the day's rainfall and darkness dispersed the musicians and their fans.

Flerlage had gone to the market on Big Bill Broonzy's recommendation. Broonzy (1903–1958), the celebrated bluesman who mentored so many of the younger players then coming north to the city, and whose own career reached from fiddling for countryside dances to singing at Carnegie Hall, told him of "the folk singers who gathered . . . near the hucksters' stands on Maxwell Street."[68] One or another of these players, Flerlage surmised, might supply "talent for 'Hoots,'" the performer-led sing-alongs that formed a primary activity of People's Songs. Broonzy had performed at the first of these hootenannies (or *hoots*) since the branch's launch that September in Chicago.[69] Come mid-November, another locally hosted People's Songs hoot featured folk luminaries Lead Belly and Woody Guthrie. The two had traveled from New York and spent that evening, emceed by radio host Studs Terkel, performing alongside local folksinger Win Stracke, as well as Josh White, who had recently concertized at Orchestra Hall, also under People's Songs auspices. A letter Flerlage sent to Pete Seeger shortly after the gathering conveys the evening's energies, one attendee calling the hoot "the greatest party ever to hit Chicago."[70] Later that weekend, Guthrie and Lead Belly made solo appearances—their performances each only eight minutes long—at a mass meeting hosted by the Communist Party at the Ashland Auditorium. The event successfully drew 3,500, a thousand of whom, Flerlage estimated, had come there just for the two musicians. In the same note, he added that at least 200 would likely attend the next month's hoot, so much so "that looks like a cinch." From its founding, wrote Mike Scott in the *People's Songs* bulletin, "Chicago is full of people who sing songs of the people."[71]

The People's Songs organization, led by Pete Seeger and headquartered in New York, was formed at the close of 1945 to "create, promote, and distribute songs of labor and the American people."[72] Emerging in the wake of World War II, People's Songs Inc. (PSI) extended Popular Front sensibilities of the 1930s. Essentially a songwriting and song-disseminating venture that over its three-year lifespan published 315 songs in its bulletin and counted at its height two thousand members spread across the forty-eight states, PSI spliced folk-based music with progressive politics. It launched in the hope that these songs would serve trade unionists and their causes. People's Songs's organizer and editor Irwin Silber set this purpose in a personal context: "We believed that the world was worth saving and we could do it with songs. . . . We called the product of this union 'people's' songs—not exactly folk music, but directly in the line of succession."[73] Another guiding member, Alan Lomax, introducing the organization's 1948 songbook, noted,

> At first, I did not understand how these songs related to the traditional folk songs. . . . Slowly I began to realize that here was an emerging tradition that represented a new kind of human being, a new folk community composed of progressives and anti-fascists and union members. These folk, heritors of the democratic tradition of folklore, were creating for themselves a folk culture of high moral and political content.[74]

Lomax's comments reflect an ideal that sociologist R. Serge Denisoff termed "folk consciousness," a mentality that "motivated its adherents to present rural music as the genre of the urban proletariat; to emulate Okie attire; and to define middle-class intellectuals as 'folk singers' and genuine rural songsters as 'people's artists.'"[75]

Denisoff traced PSI's source to Southern strike actions of the late 1920s and early 1930s that included beleaguered coal miners of Harlan County, Kentucky, and textile millhands of Gastonia, North Carolina. Northern intellectual support coupled with radical organizing and unionization efforts in these locales coalesced around the plight of the strikers and the repressive violence they faced. Songs about these events from community-bred songwriter/activists such as Aunt Molly Jackson and Ella Mae Wiggins reached northern hoots and rallies. Years earlier, Industrial Workers of the World stalwart Helen Gurley Flynn predictively, if inadvertently, identified this arc. In 1915, she characterized the work of IWW songwriter and martyr Joe Hill as having "crystallized the organization's spirit into imperishable forms, songs of the people—folk songs."[76] In this pairing, writes Denisoff, Flynn captured "the entire ethos of . . . People's Songs."[77] By the time Woody Guthrie reached New York in 1940, his guitar soon emblazoned with a sticker that read "This Machine Kills Fascists," the spirit that would animate People's Songs Inc. was already present. For these musical devotees, the idea expressed by the Rebel Poets' 1928 motto "Art for Humanity's Sake," which emerged following the Sacco-Vanzetti executions, had not tarnished with age.[78] Irwin Silber's later observations about the spirit of those times point to three animating forces that infused People's Songs Inc. The first was the massive union participation of the 1930s and 40s, which included the role played by American communists (like himself) within the Congress of Industrial Organizations (CIO). The second was an ardent belief in interracialism. The third was the New Deal vision that culminated in Henry Wallace's 1948 Progressive Party's presidential campaign.[79] All these initiatives were celebrated by song performances and memorialized in their lyrics. In short, "The American Left adopted," writes chronicler Shelly Romalis, "folksong as a weapon for social change."[80]

Yet in 1961, founder Pete Seeger, looking back on People's Songs Inc. and its abbreviated tenure, acknowledged, "How our theories went astray! Most union leaders could not see any connection between music and pork chops . . . 'Which Side Are You On' was known in Greenwich Village but not in a single miner's union local."[81] The organization had fundamentally misunderstood, Denisoff explains, "the common sense world," that is, the musical preferences, let alone political drift, of most working-class Americans.[82] Still, Seeger noted that while unable to financially survive—the organization insolvent by spring 1949—its fervor did not abate. Urban-bred folk music performers like himself found new followers, not only from the hit parade success that his group, The Weavers, soon enjoyed, but in the years that followed through personal appearances at summer camps, college campuses, nightclubs, and concerts. In turn, many of those listeners took up guitar and banjo playing themselves. Politically charged, socially conscious songs tendered in familiar folksong styles and responsive to current events extended the People's Songs model. As Seeger wrote, "our theory about singing them in an informal and enthusiastic way was correct."[83]

The passions that Pete Seeger identified among this burgeoning city audience and their participatory ethic arose most prominently between 1957 and 1965, the headiest years of the Folk Boom. While that phrase, used interchangeably with the urban folk revival, denotes the popularity of folk music that ascended with the Kingston Trio's rendition of "Tom Dooley," its core ideals reached back to the time of People's Songs. Alan Lomax, writing in the December 1, 1946, issue of *Vogue* magazine, begins with this statement: "Nineteen forty-six will be remembered among other things as the year that American folk songs came to town."[84] Then he names several of New York's most prominent concert halls and forums, along with commercial films, radio documentaries, and record companies that had lately welcomed this material. A month later in the *New York Times Magazine*, he added to that list Disney cartoons, Benjamin Botkin's best-selling *A*

Treasury of American Folklore, and People's Songs hootenannies, then playing to "packed houses from Los Angeles to Manhattan."[85] That same month Lomax could have added, too, the Broadway opening of *Finian's Rainbow*, which included in its cast the celebrated roots musician Sonny Terry and People's Songs sponsoring board member (as well as writer of "Over the Rainbow"), Yip Harburg as its lyricist. Further downtown, at the New School, Lomax might also have mentioned a concurrent production of John Steinbeck's *Of Mice and Men*. The play included ballad singer Jared Reed, whose younger sister, Susan Reed, numbered among those named in the *Vogue* piece. At the time, she, along with Pete Seeger, Woody Guthrie, Lead Belly, Josh White, and Tom Glazer, all appeared on local stages, "with songs as old as Scotch heather and as new as last week's headlines."[86] That a high-fashion magazine like *Vogue*, and its equally elite counterpart at the *New York Times*, found this music worthy of mention only confirmed its growing acceptance among urban sophisticates.

Lomax wrote "The Best of the Ballads" as a guide for *Vogue*'s readers seeking Christmas gifts, and in particular, for those building their record collections. Prefacing his list of recommended folk albums, he enumerated four interpretative styles, beginning with traditional performers, the "unsophisticated singers" who fill the anthologies issued by the Library of Congress's Archive of American Folk Song, such as Vera Hall and Smith Casey.[87] Before naming eleven of these titles, he praised these performances for their intrinsic folkloric value. Then he cited commercial recordings as providing "a new sort of small-town folk music." These included people like Tex Ritter and the Two Gospel Keys. His third category, called "the city-billy ballad singers of the big towns," were those who sang in styles he thought most accessible to *Vogue*'s readers and who offered "the best repertories." Examples included Pete Seeger and Frank Warner. He closed with the "art singers," whom he deemed of least interest, including examples such as Conrad Thibault with his concert hall renditions of Ohio River roustabout songs. He considered such formalized performances, however suited for recitals, as lacking "the original earthy essence of country music." From this taxonomy he then identified the albums themselves, highlighting favored songs. In a few cases, Lomax pointed out where "an authentic folk song [appears] in a group of non-authentic folk songs." The latter category, while inconsistently applied throughout the whole, amplifies the value he placed on tradition. Yet Lomax did so without diminishing the newly composed titles. In his survey, both types coexist, much as did that era's folksong interpreters and the traditional artists residing in New York who shared concert stages alongside them and collaboratively played at the same hoots.

Raeburn Flerlage, then in his early thirties, encountered a similarly rich creative environment astir in the Midwest. Between March and June 1946, he conducted a sixteen-part series of free public lectures titled "The People in Their Music."[88] During those evenings, he explored different themes, using phonograph records as his examples, prefacing each with his commentaries. Flerlage explained that "to understand the culture of peoples of different national and/or racial origins, a knowledge of their culture—and their characteristics as expressed through that culture—is of tremendous importance."[89] Timely discussions of Jim Crow segregation, political freedom, protest, insurgency against dictatorship, prison life, and the "heartlessness" expressed in some folk balladry dominated his presentations.

Flerlage used recordings of city-based folk performers much like those Lomax had identified in his articles. Flerlage called them "interpreters of this music," including examples from Lead Belly, Woody Guthrie, Josh White, Burl Ives, the Almanac Singers, John Jacob Niles, and Richard Dyer-Bennet, supplemented with records by Billie Holiday, Dorothy Maynor, Marion Anderson, Sonny Terry, the Golden Gate Singers, and Paul Robeson. In only a few instances did he draw upon American traditional music performers from outside the folk revival. At one point he played Kelly Harrell's 1926 Victor recording of "Bye And Bye You Will Forget Me," making special note of the plaintive fiddle that accompanies his voice calling it: "heart-wringing violin accompaniment that would do justice to a Mischa Elman or a Fritz Kreisler for beauty of tone and phrasing."[90] In praising it this way, he encouraged his audience to hear differently and expand their musical standards. In another program, a portion of which he devoted to the blues, he played Bukka White's 1940 OKeh recording of "Aberdeen Mississippi Blues," as well as Peetie Wheatstraw's "Sweet Home Blues," and Jazz Gillum's "Down South Blues." He presented them alongside artists familiar to his listeners, beginning with Langston Hughes reading one of his poems on the blues. A Bessie Smith record she made with Louis Armstrong followed. Still, Flerlage never shied away from pointing out those performances more traditionally steeped than others, sometimes playing three recordings of the same song in a sequence, each bearing increasingly idiomatic traits. He differentiated them and separated those most rooted from those he deemed "over-polished."

Flerlage believed that musical appreciation of others encourages social acceptance. His selections spanned gypsy music to Count Basie and Paul Robeson performing a song about Joe Louis to a Bolivian folk dance. He included composer Roy Harris's works, cited Sandburg's *American Songbag,* played numbers from jazzman Sidney Bechet, presented an Indian raga, compared a Turkish oud rendition with a big band version of "Miserlou," and read aloud from the Lomaxes' 1936 book on Lead Belly before playing his "Goodnight Irene." Nor did he exclude a Moussorgsky composition protesting war. He featured, as well, recently recorded artists from afar: South African Josef Marais, Brazilian Elsie Houston, Romanian pan pipe virtuoso Georges Stefanescu, the Red Army Chorus, classical Chinese singer Wei Chung Loh, and flamenco vocalist La Niña de los Peines. Their records, reflecting the formal music of their lands as well as the traditional, enhanced, he said, "understanding of common goals, hopes, plans of all peoples—as well as of their resentments. The world will be a better place if the spirit of cooperation is deepened in us all."[91]

"The People in Their Music" series arose, Flerlage noted, at a moment when "folk-music and people's music in general were 'the coming thing.'"[92] In this postwar environment, he warned against "a narrow nationalistic use of folklore," a distortion still seared in recent memory that had marked the Third Reich's deployment of folk material. Flerlage read aloud from Meridel Le Sueur's 1945 *North Star Country*: "Folklore is the hieroglyphics of all man's communication, both obvious and subterranean, as he struggles with growing society . . . to create a place, a community, a nation."[93] On that same page, in his handwriting, Flerlage jotted a personal reminder to mention the songs "Casey Jones" and "John Henry" as illustrative of Le Sueur's thought, and then added Lead Belly's version of "T.B. Blues" (taken from Victoria Spivey) and Josh White's "Bad Housing Blues." He connected all these songs of labor and social protest, the last two addressing ghetto conditions and illness arising from that deprivation, to folklore's role in a democracy. As he had said a few days earlier at his first meeting, his script highlighted with marginal notes, "Basically, folk music is folk-lore SUNG—set to music—expressed musically."[94]

For his opening lecture, Flerlage invited author Jack Conroy to discuss folklore.[95] In his introductory remarks, Flerlage celebrated Conroy's openness to others, in particular his biracial collaborations. Conroy, who by then worked as a full-time writer and editor, had grown up as an industrial laborer. He had entered the workforce in adolescence and been raised in a Missouri coal mining community where Black and white miners worked side by side. A non-doctrinaire Midwestern radical, he had been the first to publish Richard Wright. He also co-authored with Arna Bontemps, who gained repute in the Harlem Renaissance, a sociological study of Black migration, as well as two children's books, each based on industrial folktales and shortly to go into print. Conroy's place of honor in Flerlage's series attested to the democratic principles he valued.

In a 1992 interview, Flerlage briefly alluded to a book that for him captured the People's Songs sensibility shared among its folk music followers. He referred to Chicago-based community organizer Saul Alinsky, who, in 1946, published *Reveille for Radicals*.[96] Its anthemic opening includes language that Flerlage soon reprised in "Folksong Street":

> The people of America live everywhere from Back Bay Boston to the Bottoms of Kansas City. From swank Highland Park, Illinois, to slum Harlem, New York. From the gentlemen farmers of Connecticut to the share-croppers of Arkansas. From the marble swimming pools of magnificent Bel-Air, California, to the muck of the Flats of Cleveland. From sooty Harlan County, Kentucky, to impeccable Bar Harbor, Maine.
>
> The people of America are Red, White, Black, Yellow, and all the shades in between. Their eyes are blue, black, and brown, and all the shades in between. Their hair is straight, curly, kinky, and most of it in between. They are tall and short, slim and fat, athletic and anemic, and most of them in between. They are the different peoples of the world becoming more and more the "in between." They are a people creating a new bridge of mankind *in between* the past of narrow nationalistic chauvinism and the horizon of a new mankind—a people of the world. Their face is the face of the future.[97]

Ray Flerlage's view of culture developed early in his life. A Cincinnati native raised in a middle-class home, he was exposed to a breadth of music available on recordings as well as broadcasts. He recalled during boyhood the nearby Covington, Kentucky, radio station that featured singer Bradley Kincaid, who, like others there, performed "country music or whatever you wanted to call it, folk music."[98] He also saw hillbilly singer/guitarist Riley Puckett perform in a suburban Cincinnati theater. The blind Georgian, he said, "brought lumps to the throats and tears to the eyes" of the assembled audience.[99] Flerlage was a feisty child not averse to physical altercation, and this led to a stricter Catholic schooling, despite his coming from a non-practicing Protestant background. He flourished in this more disciplined environment, and teachers there encouraged his literary abilities. Though he ultimately recognized that his talents did not mark him, as he said, "the new Thomas Wolfe at least," in 1938 he began writing "The Magic Groove," the first of his music columns.[100] He confessed that "I wanted to get a lot of records." He didn't limit his interests to folk music but equally embraced operatic and jazz performances. He found record companies willing to send him their releases in exchange for press exposure.

His writing led to personal interviews with Louis Armstrong, Paul Robeson, Marion Anderson, and Jarmila Novotná, and for two years he ran a series called "The Gramophone Society," where he lectured on classical music with phonographic examples. This work, which he described as "interpreting recorded music," landed him a reviewer's position at *The Cincinnati Post*.[101] That employment lasted briefly, and by then, married with two children and facing the draft, he interviewed at a nearby wartime aircraft plant. The job required him to lead the company's recreational employee music programs. There he encountered competing rehearsal slots assigned to the Black and white singing groups, with front office management dictating preferential treatment for the latter. This discriminatory policy repulsed him to such an extent that it marked a turning point, in which he chose, as a white man, to spend the rest of his life as a resident within the Black community: "That's where I first crossed over," he recalled in 1992, and "where I've stayed ever since."[102]

On leaving Wright Aeronautical in 1944, Flerlage resettled in Chicago, moving to its South Side, where he continued to write about music for local newspapers and national periodicals. His 1946 "People in Their Music" lectures gave rise to speaking invitations from other hosts in Chicago, one of whom had connections with the New York office of People's Songs. Word of Flerlage's presentations led, that fall, to his becoming the organization's first Midwest executive secretary.

At that time Flerlage was writing a monthly review titled "The People's Music" for the Farm Equipment Workers union. Tellingly, one of his first articles there bore the title "Music for Democracy."[103] He then began writing for *People's Songs* as well. In December 1946, Flerlage launched a column at Pete Seeger's suggestion called "On the Record."[104] It called attention to recent releases, and within its limited space, emphasized those city-based performers best known to the People's Songs audience, with albums by Josh White and Lead Belly frequently occupying his pen. He knowledgeably compared their new works to their past commercial releases, drawing attention to notable as well as lesser song

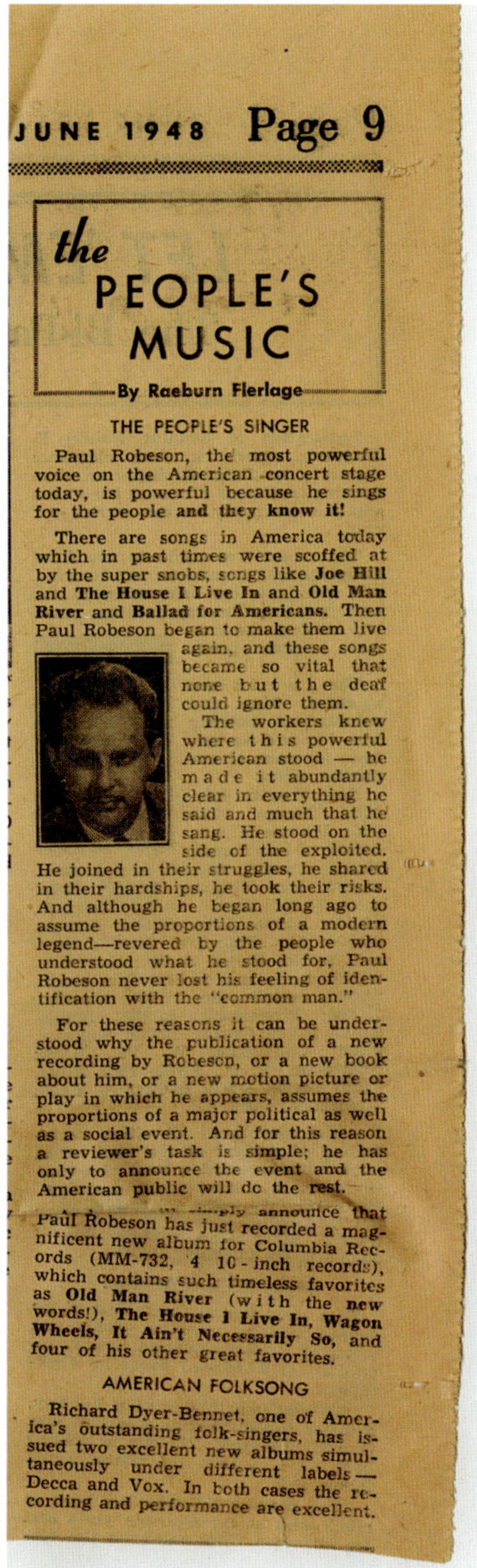

JUNE 1948 **Page 9**

the PEOPLE'S MUSIC

By Raeburn Flerlage

THE PEOPLE'S SINGER

Paul Robeson, the most powerful voice on the American concert stage today, is powerful because he sings for the people **and they know it!**

There are songs in America today which in past times were scoffed at by the super snobs, songs like **Joe Hill** and **The House I Live In** and **Old Man River** and **Ballad for Americans.** Then Paul Robeson began to make them live again, and these songs became so vital that none but the deaf could ignore them.

The workers knew where this powerful American stood — he made it abundantly clear in everything he said and much that he sang. He stood on the side of the exploited. He joined in their struggles, he shared in their hardships, he took their risks. And although he began long ago to assume the proportions of a modern legend—revered by the people who understood what he stood for, Paul Robeson never lost his feeling of identification with the "common man."

For these reasons it can be understood why the publication of a new recording by Robeson, or a new book about him, or a new motion picture or play in which he appears, assumes the proportions of a major political as well as a social event. And for this reason a reviewer's task is simple; he has only to announce the event and the American public will do the rest.

... announce that Paul Robeson has just recorded a magnificent new album for Columbia Records (MM-732, 4 10-inch records), which contains such timeless favorites as **Old Man River** (with the new words!), **The House I Live In, Wagon Wheels, It Ain't Necessarily So,** and four of his other great favorites.

AMERICAN FOLKSONG

Richard Dyer-Bennet, one of America's outstanding folk-singers, has issued two excellent new albums simultaneously under different labels — Decca and Vox. In both cases the recording and performance are excellent.

FIGURE 59. Raeburn Flerlage, newspaper clipping from his column, "The People's Music," *Farm Equipment Workers* newspaper, June 1948. Chicago History Museum, ICHi-189041.

performances. In the inaugural column, for instance, Flerlage writes of Josh White, admiring his modernity and musical ease, "although Josh's stylized approach is obviously not genuine 'folk singing,' it is highly effective."[105] Here, as in his lectures, Flerlage remains aware of White's homegrown origins, from his traditional music background to his fully developed cosmopolitan style:

> Josh White might serve as an example for almost any other folk-singer, since he combines technique, understanding, showmanship and most of the other good qualities of a folk-singer. If he could dispense with a few of his occasional affectations, and carry a little of the raw roughness and naturalness of Lead Belly, we'd have the perfect folk-singer. But when have we begun to expect perfection of anyone?[106]

This favored folksinger theme dominates his reviews. In Flerlage's next column, which appears in the same issue as "Folksong Street," he lists "the best material now on records."[107] Nearly all of the thirty-eight albums he names (in addition to noting the Library of Congress's series of folk albums) represent what he terms "People's Songs Artists." He includes *Smoky Mountain Ballads* among this list. Even with its traditional contents, it, too, represented a product intended for the city audience, though he noted that it had lately gone out of print. The following month, April 1947, on a page that includes the lyrics to May Day songs intended for union rallies, he discusses Lead Belly, Earl Robinson, and Paul Robeson along with a current album of Josef Marais's South African songs of the veldt. If that roster formed a familiar litany of artists, Flerlage introduced something else into the discussion. He writes, "Let's not overlook the 'singles.'"[108] He names some recent blues releases from Big Bill Broonzy and Josh White, artists well known to People's Songs followers. But then he identifies others familiar to the Black community more than to folk revivalists: Blind Boy Fuller, Big Maceo, Sonny Boy Williamson, Jazz Gillum, and Lonnie Johnson.

In calling attention to these performers and their songs, like the players and music he witnessed at Maxwell Street, Flerlage recognized they served a different constituency and reflected another aesthetic. He brought this awareness to the next month's issue, in which he focused on two more efforts that operated along this divide: the new American folksong series on the Decca label, and two new releases from the King label, headquartered in Cincinnati. In the latter, which he subheads in bold type as "Discovery," he notes how readers of *People's Songs* "might not ordinarily run across" products from this label. Indeed, Syd Nathan's King Records long served blue-collar audiences from among both country and western and rhythm and blues listeners.[109] Flerlage is citing Western Swing performer Ocie Stockard's "OPA Blues" and J. E. Mainer's "John Henry." Stockard sings in rhyme a series of complaints stemming from oversight failures by the Office of Price Administration, which leave "no bottoms on my shoes," a wife who has fled their straitened circumstances, and the steep costs he finds at the grocery counter. "The [OPA] 'Blues,'" writes Flerlage, "is the kind of protest number you might expect to encounter in the Bulletin, and the 'John Henry' is a good folksy warbling of the old perennial."

In contrast to these hillbilly performances, Flerlage focuses most of the column on the nascent American Folk Music Series, recently undertaken by Alan Lomax. Its first release, titled *Cowboy Songs and Negro Spirituals*, featured Carl Sandburg. The 1947 album includes a full-sized "Sing-Along Book" with words, musical notation, and guitar chords to augment the eight songs found on the set's four ten-inch records. Decca's archives, says the album's brochure, written presumably by Lomax, brim with "hundreds of records of country singers," country singers ranging from the Southern mountains to the Spanish Southwest, from Black sources to Louisiana Cajuns. "These rare records—collectors' items, gems of American folk song that can never be recorded again in the same way—will be released in the American Folk Music Series, alongside of new recordings of the best ballad singers of today—singers like Burl Ives, Josh White, Richard Dyer-Bennet, and Carl Sandburg."[110] Flerlage applauds the new undertaking but is restrained in his praise of Sandburg's vocals.

Related folk music anthologies proliferated during that time. For the June issue of *People's Songs*, an unsigned "On the Record" column—the author I take to be Flerlage—names eleven albums whose publication began in 1942, issued by the Library of Congress. "In this reviewer's opinion," the columnist writes, "these records are incomparably more valuable than practically any commercial album."[111] In the following issue, Professor Mary Elizabeth Barnicle chronicles "The Death of Harry Simms," a Kentucky strike song written by miner/singer Jim Garland, which, by then, had

FIGURE 60. *Listen to Our Story* album cover, 1947. This copy belonged to Fleming Brown, one of the first albums of this music that he acquired.

become known to New York folksong listeners via his balladeer sister, Aunt Molly Jackson. It concerns the February 1932 murder of twenty-year-old labor organizer Harry Simms. Garland was walking by his side when two local "gun-thugs" felled the unionist. The shock of this assassination and the ballad that emerged became one of the building blocks of the People's Songs movement. Garland's song opens, "Come and listen to my story, come and listen to my song/I will tell you of a hero that is now dead and gone."[112] In 1935, Alan Lomax recorded Aunt Molly's performance for the Library of Congress, and now, twelve years later, Lomax adapted its opening stanza as a title for a new collection of previously issued Brunswick records, by then transferred to the Decca label's ownership. The title was *Listen to Our Story*.[113]

Under the banner "American Folk Music," the July-August column announces the album's release without actually naming it: "If you're one of the folk-music fans who have long been unable to get Victor's 'Smoky Mountain Ballads' (a Lomax compilation of pre-Acuff hillbilly recordings) you will want to trot right down and buy a similar album compiled from old Brunswick masters by Alan Lomax."[114] The collection indeed formed the successor to its Victor antecedent, now including Black as well as white performers. It also includes two numbers by Uncle Dave Macon, as well as performances from Buell Kazee, Furry Lewis, Dock Boggs, Bascom Lunsford, Reverend Edward W. Clayborn, and Dick Rinehart. Lomax, in his introductory essay, writes:

> The country people, the small townfolk, bought their records and others like them, by the thousands, recognizing in these singers members of their own cultural family. . . . If you wish to hear such music today, you will have to go to the folklore collections or into the backwoods of the South or the 'black ghettos' of certain middle western cities.[115]

Each of Lomax's song notes, several of which are based on first-person contact with the artists, ends with the refrain "listen to our story." Lomax heard this imperative as both a cry for social justice and an invitation to hear the breadth of stories noted in the album's subtitle: *A Panorama of American Ballads*. Earlier, he had voiced this twined theme of cultural democracy in his *New York Times Magazine* piece published in January 1947, as well as in his address at the People's Songs convention held that October in Chicago.

That socially inclusive musical consciousness permeated the remaining "On the Record" columns in the *People's Songs* bulletin. With or without a byline, they explored releases that amplified this message of diversity in democracy. The July-August 1948 issue welcomed Victor's re-release of *Smoky Mountain Ballads*. The next month's issue quotes Ray Flerlage's review that appeared earlier that summer in the Farm Equipment Workers newspaper, in which he celebrated the latest Paul Robeson album: "He sings for the people and they know it!"[116] Flerlage is possibly the anonymous writer in the November bulletin who states:

> Many academic folklorists are unaware that during the depression literally hundreds of blues and hill-billy songs were commercially recorded, which gave the average American's reaction to unemployment and hard times. Look through the old Vocalion and Bluebird catalogues, and you'll see such titles as "C.C.C. Blues," "Unemployment Stomp," and "Working on the Project."[117]

In keeping with the hootenanny energies of People's Songs, the same commentator notes that on such topics, "millions of Americans could add their own verses." Finally, the last "On the Record" column, which appeared in December 1948 shortly before the organization closed down, recalled the earlier piece that had highlighted Library of Congress folk albums. This new entry enumerated ten more collections since published. These included several Latin American studies, as well as George Korson's recordings of northeastern Pennsylvania anthracite miners and their songs. The review concluded, after lightheartedly comparing Lead Belly to Guy Lombardo as to who might better represent the American voice, with this thought: "These [albums], we stress, are classics of people's music."[118]

For Ray Flerlage, the ideological aspirations of people's music and the down-home musicians he found at Maxwell Street formed an affinity. The outdoor players he saw there were living embodiments of the tradition bearers that appeared on the hillbilly, race, and documentary records he recommended to his readers and listeners. If some of the musicians he saw on the street were less talented than those found on disc, others like Jimmy Rogers (née Jimmy Lane) did achieve celebrated careers as recording artists. Either way, music formed a means, Flerlage wrote, of overcoming distrust of people with different backgrounds, and recorded sound offered an effective medium, equipped to demonstrate that "the bonds that unite all peoples are reaffirmed in their folksongs."[119]

While his tenure as Executive Secretary of People's Songs lasted only months—by the end of December 1946 he was already writing preparatory letters to his successor, singer Bernie Asbell—Flerlage's communications from that time, coupled with his later recollections, reveal the job to have been intensive and low paying, but spiritually uplifting.[120] His commitment to this music never flagged, and in fact, his contact with traditional musicians only increased with the years. Eventually, he became a full-time record sales representative and wholesale record distributor specializing in folk music. During those years he also hosted a series of radio shows and began his celebrated career as a photographer of blues and folk musicians.

The tattered but scrappy musicians who inhabited Folksong Street, like the citified artistry of People's Songs performers that included Pete Seeger, Woody Guthrie, and Josh White, collectively attested to the cross-cultural understanding Flerlage sought to inspire in his "People in Their Music" lectures and his work with People's Songs Inc. After all, he initially went to this outdoor emporium to locate hootenanny performers. He left there with a camera eye of images, a verbal newsreel of peddlers, players, and listeners united by a common passion:

> The hucksters begin to pack their wares. . . . the rain increases . . . the crowd hangs on, unwilling to turn away from the sounds. . . . but now the guitars are getting wet and it's getting dark—it seems much wetter and colder in the dark. . . . the musicians start to pack their equipment. . . . the crowd slowly becomes resigned to the idea . . . . see you next Sunday on Maxwell Street.[121]

• • •

Nearly thirty years stood between the earliest reports of Lloyd Lewis's folksong gatherings at his Chicago apartment and Indiana Dunes vacation retreat, and Ray Flerlage's public lectures at Parkway Community House, an interracially run, South Side neighborhood institution that primarily served its nearby Black clientele. For both Lewis and Flerlage, no matter how dissimilar these settings, the personal longings the music stirred in Lewis, and the social vision it motivated in Flerlage, coalesced. Though I cannot say if the two men ever met, they presented to their friends, readers, and listeners a comparable view of folk society. For Lloyd Lewis, a supporter of Franklin Roosevelt and the New Deal, traditional song summoned in him an earlier, agrarian America, and with it, a vision of Jeffersonian democracy that ameliorated present-day industrialism. When he compared sheepman Oscar Collett's perceptiveness to Benjamin Franklin, Voltaire, and Anatole France, Lewis tied a common thread from the herder's trail-savvy intellect to these book-smart predecessors. He also granted, in his work as a biographer of Lincoln and his generals, the power of folklore to shape public understanding. Similarly, for Ray Flerlage, like others in the People's Songs movement, rural folk music—a form largely unfamiliar to an urban audience—joined with liberal pluralism to make an internationalist statement. Carl Sandburg, a friend of both Lloyd Lewis and Ray Flerlage, poetically crystallized this humanistic spirit in the aptly named 1955 photographic exhibition, *The Family of Man,* for which he had contributed its written prologue. No coincidence that Flerlage, who photographed the poet in 1961, took a verse from *The People, Yes,* as the epigraph for his own book of photographs:

> What are these dialects deep under the bones
> whereby the people of all ages and races far apart
> reach out and say the same clay is in us all,
> bringing out men whose eyes
> search the earth and see no aliens anywhere,
> pronouncing across the barriers the peculiar word:
> "Brother"?[122]

Admittedly, within these aspirations also dwelt a lighter impulse. Both Lewis's and Flerlage's listeners enjoyed this music for the sake of their informal playing and singing. These energies reached from Lewis's literati-rich musicales to the hoots that Flerlage staged, frequently in the homes of well-heeled folk enthusiasts. A 1960 article in the *Chicago Tribune* sums up how this participatory ardor had grown among this audience. It bore the headline "Are You a Folknik in a Hootenanny?" which it subtitled, "Then You're Having Fun in Music Craze." A key line within the piece reads, "It's the cultured people's way of listening to hillbilly music."[123] Those words capture a class distinction, revealing both the folk and the folkie.

In December 1957, Chicago's Old Town School of Folk Music, now the largest, independent, not-for-profit community arts school in the United States, opened in the city's Near North Side neighborhood.[124] Located at 333 W. North Avenue, it stood down the hall from the Proletarian Party and the nation's leading radical press, the Charles H. Kerr Publishing Company. While the school never stressed the ideologies of these neighbors, it implicitly extended its egalitarian commitment to workers' education and industrial justice. In a recent letter, the Old Town School's first teacher, Frank Hamilton (born 1934), expressed the educational philosophy he intended with "social teaching," a term he had expressed to Ray Flerlage back in 1962.[125] "Education is a round table," he now wrote. "We learn from a community of people rather than through the dictates of the venerated learned. . . . The community is the library. . . . In short, knowledge grows into wisdom by wrestling it from elitism."[126] Hamilton's words about the teaching of folksong at the Old Town School of Folk Music comport with the philosophy that inspired its fellow occupants, the past inhabitants of the building it originally occupied.

Old Town School credits one particular song as an essential part of its formation.[127] During a suburban gathering of neophyte guitarists and banjoists, Frank Hamilton, then performing at Chicago's first professional folk nightspot, The Gate of Horn, taught "Sloop John B." using a method he gleaned from John Lomax's daughter (and Alan Lomax's younger sister), Bess Lomax Hawes.[128] By the early 1950s, Hawes (1921–2009) had devised a group technique in which she instructed classes of informal adult learners to develop their musical personalities with a selection of uncomplicated songs they harmonized by ear.[129] One of those in attendance at the October 1957 session was bass singer and performer Win Stracke (1908–1991), a past board member of People's Songs, and who, as mentioned earlier, had led local hoots organized by Ray Flerlage in the 1940s. Now, as Frank Hamilton worked through this number, Stracke leaned over to Ted Johnson, a novice guitarist sitting beside him. Johnson recalled, "Frank was giving his class, handling a group of people with differing abilities, and getting them to play together. Win turned to me, and said, 'I'm going to start a school around this.'"[130] When the school opened two months later, Hamilton again led the students that first night in "Sloop John B."

The school's earliest songbook, consisting of mimeographed pages gathered into a three-ring, loose-leaf binder, bore this headnote for "The Sloop John B.": "This song was brought back to Chicago by the well-known cartoonist John T. McCutcheon, in the early 1920s. He collected it at his island home in the Bahamas."[131] A traditional song of Bahamian sailors first documented in 1916, it was picked up by folk aficionados in Chicago and thence included in *The American Songbag* a decade later, which, in turn, led to a 1950 record made by The Weavers, who credited "Sloop John B.'s" authorship to Carl Sandburg, along with their own Lee Hays. From there Frank Hamilton learned the song, and it became part of the creation of the Old Town School of Folk Music. Soon after, the Kingston Trio recorded it in 1958, and then the Beach Boys reworked it into a mid-1960s *Billboard* chart-topper. This trajectory, spanning usage, community, geography, audience, style, and mercantile objective, speaks of a larger cultural breadth crystallized in *Smoky Mountain Ballads*, let alone in the values that Lewis, Flerlage, and Sandburg communicated throughout their various presentations of folksong.

Smoky Mountain Ballads, despite its modest sales and briefly revived shelf life, formed the preface for what became an enormous audio encyclopedia of American vernacular music. With the advent of long-playing records in 1948, to say nothing of subsequent compact disc collections, and now, online resources, there arose hundreds of albums, and a multitude of record labels, both major and specialty, that reissued traditional and traditionally based performances in country, blues, gospel, and ethnic categories.[132] Musician John Cohen, a founding member of the New Lost City Ramblers, spoke for his fellow players when he said, "One cannot underestimate the visionary importance of early reissues on Decca and Victor. *Smoky Mountain Ballads*, issued in 1941, was the first."[133] He began that thought, noting, "these reissues became the central influence in shaping the direction of the traditional music aspect of the Revival. They offered access to and continuity with an oral tradition—style, tune, and text intact." For Cohen and other devotees of Southern string band and vocal music, these records became models, much as their blues revival contemporaries turned to similarly prized performances in that idiom. From studying the names printed on the original discs, and even at times, directed by the content of the lyrics heard there, some of these young converts and record collectors journeyed into the countryside to find the performers themselves. While many had passed away, a revered cast of surviving senior players became, in the terms of the day, "rediscovered."

"The folk music revival," wrote musicologist Charles Seeger, "was an American shotgun wedding of oral (folk) and written (fine and popular art)

FIGURE 61. Ted Bogan, a veteran string band musician, wearing his University of Chicago Folk Festival performer's badge, plays after hours during the Smithsonian's Festival of American Folklife, Washington, D.C., June 27, 1986. Photo by Stephen Wade.

idioms."[134] This encounter led to traditional players making new records. Others of their generation and comparable artistry were also recorded and presented at folk festivals, campus concerts, and coffeehouses. The evening performances given at the first University of Chicago Folk Festival that launched in February 1961, and which for a decade, Ray Flerlage documented on camera, formed a pantheon of that time: Arvella Gray, Jean Carignan, Horton Barker, the Stanley Brothers, Elizabeth Cotton, Roscoe Holcomb, Bob Atcher, Frank Proffitt, Memphis Slim, and Willie Dixon. These musicians appearing in Mandel Hall faced an entirely different audience than what they had known among their neighbors, townsfolk, churches, medicine shows, variety theaters, taverns, and dance halls.

Revealingly, not long after the Chicago folk festival, Memphis Slim (Peter Chatman) observed, "I'm a folk singer in one place and a blues singer in the other place, but I'm singing the same thing in both places."[135] Arvella Gray might have said the same. Blind and missing some fingers, he played a weathered steel-bodied guitar and knew seemingly endless verses for the ballad "John Henry." After Mandel Hall, he returned to Maxwell Street market, his daily venue.

Before the University of Chicago Folk Festival's launch, many urban-based traditional music enthusiasts celebrated a resource that exceeded *Smoky Mountain Ballads* in its influence: the 1952 *Anthology of American Folk Music,* edited by Harry Smith. In this eighty-four-track collection of commercially recorded pieces made between 1927 and 1932, Smith thematically organized its three double-LP sets into ballads, social music, and songs. The jackets listed their contents on each cover and were set under two parallel columns that bordered a central image, a drawing of Robert Fludd's 1618 celestial monochord. Smith (1923–1991) amplified this iconography with brief yet informed album notes. His précis for a 1928 version of "Froggy Went a-Courting," performed by WLS radio singer/banjoist Chubby Parker, captures Smith's ebullience, its language suggesting, too, his intended audience, one clearly distant from those who had originally purchased these recordings: "Zoologic miscegeny achieved in mouse frog nuptials, relatives approve."[136] Yet for all of Smith's beatnik-era idiosyncrasy, the original motivation for his work stemmed from a library book his father had once brought home: a copy of Carl Sandburg's *American Songbag.*[137] Following that, he came in contact with Alan Lomax's 1940 "List of American Folk Songs on Commercial Records" and *Smoky Mountain Ballads.* From that point on, Smith intensified his 78-rpm record collecting, which eventually led to the *Anthology.*

Two precedents that Harry Smith didn't mention also foreshadowed his work. Like *Smoky Mountain Ballads,* these anthologies, compiled and edited by Alan Lomax, appeared as 78-rpm releases: *Listen to Our Story* and *Mountain Frolic.* The latter album, which came out a few months after the first, also in 1947, bore the subtitle "Square Dance Pieces and Hoedowns from the Southern Mountains." Its second subtitle indicates the energies that animated its printed insert: "The tale of a Tennessee Frontier dance in

1840."[138] A number of the artists included in the two compilations subsequently appeared in Smith's anthology, albeit performing different songs. Among them were Buell Kazee, Dock Boggs, and Furry Lewis, all of whom found their way in later years to the stage of the University of Chicago Folk Festival and like events, while another artist, Bascom Lunsford, remained in the public eye as well, leading his festival in Asheville, North Carolina.

In the spring of 1948, musicologist Charles Seeger penned the first record review to appear in the *Journal of American Folklore*.[139] He took as his subject four albums that Alan Lomax had recently marshaled into production. The first two were, once again, titled *Listen to Our Story* and *Mountain Frolic*. The remaining works featured in Seeger's review, *Sod Buster Ballads* and *Deep Sea Chanteys and Whaling Ballads*, consisted of new recordings, made during a single afternoon session overseen by Lomax in July 1941 for the General label (subsequently transferred to Commodore Records by the time of Seeger's review). Members of the Almanac Singers, then consisting of Woody Guthrie, Lee Hays, Millard Lampell, and Pete Seeger, performed all the pieces. In his review, Seeger divided the two pairings as signs of "what has been" and "what is coming to be."[140] They illustrated what he later termed, drawing on B. A. Botkin's 1937 essay "The Folkness of the Folk," a ceaselessly flowing dialectic of "folkness" and "non-folkness."[141]

Seeger analyzed these four works across two stylistic arcs. One involved the movement of "authentic folk idiom" to "authentic fine art or concert idiom."[142] In addition, Seeger explained that American music originated from two channels, one sourced in African heritage and the other European. In the case of Black music, it moved from tribal, to dance band, to blues and swing, to Gershwin-style Broadway jazz and back again, while white music moved from folk to hillbilly to citybilly to concert performance. Black and white musicians had both traversed the figurative highway of folk to concert idiom from either direction. By way of example, Seeger briefly mentioned the performer John Jacob Niles. Of Kentucky origin, Niles took countryside material he had known from there and translated it into conservatory form. Similarly, Woody Guthrie, "a man of oral tradition," cast his lot with the literarily guided citybillies. With "fatherly solicitude," Seeger admits that his son, Peter, raised with classical music, but now with banjo clasped in hand, took the opposite route, tirelessly seeking the unlettered world of folk tradition.[143] (Seeger does not give any Black examples.) However far these performers pursued their chosen stylistic throughways, their life histories revealed that "inheritance always shows, no matter how extreme the adaptation to environment."[144]

Charles Seeger published one additional record review in the *Journal*, analyzing four more albums that Alan Lomax produced in the Decca "Personality Series." In this and subsequent writings, he continued to explore the movement between folk and formal, book learning and home learning, amateurism and professionalism, "'hick stuff' and fine art," differentiating "data (fact) from dicta (value)," and folkness from nonfolkness.[145] He saw these qualities, however, not as opposites, but "as potentially two segments of a single strand."[146] Folk music did not present to him a closed account, even in an urban, industrial world that left behind some venerated ballads instead of others, as people adapted to new ways of life and evolved new musical styles. Despite intensive efforts by formal educators and commercial enterprises to fix music to literacy, given time, he observed, oral tradition would still emerge, adapt, and develop. "Rather than say 'the folk is dead' and attempt to keep folk song alive as something quaint, antique, and precious, let us say 'the folk is changing—and its songs with it.'"[147]

From the start of his discussion of *Listen to Our Story* and *Mountain Frolic*, Seeger framed folksongs as examples of acculturation. He defined this process as "contact between strata within a culture community as well as between whole culture communities."[148] One byproduct of this movement lay in reawakening interest in such recordings in the communities from which they originated. In the same 1969 magazine that Harry Smith discussed his anthology and its development, another article there centered on reissues. New York–based label owner David Freeman of County Records, which he debuted in late 1963, noted a change in buying habits among his customers. He specialized not only in new releases of older, recorded Southern mountain music but in making recordings of current traditional musicians from the same region. Freeman noted that while record store sales to city-based buyers, "the folk-oriented college age group," for the older material had diminished, he found that 60 to 65 percent of current sales now went to "country-oriented rural customers." He added, "Though it may seem strange, it has been my experience that the country-oriented rural customers are decidedly more liberal and flexible in that they purchase . . . new rural recordings as much as, or more than, the re-issues."[149] As a result, County Records began taking ads in "farm journals rather than in folk music magazines." This cycling from root to branches and back again extends well into the first quarter of the twenty-first century, as Blue Ridge educators embrace once-scorned hillbilly music, while out in Oakland, California, young players build gourd instruments and learn the Black banjo music of their forebears. These reclamations necessarily call on older recordings as both reference sources and artistic models.

In this way the significance of *Smoky Mountain Ballads* becomes clear. Beyond its historical place as a unique commodity briefly marketed by a major record label, the album augured a devoted audience. Bess Hawes, whose brother assembled the music for *Smoky Mountain Ballads,* and whose father made its final choices, once wrote me in a letter: "You know, most people now recognize (which they didn't a century ago) that ordinary Americans created a great new cultural resource with their cowboy songs, corridos, worksongs, spirituals etc. ad infinitum."[150] These all afforded, she observed, "glimpses into the truth of our nation." Another truth of our nation that Bess surely would have acknowledged stemmed from her own experience of formulating an instructional approach that has touched thousands of learners, one that brought an essentially rural music to the city. Her sing-alongs admitted all levels of proficiency, and in that consciously open design, they could not plumb the depths of a given tradition or deconstruct the styles of its greatest proponents. However, a resource like *Smoky Mountain Ballads* offered a means to study and immerse oneself in the artistry of a seemingly distant musical culture, whatever one's birthright.

For some students, *Smoky Mountain Ballads* communicated its lessons in a fluorescent-lit classroom in Chicago, when Old Town School of Folk Music teacher Fleming Brown played "Train 45" on his banjo, summoning in his voice and his fingers a song he had first heard on that collection. Later, I watched this happen again in a house on Washington's Capitol Hill. One of the primary figures in the folk revival, Ralph Rinzler, placed the Carter Family's 1935 recording of "Cannon Ball Blues" on his turntable.[151] Over and over, Ralph dropped the stylus arm onto one spot of the spinning 78-rpm disc. He kept replaying this single instrumental passage, marveling over the authority Maybelle Carter possessed on her guitar and transmitted in that performance. "The way she comes down on those first notes," he reflected. "Even after thirty years, I'm still getting more out of it."[152] Ralph Rinzler embodied at that moment, as Fleming Brown demonstrated at the Old Town School, what Professor D. K. Wilgus called the challenge and responsibility of "a non-folk singer in the traditional idiom."[153]

Smoky Mountain Ballads represents, then, a crossing. It joins a larger current of American life, inviting, like folklore itself, an endless round of cultural borrowing and lending. The album forms what Houston Baker terms a *matrix*, "a point of ceaseless input and output, a web of intersecting, crisscrossing impulses."[154] Baker sees the blues as a matrix, and indeed this musical reference also finds meaning in the physical manufacture of phonograph records themselves. Here a matrix signifies a process that extends from the master to the finished record. A single spiral traces across a wax surface to make an undulating trough that moves from side to side. These shapes are then reversed, and the matrix forms an electroplated die from which duplicates are mass-produced. *Matrix*, which derives from Latin for "womb," is the structure that holds something in place, in this case, sound waves.

Smoky Mountain Ballads continued what Carl Sandburg had earlier assembled in his songbook, a product substantively indebted in turn to Lloyd Lewis. Likewise, what Ray Flerlage found in the agora of Maxwell Street forged another matrix. Renamed by him as "Folksong Street," this jumbled tableau of humanity and hardship, a first home for immigrants, a beginning point for their efforts and aspirations, bore witness to countless transactions. Repeatedly, denizens in search of dimes or dollars reflected their experiences in song. What they sang, like the performances caught in the grooves of *Smoky Mountain Ballads*, launched a new matrix for us all.

· 11 ·

A Storyteller's Story

A *Story Teller's Story* is the title of Sherwood Anderson's 1924 autobiographical memoir. Anderson, best known for his novel, *Winesburg, Ohio*, came to prominence during the Chicago Renaissance, a period of intensive literary activity beginning in the late nineteenth century. Anderson and his contemporaries—poets, novelists, and critics that included Floyd Dell, Carl Sandburg, Theodore Dreiser, Edgar Lee Masters, and Vachel Lindsay, as well as editor-publishers Harriet Monroe and Margaret Anderson—fashioned a body of letters that explored reality in both modernist and vernacular terms. Their collective efforts reached a crescendo in 1917 when critic H. L. Mencken acknowledged, "I give you Chicago. It is not London-and-Harvard. It is not Paris-and-buttermilk. It is American in every chitling and sparerib, and it is alive from snout to tail."[1] Three years later, Mencken amplified this characterization with an even broader pronouncement. In describing the city as "the gargantuan and inordinate abattoir by Lake Michigan," he deemed it "the literary capital of the United States."[2]

The writing that Mencken championed in Chicago departed from genteel tradition to highlight instead a literature steeped in the common life.

This body of work extended the colloquial artistry Mark Twain achieved in *Huckleberry Finn* with its evocation of provincial dialect and oral anecdote from the rural Middle West. The writers of the Chicago Renaissance shaped a streetwise literature adapted to a new civil society. The plain-spoken eloquence and rustic humor that Abraham Lincoln brought to his orations, like the call-and-response testimonials that camp meeting preachers inspired among their congregants, both Black and white, shifted now into speech forms suited to the city and its enclaves.

For Chicagoans, this literary renaissance built on what they could already find in their daily newspapers. Journalist George Ade wrote a prolific series for the *Chicago Record* titled "Stories of the Street and of the Town," later referring to them as "little yarns about shop girls and stray dogs and cable car conductors."[3] Likewise, sports writers, including Ring Lardner, whose ballgame reports appeared as front-page news in the *Chicago Tribune*, brought fresh energies to the written word with phrases like "clout the sphere," "the initial sock," and "slam the pill."[4] Dialect humor found enormous readership via Finley Peter Dunne, who penned hundreds of columns commenting on the world at large through doings at home. He voiced these wry observations through the character of a sagacious Irish immigrant, the neighborhood bartender he called Mr. Dooley. Addressing his long-faithful customer, Mr. Dooley explained in his County Roscommon brogue: "I know histhry isn't thrue, Hinnessy, because it ain't like what I see ivry day in Halsted Shtreet . . . histhry is a post-mortem examination. It tells ye what a country died iv. But I'd like to know what it lived iv."[5]

This literature of locality corresponded with other cultural developments arising in the city. Mencken celebrated the emergence of Maurice Browne's Chicago Little Theatre with its contemporary stagings. He likewise mentioned the city's skyscrapers as a new contribution to the world's architecture, silently saluting their master builder, Louis Sullivan. Mencken further applauded the founding of *Poetry* magazine by Harriet Monroe and *The Little Review*, led by Margaret Anderson, both open to modernity. Mencken's catalog of the city's quenchless intellectual ferment—"this place engaged in the grand clash and clatter of ideas"—implicitly includes the pragmatist philosophy espoused at the recently founded University of Chicago, along with the educational theory expressed there by John Dewey, who perceived, not unlike Mencken, a continuity of life and art.[6] As Dewey himself said, "There is more than a verbal tie between the words common, community, and communication."[7] For its vitality, both commercial and creative, Mencken deemed Chicago "the most thoroughly American of American cities."[8] He found there what his predecessor William Dean Howells had earlier perceived about its homegrown fiction: "the American as the American knows himself."[9]

As someone raised in Chicago, I owe much to this history and to that midpoint on the American map. From its skyline to its neighborhoods, I sensed, along with so many others, a quality that Nelson Algren commemorated in his rhymed prose: "The city's rusty heart, that holds both the hustler and the square. Takes them both and holds them there."[10] Vibrant cultural forces thrived in what Algren termed this "cagework city beneath a coalsmoke sky."[11] Part of that atmosphere lingered in the whiskey fumes and cigarette stubs that permeated the saloons where I first performed. By then, the butcher block gusto that Mencken summoned in his lakeshore abattoir, unabashed if bloodied, had long permeated the city's music, theater, speech, and literature.

• • •

Jack Conroy (1898–1990), seen in this 1957 photograph taken during opening night at Chicago's Old Town School of Folk Music, first came to Chicago in 1938 at the invitation of fellow writer Nelson Algren. He joined the city's unit of the Federal Writers' Project. Jack, a native of Moberly, Missouri, and already author of the celebrated Depression-era novel *The Disinherited*, brought to his new home a personal knowledge of folklore and traditional music. His comments, recorded in notes taken during a July 1939 Illinois Writers' Project meeting in Chicago, reveal his interest in this material, as he, Algren, and their colleagues discussed an incoming assignment from the national office in Washington, charging them to undertake a series of industrial folktales.[12]

The previous month, Benjamin A. Botkin, national folklore editor for the Federal Writers' Project, had addressed the Third American Writers' Congress in New York, where he spoke of folklore as "not something far

FIGURE 62. Jack Conroy (foreground pictured left) attending opening night, Old Town School of Folk Music, Chicago, Illinois, Dec. 1, 1957. Courtesy of Old Town School of Folk Music Resource Center & Archives.

away and long ago but real and living among us."[13] Now, at the Chicago meeting, Jack referred to Botkin's words and soon began to create a series of updated tall tales. These were based in part on his own experience as an industrial laborer. He had left school at thirteen to work in Moberly's Wabash railroad yards, where he heard stories told by the older hands. He began collecting from other living sources in Chicago but also drew from his wide reading of frontier humor reaching back to the 1830s. His methodologies included going into a North Clark Street tavern, buying thirty shots at once, lining them up on the bar, and then offering any taker: "You tell me a story and I'll give you a drink."[14] The gambit worked.

Jack's industrial folktales—they number well over a dozen—were originally scheduled for a publication called *A Tall Chance of Work.* While that volume never materialized, several of Jack's pieces, along with others reflecting on contemporary life, found print in 1944 in Botkin's best-selling book, *A Treasury of American Folklore.* Jack's old friend, Carl Sandburg, wrote the book's foreword. He cites something "rather sweetly modern and quite impossible to see as coming alive out of any former generation."[15] Sandburg then identifies Jack's story of "Slappy Hooper, the World's Biggest, Fastest, and Bestest Sign Painter" as a modern masterpiece. Jack's source for it, a coworker on the Writers' Project in Chicago, who, in turn, heard it from his father-in-law, had given him the kernel.[16] From there, Jack built out the tale.

Slappy's biggest sign, for instance, stretched the length of the Union Pacific Railroad. It required him to set off cannons for his sky hooks that supported his sky painting scaffold. Unfortunately, stray airplanes, often as not, tangled the lines, and when it rained, his colors all jumbled together. This, by the way, created the meteorological condition that people nowadays call a rainbow. Slappy also found that another by-product of his Union Pacific sign was that it made people's necks stiff from reading it. Fortunately for him, Sloan's Liniment, an ointment they would all need, paid him for one displayed right at the railway's end.

Stories like this and anthologies like Botkin's furnished the core of what eventually became *Banjo Dancing.*[17] Along the way, those sources led me to related anthologies, unpublished manuscripts, other collectors as well as archivists, humor scholars, and past members of the Federal Writers' Project. Best of all, this work led to my closeness and collaboration with Jack Conroy. But before any of those efforts, and before my having read a word of Botkin's treasuries, I encountered a piece that anticipated all my future storytelling. It transcribes the thundering of a mythical Arkansas legislator:

> The man who would change the name of Arkansas is the original, iron-jawed, brass-mounted, copper-bellied corpse-maker from the wilds of the

> Ozarks! Sired by a hurricane, dammed by an earthquake, half-brother to the cholera, nearly related to the smallpox on his mother's side, he is the man they call Sudden Death and General Desolation![18]

The grandiloquent oration continues, piling on increasingly elaborate comic boasts. It also appears in varied renditions, attesting to a lively, living tradition. One need only examine James Kirke Paulding's 1830 two-act farce titled *The Lion of the West* to recognize a recurring pattern. At the invitation of the celebrated American stage actor James H. Hackett, who offered at that time $250.00 for a three-act play "dramatizing the manners and peculiarities of our country," Paulding created the first Western frontier character to inhabit the American stage.[19] To do so, he parodied an already myth-encased congressman from eastern Tennessee, David Crockett. The play brims with boisterous poetry: "Ain't I the yaller flower of the forest, and I'm all brimstone but the head, and that's aquafortis."[20] Crockett, personified here as Colonel Nimrod Wildfire, crows that he's "half-horse, half-alligator, and a touch of the earthquake—that's got the prettiest sister, fastest horse, and ugliest dog in the district and can outrun, outjump, throw down, drag out, and whip any man in all Kaintuck." Soon, Paulding's words—themselves documented in living speech among Natchez-based rivermen as early as 1808—like other passages he wrote, would reappear in the Crockett almanacs.[21] These unsigned, pocket-sized paperbacks were annually published for some twenty years, both preceding and following Crockett's death at the Alamo. In an instance where art truly meets life, Hackett, performing in Washington in December 1833 as Nimrod Wildfire in *The Lion of the West*, exchanged bows with Crockett, who attended the show.[22]

Nor did the exultant brag end its course at the apron of that antebellum theatre. More than a century later, it surfaced in the Mississippi folk toasts that Bo Diddley unspools in "Who Do You Love": "I walk 47 miles of barbed wire/I use a cobra snake for a necktie/I got a brand new house on the roadside/Made from rattlesnake hide."[23] Early in his boxing career, Muhammad Ali employed similarly rhymed hyperbole that delighted his fans as it irritated his opponents. This impulse, which Botkin called "making a noise in language," reflects an unmistakably American idiom.[24] It also formed the keystone of *Banjo Dancing*. "Change the Name of Arkansas"

FIGURE 63. Davy Crockett almanac, 1839.

marks the first monologue I ever performed. As the unstoppable legislator said, "Hide the stars in a nail-keg . . . unbuckle the belly-band of Time, and turn the sun and moon out to pasture; but you will never change the name of Arkansaw!"[25] In tall talk, the sky's the limit.

For me, these words found dramatic realization at a local tavern on Chicago's North Avenue called the Saddle Club. Beginning in the mid-1960s, starting around 10:45 p.m. every Thursday, the Old Town School of

Folk Music reconvened there after classes. Students, teachers, and visiting professionals, who, in the words of the school's founder, Win Stracke, came without "thought of paltry or pelf" to play and sing "for friends and strangers alike."[26] In 1972, my teacher at the school, Fleming Brown, insisted I appear there too. He felt I needed to work on stage to test how well I had learned a given tune. While during my first Saddle Club appearance, I delivered a trio of banjo tunes that met with increasingly tepid response as the set wore on, I returned the following week with the Arkansas legislator's speech tucked in my back pocket. Now, with one hand picking the banjo and the other holding up this text, I found not only interest among the Saddle Club's listeners, but recognition. The audience claimed these comic epithets for their own, the spread-eagled bluster clearly familiar to them, their declarations of independence worn deep in the American grain. Someone exultantly shouted, "Sooey!" and for this still-teenaged banjoist, the path I would eventually follow as a performer stemmed from that jubilant moment.

Those Saddle Club denizens who enjoyed the words of the voluble Arkansas legislator doubtlessly knew that just around the corner stood Chicago's Second City and its improvisational comedy troupe. Originally, Paul Sills directed its ever-changing and continually illustrious cast. He based his creative technique on ideas he credited to his mother, Viola Spolin. Spolin, author of *Improvisation for the Theater,* in turn repeatedly acknowledged Neva Boyd, her teacher at the nation's first social settlement, Chicago's Hull-House. Hull-House's theater program began in 1899, and it soon became a nationally known endeavor, presenting national premieres of plays by Shaw, Galsworthy, Lady Gregory, and Synge. Its noncommercial ventures into social realism placed it well outside the variety theater of that era. By 1912, Hull-House so influenced Maurice Browne that he established the Chicago Little Theatre, a flagship of art theater that galvanized kindred institutions across America. While some of these endeavors survived longer than others, this model led not only to the Federal Theatre Project of the Works Progress Administration of the 1930s but to the flowering of regional theater in postwar America.

As for Paul Sills, following his tenure at Second City, his energies to forge innovative performance continued unabated. In 1969, with his Story Theater company spanning Ovid's *Metamorphoses* to Grimm's fairy tales, he also helped launch (and name) the Body Politic, a newly founded arts venture set up in a former bowling alley and slicing machine works located in the Lincoln Park neighborhood.[27] The resulting off-Loop theater movement that Sills and like-minded creators instigated found enthusiastic support in Ray Nordstrand, president of the city's fine arts radio station, co-host of the *Midnight Special*, its weekly folk music-and-comedy program (initially introduced by Fleming Brown and Sills's former colleague, Mike Nichols), and publisher of *Chicago* magazine.

Convergence, more than coincidence, arises when recalling *Banjo Dancing*'s theatrical origins. The show was Ray's idea, one that he suggested over dinner following a 1975 benefit at Second City where we both appeared, he in the role of emcee and me as one of the performers. He mentioned Hal Holbrook's *Mark Twain Tonight!*, which stood out at that time as the preeminent model of solo American theater pieces. Three years later, when I thought I had assembled enough material to venture my one-person play, itself steeped in native materials, Ray suggested that I contact the Body Politic as a possible venue. They might take a chance on an unknown. It fit their adventurous streak, he thought, and clearly, it sustained a tradition that Paul Sills, Viola Spolin, and Hull-House had established. Once again, a congeries of institutions and individuals, open to localized expression, paved a route that I was fortunate enough to follow.

• • •

Another cultural gathering point also within walking distance of the Saddle Club was Chicago's open-air speakers' forum long known as Bughouse Square.[28] Donated to the city in 1842 as a public commons and formally named Washington Square Park, by the early twentieth century, it became a widely recognized informal outlet for soapbox orators. For those who attended these lectures, before home air conditioning and the allure of television, Bughouse offered fresh-air summertime relief, while its cast of characters conferred its greatest atmosphere. Bughouse, along with kindred free-speech gatherings found elsewhere in the city, included verbal scrappers like the one Studs Terkel remembered, a fellow who silenced a heckler by informing him that, "If brains was bedbug juice, you couldn't drown a nit."[29] Saul Bellow, too, embraced Bughouse for its oral torrents. He attributed the square's vitality to a disappearing strain, the "hobo intellectual."[30] In the late 1930s, while employed by the Federal Writers' Project and doing research at the Newberry Library, which stands astride Bughouse Square, he gathered enough impressions to pen "A Sermon by Doctor Pep." In this 1949 story, which he did not consider a work of fiction, Bellow offered a hymn to the square's stump speakers and their soliloquies. Here, Dr. Pep lectures on "true and false nourishment," promising at the outset:

> First-off I want to say that I'm not going to discuss anything so obsolete as the effects of Dogstar rains or descending phlegm in humid natures; nor will you hear anything from me, more recent, for or against psyllium seeds or senna leaves for regularity, or yogurt and the parasites of carp for old age; or any of the stuff you hear from radio doctors about health-bread or the evil of polished grain and false, agenized bleached flour or digging your grave with your teeth. No, it's something else I have in mind. . . . [31]

In colder months, Bughouse's firebrands and their listeners, if not warming themselves within the Newberry Library, convened at a nearby winter headquarters, the Dill Pickles Club. Founded in 1917, it was entered through an alleyway entrance whose doorway sign read "Step High, Stoop Low, Leave Your Dignity Outside." Here, nearly all the writers associated with the Chicago Renaissance mingled alongside "professors and politicians, hopheads and whores, gangsters and labor organizers with lawyers and social workers."[32] Like Bughouse Square with its spit-and-argue ambience, people came to Dill Pickles to both speechify and socialize. Sherwood Anderson captured its ecumenical spirit when he reported on its founder, Jack Jones: "'There it is, don't you see,' said Jones, chuckling and wagging his head, 'the proletariat and the stiffs are just like the painters and the poets. They'll laugh if you give them a chance.'"[33]

Alongside this hurly-burly of oratorical energy, a parallel movement equally dedicated to public speech took hold. By the second half of the nineteenth century, writers from Oscar Wilde to Edgar Allen Poe, Charles Dickens to Mark Twain, and in later years Arthur Conan Doyle and Carl Sandburg followed the platform circuit, a more polite counterpart of that era's elocutionary passions. For many of those platform readers, whose appearances became increasingly viable as railroad travel increased, their presentations of spoken literature found widespread audiences.

These storytellers billed themselves in various ways: from dramatic reader to character artist, elocutionist to monologist, impersonator to expressionist. For an entire century, in three successive waves, the first beginning in 1826 and ending in 1850, organized platform performance took place in lyceums; then, from 1851 to 1874, via the lecture system; and finally, between 1874 and 1925, in the Chautauqua-lyceum. Throughout this period, McGuffey Readers dominated the educational system. These manuals not only taught literacy to generations of America's school children but also did so by teaching them *aloud.* The spoken word, from schoolhouse recitation to platform performance, resounded across the nation.

For women, the elocutionary movement provided opportunities to move outside the household and still uphold feminine respectability. Their performances, held in women's clubs and similarly discreet settings, took place outside the theater environment, bypassing the opprobrium long associated with show business. By 1850, an ever-increasing number of oratory departments allowed women new employment that frequently coupled literary recitation with musical accompaniment. Musicalized poetry readings, Delsarte movement, hymns reinterpreted as religious love songs, choral speaking, and pianologues—words again supported by music, much of which was created by female composers—gave rise in those years to a widely witnessed body of spoken-musical work.[34]

All this to say that *Banjo Dancing* had precedents that reached not only back to exemplars like James H. Hackett and *The Lion of the West,* but to generations of platform speakers and elocutionary artists, men and women both, who often entertained audiences with native humor, and not infrequently, via recitations accompanied by music. Before *Banjo Dancing*'s opening, I had scant knowledge of these forebears. I had only the vaguest notion that beginning in 1930 Chicago served as a center of the nation's humor studies, led at the University of Chicago by Walter Blair, and pioneered by his collaborator, bibliophile and author Franklin Meine.[35] I had no idea either that in the wartime years—the same period that Jack Conroy's stories first appeared in Botkin's *Treasury*—Jack worked as an editor at an encyclopedia that Meine oversaw.

My reference points for musically accompanied spoken-word pieces, instead, centered on a diverse body of talking songs that traditional musicians across America had long performed. In Chicago, I witnessed this in the chanting recitation of the magical powers Muddy Waters brought to "Hootchie-Coochie Man," in Doc Hopkins's talking banjo song, "Trouble at the Coal Creek Mines," and during African American church services, where live music both underscored and punctuated sermons that stirred worshippers and ministers alike. Additionally, I found myself drawn to documentary field recordings that ranged from roosters crowing while rural fiddlers played to sidewalk vendors who hawked fountain pens that "will write in any language."[36] Long before all that, I had encountered Chicago's beloved Casey Jones, the Chicken Man (see preface to *The Beautiful Music All Around Us*), who unforgettably roved the city with his accordion and his chickens, each of them named Mae West.[37] He showed up, among other places, at Bughouse Square, where I glimpsed him for the last time.

In this meditation on *Banjo Dancing*'s sources, I recognize that I instinctively, if unknowingly, observed the more formal structures employed by the nineteenth-century platform speakers, even as I consciously emulated their folk counterparts. The elocutionists' stable texts and notated musical scores reflected the stories I performed: carefully crafted, written evocations of oral tales. Their verbal detail, as well as the need for dramatic characterization, called out for memorization. This self-appointed task no doubt reflected my upbringing and schooling. That deliberative method stood apart from the warmly casual improvisations that better suited the saloons where I played. Yet on entering the theater, that priority suddenly changed. Theaters called out for scripts, fixed products that could coordinate with lighting cues, and meet mandated time requirements for stagehands, administrators, and audiences alike.

FIGURE 64. Aboard the Mariposa Folk Festival performers' launch. (l-r) John Prine, Stephen Wade, and Steve Goodman. Harry Waller, in a cowboy hat, sits behind. Toronto, Ontario, June 20, 1975. Photo © 2017 by Arthur Usherson.

Any single recitation of sources cannot sufficiently acknowledge the numerous individuals who helped bring *Banjo Dancing* to the stage. Here is one, captured in a June 1975 photograph. It shows John Prine, Steve Goodman, Harry Waller, and me in Toronto at the Mariposa Folk Festival. The picture was taken aboard the performers' launch that shuttled between the city and a nearby island where the festival annually took place. Our

Canadian trip marked a busman's holiday for Goodman and Prine, who brought me there, housed me, introduced me around, got me on stage, and picked up the phone a few days later to obtain work on my behalf. Their intercession led to my finding a career beyond Chicago and launched a process that four years later culminated in *Banjo Dancing*.

Looking back at this image of Steve Goodman (1948–1984) with his luminous smile, I wish I had asked him when the words first came for "City of New Orleans," his great train song, whether he consciously saluted Carl Sandburg in his refrain, "Good morning, America, how are you?" It echoes the 1928 title Sandburg had taken for one of his most celebrated volumes. I am certain Goodman knew it—after all, he never forgot a single joke he ever heard. He stayed vigilantly attuned to Chicago, its folkways, and its voices. I am certain, too, that Richard Wright's *Native Son* informs Goodman's next line, "Don't you know me? I'm your native son." Here, as in other songs as well as his stage performances (and personal interactions), Goodman habitually invoked familiar sayings and accumulated wisdom. He drew larger resonances from them, assured that his listeners would recognize their perennial truths. Such threads turn ancestries into continuities.

Much the same could be said for the Mariposa banjo workshop. It took place on June 20, 1975, during the second hour of the festival's opening day.[38] A sizable crowd assembled, with Steve Goodman standing at the back edge beside the festival's director, Estelle Klein. He wanted her to see me play. On stage, banjoist Art Rosenbaum, who moderated the hour and who had invited me to join in, seated himself on one end to introduce the participants. These included Buell Kazee (1900–1976), the eastern Kentucky minister, who, between 1927 and 1929, released fifty-two sides for the Brunswick label. Though he declined a professional career as a musician and pursued the ministry, he sustained his music, remaining as adept with centuries-old ballads as with mountain frolic songs. Early in the urban folk music revival, his recordings, which included such ancient plaints as "Lady Gay" and "The Wagoner's Lad," as well as mid-nineteenth-century laments like "The Orphan Girl," had become prized models for city players, let alone valued items among Kazee's neighbors back home, who recognized his gifts.[39] To all, he spoke knowingly about songs and playing styles. I felt honored that minutes after the workshop concluded, Reverend Kazee invited me to come see him in Winchester, Kentucky, an invitation sadly never fulfilled due to his death the following year.

Another of the workshop's participants consisted of the team of William Miles (1878–1979) and Scott Didlake. Miles, then ninety-seven, played in the "classic" banjo style, a complex, guitar-derived technique guided by written notation. Its body of marches, schottisches, and overtures played on gut, and later, nylon strings flourished in the ragtime era. Miles, a witness to those years, had studied under Alfred A. Farland (1864–1954), a much-celebrated banjo virtuoso who moved beyond his minstrel show beginnings to perform concert hall arrangements of Schubert, Schumann, Rossini, and Chopin. Scott Didlake provided a second banjo, a common pairing in that style. Paramount in Miles's value system, Scott recalled, was his belief that music is best transmitted not on recordings, but through direct exchange and personal contact. For William Miles, music resided in the lived experience of the participants.

A few years later, Scott (1948–1994), a native Mississippian, returned to the United States following President Carter's 1977 pardon for Vietnam draft resisters. Once back home, after reading Dena Epstein's published research on Black banjo, in particular her landmark book, *Sinful Tunes and Spirituals,* Scott began in 1984 to make calabash banjos of the sort she had documented. (Soon after he launched this work, I purchased one of his first gourd banjos, a replica of a ca. 1770 instrument made in Surinam. From that point on, I closed every performance of *Banjo Dancing* with its low, grumbling tones.) Early in those years, Scott frequently wrote me, sending photographs of his latest gourd crops, while passionately applauding the unknown, enslaved musicians who cultivated and then crafted these banjos from the earth. Not without reason, Scott Didlake called himself an "apprentice to ghosts."[40]

But that lay in the future. Here at Mariposa, I sat between Don Stover and Ola Belle Reed, two people I would also come to know in the years ahead. Raised in the rural West Virginia coal mining community of White Oak, Don (1928–1996) began learning old-time banjo at age seven from his mother, Norma Stover. He grew up watching her play at neighborhood dances and spoke of the "roaring tone" that she produced on her banjo.[41] In late 1945, after hearing Earl Scruggs with Bill Monroe, Don began sorting out the intricacies of Scruggs's bluegrass picking. Don was stymied at first as he was using only two fingers to execute Scruggs's style. He recalled that "a traveling salesman came through town and said Scruggs was using three metal picks on his banjo, wears his picks backwards, upside down. I made some picks out of an old Prince Albert Tobacco tin right after the salesman told me."[42] By 1952, Don had achieved enough command of the style that he left his old work as a coal loader in the mines and became a professional banjo player. He first performed with his childhood friends, the Lilly Brothers (who also appeared at the 1975 Mariposa festival), followed by stints in Washington, D.C., and Shreveport, Louisiana, with bluegrass mandolin virtuoso Buzz Busby. In 1957, Don joined Bill Monroe's Blue Grass Boys, recording eleven songs, nine of which appeared on Monroe's first LP, *Knee Deep in Bluegrass*. In later years, Don's autobiographical song "Things in Life" reached both his peers and parking lot pickers, the song appealing to bluegrass and old-time devotees alike. In a 1997 film titled *Banjo Spirits*, which appeared within a year of his death, Don quotes its closing verse, saying how he hoped he might be remembered by these words: "Now when they lower my casket down/In some lonesome grave to rest/And you take your last look at my face/You can say I did my best."[43] Don Stover's epitaph, his followers agree, has proven true.

Ola Belle Reed (1915–2002) attained comparable esteem. The venerated singer, songwriter, and player was a native of Ashe County, North Carolina, located along the New River. She grew up in a large, music-playing family that included schoolteachers, ministers, farmers, and country store merchants. In 1934, during the Great Depression, they moved en masse from the mountains to Rising Sun, Maryland, in search of greater economic stability. Following his return from the war, Ola Belle's younger brother, Alex Campbell, reinstituted their family band, the New River Boys and Girls. The siblings began making local radio appearances in this borderland area of Maryland-Delaware-Pennsylvania, a region much populated with fellow Appalachian migrants. In 1949, Ola Belle wed Bud Reed, who, like her, had grown up in a large musical family, long settled in this part of Maryland athwart the Mason-Dixon line. Two years later, Bud began construction of the New River Ranch, an outdoor country music park near Rising Sun. This down-home venue, illuminated by two bare light bulbs jury-rigged from an adjacent highway pole, opened with a performance by Lester Flatt and Earl Scruggs. It became a requisite, if rough-hewn stop for that era's top bluegrass and country stars. Audiences sat on benches to see performers from George Jones to Skeeter Davis, Don Reno to the Stoneman Family, Ernest Tubb to June Carter and Johnny Cash. No structures, apart from the stage itself, separated the artists from the audience, and often the entertainers shared picnic tables and dined with their fans. For Ola Belle, this proximity made sense: "You cannot separate your music from your lifestyle. You cannot separate your lifestyle, your religion, and your politics from your music. It's a part of life. That's what our music was in the mountains. It was a part of our life."[44]

Likewise, at Mariposa, Ola Belle voiced this seamlessness during the festival's workshops. For a session titled "Strong Women: Purpose and Protest," Ola Belle introduced a song she had written about romantic fealty. She titled it "Only the Leading Role Will Do." She began by saying:

> When you speak of freedom, you're speaking of a mighty big word. I think, really the way that a person like me, the way that I been free, is that I call myself a free spirit. And when you're a free spirit, anything can happen . . . and nobody can take that away from you. 'Course, I was an independent cuss when I was ten years old. I used to go play the banjo for people who didn't believe in banjos.
>
> I used to go and visit an old family, a man and woman. . . . They lived across the hill from where I did. They were good people. But they weren't used to a banjo and they weren't used to a woman a-doing the Charleston. So, I used to go and pick the banjo and I used to dance for 'em . . . I done all them old dances, and they used to watch me. And they wasn't mad!
>
> So I think that all of my life. . . . They always say, 'Don't try to change her, 'cause she'll have her way' . . . that's what they tell me ever since I was small. Said I always thought I could do something about it, no matter what it was. . . .

Then Ola Belle ended her remarks, returning to the song she soon began to play. She said, "This is a love song that ended up not a love song."[45]

Soon after the festival, I visited Ola Belle and her family in Rising Sun. She showed me the general store in Oxford, Pennsylvania, where she and her brother broadcast their live country music and bluegrass radio show, as well as the former site of New River Ranch. We also dropped in on her longtime Dobro player at his barbershop. Deacon Brumfield kept spare instruments set in reach for jam sessions. Yet for all these ventures we made around town and thereabouts, I realized that music did not dominate Ola Belle's focus. For years, she, along with Bud, provided a home for runaways, giving shelter to the needy and the lost, regardless of age or race. No wonder, as their guest, I stayed in what looked like a dormitory, a large room stocked with bunk beds. Her songs made her famous, but she never considered herself a professional musician. Something else moved her, and it tied to her view of service.

"There's something about Ola Belle that most people don't know," recalled Bud Reed in 2009. "She was a great humanitarian. We used to take in kids. We took in all kinds of kids. They'd come and find us . . . I don't know how many kids we raised. I used to get up Saturday mornings and the house would be full. Boys and girls, and I'd start cooking them hotcakes and set them down at the table . . . they'd have to take turns sitting. You know, that was a joy." Bud and Ola Belle's son, David, added, "That was the best part of her."[46]

Thoughts of Ola Belle provoke more memories, including those of others whom she knew, among them, Bill Monroe. Sometime in the mid-1970s, he played a Chicago nightspot with his band. I had come early to the venue where he was scheduled that evening. However, the club was empty, except for its afternoon staff. When I opened the door to the performers' back room, seeking a place to wait until showtime, I found Bill Monroe sitting by himself looking straight ahead, as if he expected company. Suddenly face-to-face with him, I mentioned Doc Hopkins. I still worked as Doc's accompanist, and Doc numbered among the musicians Bill had first known in Chicago in the early 1930s. While employed with his older siblings at an oil refinery near Whiting, Indiana, Bill sometimes appeared on WLS as an exhibition square dancer. He fondly reminisced about those times at the outset of his career with Doc, a fellow Kentuckian, among the station's performers. He bid me to draw up a chair.

Bill Monroe sang with enormous physical volume on stage, but here in the quiet, he whispered the entire time we spent together. It was Christmas season, and I had just come from the Art Institute where I had purchased some modern art books as family presents. Bill asked to see them, and he looked at each volume, quietly paging through them. For all the tradition he embodied, Bill Monroe certainly defied any blithe assumptions about his interests. He took his time with these images of paintings and sculptures. Not unlike those artists, he, too, was an innovator. Then he picked up his 1923 Gibson F5 mandolin. Signed by acoustician and craftsman Lloyd Loar, it had become so iconic that amateur and professional players alike have, for generations, come to recognize it for its singularity.

While it gave voice to Bill Monroe's art, it also reflected his temper. Years before, in anger over a botched repair job undertaken by the company, he gouged out their pearl-inlaid brand name from the peghead with his jackknife. Now Bill passed me the weathered instrument to play. Over the next hour, it went back and forth between us.

He pointed to a distressed area on the mandolin's surface, a bare spot just below the neck near the lower F-hole where he picked and strummed. Its varnish gone, the exposed wood had stripped and serrated. He touched the wound and wondered aloud which would go first, the mandolin or himself. A few years later, using this same instrument, he composed a tune he called "My Last Days on Earth." Though Bill Monroe's Gibson, serial number 73987, now resides in a sealed display case at the Country Music Hall of Fame and Museum, that elegiac composition, like the rest of his music, survives his stilled and silenced mandolin.

Matters of mortality, let alone greater spiritual purpose, repeatedly surfaced among these players and singers. Ola Belle Reed and Don Stover contemplated larger realities in their songs, let alone by their words and actions, much as William Miles and Scott Didlake recovered ancestral continuities in their musical archeology. Buell Kazee situated the decorum of his banjo playing in relation to the practice of his faith, while Bill Monroe posed a question about his mandolin, his music, and his own final days. Fortunately, I have on videotape a statement about this continuity of life and music that might speak for them all. It arose in the home of two fellow players and contemporaries, Virgil and Mabel Anderson of Rocky Branch, Kentucky. Beginning in the early 1980s I visited the Andersons, and on one of these trips, I came with a camera operator, producer, and sound recordist to film Virgil and Mabel for a public television documentary about the musical sources of *Banjo Dancing.* The hour-long program, *Catching the Music,* focuses on my teachers and their counterparts, their learning, and their lessons.[47]

Virgil (1902–1997) and Mabel (1908–2006) lived on the Cumberland plateau near the Tennessee state line. To get to their house, one had to cross the Little South Fork either with a high-sprung truck or on foot via a swinging rope bridge that Virgil had strung up. He called it "walking them cable lines." At the bridge's end, in the cement footer, Virgil had carved the initials "USA." He did that, he told me with a twinkle, to assure people that no matter how far they had come they were still in the United States. His good humor appeared in other ways too. He called their home "Wildcat Rock City," and there in the middle of the woods, by his house, he had put up municipal street signs as if they lived on some city block. He said that he liked cities for their bustle and crowds, notions expressive of his amiable extroversion, even though he lived a rural life.

During the second day of our taping, in a wholly unscripted scene, Virgil began teaching me a banjo tune called "The French Waltz." A chorded piece related to the "Spanish Fandango" prototype, and set in an unusual tuning, it connected to the doughboys serving overseas during the First World War. According to Mabel's younger brother, Clyde, himself a musician, it came from a banjo-playing Frenchman and was transmitted to a musical neighbor of theirs who brought it home from service.[48] Without saying a word, Virgil started playing the tune. He began repeating it, allowing me to absorb the melody and follow his hands.

Mabel sat between us attentively. In her youth, she had learned to play the five-string banjo from her father, Jasper Troxell, and her grandfather, Al Davenport, a former medicine show performer. In turn, early in their courtship, she showed Virgil such numbers as "Wild Bill Jones," "Muskrat," and "Rainbow Schottische," all pieces that he came to perform. By the time of our taping, Mabel remained surrounded by the banjo, guitar, and fiddle playing of her family members. Her brothers, Clyde and Ralph living nearby, still actively made music, as did the Andersons' children and grandchildren. But a family tragedy from years before caused Mabel to stop playing. Her withdrawal was an act of mourning that she sustained

FIGURE 65. Mabel Anderson responding to the music making in her home, Rocky Branch, Kentucky, May 1987. Photo by Milton Kramer.

to the present day. Though this decision severed her from the banjo, her joy in its music and what others might play never lessened.

Virgil finished the tune and Mabel gently clapped her hands at each of us. Then Virgil began to talk. At first, he spoke humorously about me and the tune: "He's as full of music as a dog has fleas. . . . He's got it."[49] Then his thoughts turned contemplative. "Music is something to think about," he said. "It's a charm to the world." With Mabel listening by his side, Virgil continued,

> Music is a thing that should be honored and respected because it is a gift of God. God gave it to us as a pastime here. Just think about how good God is! What else could He done? He even gave us the talent for music. There has to be people for all things. Some to entertain others. And here we are, trying to entertain others. God knows what He's doing.

• • •

On Labor Day in 1979, I found myself at the White House. This most unexpected invitation stemmed from a review of *Banjo Dancing* that ran that June in *Time* magazine, and which Rosalynn Carter had read.[50] A week before the event, which featured an old-fashioned picnic on the grounds, three staffers, including the White House's social secretary, flew out to Chicago and attended the show. Plans called for me to close the evening, playing at the outdoor bandshell that faces the South Portico. Were rain to descend, however, I would perform in the East Room. Mercifully, Hurricane David avoided Washington throughout the holiday weekend. That night, President Carter, before sitting down on the South Lawn beside the First Lady, addressed an audience of more than a thousand guests, consisting largely of labor movement leaders and their families. The principal number the White House requested I perform fit the day's symbolism. They wanted the second chapter of *Tom Sawyer* in which Tom cons his friends into whitewashing the fence, transforming that task of work into the joyfulness of play. The *Time* review had mentioned the piece, and both its steamboat and fence painting imagery seconded the First Family's own travels.

A few days before this White House concert, the Carters had gone aboard the *Delta Queen* for a vacation. During a stopover in Hannibal, Missouri, they attended a performance that featured some of the leading characters from Mark Twain's writings. The president described Tom Sawyer as sometimes philosophical, and he paraphrased his words when Tom recognizes at the newly restored fence that "Work consists of whatever a body is *obliged* to do, and that Play consists of whatever a body is not obliged to do."[51] Now President Carter extended that thought to the assembled Labor Day audience:

> I think one of the great things about the trade union movement that has made you great are the things that you were not obliged to do. And I've been impressed with your unselfishness, the fact that many times you would take a stand or espouse a cause or fight a battle when there's not any direct benefit in it for you, but there's a benefit for others who are not quite so secure or quite so organized or quite so prosperous.[52]

Then, with a few more words, the president brought me on stage.

• • •

Two years earlier, I had begun performing the piece, committing it to memory and then setting it within a musical and clog-dancing framework. Like so many, I first read that chapter as a child. Years later, I gleaned it from Botkin's *Treasury of American Folklore,* intrigued by Alfred Bigelow Paine's observation cited there that for the average person, the sheer mention of Mark Twain's name reflexively summons this scene. "The Glorious Whitewasher" had entered popular folklore, becoming a cultural property shared by many, if not most, Americans. The breadth of that commonality became stunningly clear at the 1977 Philadelphia Folk Festival during the storytelling workshop. Blues guitarist and banjoist John Jackson of Rappahannock County, Virginia, attended that session. Afterward, John remarked that while he'd heard me play at other festivals, he had never heard any of the stories I did. This one, he noted, especially interested him. "I always wanted to know what happened with Tom Sawyer and that whitewashed fence, because, Steve, I can't read."

In that moment that gave me chills, I felt useful in a way I had never known before. John's world of orality and mine of literacy came together in this piece we had just shared. He knew countless songs through his gifts of memory and discernment, just as his wife, Cora, could tell story upon story: like the one about the Irishman who gave his wife "enough money to get twenty-five hens and one rooster. She goes and gets twenty-five roosters and one hen. So he said, 'Law, honey, what have you done? You got twenty-five roosters and one hen.' She said, 'Well, I don't want that hen to suffer like I do.'"[53]

John Jackson summoned in that utterly candid inquiry not only his life and that of his neighbors, but the Blue Back Spellers, McGuffey Readers, and recitations of an earlier time. When he wanted to know what happened when Tom Sawyer whitewashed the fence, John returned that fable to his lived experience, the spoken word that constitutes the storyteller's story.

John Jackson's seventy-seven-year engagement with the world and its stories stilled on January 20, 2002. At the moment of his passing, I stood at his bedside, banjo in hand, quietly playing. A few days earlier, on the last day he still had the power of speech, he had invited me to come over to his house sometime that week and play for him. During that call, he addressed his impending death, speaking with patience and acceptance. For John Jackson did not solely make his living as a musician. He also worked as a gravedigger, so when he said, "this happens to everyone," he acknowledged with back-breaking comprehension of the human condition.

John Jackson possessed the same kind of generosity that President Carter identified within the labor movement. Like Doc Hopkins, "America's Favorite Folk Singer," John remained continually open to others and the inherent value of their renditions. Unfailingly friendly, both John and Doc had a warmth that permeated their music and touched their acolytes and listeners.

In the best of cases, these warm and supportive connections between performers extended into their relationships with their audiences. Fleming Brown called himself a conduit. John, too, took on that role, bringing contemporary listeners into the increasingly distant songs of Blind Blake and Mississippi John Hurt. In playing for those outside his family and community, John brought an artistry that became, however fleetingly, part of the lives of people raised in circumstances wholly unlike his own. He epitomized Fleming Brown's greatest lesson: respect for those who came before while sharing their music across divides. John takes his place alongside others in this book beginning with Honeyboy Edwards and Jim Schwall, Joe and Odell Thompson, Hobart Smith and William Sidney Mount. Each of them began by paying heed to the senior musicians they most admired. Like those who set *1000 Fiddle Tunes* on their music stands, these players reworked and renewed their sources in fluid ways, personalizing the notes as they caught the music and passed it to their listeners.

From this foundation, the performers here amplified tradition's gifts. Lead Belly, for example, took "Old Man," a song that flourished in multiple settings and made it into a lyric of resistance against the grinding pressures of roustabouts' toil as they loaded and unloaded steamboats. The words mocked their indifferent bosses while sustaining the singers. This steamboat song extended like a rhizome, bearing in its roots a truth about labor that shipwright-scholar Archie Green pursued throughout his life: the inherent value of the worker. In "The Sound Wagon," Thaddeus Willingham himself, too, a manual laborer, found in his own quiet voice and graceful, swaying banjo playing, a way of easing the hungry nights that he and his children repeatedly faced. They found solace and unity, their legs hanging off the porch, as they sang together. In some of the harshest years of Southern segregation, he had absorbed the music of his Black childhood playmates, demonstrating in his renditions that culture emerges as a product of choice and environment.

Folk creativity, as Bertrand Bronson notes, "at its vital best" forms "a marriage of opposites . . . half recollection, half improvisation."[54] That creativity flows through Helen Marie Rowe's time-tested stories that she brought to her brood of children, easing them to sleep. It permeates Will Keys's inventions as he turned materials that lay at hand into an art all his own. Uncle Dave Macon's traditional resources and compositional methods employed in "Arcade Blues" similarly speak to an idea of properties held in common and then individually recast. When John Jackson heard Uncle Dave's broadcasts on the *Grand Ole Opry*, he thought him a Black musician, and by doing so, stunningly suggested how style had outwitted the segregation of the Jim Crow era.

In turn, the transference of this regional music to the recordings that stirred Lloyd Lewis and Carl Sandburg, and whose social content inspired Ray Flerlage in his own life choices, let alone his work to document and transmit it, helped forge another folksong audience. Finally, a rhythmically inspired spiritual that Wash Dennis and Charlie Sims sang while under state confinement spanned an even broader distance, their sampled voices filtered into a passing moment of a Hollywood movie. Once again, this malleable music reached across the social polity, inviting new listeners and participants.

The irrepressible process of re-creation within these songs and stories confirms what Ben Botkin repeatedly found to be true of folk storytellers and singers everywhere: They draw on "the bonds of common meaning and shared emotion" that join performer to audience.[55] These artists operate in a balance "between remembering and inventing . . . fitting new words to old tunes and old texts to changing circumstances." In this living transfer, bequeathed through craft, knowledge, and skills, lies a profound resourcefulness. It demonstrates a larger reality of American life, one expressed in its founding charter. The Constitution of the United States, in its masterful ordering of restraint and abstraction, limits the powers of government to dictate affairs of daily life, of the common life. In doing so, it takes a great risk but allows the creative ingenuity of its citizens to flourish, locally, independently, colloquially, and casually. In the end, this freedom of imaginative expression can move into still deeper waters, as most eloquently voiced by Preacher Casy in *The Grapes of Wrath:* "I know a bunch of stories, but I only love people."[56]

Notes

PREFACE

1. Beginning in 1928, Bascom Lunsford established the annual "Mountain Dance and Folk Festival." Following its first year, the festival's name became numbered, as in "The Second Mountain Dance and Folk Festival." The numbering continued on, well past the forty-sixth in 1973, the year of his death.

2. I recorded "The Far-Famed Fairytale of Fenella" on *A Storyteller's Story: Sources of Banjo Dancing.*

3. From Joseph Mitchell's *McSorley's Wonderful Saloon,* 91.

4. Wade, notes to *Dancing Home.*

5. Rosenberg, "'An Icy Mountain Brook,'" 180–81.

6. Thanks to *Weekly World News* managing editor Susan Jimison for our May 1999 communications that culminated in a telephone interview on May 11, 1999. Jimison likened the tabloid to the *Ripley's Believe It or Not* series, as well as to campfire tall tales. After combing through current newspapers and magazines, she said, "We try to find the most bizarre and entertaining [stories] to tell a ripping good yarn," and "let the readers decide" about the authenticity of any given piece.

7. Botkin, *A Treasury of American Folklore,* xxii.

8. See chapter nine, "Hands on the Tune."

9. I previously discussed these keywords in relation to Ball in *The Beautiful Music All Around Us,* 21–23.

10. Green, *Wobblies, Pile Butts, and Other Heroes,* 316.

11. Parsons, "Special Report: Performers, Collectors, and the People of the United States," January 7, 1991. It was later reprinted in *Folklife Center News* XVII, no. 1 (winter 1995): 7–10. I previously discussed Gerry's work and this research method in "A Matrix of America."

12. Langer, *An Introduction to Symbolic Logic,* 22.

13. Parsons, "Phenomenology and Folklife Research," 115.

14. Parsons, "Phenomenology and Folklife Research," 114.

15. Parsons, "Phenomenology and Folklife Research," 116.

16. Hood, "The Challenge of 'Bi-Musicality.'" Thanks to Erika Brady for this reference.

17. Parsons, "Phenomenology and Folklife Research," 116.

18. Macon, *Laugh Your Blues Away.*

19. This is the hatbox of records referred to in this book's chapter three, "The Conduit."

20. Macon, "Banjo Heritage."

CHAPTER 1. OUR COMMON LIFE

1. Bellow, "Chicago and American Culture." See also his "Starting Out in Chicago."

2. Bellow, "Chicago and American Culture," 87.

3. *Oxford English Dictionary.* Also, for "common," see Williams, *Keywords,* 70–72.

4. For more on the commons, see Hyde, *Common as Air.* Raymond Williams also addresses the commons in "Enclosure, Commons and Communities," 96–107.

5. Williams, *Keywords,* 71.

6. Howard Finster appeared on *The Tonight Show* on August 5, 1983, and his twelve-minute interview can be accessed on YouTube and Vimeo. https://www.youtube.com/watch?v=YweCaFHEZ50.

7. Vlach, "Vernacular," 734. See also Green, "Vernacular Music," and Green, "Vernacular Music Albums."

8. Overheard at the Weenie Beenie snack shop, Shirlington, Va., ca. 1987. Thanks to Jackson Frost.

9. Rourke, *Roots of American Culture,* 244.

10. Bayard, "The Materials of Folklore," 8.

11. I'm indebted to Archie Green for these terms, which appear in his *Wobblies, Pile Butts, and Other Heroes,* 26 and 33, as well as our own conversations about these matters during the summer of 1993 in San Francisco, shortly before publication of that book.

12. Ivey, Statement at the hearing on the American Folklife Center.

13. For an overview of the event from an informed, administrative perspective, see Richard Kurin's essay, "What Is It? The American South at the Olympics," 239–64.

14. Holt, letter to presenters at Southern Crossroads.

15. The performer was Steve Chappell of Augusta, Georgia, who has had a long and celebrated career as an Elvis tribute performer. At the time of the Atlanta Olympics, he was performing a piece he titled, "Elvis Lives!" A decade later, during a 2006 show, this tireless singer explained his motivation as "music for the King." He surely fulfills that commitment to Elvis's repertory and style.

16. See Schrager, "Trial Lawyers as Storytellers," 12–16, and Hatch, "Some Green Sand Hogs and Others," 282–84.

17. Botkin, *A Treasury of American Folklore*, xxi.

18. Bayard, "Materials," 12.

19. Botkin, *Treasury*, xxii.

20. Twain, *The Adventures of Huckleberry Finn*, 14. Cited in Wolfe, "Musical Roots of the South," 2.

21. Addams, "The Subjective Necessity for Social Settlements."

22. See Lissak, *Pluralism and Progressives*. See also Gleason, *Speaking of Diversity*.

23. Polacheck, typescript, American Folk Stories, Illinois Writers' Project, 1937. A similar but not identical account appears in her memoir, *I Came a Stranger: The Story of a Hull-House Girl*, 51–52.

24. Claxton, "An Opportunity to Help in an Important Work," 1.

25. Smith, "A Great Movement in Which Everyone Can Help," 4.

26. Smith, "A Great Movement in Which Everyone Can Help," 3.

27. "Ballads in America," *The Nation*, 129. Spelling as in original.

28. Bradley, "Song-Ballets and Devil's Ditties," 914.

29. Smith, "Ballads Surviving in the United States," 111.

30. Smith explored this idea in various Virginia newspaper articles that announced the ballad collecting project in 1914.

31. See Belden, "Balladry in America."

32. Davis, *Traditional Ballads of Virginia*, 14.

33. Davis, *Traditional Ballads of Virginia*, 15

34. Davis, *Traditional Ballads of Virginia*, 14.

35. Davis, "Miscellaneous Material re Ballads & Ballad Collecting."

36. Davis, *Folk-Songs of Virginia*, xxx.

37. Davis, "Some Recent Trends in Field of Folksong," 23.

38. Malone, "Music," 131.

39. Malone, "Music," 132.

40. Green to author, Aug. 2, 1993.

41. Green, Hearing on American Folklife Center, 62.

42. Green, "The Folklife Act in the Ninety-Third Congress," 2. See also "P.L. 94–201—A View from the Lobby," 269–281; and his Introduction to *Folklife and Federal Government*, 1–9; and Bressler, *Culture and Politics*. Thanks to David Taylor for sharing some of these materials following our September 14, 2009, memorial to Archie held at the University of Illinois, School of Labor and Employment Relations.

43. See Senator Richard S. Schweiker's essay, "Ethnic Studies," 63- 71; and Roman Pucinski's "Ethnic Studies and Urban Reality," 73–88. See also Congressman Pucinski's hearings on "Ethnic Heritage Studies Centers."

44. Green, "The Archive's Shores," 70.

45. Downey, *Congressional Record*, September 8, 1975, 27920. The congressman

was quoting lyrics from a song one of his staffers had written, "The Ballad of the Folklife Preservation Act."

46. Gross, *Congressional Record,* December 16, 1974, 40142.

47. See Stearns, *Civilization in the United States,* vii.

48. "Immigrants came to this small Wisconsin city. So did the political rhetoric," WBUR radio broadcast, aired November 5, 2024.

49. Rubio, "Rubio Sees a 'Remaking' of the Republican Party."

50. Ellison, "The Little Man at Chehaw Station," 21. Ellison first published the essay in *The American Scholar,* Winter 1977/78. For more on "liberal pluralism," and its counterpart, "corporate pluralism," see Gordon, "Models of Pluralism," 178–88.

51. Ellison, "Going to the Territory," 139.

52. Ellison, "Little Man," 27. Emphasis as in original.

53. Ellison, "Going to the Territory," 136.

54. Louis Menand addressed this idea too. See his "Diversity," 352.

55. Ellison, "Little Man," 31. Thanks also to gospel scholar Doug Seroff for information on Hazel Harrison. Italics as in original.

56. Ellison, *Invisible Man,* 503.

57. Shahn, personal communication with author, Dec. 9, 1994. Bernarda, Ben Shahn's wife, recalled this title as one of the tunes the siblings played that day. Ben Shahn was further exposed to it by fellow artist Bernard Steffen. In June 1936, musicologist Charles Seeger recorded Bernard Steffen and Charles Pollock playing it as a harmonica duet, AFS 3304-A4. Thanks to Eleanor Steffen for her generous 2015 communications about her husband, his art, and his music. Together these social realists and fellow regionalists, many of them inheritors of the earlier Ashcan movement, expressed what the Rebel Poets organization used as their slogan: "art for humanity's sake." In their representational art they often depicted scenes of daily life that the Musgrove brothers playing music among themselves on that Pennsylvania roadside embodied. For more discussion of this motto and musical sensibilities surrounding it, see chapter ten, "Folksong Street." See also Cowell, "Charles Seeger (1886–1979)," as well as Pescatello, *Charles Seeger: A Life in American Music,* 133; Kaskowitz, *A Chance to Harmonize,* 86; and Wixson, *Worker-Writer in America,* 163.

58. Recorded on January 16, 1987, this performance, titled "Chicago," appears on *A Storyteller's Story: Sources of Banjo Dancing.*

59. Treadway, interview, Feb. 27, 2014.

CHAPTER 2. CATCHING THE MUSIC

1. Letter from Robert Nelson Mount to William Sidney Mount, July 28, 1840. Cited by Pike, *Catching the Tune,* 8. Spelling as in original.

2. See Smith, *The Creolization of American Culture.* Smith cites this letter, dated January 17, 1841, in endnote 149, p. 269.

3. Mount, from his diary, dated July 10, 1866, cited in Frankenstein, *William Sidney Mount*, 425.

4. Jabbour, Introduction to *Folk Roots, New Roots: Folklore in American Life*, 10.

5. Letter from William Sidney Mount to C. M. Cady, Nov. 24, 1853. Cited by Pike, *Catching the Tune*, 13. Punctuation as in original.

6. See Ben-Amos, "The Seven Strands of Tradition." David Evans adds that in Latin *tradere* expresses the idea to transmit, but in a very personal, conscious, and direct process. He further notes, however, that "It can also mean to give up or surrender something. It's a pretty flexible word for various ways of transferring something." Evans to author, Apr. 28, 2024.

7. Walker, *Blues Unlimited*, 14.

8. Lundy, interview, Archive of American Folk Song recording. Quoted in Thomas Carter's notes to *Emmett W. Lundy, Fiddle Tunes from Grayson, County, Virginia.*

9. Mose Rager quote from Lightfoot, "A Regional Musical Style," 129.

10. Mercer quote in Miller, *Traveling Home*, 205. Italics as in original.

11. Vera Hall quoted in Sandburg, *New American Songbag*, 84. For more on Vera Hall and this song, see *The Beautiful Music All Around Us*, 153–78.

12. "Kyle Creed: A 1966 Interview by Charlie Faurot with Tom Mylet and Kirk Sutphin," 23–32. Kyle Creed's quote appears on p. 31.

13. Thanks to Scott Odell for his research into John Snipes's birth year. Email to author, Jan. 12, 2022. "Catch" appears in a quote from Snipes in Conway, *African Banjo Echoes in Appalachia*, 10.

14. Conway, *African Banjo Echoes in Appalachia*, 374. Italics as in original.

15. Conway, *African Banjo Echoes in Appalachia*, 380.

16. Thompson, interview, Nov. 3, 1987. See also Menius, "The Marrow of Tradition," 33–35. Joe Thompson's interest in audio documentation extends more broadly too. At the outset of the Seventh Day Adventist Choir's 1926 release, "On Jordan's Stormy Banks We Stand" (Columbia 14178-D), Brother Hubbard offers "a special prayer on the man that's a-catching the record for you." See John Minton's remarkable study, *78 Blues*, 95–96, 103.

17. I wrote this statement for Alan Jabbour as well as his other lines that appear in *Catching the Music*, a 1987 WETA-TV documentary, accessible on the Folkstreams website. For a profound discussion of early cylinder recording and ethnography, in particular the values and experiences of the people recorded, see Brady, "Performers and the Phonograph," 89–117.

18. Scarborough, *On the Trail of Negro Folk-Songs*, 4.

19. Stearns, "Critic Praises Dorothy Scarborough's Song Catcher in Southern Mountains," 23.

20. Fewkes, in May 2, 1890, issue of *Science*, quoted by Joseph C. Hickerson in "Early Field Recordings of Ethnic Music," 68. See also Brady, *A Spiral Way*. On pages 56–57, Brady points out that Fewkes's colleague, Frank Hamilton Cushing, may have made the first ethnographic recordings.

21. See Ward and Huber, *A & R Pioneers*. See also the great indexes of commercial vernacular recordings about this period: Tony Russell's *Country Music Records, A Discography 1921–1942*, *Blues and Gospel Records 1890–1943*, fourth edition, by Robert M. W. Dixon, John Godrich, and Howard W. Rye, and *Ethnic Music on Records, A Discography of Ethnic Recordings Produced in the United States, 1893–1942*, by Richard K. Spottswood.

22. From Ginell, *The Columbia 15000-D-Series Discography (1924–1933) Familiar Tunes Old & New.*

23. Evans to author, Apr. 28, 2024.

24. Maloney, "Irish Ethnic Recordings and the Irish-American Imagination," 97.

25. Archie Edwards in Barry Lee Pearson's "Appalachian Blues," 41.

26. For more on John Jackson, see this book's closing chapter, "A Storyteller's Story."

27. John Jackson's quote appears in Pearson, "Appalachian Blues," 41.

28. Smith, transcribed in author's notes to *In Sacred Trust: The 1963 Fleming Brown Tapes*. See track 34 to hear Hobart Smith make this October 1963 statement. I also recorded a portion of these words on *A Storyteller's Story: Sources of Banjo Dancing*, as "Hobart Smith on Music/Cumberland Gap," track 11.

29. Ebert, "A Hard Day's Night."

30. Likewise, piano maker Baldwin on the next block carried the imported if lesser lines of Hagstrom and Vox guitars. A few doors away, Eric Praeger and Wolfgang Ritter enlarged their trade in classical stringed instruments by adding "Chicago Guitar Gallery" to their business cards. A walk-in vault still safeguarded their inventory of old-world violins, while the main showroom now reached back with guitars of every description. At Kagan and Gaines nearby, which primarily served the needs of the Chicago Symphony Orchestra, its back shelves spilled with trapezoid-shaped cardboard boxes of low-priced electric guitars.

31. Grano, interview, Sept. 11, 1991.

32. As Rob Cook reports in *Franks for the Memories*, the store, after coming under the Lishons' ownership, chose not to use the possessive in its name, p. 61.

33. Seeger, "Prescriptive and Descriptive Music Writing," 168.

34. From *Chicago American*, December 17, 1836, quoted in Epstein, *Music Publishing in Chicago before 1871*, 3. Within a decade of Osbourn and Strail's establishment, Chicago's first music store opened, and in late 1853, its proprietor published the "Garden City Polka," written by Christopher Plagge, director of the Chicago Philharmonic Society. It became the earliest copyrighted piece printed in Chicago. Two years later, siblings A. J. and H. M. Higgins founded the city's first music publishing company in addition to dealing in instruments, accessories, and instruction books, as well as offering lessons. Higgins Brothers soon added a monthly magazine devoted to musical pursuits, *The Flower Queen* (later, *The Chi-*

cago Musical Revue), named after the 1851 cantata by composer George F. Root. The *Revue*'s editor was C. M. Cady, who, in 1859, partnered with Root to form Root & Cady. Along with song publishing, they, too, opened a music store selling a gamut of instruments—from pianos to banjos—along with offering repair services, to become the city's leading retail music outlet.

35. Cohen, *Folk Song America*, 5. See also his more extensive exploration of this idea in his *Long Steel Rail*, 21–38. Earlier yet, he proffered this definition in "Tin Pan Alley's Contribution to Folk Music," 15. In his 1998 Phillips Barry Memorial Lecture, which appears in *Southern Folklore* 56, no. 1 (1999), 3–26, "The Sinking of The Titanic and the Floundering of American Folksong Scholarship," he broadens his analysis, to distinguish between traditional songs and folksongs.

36. In this period, too, local banjo makers included Joseph Bohmann in 1876, followed by Edwin Cubley and J. B. Schall. Other Chicago-based instrument makers who achieved national prominence in that period included Holton and his circular bass tubas, Wunderlich and his cornets, and Guyer and his French horns. Come the twentieth century, similar renown was attached to Ludwig drums, famously used by Ringo Starr in the 1960s, and Deagan vibraharps, played by Lionel Hampton and Milt Jackson. See Brubaker, "Instrument Manufacturing," 56–61.

37. Cronon, *Nature's Metropolis*, 338.

38. Sky, *Mel Bay Presents Ryan's Mammoth Collection [of] 1050 Reels and Jigs, Hornpipes, Clogs, Walk-arounds, Essences, Strathspeys, Highland Flings and Contra Dances.* With a preface, introduction, notes, bibliography, and author's biographical sketch by Patrick Sky.

39. Ad for *Ryan's Mammoth Collection*. Reprinted in Wells, "Elias Howe, William Bradbury Ryan, and Irish Music in Nineteenth-Century Boston." Reproduction appears on p. 416.

40. Wells, "Elias Howe, William Bradbury Ryan, and Irish Music in Nineteenth-Century Boston," 418.

41. Wolfe, "The Fiddler's Bible," 43.

42. From cover of O'Neill's *Music of Ireland*, reproduced in *Making Music, Chicago Style*, 43.

43. The 1940 edition fit with other M. M. Cole publications also marketed by mail order. These included several prominent radio barn dance shows, like their *Grand Ole Opry* sampler. Each of these collections featured performers and songs associated with those broadcasts. Principally, though, M. M. Cole promoted country artists like Gene Autry, Red Foley, and Doc Hopkins, who had appeared on the WLS *National Barn Dance*. All these songbooks came printed "in regular sheet music size," supplemented with guitar chords and lyrics to constitute "the greatest selling books ever published." These quotations from the back cover of *Doc Hopkins and His Country Boys, Deluxe Edition*.

44. See in this book chapter four, "America's Favorite Folk Singer," which focuses on Doc Hopkins, calling attention to these Cole transcriptions.

45. This anecdote appears in Wolfe, "The Fiddler's Bible," 44. Doc Hopkins also told me this story of Alan Crockett's note-reading facility and often cited his superb musicianship.

46. Charlie Walden, quoted in Marshall, *Play Me Something Quick and Devilish*, 18.

47. See Marshall, *Play Me Something Quick and Devilish,* for portraits of these players, all of whom credited Cole. Beyond them, still more affected by Cole appear in Marshall's book.

48. See Marshall, *Play Me Something Quick and Devilish,* 99.

49. From back cover of *1000 Fiddle Tunes.* No date, beyond the 1940 copyright, renewed in 1967. Charles Wolfe identified this edition as 1984, which conforms with my own memory of acquiring it then.

50. Maloy in *Devil's Box,* 50.

51. See Wells, "Elias Howe, William Bradbury Ryan, and Irish Music in Nineteenth-Century Boston," 406–7, for this insight.

52. Marshall, *Play Me Something Quick and Devilish,* 252.

53. See *Corky Siegel with Seji Ozawa and the San Francisco Symphony Orchestra, Russo: Street Music; Three Pieces for Blues Band and Orchestra, featuring the Siegel/Schwall Band.* Added thanks to Corky Siegel for our clarifying conversation about his band's history on June 14, 2022, just five days before Jim Schwall's unexpected death.

54. Schwall, interview, Feb. 26, 2022.

55. Schwall, interview, Oct. 14, 2021.

56. Flerlage, interview, in Cushing, *Pioneers of the Blues Revival,* 198. For more on Flerlage in this book, see chapter ten, "Folksong Street."

57. Son House quote in Flerlage, *Chicago Blues as Seen from the Inside,* 76.

58. Muddy Waters, in Palmer, *Deep Blues,* 260.

59. Charlie Musselwhite, quoted in Pearson, *Pioneers,* xix.

60. Flerlage, *Chicago Blues as Seen from the Inside,* 60. Italics as in original.

61. Melford, interview, Nov. 6, 2021.

62. Bruynoghe, "Chicago, Home of the Blues." Both quotes appear on p. 69. See also *Blues Unlimited: Essential Interviews.* Greensmith's introduction, which mentions this article, set it in context of other blues writing of the time. My thanks to Chris Smith for obtaining and sharing Bruynoghe's article.

63. Charters, Notes to *Chicago/The Blues/Today, Volume One,* 29. He made these recordings in winter 1965.

64. Charters, Notes to *Chicago/The Blues/Today, Volume One,* 23.

65. Schwall, interview, Oct. 14, 2021.

66. Schwall, interview, Feb. 26, 2022.

67. Schwall, interview, Feb. 26, 2022.

68. Schwall, interview, Oct. 14, 2021.

69. See Cohen and Riesman, *Chicago Folk*.

70. Schwall, interview, Oct. 14, 2021.

71. Schwall, interview, Feb. 26, 2022.

72. Schwall, interview, Oct. 14, 2021.

73. Pearson, notes to *Honeyboy Edwards, Mississippi Delta Bluesman*, 9.

74. Edwards, interview, undated, ca. late 1996/early 1997. Thanks to Michael Frank and Marty Salzman for their efforts to recover Honeyboy's travel itinerary.

75. Edwards, interview, Aug. 6, 1998.

76. Edwards, interview, Aug. 6, 1998.

77. Edwards, interview, Aug. 6, 1998.

78. Edwards, *The World Don't Owe Me Nothing*, 117.

79. Edwards, interview, *Living Blues*, 20.

80. Edwards, interview, Aug. 6, 1998.

81. Edwards, interview, Aug. 6, 1998.

82. Edwards, interview with Pete Welding, *Blues Unlimited*, 5.

83. Edwards, *The World Don't Owe Me Nothing*, 118.

84. Palmer, David "Honeyboy" Edwards, *Mississippi Delta Bluesman*, 2. Palmer further explores this idea in relation to Edwards in "Pure Honeyboy Edwards."

85. Work, Jones, and Adams, *Lost Delta Found*, 87.

86. Edwards, interview, Aug. 6, 1998.

87. Edwards, interview, Aug. 6, 1998.

88. Junior Wells, quoted in Rowe, *Chicago Blues*, 117. Italics as in original. Both Barry Lee Pearson in *Sounds So Good to Me* and David Whiteis in *Chicago Blues: Portraits and Stories* invoke this well-told story. It even appears on Junior Wells's Wikipedia site (accessed Feb. 27, 2022).

89. Charters, *Chicago/The Blues/Today!*, notes to vol. 2, 39.

90. Henry Thomas earlier recorded for Brunswick in Chicago in 1927, much as Dave Macon did so again in 1929.

91. For more about Uncle Dave Macon, his acolytes, and collaborators, see in this book chapter nine, "Hands on the Tune."

92. See Cantwell, *Bluegrass Breakdown*, xi.

93. The album, *CORE Sit-In Songs: Songs of the Freedom Riders*, features on its inserted booklet's cover not two but four ledger lines of lunch counter seats arranged on the staff.

94. Robert Moses from a 1961 letter quoted in Danny Lyon's *Memories of the Southern Civil Rights Movement*, reprinted in "SNCC's Staff Photographer Reflects on Civil Rights Struggle in Mississippi."

CHAPTER 3. THE CONDUIT

An earlier version of this essay appeared in *The Journal of Country Music*, vol. 17, no. 3, 1995, pp. 7–12.

1. With the exception of these remarks and a few others remembered from over the years, most quotes here come from a taped interview I conducted with Fleming Brown on May 24, 1983. Author's collection.

2. Fleming put together this verse by combining "Lost John" with Furry Lewis's performance of "Kassie Jones," which appears on the Harry Smith anthology. Fleming knew that collection inside and out.

3. See Jones, *Minstrel of the Appalachians*, 77, 169–76.

4. Seeger, *How to Play the 5-string Banjo*, 2.

5. For much more on ownership and stewardship in folk culture, see the writings of professor Jeff Todd Titon. These include his 1991 paper, "Repertoire, Technique, and the Gift of Music among Three Kentucky Old-Time Fiddlers: Isham Monday, John M. Salyer, and Clyde Davenport."

CHAPTER 4. AMERICA'S FAVORITE FOLK SINGER

1. This characterization appeared on Doc's personal stationery that he received from WLS, as well as in their printed advertisements that included the periodical *State Fair Barn Dance Jamboree*, no. 1, 1947, p. 12. Along with other pictured stars of the WLS *National Barn Dance*, the caption identifies Doc Hopkins as "favorite singer of folksongs." His 1945 songbook, M. M. Cole's *Deluxe Edition, Doc Hopkins and his Country Boys*, also introduces him as "America's Favorite Singer of American Folk Songs," again in connection with the *National Barn Dance*. This branding of Doc by the station as a "folk singer" in the mid-1940s fit a trend in the country music industry as it moved towards finding a respectable term to replace "hillbilly" and "old time" for rural performers and their offerings. For Doc, the folk singer's mantle was set in motion as early as 1930, when Doc's predecessor at WLS, Bradley Kincaid, drew a value-laden distinction between "these fine old folk songs of the mountains, and the so-called Hilly Billy songs." Kincaid, *Favorite Old-Time Songs and Mountain Ballads*, 6.

2. Hopkins, "Studs Terkel with Doc Hopkins and Stephen Wade."

3. Hopkins, interview with Kahn, July 8, 1961.

4. Personal communication with author, spring 1987.

5. Hopkins, undated cassette tape letter, ca. 1983, with Doc's inscription, "From Doc to Steve."

6. Botkin, Introduction to *A Treasury of American Folklore*, xxii.

7. A number of citations reverse Doc's first name, Doctor, with his middle name, Howard, including his Chicago newspaper obituaries and on his gravestone, which his wife, Mary Locke Hopkins, elected to do, feeling, as she explained

to me, socially embarrassed if stated otherwise. Indeed, Doc himself at times flipped the two names, beginning at his elementary school where he was told that he needed to use Howard for the sake of clear communications in the classroom, rather than Doc or Doctor. See his interview with Ray Nemec, Apr. 17, 1969, which Ray kindly shared with me. The same tape, RP-OR-10-001-03 C, Side A, which includes this story, is housed in the Doc Hopkins, Audio Recordings Reference Collection, Berea College Department of Special Collections. Similar confusion attends the year of Doc's birth. He was born in 1900, but in order to enlist in World War I, he gave the year as 1899. He sometimes used that in later interviews, but the true date was 1900, just as his given name was Doctor Howard Hopkins. For more on Doc's past, see his interview with Berea College professor Loyal Jones, Oct. 24, 1975. There, too, Doc discusses altering the sequence of his name.

8. See Sterkert, "Focus for Conflict," 120. See also Brown, "Popular Beliefs and Superstitions," 38 and 66.

9. Hopkins, interview with Kahn, July 7, 1962.

10. Hopkins to author, "True History of Doc Hopkins," handwritten letter.

11. Hopkins, "Studs Terkel with Doc Hopkins and Stephen Wade."

12. Hopkins, "Studs Terkel with Doc Hopkins and Stephen Wade."

13. Hopkins, interview, Dec. 17, 1982.

14. Hopkins, interview with Kahn, July 8, 1961.

15. Hopkins to author, "To Steve from Doc," undated tape-recorded letter, ca 1983.

16. Hopkins, interview, Sept. 15, 1986.

17. Doc Hopkins, first quote, "I'll go there no more," from personal communication with author, ca. fall 1981. Last two quotes, interview, Dec. 17, 1981.

18. Hopkins to author, Nov. 28, 1983.

19. Cited in McCusker, *Lonesome Cowgirls and Honky-Tonk Angels*, 35.

20. Williams, *Staging Tradition*, 59. For more on Lair, see Williams, especially chapters 3 and 4.

21. Hopkins, interview with Kahn, July 8, 1961, part two. This Bill Cox is not the same as the hillbilly recording artist by that name who extensively recorded for Gennett, beginning in 1929, and later, for the ARC label and its affiliates.

22. Hopkins, interview with Green, June 11, 1974, transcript, 47, 49.

23. Hopkins, interview with Green, June 11, 1974, transcript, 48.

24. Wilgus, "Country-Western Music and the Urban Hillbilly," 143.

25. Quoted by Wilgus from back jacket of *Doc Hopkins* LP, Birch 1945 (1971). In addition to his extensive liner notes there, Wilgus also wrote about Doc Hopkins in "An Introduction to the Study of Hillbilly Music," *Journal of American Folklore*, 197. He mentions Doc Hopkins in connection to "Bradley Kincaid," in *Stars of Country Music: Uncle Dave Macon to Johnny Rodriguez*, edited by Bill C. Malone and Judith McCulloh, 92. Thanks to Erika Brady, emeritus professor of folklore from Western Kentucky University, who pointed out in her reader's report for

this book, that before Wilgus came to UCLA he taught at her school, then called Western Kentucky State College from 1955–1963. She writes, "His important—and at the time radical—attention to the interplay of commercial and 'front-porch' music derives from his fieldwork from this period."

26. "Greetings from Allan M. Trout," item 3, *Louisville Courier-Journal*, 33.

27. Wilgus, "The Text Is the Thing," 251.

28. Hopkins to author, Sept. 22, 1986.

29. Hopkins, interview, Sept. 15, 1986. See also "Voice of America Broadcast with Doc Hopkins" from July 16, 1982, which appears on *A Storyteller's Story*.

30. "*National Barn Dance* WLS Performances," April 10, 1942, broadcast.

31. Hopkins to author, Sept. 22, 1986.

32. Hopkins, tape-recorded letter, "Songs and Gags & Etc." Oct. 1983.

33. Hopkins, undated tape-recorded letter, ca. 1983, with Doc's inscription, "From Doc to Steve."

34. Hopkins, interview, Sept. 15, 1986.

35. See Bertrand, "Race and Rural Identity," 130–52. See also Brooks, *The Blackface Minstrel Show in Mass Media*.

36. Hopkins, interview, July 12, 1983.

37. This tearful evocation of a Black child's memorial service found its way from Doc's locker at WLS—from which, he ruefully noted, Karl Davis had taken it without his permission. Davis passed "The Funeral" along to Red Foley, whose use of it in "Steal Away" brought the latter considerable success. In turn, Foley's recording led to Hank Williams's 1950 rendition under its original title. Black versions include those recorded by the Morning Stars of Savannah, ca. 1980, Nashboro 7231 (LP) and the Staple Singers, early April 1965, Epic 9825 (45) LP/LP 24163. Thanks to David Evans and the Mighty Gospel Friends internet group for copies of these two stirring performances.

38. "The Old Chain Gang," in Doc Hopkins and Karl and Harty of The Cumberland Ridgerunners, *Mountain Ballads and Home Songs*, 7. The band is sometimes named as The Cumberland Ridgerunners and sometimes as the Cumberland Ridge Runners.

39. "Pickin' on the Old Banjo," in *Deluxe Edition, Doc Hopkins and His Country Boys*, 6.

40. Hopkins, interview, Sept. 15, 1986.

41. See Linn, *That Half-Barbaric Twang*.

42. Hopkins, interview with Kahn, Jan. 7, 1962.

43. Jones and Jones, in *Blues Unlimited*, 134–35. Moody Jones also conflates, understandably enough, the Prairie Ramblers band with the *Prairie Farmer* newspaper, which, for a time, owned WLS, where Doc performed in close association with the Prairie Ramblers.

44. Hopkins, interview with Nemec, Apr. 17, 1969.

45. Hopkins, "Tape of Doc to Steve," ca. 1986.

46. Hopkins, interview with Kahn, July 8, 1961.

47. Hopkins, personal communication with author, Summer 1982.

48. Burnett, interview with Archie Green and Eugene Earle.

49. Burnett, interview with Archie Green and Eugene Earle.

50. Dick Burnett, quoted in Charles Wolfe's notes to *A Ramblin' Reckless Hobo, The Songs of Dick Burnett and Leonard Rutherford.* Wolfe's interview with Burnett occurred in September 1974.

51. For a fuller discussion of this song-story, see Wade, *The Beautiful Music All Around Us,* 227–29. See also Archie Green's unsigned notes for "Trouble at the Coal Creek Mines" in *Doc Hopkins,* Birch 1945. For more on this piece, see my track notes in *Across the Amerikee: Showpieces from Coal Camp to Cattle Trail,* 25–26.

52. See Burnett's ca. 1913 songster, *Songs Sung by R. D. Burnett, The Blind Man, Monticello, Kentucky.* "The Jolly Butchers."

53. See Wilgus's notes to "Wreck of the Titanic" in *Doc Hopkins,* Birch 1945. The text to the Burnett song appears in his songster named above.

54. All quotations from Burnett's "Song of the Orphan Boy" appear in his songbook. That page is also reproduced in Dick Spottswood's *The Blue Sky Boys,* 212.

55. From 1962 Green/Earle interview with Burnett. Thanks to Dr. David Evans for his transcription of this melody, and to Robert Tucker Nance for transferring that handwritten notation to machine-readable form.

56. Hopkins, interview with Kahn, Jan. 7, 1962.

57. Hopkins, interview with Kahn, July 8, 1961.

58. Hopkins, interview with Green, June 11, 1974, 56.

59. See "Song of the Blind," in *Mountain Ballads and Home Songs,* 9.

60. See Spottswood, *Blue Sky Boys,* 211.

61. Hopkins, interview, Nov. 28, 1985.

62. Hopkins, interview with Nemec, Apr. 17, 1969.

63. Hopkins, "Studs Terkel with Doc Hopkins and Stephen Wade."

64. Hopkins, personal communication with author, ca. summer 1981.

65. "Dakota Jack," *The Maryville Times,* 3.

66. Uhl, "How Dead Is Herb-Doctoring?," 36. In this article the paper identifies Charlie White Moon as "J. C. Bunce," and on May 21, 1944, the paper names him "Charlie Bunce."

67. Hopkins to author, Sept. 22, 1986.

68. Hopkins to author, Sept. 22, 1986.

69. Hopkins to author, Dec. 18, 1983.

70. Hopkins, "Studs Terkel with Doc Hopkins and Stephen Wade."

71. "Dakota Jack," *The Johnson City Staff,* 6.

72. "A Message of Hope to the Sick and Afflicted," *Interior Journal*, 4.

73. "Victory for Dakota Jack, and Com-Cel-Sar," *The Owensboro Messenger*, 6.

74. Hopkins to author, personal communication, spring 1986.

75. Hopkins to author, personal communication and handwritten notes, spring 1986. I drew on these words for Doc's portion in the 1987 public television documentary *Catching the Music*.

76. Hopkins, interview, Dec. 17, 1981.

77. Hopkins, interview, Sept. 15, 1986.

78. Hopkins to author, Sept. 22, 1986.

79. Hopkins, interview, Sept. 15, 1986.

80. Hopkins, interview, Sept. 15, 1986.

81. Hopkins to author, Sept. 22, 1986.

82. Hopkins, personal communication with author, May 25, 1983.

83. Hopkins, interview, Sept. 15, 1986.

84. Hopkins, interview with Kahn, July 8, 1961.

85. Hopkins, interview, Dec. 17, 1981.

86. Brown, "Popular Beliefs and Superstitions," 446.

87. Hopkins, interview, Dec. 17, 1981.

88. Hopkins, interview, Dec. 17, 1981.

89. Hopkins, interview with Nemec, Apr. 17, 1969.

90. Hopkins, interview with Nemec, Apr. 17, 1969.

91. Hopkins to author, undated letter, ca. 1981, titled "Early Days at the Start of the Cumberland Ridge Runners, Doc Hopkins, Karl and Harty, and All the Others that Came into the Act Afterward."

92. Hopkins, tape, "Jokes and Gags," Sept. 1, 1984.

93. Hopkins, interview with Nemec, Apr. 17, 1969.

94. "Continue Regular Scheduled Programs at Buck Lake Ranch," *Angola Herald*, 1.

95. Quoted in liner notes to *Doc Hopkins*, Birch 1945.

96. Hopkins, interview with Kahn, July 8, 1961.

97. Hopkins, interview with Nemec, Apr. 17, 1969.

98. Hopkins, interview with Green, June 11, 1974, 46. See Macon, *Songs and Stories of Uncle Dave Macon*. Song No. 3 is Macon's arrangement of "You Can't Do Wrong and Get By."

99. Wilgus, notes to *Doc Hopkins*, Birch 1945. During Doc's residency in Los Angeles, when he was working as a machinist, Wilgus contacted him. The two met through the professor's UCLA colleague, Ed Kahn, whose research on "Coal Creek March" had led him to Doc Hopkins. Wilgus, with Barrett Hansen, recorded the contents of Doc's album on July 19, 1965.

100. Everlasting thanks to my oldest friend, Fred Ordower, who introduced

me to Doc. The two met at a Chicago venue where Doc was performing. When Doc recounted his musical past, Fred noted that he had taught Fleming Brown. Happily, Fred, then a nascent booking agent, soon became Doc's representative, which, in turn, led to our meeting at a gig Fred had booked. Doc and I began working together from that point on.

101. Hopkins, personal communication with author, Dec. 24, 1987.

102. Hopkins, "Studs Terkel with Doc Hopkins and Stephen Wade."

103. In 1948, Doc said this to Fleming Brown when Fleming first contacted him for banjo lessons. For an account of that conversation, see previous chapter, "The Conduit."

CHAPTER 5. ARCHIE'S "OLD MAN"

1. Archie dated the first draft as February 12, 1997, and the second, while undated, he accompanied with a letter dated March 25, 1997. Called "Green ms." hereafter in these notes.

2. Green, interview, Aug. 2, 2006.

3. "Old Man" aired on NPR's *All Things Considered* on August 23, 2006. It remains accessible on the NPR website as "Leadbelly's 'Old Man' and the Work Song Tradition."

4. Green ms., second draft, 3.

5. Green ms., second draft, 18.

6. Green ms., second draft, 2.

7. Green to author, May 5, 2003.

8. Green, interview, Aug. 2, 2006.

9. Distler, notes to *Work Songs of the U.S A. Sung by Lead Belly*. Spelling as in original.

10. Lomax, "Work Songs" in notes to *Negro Sinful Songs*.

11. Smith, "King of the 12 String Guitar." This review, which draws on Smith's interview with Lead Belly shortly before the album's release, originally appeared in *Jazz Magazine*, no. 4, 1942, and was reprinted in Jones, McCarthy, and Ramsey, *A Tribute to Huddie Ledbetter*, 4–6. Another review of the album by Charles Wilford appears in the same publication, 19–20.

12. For more on the origin of "Rock Island Line" and Lead Belly's creative reinterpretation of it, see chapter two of *The Beautiful Music All Around Us*.

13. "Haul Away Joe" on Lead Belly, *Bourgeois Blues, Lead Belly Legacy Vo. 2*.

14. For this usage, see "The 'Old Man,'" chapter nine, 71–77, in Merrick, *Old Times on the Upper Mississippi*.

15. "Old Man," Asch 103 B, on *Work Songs of the U.S.A.* Author's transcription.

16. "The River: Weather and Business—Arrivals and Departures of Steamboats," *Times-Picayune*, 2.

17. Freight list from "Boats Leaving To-Day," *Daily Memphis*; "Gentlemen" from "Boats Leaving To-Day," *New Orleans Republican*; "crowds" from "Ledger Lines," *Memphis Public Ledger.*

18. "River Intelligence," *The Cincinnati Daily Enquirer*, Jan. 27, 1868, 4.

19. Hearn, *Children of the Levee*, "Levee Life," 68–69.

20. Wheeler, *Steamboatin' Days*, 19.

21. See Wheeler, *Steamboatin' Days*, 35–37. See also Wheeler's correspondence with Joe Curtis at the Memphis *Commercial Appeal*, August 20, 1940, followed by letters dated August 22 and August 27, 1940, from Department of Commerce inspectors headquartered in New Orleans. In all these responses the steamboats *Richmond* and *Belle Lee* appear together. This association evidently informs Wheeler that her source for "Oh, Annie Oh!" refers to the *Belle Lee*. In Wheeler's note 18 to the song on page 37 in *Steamboatin' Days*, I think she conflates the earlier *Belle Lee* with the larger vessel completed in 1868.

22. Alden, "Sailor Songs," *Harper's Magazine*, 281.

23. Hazel, AFS 3098 B.

24. Hazel, AFS 3097 B. Kentucky-bred chronicler Ben Lucien Burman reiterates these extraordinarily long hours, writing, "Several times when in some emergency the roustabouts had been toiling for thirty-six hours without respite." Burman, "Mississippi Roustabout," 636.

25. "Lead Belly Radio Show WNYC, 1/13/1944 (ACT-392.)" Thanks to Jeff Place of Smithsonian Folkways archives for dub of this appearance.

26. The Library of Congress index card catalogue for "Black Gal," AFS 253-A-2, names the singers as "unidentified," but as John Lomax's personnel announcement reveals elsewhere during this recording session, as well as discernible from their distinctive performance style, the individuals named here sang this piece. I'm much indebted to discographer and scholar Chris Smith for this information.

27. The letter referenced here Alan Jabbour sent to Judith McCulloh, dated October 10, 1969. She mentions it on page 306 of her 1970 doctoral dissertation for Indiana University: "'In the Pines': The Melodic-Textual Identity of an American Lyric Folksong Cluster."

28. See AFS 253 A-1, "Longest Train I Ever Saw."

29. See "Old Man, Will Your Dog Catch a Rabbit?" *Lead Belly's Last Sessions.*

30. Brown, "Songs of the Slave," 620. Earlier, "roustabout" appears in "Affray on Steamboat," unsigned article in the *Daily Missouri Republican*, 3. Eileen Southern cites a ca. 1800 roustabout song text she found in Scharf's *History of Philadelphia*, 931. See *The Music of Black Americans, A History*, 148. Thanks to Ryan Benyo and Mike Monseur for their notational help with "Steamboat Song" and "Woman, Woman."

31. "Solo," italics as in original, Brown, "Songs of the Slave."

32. See "I'm Gwine to Alabamy" in *Slave Songs of the United States*, 89.

33. See Bertha Wheeler Wenzel's album, *Steamboatin' Songs, Authentic Americana 1860–1900*, recorded 1964, and resissued on CD, self-published, n.d., accompanied by Bill Small. No label or number is indicated on the product, a gift from the artist to the author. I visited Mary Wheeler's collection on September 29 through October 1, 2006, as well as called on Bertha Wenzel, with whom I continued to correspond. Lasting thanks to both her and to Vonnie Shelton, reference librarian at the McCracken Public Library, Paducah, Ky., for making this visit so richly rewarding.

34. See "Woman, Woman, I See Yo' Man," in Wheeler, *Steamboatin' Days*, 118.

35. Miss Jerome Sage's four-page typed document, dated May 17, 1939, appears with the papers pertaining to the 1939 recording expedition housed at the Mississippi Department of Archives and History. Herbert Halpert recorded James Archer on May 29, 1939.

36. See Eskew's 1939 "Coonjine in Manhattan" for additional steamboat reference to "Rango." p. 7. Also, see Abbott Ferriss's field notes to "Folk Music Recordings Made in Mississippi by Herbert Halpert, May 1939," 414–15.

37. Jerome Sage spells "Rango" as "Wrango," but otherwise her transcription of the verse closely approximates Ferriss's. Capitalization as in original.

38. See Archer, "Rango."

39. AFS 3076 B1, "Steamboat Song," sung by Emmett Jackson, and recorded on May 30, 1939. Abiding thanks to Matthew Barton of the Library of Congress's Recorded Sound Division and Todd Harvey of its folk archive for providing this recording and other much-needed audio resources during the pandemic that closed otherwise open collections to public view.

40. See Ferriss, field notes, 424–25. Emmet Jackson's discussion appears on AFS 3076 A2, "Steamboat Song."

41. See AFS 3081 A, Jackson and Floyd, "Old Steamboat, Roustabout Song." See also Ferriss, field notes, 441.

42. Shores's sounding calls have appeared both on published records and in print. Among the earliest, see "Mississippi Sounding Call," in Botkin's *A Treasury of Mississippi River Folklore*, 572–73. Before that, Shores's recording appeared on *Negro Work Songs and Calls*, AAFS, album 8, which Botkin edited in 1943. In the mid-1980s, Erika Brady, then living in Cape Girardeau, Missouri, took Archie Green to see "a few older deckhands who could 'perform' sounding calls. Archie, visiting at the time, was completely enthralled by observing this in action." From Brady's reader's report for this book.

43. AFS 3094 B2 and 3095 A1. Shores, "Roustabout Song." See Ferriss, field notes, 488–90. On the second take, Shores calls it "Roustabout Corn Song."

44. For its whaling usage, see William Alden's discussion of "Randso" in "Sailor Songs," 284.

45. Green ms., second draft, 19.

46. See Snyder, "Leadbelly and His Windjammer."

47. Hally Wood's transcription of "Old Man" first appeared in *The Leadbelly Legend*, edited by John and Alan Lomax, 58. She reprinted it in her liner notes to *Songs to Live By*. Her source comes from Lead Belly's 1948 recording, made by Frederic Ramsey Jr. Another transcription of the song, following the same melody, but set in a different key by Jerry Silverman, appears as "Old Man, Will Your Dog Catch a Rabbit?" in Moses Asch and Alan Lomax, *The Leadbelly Songbook*, 49. It begins with the same 1948 text that Wood used, plus four additional verses.

48. Wood, notes to "Poor Howard," *Songs to Live By*.

49. For "Red Bird" see Lead Belly, *Bourgeois Blues*. Thanks to Norm Cohen for his invaluable thoughts about "Spike Driver Blues" and "Old Man."

50. See Bascom Lamar Lunsford's "Swannanoa Tunnel" on *Smoky Mountain Ballads*, Folkways FA 2040, 1953. Recent research on its Black origins appears in Kehrberg and Keith, "Somebody Died, Babe."

51. I'm indebted to Dr. David Evans for these insights. Evans to author, Sept. 28, 2020.

52. Lead Belly, AAFS4469-B (a) "Monologue on Square Dances [or] Sooky Jumps."

53. Alden, "Sailor Songs," 285.

54. Burman, "Mississippi Roustabout," 636–37.

55. See Davenport, "Old Cow Died in the Forks of the Branch."

56. See my notes to "Chatham Hill Serenade," in Smith, *In Sacred Trust: The 1963 Fleming Brown Tapes*.

57. Tross, "Old Man, May I Have Your Daughter." See also "Clarence Tross, Hardy County Banjoist," by Kip Lornell and J. Roderick Moore in *Mountains of Music, West Virginia Traditional Music from Goldenseal*. See also Milnes, "The Banjo in West Virginia."

58. Smith, "King of the 12 String Guitar," in *A Tribute to Huddie Ledbetter*, 6.

59. Paley, "Salty Dog," *Hard Luck Papa, Old Time Picking Styles & Techniques*. For more on Tom Paley's visits with Lead Belly, see p. 63 in *The Beautiful Music All Around Us*.

60. From "Corn Bread Rough" on *Work Songs of the U.S.A.*

61. Smith, "King of the 12 String Guitar," 4. Italics appeared in the original.

62. Cohen, "Old Man," performed by Hally Wood, in *Folk Song America, A 20th Century Revival*.

63. Green, interview, Aug. 2, 2006.

64. Green ms., second draft, 19.

65. Green, interview, Aug. 2, 2006.

66. "Old Man, Can I Have Your Daughter," *The Hammons Family: The Traditions of a West Virginia Family and Their Friends*, 74.

67. Proffitt, "Sourwood Mountain."

68. Evans, *Afro-American Folk Music from Tate and Panola Counties, Mississippi*, 32–34. See also Talley, *Negro Folk Rhymes*, "Chicken in the Bread Tray," 6. For more references, see Belden and Hudson, *Frank C. Brown Collection of North Carolina Folklore III*, 205–6.

69. Scarborough, *On the Trail of Negro Folk-Songs*, 194.

70. Ford, *Traditional Music of America*, 36. See also entry in Bayard, *Dance to the Fiddle, March to the Fife*.

71. Tucker, "Hog Eye."

72. "Hog Eye," from Pope's Arkansas Mountaineers.

73. Quoted from "Hog Eye," Traditional Tune Archive, retrieved Jan. 28, 2021. https://tunearch.org/wiki/Annotation:Hog_Eye_(1). Quotation from Legman, *Roll Me in Your Arms*.

74. See Mack McCormick's notes to "Boar Hog Blues," 5–6, on *The Unexpurgated Folk Songs of Men* where he discusses the "Hog-Eye" symbol. As McCormick rightly observes, Texas Alexander recorded this title as "Boe Hog Blues," March 10, 1928 (OKeh 8563).

75. David "Stringbean" Akeman quote from "Say Old Man Can You Play the Banjo" on *Hee Haw Corn Shucker*.

76. "Hard of Hearing," from Belden, *Ballads and Songs Collected by the Missouri Folk-Lore Society*, 265.

77. See Charles K. Wolfe's headnote to "Old Woman" in *Folk Songs of Middle Tennessee: The George Boswell Collectio*n, 128.

78. For just two of the many times this verse has appeared in print see Wheeler, *Steamboatin' Days*, 6, and Eskew, "Coonjine in Manhattan."

79. Macon, "The Cross Eyed Butcher And The Cackling Hen." Capitalization as in original. In this book's chapter nine, "Hands on the Tune," see its discussion of the roustabout song "Rock About My Saro Jane."

80. Green, interview, Aug. 2, 2006.

81. Green ms., second draft, 24.

82. Green to author, memo, Feb. 12, 1997.

83. Green ms., second draft, 26.

84. Green ms., second draft, 24.

85. Green, interview, Aug. 2, 2006.

86. This number of interviews as of March 2025.

87. Harris, AFC interview, Nov. 16, 2011.

88. See "coonjine," in *Dictionary of American Regional English*,765–76. See also Eskew, "Coonjine in Manhattan." Near the end of his 1939 report, Eskew refers to "an accomplished musical composer in Paducah, Kentucky," who is planning "to bring out a book of Coonjine songs with music." Calling it "an invaluable addition

to our vanishing Americana," he is surely referring to Mary Wheeler, who, by then, had completed her master's thesis that she was transforming into what became *Steamboatin' Days* five years later. A thorough study of "Coonjine" appears in Lynn Abbott and Doug Seroff, *Out of Sight*, 308–12.

89. Green, interview, Aug. 2, 2006.

CHAPTER 6. THE SOUND WAGON

1. Ferriss, interview, Jan. 20, 1997.

2. Willingham, interview, June 10, 1939.

3. Dodge, interview, Feb. 2, 1997. Second quote from her personal memoir, "We All Have a Past," 1. Third quote, personal communication with author, early 1997. Forever thanks to Steven Dodge for sharing this written account from his mother, and those penned by his aunts Mary and Carolyn.

4. Kerns to Douglass, Apr. 21, 1939.

5. Mary Emma Willingham, "Mary's History," 13.

6. Family memories date Willingham's coming to Gulfport a few years later than 1902 as reflected in Clarence Kerns's account in the field notes. Willingham's first child, Ona Mae, by his previous marriage to Ona White, was born in Jackson in 1914. Following the death of his wife, he entered into his second marriage to Larlie Warden, eight years or so later. Their marriage bore eight more children.

7. Dodge, interview, Feb. 2, 1997.

8. Bishop, telephone conversation with author, July 7, 2011.

9. Dodge, interview, Feb. 2, 1997.

10. During playback, others may adjust the pitch of his strings a step higher. Either way, he set his banjo in accordance with open G tuning (gDGBD) or double C (gCGCD).

11. Willingham to Halpert, AFS 3113 A.

12. This picture appears on the back cover of *The Beautiful Music All Around Us.*

13. Willingham to Halpert, AFS 3118 B2.

14. Gordon, "Banjo Songs," 79.

15. Willingham, "Roll on the Ground." This recording first appears on Folk Music of the United States, Album II, *Anglo-American Shanties, Lyric Songs, Dance Tunes and Spirituals* (1942), and beginning in 1956, subsequently reissued on LP. I also included it, with Willingham's comments and Halpert's questions, on *A Treasury of Library of Congress Field Recordings.* See note 19 for the song's text, tablature, and musical notation, which appear on pp. 390–91, in Bolick and Austin, *Mississippi Fiddle Tunes and Songs from the 1930s.*

16. Dodge, interview, Feb. 2, 1997.

17. Gordon, "Banjo Songs," 84.

18. Dodge, interview, Feb. 2, 1997. She repeated this thought, in these words, during our two subsequent visits in 1998 and 1999.

19. AFS field notes, "Folk Music Recordings made in Mississippi by Herbert Halpert," 538. Clarence Kerns's interview with Willingham also included song transcriptions taken down by dictation and later incorporated in the field notes that Ferriss submitted at the trip's conclusion. For more of Kerns's notes (attributed to Ferriss, but in truth, Kerns's handiwork, which Ferriss explained during our conversations), see Bolick and Austin, *Mississippi Fiddle Tunes and Songs from the 1930s*. The authors include their musical notations and banjo tablatures of the songs Willingham played during his session, 375–403. See also Harry Bolick's compilation of Willingham's recordings on *Mississippi Fiddle Tunes and Songs from the 1930s*. Disc three, tracks 13–31.

20. Dodge. First quote from "We Have a Past" memoir. Second quote from Dodge, interview, Feb. 2, 1997.

21. Mary Willingham, "Mary's History," 11. The "rabbit tobacco" she mentions here is a medicinal herb.

22. Dodge, "We Have a Past."

23. Dodge, "We Have a Past."

24. Dodge, interview, Feb. 2, 1997.

25. Dodge, interview, Feb. 2, 1997.

26. Dodge, interview, Feb. 2, 1997.

27. Dodge, interview, Feb. 27, 1999.

28. Dodge, interview, Feb. 2, 1997.

29. AFS field notes, 539.

30. Halpert quoted in an unsigned article by Abbott Ferriss, *Memphis Commercial Appeal,* July 23, 1939.

31. Hazel, notes, Negro Roustabout Songs, "Folk Music Recordings made in Mississippi by Herbert Halpert," hand-numbered page 492.

32. Halpert, "Federal Theatre and Folksong," 83. In his 1939 notebook, under the heading of "Halpert on Miss. Songs," Ferriss writes in reference to Sam Hazel, "This shows conclusively the fact that not race but environment is the basis for culture." Notebook 7, Mississippi Department of Archives and History.

33. Halpert, interview with Farber, Kodish, and Parsons, Nov. 17, 1978.

34. See Mead, "Roll the Cotton Down!" See also both Hugill, *Shanties from the Seven Seas*, 123–28; and Doerflinger, *Songs of the Sailor and Lumberman*, 32–34, 350–51.

35. Bolick and Austin, *Mississippi Fiddle Tunes and Songs from the 1930s*, 108.

36. Advertisement from Victor catalog reprinted in Russell, *Blacks, Whites and Blues*, 19.

37. Thanks to Kurt Nauck, David Giovannoni, Gerald Fabris and the Thomas Edison National Historical Park, David Seubert, Jay Bruder, Tom Mindte, and Tim Brooks for their help with Billy Golden research. Thanks also to Norm Cohen for his guidance regarding nineteenth-century published minstrel songsters.

38. See Hearn, "Dolly/An Idyl of the Levee," in the *Cincinnati Commercial,* reprinted in *Children of the Levee,* 21. He also mentions the song in "Banjo Jim's Story," first published on October 1, 1876, in the *Cincinnati Commercial,* and reprinted in *Children of the Levee,* 27.

39. See Talley, *Negro Folk Rhymes,* 217–18.

40. See "Workin' on the Levee, Sleepin' on de Ground" sung by Jim Henry, AFS 941-A2. This appears on *Mississippi: Saints & Sinners, From Before the Blues and Gospel.* See Jones ms. "The Mississippi Delta," 15. For wheel rolling songs and the laboring they represent, see Archie Green's discussion of the "roll on, buddy" verse in "Nine Pound Hammer" in *Only a Miner,* 329–69.

41. Mainer, interview, July 22, 1999

42. Logan, interviews, Oct. 4, 2001, and Oct. 18, 2001.

43. "A Page of Breakdowns," *People's Songs,* 3.

44. Mary Willingham, "Mary's History," 13.

45. Botkin, "The Function of a Folk Festival," 3. See also Mark Davidson's extensive discussion of this passage, its context, and its wider ramifications in his 2015 University of California–Santa Cruz dissertation, "Recording the Nation: Folk Music and the Government in Roosevelt's New Deal 1936–1941."

46. Abbott Ferriss used this phrase during our 1997 interview. He originally titled it for his essay on the trip, "Music Tour Remembered," that appeared in the liner notes to *Great Big Yam Potatoes: Anglo-American Fiddle Music from Mississippi.*

47. Halpert, interview, 1978.

48. Halpert to author, first quote, Feb. 10, 1997. Second quote, Jan. 28, 1997.

CHAPTER 7. ANY WAY YOU CAN

1. This was the "Mountain Banjo: Will Keys and Lee Sexton with Doug Dorschug and Rich Kirby" workshop that took place on July 4, 2003, between 3 and 4 p.m. at the Bristol Mural Stage in the "Appalachia: Heritage and Harmony" program. I served as the workshop's presenter.

2. Will Keys to author, Sept. 18, 1986. Punctuation as in the original letter.

3. Will Keys to author, June 23, 1996.

4. Will Keys with Kuhns and Smith, *Oldtime Banjo from Blackley Creek.*

5. Will Keys with Kuhns and Smith, *Oldtime Banjo from Blackley Creek.*

6. Doug Smith and Barb Kuhns also noted Will's talent for finding four-leaf clovers at festivals, and bequeathing them to his friends. "It seems whenever Will was on a smoke break, especially when sitting on the doorway to the bus, which is lower than the average chair, he was on the lookout for four-leaf clovers. He would present them to whoever was nearby. A pretty sweet gesture, and perhaps another aspect of his active mind." Smith to author, Mar. 9, 2021.

7. *Oldtime Banjo from Blackley Creek.*

8. Bill Keys to author, May 8, 2021. Here, Bill is quoting his father.

9. Bill Keys to author, Mar. 9, 2021.

10. Will Keys's "cattle" quote appears in the notes to *Sweet Marie,* a published cassette featuring Will Keys, and accompanied by Barbara Kuhns and Doug Smith. Additional information about the family relationship comes from Jerry Keys, who described his mother's relationship to Bob Clark. From a recorded interview with the author, March 28, 2021.

11. Robert Taylor quoted in Charles K. Wolfe, *Tennessee Strings,* 23 and 25.

12. See [Ex-Governor] Alf. Taylor entry, in Russell, *Country Music Records,* 892.

13. Bill Keys to author, Mar. 12, 2021.

14. Bill Keys to author, May 4, 2021.

15. Jerry Keys, interview, Mar. 7, 2021.

16. Will Keys, interview, July 1, 1986.

17. Bill Keys to author, May 5, 2021.

18. Bill Keys to author, May 5, 2021.

19. Bill Keys, interview, Mar. 2, 2021.

20. *Oldtime Banjo from Blackley Creek.*

21. Will Keys, banjo workshop, July 4, 2003.

22. Bill Keys to author, Mar. 4, 2021.

23. Will Keys, personal communication with author, July 1986.

24. Lloyd, interview, Mar. 5, 2021.

25. Bill Keys, interview, Mar. 2, 2021.

26. Will Keys interview with Jerry Keys, *Banjo Newsletter*, 7.

27. Will Keys to author, Sept. 18, 1986.

28. Will Keys interview in *Banjo Newsletter*, 7.

29. Bill Keys to author, Apr. 19, 2021.

30. Bill Keys to author, Apr. 19, 2021.

31. Will Keys in Paine-Brooks, "Banjo Picker's Style Earns Award," 1.

32. Mindte, unpublished remembrance of Will Keys, May 2006. Thanks to Tom Mindte for his affectionate essay.

33. Will Keys, interview, July 1, 1986.

34. *Oldtime Banjo from Blackley Creek.*

35. Jerry Keys, interview, Mar. 7, 2021.

36. Will Keys, quoted in Wald, "Banjo Strummin,'" 112.

37. Jerry Keys, interview, Mar. 7, 2021.

38. Quoted by Bill Keys, interview, Mar. 2, 2021.

39. See James, *The Complete Bloomington Concert- Part I (March 30, 1968),* track 2, titled "Skip James Talking," Also, see Hurston, "High John de Conquer," 107. I discuss her usage of the phrase in "A Straight Lick and a Crooked Stick,"

Polk County, Performance Journal, 20–21. Tayari Jones and Genevieve West cite additional uses in *Hitting a Straight Lick with a Crooked Stick*, ix-xliii. A 2019 CD by Marietta Simpson, titled *Crooked Stick: Songs in a Strange Land*, invokes the expression for this eclectic musical interpretation of Black spirituals.

40. For more on mother wit, see Safire, "The Way We Live Now." See also Dundes, *Mother Wit from the Laughing Barrel*. Beginning with "custom and wisdom . . . ," I previously used these words to define folk practice in *The Beautiful Music All Around Us*, p. 204.

41. Will Keys, *A Banjo Original*.

42. 1996 National Endowment for the Arts, *National Heritage Fellowships Program Book*, 10.

43. Fulcher, personal communication with author, Sept. 28, 1996.

44. Bill Keys to author, July 15, 2021.

45. The Galax Convention inserts the apostrophe as "Old Fiddler's" rather than "Old Fiddlers."

46. Lloyd, interview, Mar. 5, 2021.

47. Glassie, "Tradition," 177.

48. Barry, "The Part of the Folk Singer in the Making of Folk Balladry." See discussion of this quote in *The Beautiful Music All Around Us*, note 103, p. 406. Italics as in original.

49. Barry, "The Part of the Folk Singer in the Making of Folk Balladry," 61. Also, see note 105 in *The Beautiful Music All Around Us*, p. 407.

50. Work III, "Folk Songs of the American Negro," 32.

51. Will Keys to author, June 23, 1996.

52. Will Keys, *Banjo Newsletter*, 7.

53. Will Keys, *Banjo Newsletter*, 6.

54. Blaustein, notes to *Down Around Bowmantown*, 3.

55. Will Keys, *Banjo Newsletter*, 7.

56. Smith, quoted in the liner notes to The Home Folks, *Last Chance*.

57. *Evergreen* went into publication in 1992. Cloudlands CLC006.

58. *Oldtime Banjo from Blackley Creek*.

59. Glassie, "Tradition," 176.

60. Will Keys, *Down Around Bowmantown*, 7.

61. McGee, interview, July 9, 1981. For more on Kirk McGee, see this book's chapter nine, "Hands on the Tune."

62. Bagsby, interview, July 9, 1981.

63. Wolfe, *A Good-Natured Riot*, 190.

64. Arthur Smith's 1937 Bluebird recording of "I'm Bound to Ride," Bluebird BB B-7325, provides his earliest commercially issued banjo recording. On *Milk 'em in the Evening Blues*, Folkways FTS 31007, issued in 1968, he plays it on

"Uncle Buddy," and adds his banjo accompaniment to Kirk McGee's fiddle tune, "Lafayette."

65. Forster, interview, July 9, 1982.

66. Forster, interview, July 9, 1982.

67. Stringbean, quoted in Charles K. Wolfe's liner notes to Omer Forster, banjo, featuring Houston Daniel and The Highland Rim Boys, *Flowery Girls*. See also Matt Brown's tablature of "Flowery Girls" as performed on that album.

68. Bledsoe, interview, Mar. 4, 2021.

69. Will Keys, *Down Around Bowmantown*, 8.

70. Will Keys, *Banjo Newsletter*, 7.

71. Will Keys, *Down Around Bowmantown*, 7.

72. I'm indebted to conversations and notes exchanged with Bob Sayers about these matters in December 2019 and January 2020.

73. Will Keys, *Down Around Bowmantown*, 8.

74. See Ted Olson's notes, "Fiddle Style" Banjo, in Carroll Best and the White Oak String Band, *Old-Time Bluegrass from the Great Smoky Mountains, 1956 & 1959*. See also Best, *Say Old Man, Can You Play the Banjo?*

75. Trischka, *Melodic Banjo*, 27.

76. Blaustein, *Down Around Bowmantown*, 8.

77. Jerry Keys, interview, Mar. 7, 2021.

78. Jerry Keys to author, July 18, 2021.

79. Jerry and Will Keys, *Sycamore Shoals*.

80. Jerry Keys to author, Aug. 22, 2021.

81. Bledsoe, interview, Mar. 4, 2021.

82. Will Keys, *Oldtime Banjo from Blackley Creek*.

83. Bill Keys, interview, Mar. 2, 2021.

84. Dorschug, liner notes to *Evergreen*.

85. Jerry Keys, interview, Mar. 7, 2021.

CHAPTER 8. EQUIPMENT FOR LIVING

1. *A Treasury of Library of Congress Field Recordings*. "Lead Me to the Rock," as performed by Wash Dennis and Charlie Sims, appears as track 20 on this collection.

2. For more about *The General's Daughter* and utilization of these recordings in the film, see *The Beautiful Music All Around Us*, 121–23.

3. This was Ella Hoffpauir Boudreaux of New Iberia, Louisiana, singing "Sept ans sur mer" with her older sisters, Elita and Mary Hoffpauir. For more on Ella, see *The Beautiful Music All Around Us*, 17–20. Simon West, the film's director, chose not to use this piece, leaving only three tracks from the *Treasury* in the movie. A more recent field recording from the Lomax series on Rounder was

substituted, also reshaped by Greg Hale Jones, in addition to the film's principal score and arrangements, set by Carter Burwell.

4. Helen Marie Rowe appears in chapter three, "Ora Dell Graham, A Little Black Girl from Mississippi," *The Beautiful Music All Around Us*, 91–93.

5. Rowe, tape recorded message, May 17, 2004.

6. Courlander, *Terrapin's Pot of Sense*. We also read aloud from *Go Gator and Muddy the Water, Writings by Zora Neale Hurston from the Federal Writers' Project*.

7. Brewer, *Dog Ghosts and Other Negro Folk Tales* and *The Word on the Brazos*; Hughes and Bontemps, *The Book of Negro Folklore*; Talley, *The Negro Traditions*; Puckett, *Folk Beliefs of the Southern Negro*; Abrahams, *Deep Down in the Jungle*; Roberts, *South from Hell-fer-Sartin*; Oster, "Negro Humor"; Dorson, *American Negro Folktales*; Randolph, *The Devil's Pretty Daughter and Other Ozark Folk Tales* and *Blow the Candle Out*; and Jones, "A Descriptive and Analytical Study of the American Negro Folktale."

8. Ware to author, Facebook DM communication, Sept. 4, 2024.

9. Burke, *Counter-Statement*, 143. Also cited in Abrahams, *Everyday Life*, 1. With respect to Charlie Sims, I was fortunate to visit Rev. Willie Sims and Stephanie Sims (on both March 9 and 10, 1999), a Sims family cemetery, and Egypt, Mississippi, where Charlie lived at the time of his imprisonment at Parchman. Others bearing this last name whom I visited during that time also had no relation to Charlie. In subsequent years, the Rev. Willie Sims and I remained in touch.

10. Burke, "Literature as an Equipment for Living."

11. Burke, *The Philosophy of Literary Form*, 109. Italics as in original. He reprints the original essay here too, retitled as "Literature as Equipment for Living."

12. Mississippi Department of Corrections, microfilm document checklist.

13. "The State vs. Wash Dennis, Robbery with a Firearm." Second District Circuit Court, State of Mississippi, Chickasaw County.

14. Jones to Standish, Mar. 9, 1961.

15. State of Mississippi, Monroe County, Oct. 24, 1927, handwritten grand jury document.

16. Mississippi Department of Corrections, microfilm document checklist.

17. List of "colored" educable children, town of Prairie, MS., Nov. 8, 1923, 493 and 489.

18. "The State vs. Charlie Sims, Murder." Second District Circuit Court, State of Mississippi, Chickasaw County.

19. Charlie Sims file, October 7, 1947.

20. Sgt. T. L. Gorrell memo, October 28, 1947. Charlie Sims file. Also in memo there dated November 11, 1947.

21. "Mississippi State Penitentiary, Physical Examination and Description." Charlie Sims file.

22. Although various indexes report the Wash Dennis and Charlie Sims recording of "Lead Me to the Rock" AFS 739-A, as having occurred on Thursday, April 16, 1936, Lomax verbally identifies the earlier date at the conclusion of their performance. He also specifies that date on "There Was a Man," AFS 610-B, at Camp 8 where they resided, just as he did with "John Baptize Me (Do You Know Him)," AFS 739 B-1. Of the latter, John Lomax only gives the parenthetical title as its name. Indexes further report Charlie Sims's participation on both AFS 739 B1 and B2. While this second number lacks Lomax's announcement naming the participants, the song appears on the same disc immediately following the other, and it includes the same distribution of voices.

23. Notation from listing to "Convict Groups" at "Brickyard Camp," courtesy of Chris Smith, revisions for *Blues & Gospel Recordings—1890–1943*, forthcoming fifth edition.

24. "Monologue [The Alphabet of the Parchman Penitentiary]," AFS 598 A4.

25. Lomax, *Adventures of a Ballad Hunter*, 144. David Evans cites this passage in the notes to *Deep River of Song*. Alan Lomax subsequently recorded Dobie Red at Parchman in 1948.

26. Boyd, "Calling Trains."

27. "Lord, I'm in Trouble," AFS 743-B1, sung by Joe Miller and Jim Henry, published on *Mississippi: Saints & Sinners*.

28. Evans, notes to *Mississippi: Saints & Sinners*.

29. Abrahams, *Everyday Life*, 144.

30. Psalm 61, *The Holy Bible*, 774.

31. "Lead Me to the Rock," from E. O. Excell, *Triumphant Songs. No. 5: A Collection of Gospel Hymns for Sunday-Schools and Revivals*, 122–23. "Lead Me to the Rock" in Work III, *American Negro Songs and Spirituals*, 75. An alternative refrain for "Lead Me to the Rock" appears in *Morning Light*, no. 112, n.p. Psalm 89:26, *The Holy Bible*, 794, and 1 Corinthians 10: 4., 245.

32. Odum, "Religious Folk-Songs of the Southern Negroes," 60.

33. "Lead Me to the Rock," no. 112, in *Morning Light*.

34. Dorsey, "Lead Me to the Rock That's Higher Than I."

35. Subsequent recordings include Golden Eagle Gospel Singers (Decca 7793, 1940); Mitchell's Christian Singers (OKeh 05948, 1940); Harmony Four (AFS 4723 A-2, 1941); Southern Sons (Bluebird 8808, 1941); Ada Pettway (Library of Congress AFS 5094 A-2, 1941); Middle Georgia Four (Library of Congress AFS 6992 B, 1943); Original Kings of Harmony (King Solomon 1008, 1943); Wandering Boys (Standard Program Library ET 5017, c. 1943); Four Knights (Decca 48018, 1946); Canaanites (Gotham 607, 1949). Endless thanks to Doug Seroff and to Matthew Barton for sharing these recordings.

36. Seroff to author, July 22, 2024.

37. Seroff to author, July 12, 2024, and interview, July 24, 2024.

38. Seroff to author, July 22, 2024.

39. Lomax, brochure notes to *Afro-American Spirituals, Work Songs, and Ballads*, pages 8–9 of the reissued 1978 album brochure.

40. With thanks to Mike Monseur of Nashville's Axis Audio for providing enhanced and isolated sound files. Even with this processing, he acknowledged that much remains indiscernible. "It was just a very rough recording," Monseur to author, Nov. 17, 2024.

41. Broadway interview, Oct. 25, 1997. Doug Seroff independently concluded, too, that "raising" was more likely intended than "racial." Seroff to author, July 22, 2024.

42. See chapter four of *The Beautiful Music All Around Us* for an extended discussion of the Shipp family singers and "Sea Lion Woman."

43. Both "She Began to Lie" and "Rachel Rocket" (as well as "Mighty Good Road," a reworking of "Rock Island Line") appear in the film and on the soundtrack album, *Music from the Motion Picture, The General's Daughter,* Milan 73138 35885-2, 1999. I made it a pre-condition that usages of these source recordings in the film and soundtrack include the original performers' names and their song titles. In meeting this requirement, Paramount Pictures, the film's director, Simon West, composer Greg Hale Jones, as well as Paramount's Kevin Koloff of the legal department, and Russell Ziecker of Milan Records were wholly supportive.

44. Broadway, interview, Oct. 25, 1997.

45. The church, keeping the CME initials, subsequently changed its name from Colored Methodist Episcopal to Christian Methodist Episcopal.

46. Shipp, interview, Feb. 8, 1997.

47. Broadway, interview, Oct. 25, 1997.

48. Cotton, interview, Oct. 26, 1997. For more about Ms. Cotton, see *The Beautiful Music All Around Us*, chapter seven.

49. Rowe, interview, Mar. 3, 1999.

50. Rowe, interview, Mar. 4, 1999.

51. Jones, interview, Mar. 2, 1999. I also spoke that day with Henry Johnson, an eighty-five-year-old pig farmer who had known Wash Dennis. The Rev. Willie S. Mosely Jr., of Aberdeen, was responsible for my getting in touch with Ernest Broyles, who knew both Willie Jones and Henry Johnson. I met Rev. Mosely on March 1, 1999, via Kathy Bailey of the Evans Memorial Library, Aberdeen, Mississippi.

52. Broyles, interview, Mar. 2, 1999.

53. Rowe, interview, Mar. 3, 1999.

54. Rowe, interview, Mar. 3, 1999.

55. Rowe, interview, Mar. 3, 1999.

56. Rowe, interview, Mar. 4, 1999.

57. Rowe, interview, Mar. 3, 1999.

58. Rowe, interview, Mar. 4, 1999.

59. Rowe, interview, Mar. 11, 1999.

60. It might be added that Bukka White, imprisoned at Parchman from 1937 to 1939, and who hailed from Houston/Aberdeen, Mississippi, recorded "Bukka's Jitterbug Swing" in 1940. Thanks to David Evans for this reminder. For that matter, all the musicians that Helen Marie Rowe referenced—Howlin' Wolf, Muddy Waters, and Big Joe Williams—were Mississippians.

61. Broyles, interview, Mar. 2, 1999.

62. Rowe, interview, Mar. 11, 1999. See discussion of Compton Jones playing "Shake 'Em On Down" on Evans, *Afro-American Folk Music from Tate and Panola Counties, Mississippi*, 41–44. Also, see Evans, "Afro-American One-Stringed Instruments."

63. Broyles, interview, Mar. 2, 1999.

64. Fichandler, "Toward a Deepening Aesthetic," 156. Much like Kenneth Burke's assessment of literature, Fichandler viewed theater as a three-dimensional embodiment of symbolic representation merged with lived experience.

65. Rowe, interview, Mar. 4, 1999.

66. Rowe, interview, Mar. 11, 1999.

67. Jones, interview, Mar. 2, 1999.

68. Ware, interview, July 30, 2024.

69. Ware, interview, July 29, 2024.

70. Ware, interview, Aug. 13, 2024.

71. Ware, interview, Aug. 13, 2024.

72. Ware, interview, July 29, 2024.

73. Ware, interview, July 30, 2024.

74. I am uncertain of this spelling.

75. Ware, interview, Aug. 4, 2024.

76. Ware, interview, Aug. 13, 2024.

77. Ware, interview, July 30, 2024.

78. Ware, interview, July 30, 2024.

79. Ware, interview, Aug. 6, 2024.

80. Ware, interview, July 29, 2024.

81. Rowe, interview, Mar. 3, 1999.

82. Ware, interview, Dec. 1, 2024.

83. Ware, interview, July 30, 2024.

84. Ware, interview, July 30, 2024.

85. Ware, interview, July 29, 2024.

86. Rowe, interview, July 27, 2001.

87. Ware, interview, Sept. 16, 2024.

88. Ware, interview, Sept. 16, 2024.

89. Ware, interview, July 30, 2024.

90. Ware, interview, Sept. 16, 2024.

91. Rowe, interview, July 27, 2001.

92. Ware, interview, Sept. 16, 2024.

93. Rowe, interview, Mar. 11, 1999.

94. Rowe, interview, Mar. 11, 1999.

95. Ware, interview, July 30, 2024.

96. Ware, interview, Sept. 12, 2024.

97. Ware, interview, July 30, 2024.

98. Levine, *Black Culture and Black Consciousness*, 118.

99. Rowe, interview, Mar. 11, 1999.

100. Rowe, interview, May 30, 1999.

101. Levine, *Black Culture and Black Consciousness*, 99.

102. Levine, *Black Culture and Consciousness*, 99. Emphasis as in original.

103. Ware, interview, July 29, 2024. The Hurston version appears in *Mules and Men*, 184–85. See also "Talking Bones," in Dorson, *American Negro Folktales*, 147–48. An extensive study that arose in the wake of Dorson's work appears in Bascom, "African Folktales in America."

104. Rowe, interview, Mar. 11, 1999.

105. From Mississippi files for the Federal Writers' Project, quoted in Levine, "The Meaning of the Slave Trickster," 66.

106. Rowe, interview, Mar. 11, 1999. For more on African American riddling in a living setting, see Evans, "Riddling and the Structure of Context." Among those that Helen Marie Rowe told me that evening, Evans documented many of the same in Como, Mississippi, in August 1973. These include, using his numbers, 7, 8, 18, 19, 21, 22, 24, 26, 31, and 32. His article includes extensive bibliographic references on each of these riddles.

107. For another version see Farr, "Riddles and Superstitions of Middle Tennessee," 319. Closer to Helen's is the one found in Parsons, "Notes on Folk-Lore of Guilford County, North Carolina," 202.

108. Abrahams, *Everyday Life*, 30–31.

109. Abrahams, *Everyday Life*, 38.

110. Ware, interview, Sept. 4, 2024.

111. Rowe, interview, Mar. 11, 1999.

112. Ware, interview, Sept. 4, 2024.

113. Hurston, *Mules and Men*, 133. See also Puckett, *Folk Beliefs*, 470.

114. Ware, interview, Sept. 16, 2024. This version of "The Signifying Monkey" that Helen Bell recalled as closest to her mother's, and which appears here, is

taken from Hughes and Bontemps, *The Book of Negro Folklore*, 363–66. Additional sources on the signifying monkey and its background appear in Abrahams, *Afro-American Folktales*, 316–17. See also Willie Dixon's recording of "Signifying Monkey" with the Big Three Trio.

115. Ware, interview, July 30, 2024.

116. Ware, interview, July 29, 2024.

117. Ware, interview, Aug. 23, 2024. She spoke of the second shadow hiding behind the door, "that death is following you." Helen Bell also mentioned a famous song associated with this image. One such performance, recorded in September 1959 by Mississippi Fred McDowell of "Soon One Mornin'" appears on *61 Highway Mississippi: Delta Country Blues, Spirituals, Work Songs & Dance*. Earlier still is Charley Patton and Bertha Lee's performance, as Patton and Lee, "Oh Death."

118. Rowe, interview, Mar. 11, 1999.

119. Helen Marie's exact words were "You're welcome to my coat, but he kept on going." The wording here reflects my notes with Helen Bell Rowe from August 23, 2024, during our discussion of the March 11, 1999, recording.

120. Ware, interview, Aug. 23, 2024. The bawdy stories that Helen Marie told that evening, March 11, 1999, echo, for instance, a number of similarly humorous, suggestive riddles that appear in Randolph, *Blow the Candle Out*, 824–31. For more on female bawdy lore, see Green, "Magnolias Grow in Dirt."

121. Among the many versions documented of the "Golden Arm," see the "Tailypo" story that appears in Cox, "Negro Tales from West Virginia," 341–42. See also Hudson, "I Want My Golden Arm," in *Folk Travelers*, 183–94. Much scholarship similarly surrounds "Raw Head and Bloody Bones," and one place to start are the endnote references in Leach, *Whistle in the Graveyard*, 125. See also Anderson and Fugate, "Two Versions of 'Rawhead and Bloodybones' from the Farmer-Muncy Family." For "dividing souls," see Oster, "Negro Humor." Oster also recorded musician Son House recounting this tale as "Two at the Gate," on *John and Old Marster, Negro Folk Tales.*

122. See Dorson, "Eating the Baby," 235–36. See also cognates in Abrahams, *Afro-American Folktales*, 317.

123. Rowe, interview, Mar. 11, 1999. Among the scholarship that addresses this story, see the references cited in Levine, *Black Culture and Consciousness*, note 24, p. 465, and "Coon in a Box," by Richard M. Dorson, *American Negro Folktales*, pp. 126–29. See also Minton and Evans, *"The Coon in the Box."*

124. Ware, interview, Oct. 15, 2024.

125. Ware, interview, Aug. 6, 2024.

126. Ware, interview, Aug. 4, 2024.

127. Ware, interview, Oct. 15, 2024.

128. Hurston, "High John De Conquer," 106

129. Rowe, conversation with author, handwritten notes, Mar. 11, 1999.

130. Abrahams, *Everyday Life*, 9.

CHAPTER 9. HANDS ON THE TUNE

1. Wade, *Hands on the Tune*. I have Dr. Laurie Matheson, past director of the University of Illinois Press, to thank for this phrase. She suggested "Getting Their Hands on the Tune: From the Front Porch to the Library of Congress and Back Again" as the title for the George A. Miller Lecture I gave on October 30, 2013, at the Center for Advanced Study, University of Illinois, Urbana-Champaign.

2. See my notes to Victor Furtado, *Dellorto Island*. Even more, listen to Victor's performance of "Sugar Hill" on that recording. He has since gone on to receive the 2019 Steve Martin Banjo Prize, the youngest recipient in the award's history.

3. Laws, *American Balladry from British Broadsides*. First quote, p. 121; second quote, p. 104; third quote, p. 83. Laws addresses "The Gosport Tragedy" on pages 268–70.

4. See Fowler, "The Gosport Tragedy." Fowler suggests 1727 as to when the victim's parents were possibly informed of their daughter's death. He also cited that year based on the ballad's appearance on printed broadsides and related forms, which he explores in his article's latter pages.

5. With abiding thanks to the late Gerald E. Parsons Jr. for this exploration we took into "Pretty Polly" during the last months of his life. The parable, so reflective of his insights and values, had taken form by February 1995. Gerry died that July.

6. Ball used this phrase to affectionately describe his community during a July 30, 1977, workshop at the National Folk Festival, Wolf Trap, Vienna, Virginia. His family also used it. Kathryn and Blair Reedy said the same during the first of my visits with them at their home in Rugby, Virginia, November 18, 1996.

7. Ball, National Folk Festival, workshop, July 31, 1977.

8. See liner notes to Brown, *Little Rosewood Casket and Other Songs of Joy*. I put together the LP's liner notes, written under Fleming's name, based on my interviews with him. In this quote, he was comparing the singing of a song to the stories I told in *Banjo Dancing*.

9. Brown, interview, May 24, 1983. Published in *Banjo Newsletter*, March 1984, 7.

10. Regarding "hayseed" and "man about town": I am indebted to Michael D. Doubler, great-grandson of Uncle Dave Macon and author of his biography, cited below. Michael used these characterizations during his 2019 presentation for the Tennessee Folklore Society, titled "Uncle Dave Macon: Elements of Success and Legacy."

11. Seeger, *The Music of American Folk Song and Selected Other Writings on American Folk Music*, 23.

12. Seeger, quoted in Tick, *Ruth Crawford Seeger*, 279.

13. Lomax, *Our Singing Country*, first quote, p. xvi; second quote, xiv.

14. Macon to Lomax, Nov. 26, 1947. Lomax replied on Dec. 1, 1947. I found this correspondence, then unfiled, among Alan Lomax's papers at the Association for Cultural Equity, Hunter College, New York, in December 1996.

15. See this book's chapter ten, "Folksong Street," for more discussion of *Listen to Our Story.*

16. "I learned," wrote Uncle Dave, "'Rock About My Saro Jane' hearing steamboat's colored crew singing on Front Street in Nashville, Tennessee in 1887." Macon to Lomax, letter quoted in Lomax's notes to *Listen to Our Story*. For more on this song, see Lomax and Lomax, *Folk Song U.S.A.*, 180–81; and see Boswell, *Folk Songs of Middle Tennessee*, 103–5. Wolfe also discusses the song and these sources in his *A Good-Natured Riot*, 116–17. As did others noted here, I use the name "Saro Jane" rather than "Sara Jane." The title appears on the record label as "Rock About My Sara Jane," recorded May 7, 1927, Vocalion 5152. Capitalization of this song title, and all other song titles found in this chapter, conform to the original record release labels.

17. Macon to Lomax.

18. Macon, "Arcade Blues," Vocalion 15440 and 5002, recorded in New York, September 9, 1926. It is not to be confused with Leola Manning's recording, "Arcade Building Moan," Vocalion 1492. That song pertains to a March 20, 1930, fire in Knoxville.

19. National Register of Historic Places, Inventory-Nomination Form, received April 19, 1973. Submitted and written by Mrs. Donald Drummond.

20. "Hit for Hyde's to Get Latest Musical Hits," *The Tennessean*, 38.

21. "Uncle Dave' Macon Begins His Fourth Week at Loew's Bijou," *Birmingham News*, 2.

22. For more on Lee Roy "Lasses" White (accounts vary in the spelling of his first name), see Brooks, *The Blackface Minstrel Show in Mass Media.*

23. From facsimile of copyright submission, "The Negro Blues" by Le Roy White, words and music. Courtesy of Lynn Abbott and Doug Seroff.

24. Abbott and Seroff, "They Cert'ly Sound Good to Me," 57. Italics as in original. On pages 56–57 of their essay, they reprint all fifteen of the original verses.

25. Monge and Evans, "New Songs of Blind Lemon Jefferson," 12.

26. White, *Lasses White's Book of Humor and Song.*

27. "Large Crowd Will Seek Park Program," *The Nashville Banner*, 11.

28. I'm indebted for this information to the research of Dr. David Evans and his notes to "Nigger Blues" that appear in *Let's Get Loose: Folk and Popular Blues Styles from the Beginnings to the Early 1940s*. Additional information presented here comes from Abbott and Seroff, "They Cert'ly Sound Good to Me." Further discussion of the song, equally invaluable, appears in Muir, *Long Lost Blues.*

29. Palmer, *Deep Blues*, 105–6.

30. "Arcade Blues." Transcription by author. I also recorded this song on *Banjo Diary*.

31. Cohen, "The Songs of Uncle Dave Macon."

32. See Hyland, "Songs Sung and Played by Uncle Dave Macon on Radio and Appearances."

33. Hay, *A Story of the Grand Ole Opry*, 6–7. Rinzler, notes to *Uncle Dave Macon: First Featured Star of the 'Grand Ole Opry.'* Rinzler and Cohen, *Uncle Dave Macon: A Bio-Discography*. Wolfe, notes to *Uncle Dave Macon, Keep My Skillet Good and Greasy,* and many other writings that include "Uncle Dave Macon" in *Stars of Country Music, Uncle Dave Macon to Johnny Rodriguez*. Doubler, *Dixie Dewdrop*. Hermann, "In the Good Old Days of Long Ago." Hayslett, "The Doyen of Dixie." See also Doubler, *Uncle Dave Macon: A Photo Tribute* (Macon-Doubler Fellowship, 2014), for a marvelous visual history of Uncle Dave's life.

34. Green, *Only a Miner*, 218.

35. Green, *Only a Miner*, 218.

36. For more on Ann Macon-Walling Youree, the house fire, and the loss of song drafts and related materials, see Doubler, *Dixie Dewdrop*, 211. Also, he outlines the family tree on p. 229.

37. "Walking in the Sunlight."

38. Hatch Show Print window card poster, Nashville, TN. Thanks to Tom Mindte for sharing this poster in his collection.

39. Hyland, August 1970 letter to Cohen, in *Uncle Dave Macon: A Bio-Discography,* 50.

40. Kemp, interview, July 8, 1981.

41. Hooks to author, May 31, 2016. See also his further writings on this history in *Five Stringer*.

42. Kemp, interview, July 8, 1981.

43. Uncle Dave Macon called the same downpicking technique "rapping." Both knocking and rapping employ the same fist-like appearance, as if one were knocking on a door. See also the Will Keys chapter in this book, "Any Way You Can," and Eugene Bagsby who employed "knocking" to name this style.

44. Kemp, interview, July 8, 1981.

45. Oliver and McCormick, *The Blues Come to Texas,* 388. Italics as in original.

46. The couplet appears in English divine and essayist John Brown's 1745 *Essay on Satire: Occasioned by the Death of Mr. Pope,* verse 23. Esten Macon cites it in full in his "Rambling Views" column, *The Daily News-Journal*, p. 3. Earlier references cited here include *The Twin-City Daily Sentinel,* Winston-Salem, North Carolina, Oct. 15, 1915, p. 5; and a letter to the editor from Mabel Sheldon, *Free Press Prairie Farmer,* Winnipeg, Manitoba, Canada, July 31, 1918, p. 23.

47. Macon, "Worthy of Estimation." Paul Wells hears the chorus differently: "Worthy of estimation, After long consideration, And the great reputation, I possess in the nation." See Wells, "'Worthy of Investigation,'" 23. My version of the song appears on *Hands on the Tune*, track 13. Uncle Dave's letter, dated Feb. 23, 1890, is reproduced in *Keep My Skillet Good and Greasy*, 8.

48. For more on Bughouse Square, see this book's first and last chapters, "Our Common Life" and "A Storyteller's Story."

49. Peacock's verses appear in this pattern in Beck, *Hobohemia*, 69.

50. Kirk McGee, who recorded these words on video tape at his home in Franklin, Tenn., on May 8, 1978, can be seen saying this in the 1987 WETA documentary *Catching the Music.*

51. "Sourwood Mountain Medley." For ugly man themes in American humor, see Hooper, *The Widow Rugby's Husband.*

52. *Bristol Herald*, 2.

53. See Boswell, *Folk Songs of Middle Tennessee.*

54. For more on the years Uncle Dave lived in Nashville, see Doubler, *Dixie Dewdrop*, 24–28.

55. I'm indebted to the transcription of the song's vocables in *Keep My Skillet Good and Greasy*, 86.

56. For further discussion, see *The Beautiful Music All Around Us*, 286. There I mention Uncle Dave's use of this major against minor maneuver that he and Sam McGee employed in "Death of John Henry." In "Run Nigger Run," he plays an A-major barre at the ninth fret, when set at standard pitch in open-C tuning. On the recording, he either capoed up two frets, or else tightened the strings in this setting to play at D.

57. "Mountain Farmer, With Banjo, Plays Way Into Ranks of Vaudeville Stars," *The Birmingham News*, 24. Macon mentions "Run Nigger Run" as one of the titles played during that run in "'Uncle Dave' Macon Begins His Fourth Week at Loew's Bijou," *The Birmingham News*, p. 2.

58. Macon, "My Life and Experience," 11. Lowercase usage as in original.

59. See liner notes to Jackson, *Don't Let Your Deal Go Down.*

60. Both "folk storehouse" and "common storehouse" appear in Brown, Davis, and Lee, "Folk Literature," 414.

61. Wolfe, "Rural Black String Band Music," 32.

62. Russell, *Blacks, Whites and Blues*, 26.

63. Wolfe, "Rural Black String Band Music."

64. Lornell, "Old-Time Country Music in North Carolina and Virginia," 188.

65. Kirk McGee relayed this idea of the escaping prisoner in conversation with author, July 8, 1981. Cannon's Jug Stompers recorded "Feather Bed," and Flatt and Scruggs added new words on their "Down the Road."

66. For more discussion of Uncle Dave's "Backwater Blues," see Monge, *Wasn't That a Mighty Day*, 47–48.

67. Russell, *Blacks, Whites and Blues*, 31.

68. To get this effect, Uncle Dave emphasized the dissonance of the B-flat note sounded at the third fret in open G tuning, bearing in mind that on his original recording, "Keep My Skillet Good and Greasy," recorded July 8, 1924, Vocalion 14848, he held the pattern while capoed up to B.

69. See David Evans's notes to *Will Slayden, African-American Banjo Songs from West Tennessee*. See also Smith and Evans, "Willie and India Slayton," 20–23.

70. Bailey, quoted in Gaillard, "A Parable of Integrity and Survival," posted on Chapter 16, published by Humanities Tennessee.

71. Perrow, "Songs and Rhymes from the South," 170.

72. Hudson, *Journal of American Folklore*, 187–88. Spelling as in the original.

73. Work, *American Negro Songs and Spirituals*, 244.

74. Thomas, "Shanty Blues."

75. Hemphill, "Skillet Good and Greasy."

76. Riddle, *A Singer and Her Songs*, 99.

77. Riddle was not casual about her music, nor reticent in her thoughts about it. I say this having opened a show for her in 1975 and recalling our conversation beforehand, let alone from following her work on stage and in print. In the early 1960s, she sometimes performed with Hobart Smith. They worked as a duo as part of his sets at urban folk festivals. Riddle, in effect, took the place of Texas Gladden, Hobart's then ailing ballad-singing older sister with whom he previously sang. By the time of the folk music revival, festival organizers had heard the Gladden/Smith siblings on their 1948 album, *Texas Gladden Sings Blue Ridge Ballads* (Disc 737). While "Mandy" did not arise during the Almeda Riddle/Hobart Smith performances, songs like it—more of this racially shared music of the post-Emancipation era—filled Hobart Smith's repertory.

78. "My Money Matters Easy," No. 21.

79. Harkreader, *Fiddlin' Sid's Memoirs*, 15.

80. Harkreader, interview, Aug. 19, 1979.

81. Accounts of Sid Harkreader's past include his 1972 John Edwards Memorial Foundation interview with Norm Cohen, his 1976 autobiography, and the writings of Charles Wolfe. See "Fiddling Sid Harkreader," by Norm Cohen, *JEMF Quarterly* 8; Harkreader, *Fiddlin' Sid's Memoirs*; and Wolfe, *A Good-Natured Riot*.

82. Harkreader, interview, Aug. 19, 1979.

83. Wolfe, *A Good-Natured Riot*, 100.

84. Harkreader, interview, Aug. 19, 1979.

85. My recording of "Old Joe" appears on *Dancing Home*. It was at Sid Harkreader's home that I first heard it, but I based my version on the Nashville

Washboard Band's 1942 rendition. For more on the tune, see my notes to *Black Appalachia*, Rounder 1823, 1999, and "Something Out of Nothing," chapter five of *The Beautiful Music All Around Us*, and reprinted in *Music in Black American Life, 1600–1945*. I mention Elijah Cox and this tune in *The Beautiful Music All Around Us* on p. 338.

86. Harkreader, interview, Aug. 19, 1979.

87. Earlier in 1979, John Hartford had been kindly inviting me to visit him in Nashville and stay over at his new home poised above the Cumberland River in Madison, Tennessee. I consented with the caveat that I'd only come if we took "an archeological expedition into the life of Uncle Dave Macon." John happily assented, and with a call made by Charles Wolfe to Sid Harkreader the night before, plans became set for our visit with Sid.

88. Davidson, notes to *Traditional Music from Grayson and Carroll Counties.*

89. Davidson and Newman, *Band Music of Grayson and Carroll Counties, Va.*, 8.

90. Kirk McGee, quoted in liner notes by Jon Pankake to McGee Brothers and Arthur Smith, *Milk 'em in the Evening Blues.*

91. Kirk McGee, *Milk 'em in the Evening Blues.* Emphasis as in original.

92. Evans, "The Guitar in the Blues Music of the South," 13.

93. Kirk McGee, interview, July 9, 1981.

94. Sam first learned the popular instrumental "Wheels," a 1960 hit for the String-A-Longs, having heard it over the radio. He worked it out in his style and eventually recorded it as well as played it in a duet with Kirk. As he told Mike Seeger: "I liked it and it just stayed with me and I got to playing it. I don't know whose it is." From notes to Sam McGee, *Grand Dad of the Country Guitar Pickers.*

95. See Evans, "The Guitar in the Blues Music of the South," 23.

96. Pankake, notes to *Milk 'em in the Evening Blues.*

97. The event took place on July 10 and 11, 1981. My visits with Kirk McGee occurred on July 8 and 9, 1981.

98. McGee, *Mister Kirk—54 Years of Country Pickin'.*

99. Dalrymple, "Tennessee Banjoist Reminisces of New Years On And Off Stage," 28.

100. Kirk McGee, interview, July 9, 1981.

101. Stagner, "Reminiscences of Uncle Dave by Smoky Mountain Glenn," 49.

102. Kirk McGee, interview, July 9, 1981.

103. Kirk McGee, interview, July 9, 1981.

104. Haynes, interview, July 11, 1982.

105. Oldham, "Pianist Recalls Years with Macons," 59.

106. Haynes to author, Aug. 24, 1982. Emphasis as in original.

107. Haynes, interview, July 11, 1982.

108. Haynes, interview with Charles Wolfe, June 7, 1977.

109. Archdeacon, "Uncle Dave Macon," 67.

110. Haynes, interview with Charles Wolfe, June 7, 1977.

111. Haynes, interview, July 11, 1982.

112. Other personnel in Sid Harkreader's bands appear in *Fiddlin' Sid's Memoirs*.

113. Seeger, "Who Owns Folklore?—A Rejoinder," 101.

114. Oldham, "Pianist Recalls Years with Macons."

115. Dorris Macon, interview, Aug. 27, 1979. Dorris's older brother, Archie Macon, a blacksmith, used the term "mule man" to describe Uncle Dave, who never drove an automobile. In July 1981, Archie's daughter, Mary Wren Doubler, generously gave me one of the mule shoes he had forged. For a similar account about Dorris's coming to work with his father, see Michael Doubler's biography, *Dixie Dewdrop*, 137.

116. McCormick, interview, Feb. 21, 1994.

117. Wes Sharp quoted in Glassie, "Tradition," 185.

CHAPTER 10. FOLKSONG STREET

This chapter is dedicated to Dr. Ronald D. Cohen (1940–2022) who died on December 27, 2022. Ron, a prolific historian of the urban revival, generously shared his research over the course of this chapter. He loved folk music and those who explored it, no matter how much they might differ in perspectives and priorities. For him, all knowledge was, as he said, "crucial." Across the 48 years of our friendship, he stayed unfailingly kind and encouraging. I miss him.

1. Alan Lomax, Archive of American Folk Song, Annual Report of the Librarian of Congress for the Fiscal Year Ended June 30, 1940, 152.

2. Alan Lomax to Spivacke, Mar. 8, 1939. Cited in Szwed, *Alan Lomax*, 143.

3. See Green, "Victor's 'P' Album Series."

4. John A. Lomax, album notes to *Smoky Mountain Ballads*, Victor P-79. See also Box 3D-191, John Avery Lomax Family Papers, Barker Texas History Center, now Dolph Briscoe Center for American History, Austin, Texas.

5. Taubman, "Records; The Smokies," 6.

6. I may have found this document in September 1994, possibly in Box 3D-191 noted above, among the Lomax family papers in Austin. Otherwise, I came upon it in Alan Lomax's files at the Association for Cultural Equity at Hunter College, New York City, in December 1996. Wherever it may reside at this time, there's no question about its authenticity, given Guthrie's distinctive script, his signature, and the embossed "Remember Pearl Harbor" sticker affixed to its last page. In August 2022, I checked with the Woody Guthrie Collection in Tulsa, contacting both its curator and senior archivist. They could not determine if it might have been published elsewhere. Thanks to Mark Davidson and Kate Blalack for their most generous efforts.

7. Kahn, liner notes to *Smoky Mountain Ballads.*

8. Guthrie, *Smoky Mountain Ballads.*

9. Green, "General's Folk Albums," 185, Graphics 63.

10. Lewis quoted in Lomax, *Adventures of a Ballad Hunter*, 88.

11. Sandburg, 1950 memorial tribute to Lewis, 1. Boundless thanks to Alison Hinderliter, Lloyd Lewis Curator of Modern Manuscripts and Archives, Newberry Library.

12. I'm indebted to Richard A. Reuss's discussion of folk and literary standards that appears in his essay, "Woody Guthrie and His Folk Tradition," In *Journal of American Folklore.*

13. McCutcheon, headnote to "The John B. Sails," in Sandburg, *The American Songbag*, 22.

14. Sandburg to McCutcheon, McCutcheon papers, Newberry Library.

15. Sandburg, *The American Songbag*, xii.

16. Sandburg, *The American Songbag*, xxiii.

17. Sandburg, *The American Songbag*, 92.

18. Sandburg, *The American Songbag*, xv.

19. Lewis, quoted in Lomax, *Adventures of a Ballad Hunter*, 90. Nolan Porterfield, Lomax's biographer, who located Lewis's letter among Lomax's papers, as dated June 5, 1940. See *Last Cavalier*, 225, footnote 29.

20. Lomax, *Adventures of a Ballad Hunter*, 88 and 90.

21. Lomax, *Adventures of a Ballad Hunter*, 90.

22. Sandburg, Introduction to Lewis, *Myths After Lincoln*, vi.

23. Lewis, *Myths After Lincoln*, 404.

24. Lewis, *Myths After Lincoln*, 408.

25. Lewis, *Myths After Lincoln*, vii.

26. Lewis, letter quoted in Lomax, *Adventures of a Ballad Hunter*, 90.

27. Lewis, letter quoted in Lomax, 89.

28. Lewis, letter quoted in Lomax, 88.

29. Lewis, letter quoted in Lomax, 90.

30. Green, *Only a Miner*, 38.

31. For Ford's contact with Edison, see Conot, *Thomas A. Edison*, 381–83. For Ford's engagement with traditional music, see Gifford, "Henry Ford's Dance Revival and Fiddle Contest." Thanks to Tom Mindte for recalling the Ford/Edison recordings. For Jasper Bisbee's recordings, see Russell, *Country Music Records, A Discography, 1921–1942*, 107.

32. Wilson, from liner notes to *The Hill-Billies*. See also Green, "Hillbilly Music: Source and Symbol."

33. "Sheep ranching in Colorado and Utah, ca. 1925–1930," Box 10, Folder 196. Lloyd Lewis papers.

34. "Sheep ranching in Colorado and Utah."
35. "Sheep ranching in Colorado and Utah."
36. Lomax, album notes to *Smoky Mountain Ballads.*
37. Lewis, "A Founding Father Returns," 217.
38. Botkin, *A Treasury of American Folklore*, xxvi.
39. "Last of the Troubadours," manuscript, Box 7, Folder 120. Lloyd Lewis Papers.
40. "Last of the Troubadours," 2.
41. "Last of the Troubadours," 3.
42. "Last of the Troubadours."
43. Lewis mentions Mary Garden in his letter to Lomax, p. 89, and Sandburg mentions Eddie Leonard in his 1950 memorial tribute to Lewis, p. 1, Box 1, Folder 49. Lloyd Lewis Papers.
44. Golden, *Carl Sandburg*, 83.
45. Golden, *Carl Sandburg*, 84.
46. Hopkins, personal communications with author, ca. 1981.
47. "Last of the Troubadours," 74.
48. "Last of the Troubadours," 81.
49. "Last of the Troubadours," 270.
50. Lewis to Stein, June 26, 1936. Box 2, Folder 80. Lloyd Lewis Papers.
51. Lewis, "Chicago and the Midlands," 463. In Box 4, Folder 90. Lloyd Lewis Papers.
52. Lewis, "Chicago and the Midlands," 464.
53. Lewis, "Chicago and the Midlands," 518.
54. Lewis, quoted in Lomax, *Adventures of a Ballad Hunter*, 91.
55. Butcher, "The Literary Spotlight." In Box 7, Folder 142a, Scrapbooks. Lloyd Lewis Papers.
56. Sandburg, Box I, Folder 49, Incoming Correspondence, 1933–1938, n.d. Lloyd Lewis Papers.
57. Leonard, "Tower Ticker," 9.
58. Leonard, "Tower Ticker."
59. Lomax, *Adventures of a Ballad Hunter*, 87.
60. For more on Raeburn Flerlage in this book, see chapter two, "Catching the Music." There, I note his work as a blues and folk music photographer. For some of those images, see *Chicago Blues As Seen from the Inside: The Photographs of Raeburn Flerlage*. See also Matthew Ismail's *Blues Discovery: Reaching Across the Divide*, 76–97.
61. Cutler, *The Jews of Chicago*, 58. See also Berkow, *Maxwell Street*, and *And This Is Free*.
62. Cutler, *The Jews of Chicago*, 69.
63. Figure attributed to Edward Schulz's 1954 study, "A Functional Analysis of

Retail Trade in the Maxwell Street Market Area of Chicago," and cited by Carolyn Eastwood in "The Demise of an Urban Market."

64. Flerlage, "Folksong Street," 5 and 9.

65. Rogers quoted in Goins, *Blues All Day Long,* 30.

66. Flerlage, "Folksong Street," 5.

67. Flerlage, "Folksong Street," 9.

68. Flerlage, "Folksong Street," 5.

69. For more on hootenanny's verbal roots, see Tamony, "'Hootenanny.'"

70. Flerlage to Seeger, Nov. 12, 1946. Copy of letter courtesy of Ron Cohen. The Ashland Auditorium event occurred two days earlier, on Sunday, November 10, 1946.

71. Scott, "Singing People," *People's Songs,* Oct. 1946, 2.

72. Bulletin of People's Songs Inc., 1.

73. Silber, *Reprints from the People's Songs Bulletin 1946–1949,* 4.

74. Lomax, *The People's Songbook,* 3.

75. Denisoff, *Great Day Coming,* 8. See also Denisoff, "The Proletarian Renascence."

76. Reuss, *American Folklore and Left-Wing Politics: 1927–1957,* 36.

77. Denisoff, *Great Day Coming,* 76.

78. For more on this slogan, see discussions of the Rebel Poets in Wixson, *Worker-Writer in America,* 163 and 264.

79. See Silber, in *"Wasn't That a Time!,"* 96.

80. Romalis, *Pistol Packin' Mama,* 161.

81. Seeger, foreword to *Reprints from the People's Songs Bulletin,* 3.

82. Denisoff, *Great Day Coming,* 129.

83. Seeger, foreword, *Reprints from the People's Songs Bulletin,* 3.

84. Lomax, "The Best of the Ballads," 208.

85. Lomax, "America Sings the Saga of America." Cited here from *Alan Lomax, Selected Writings 1934–1997,* 91.

86. Lomax, "The Best of the Ballads," 208.

87. Lomax, "The Best of the Ballads."

88. Flerlage, "Typescript and Manuscript drafts, 1946–1998." "The People in Their Music," Flerlage Collection.

89. From "Note for Miss Blackwell." Flerlage Collection. Blackwell was apparently the publicist for the series presented at Chicago's Parkway Community House.

90. Flerlage, program nine, "Notes," 3. "The People in Their Music," Flerlage Collection.

91. Flerlage, Program five typescript, April 2, 1946, Flerlage Collection. See also Cohen and Riesman in *Chicago Folk,* who discuss this same lecture on p. vii.

92. Flerlage, program two, March 12, 1946. "The People in Their Music," Flerlage Collection.

93. Flerlage, "Introductory Notes," March 12, 1946. "The People in Their Music." File 32.4. Flerlage Collection.

94. Flerlage, typed script for "Notes on the Records," from "The People in Their Music, Program no. 1, March 5, 1946." Spelling and capitalization as in original. Flerlage Collection.

95. For more on Jack Conroy in this book, see chapter eleven, "A Storyteller's Story."

96. Flerlage, interview with Ron Cohen, July 15, 1992. Thanks to Steve Weiss, Wiley Thornquist, and Aaron Smithers at the Wilson Library, UNC-CH.

97. Alinsky, *Reveille for Radicals*, 11. Italics as in original.

98. Flerlage, interview, July 15, 1992.

99. Flerlage, program nine, "Notes," 3.

100. Flerlage, interview, July 15, 1992.

101. "Interpreting recorded music" comes from Flerlage's self-penned biography for his handout that introduced the series. "Typescript and Manuscript drafts, 1946–1998."

102. Flerlage, interview July 15, 1992.

103. Flerlage, "Music for Democracy," in "The People's Music," May 18, 1946, *Farm Equipment Workers News*. Flerlage's files reveal he penned this series for two years. Clippings of his articles also appear in file Box 47, folder 9. Flerlage Collection.

104. Ronald Cohen quotes a letter dated Nov. 27, 1946, in which Seeger suggests to Flerlage that he pen such a column. In Cohen and Riesman, *Chicago Folk*, ix.

105. Flerlage, "On the Record," *People's Songs*, Dec. 1946, 5.

106. Flerlage, program six, "Notes," April 9, 1946. "The People in Their Music," 2. Flerlage Collection.

107. Flerlage, "On the Record," *People's Songs*, Feb.–Mar. 1947, 16.

108. Flerlage, "On the Record," *People's Songs*, Apr. 1947, 4.

109. Flerlage, "On the Record," *People's Songs*, May 1947, 5.

110. Alan Lomax (unnamed here as author), "Introduction to American Folk Music Series," for *Carl Sandburg, Cowboy Songs and Negro Spirituals.*

111. "On the Record," *People's Songs*, June 1947, 3. The first of the library's releases, dated 1942, went into public distribution in February 1943. See endnote 4, p. 362, in *The Beautiful Music All Around Us.*

112. "The Death of Harry Simms," *People's Songs*, July–Aug. 1947, 12.

113. John Szwed details how Alan Lomax earlier chose this title in 1941 for a book of first-person narratives. See Szwed, *Alan Lomax*, 178.

114. "On the Record," *People's Songs*, July–Aug. 1947, 8. Again, Flerlage isn't named here.

115. Lomax, "Sing-Along Book," notes to *Listen to Our Story.*

116. "On the Record," *People's Songs*, September 1948, 7. The cited article from the Farm and Equipment Workers newspaper appears in Flerlage's column, "The People's Music," June 1948, page 9. Thanks to the Chicago Historical Museum, Raeburn Flerlage Collection, Box 47, folder 9, for this series of reviews and for those he wrote in a column called "Record Notes" for the *Chicago Star*, folder 8. Personal thanks to CHM archivist Lesley Martin. Emphasis and punctuation as in original.

117. "On the Record," *People's Songs*, Nov. 1948, 7.

118. "On the Record," *People's Songs*, Dec. 1948, 6.

119. Brochure for "The People in Their Music" series. File 32.4. Flerlage Collection.

120. Flerlage to Asbell, Dec. 29, 1946. Copy of letter courtesy of Ron Cohen.

121. Flerlage, "Folksong Street," 9. Punctuation as in original.

122. Sandburg, *The People, Yes*, 225. This excerpt appears in Flerlage, *Chicago Blues*, vi.

123. Browning, "Are You a Folknik in a Hootenanny," 13.

124. I'm indebted for this information to Gail Tyler, former acting executive director and senior business manager of the Old Town School of Folk Music. Tyler to author, Aug. 1, 2022.

125. See Ray Flerlage's album notes to *Frank Hamilton Sings Folk Songs*, 3.

126. Hamilton to author, Nov. 6, 2022.

127. See the school's podcast on Soundcloud, "Sloop John B." in *Episode 8, Five from the Archives,* https://soundcloud.com/oldtownschool/ep-8-five-from-the-archives-sloop-john-b.

128. See Romanoski, "Dawn Greening: The Mother of Us All," 6–9.

129. See my "Old Town School of Folk Music" entry in *Encyclopedia of Chicago*, 588. Bess Hawes described her group teaching method during a tape-recorded telephone interview we had on May 20, 1998.

130. Johnson, interview, June 8, 2022.

131. Unpaginated headnote from the earliest known edition of the Old Town School of Folk Music songbook, ca. 1958. Thanks to musician Mark Dvorak for generously copying the entire book and sharing its contents.

132. See Smyth, *Country Music Recorded Prior to 1943*.

133. Cohen, in *"Wasn't That a Time!,"* 33.

134. Seeger, "The Folkness of the Nonfolk," 338.

135. Memphis Slim quoted in Wilgus, "Record Reviews," 88.

136. Smith, album notes to *Anthology of American Folk Music*, FP 251 side B, band 8. "Condensation of lyrics," entry 8 (unpaginated).

137. Cohen, "A Rare Interview with Harry Smith."

138. *Mountain Frolic*, American Folk Music Series, Album No. B-1025.

139. Seeger, Reviewed Work(s): "Listen to Our Story" by Alan Lomax; "Mountain Frolic" by Alan Lomax; "Sod Buster Ballads" by Alan Lomax; "Deep

Sea Chanteys and Whaling Ballads" by Alan Lomax, *Journal of American Folklore,* 215–18.

140. Seeger, Reviewed Work(s), 216.

141. Seeger, "The Folkness of the Nonfolk." This essay originally appeared in *Folklore and Society. Essays in Honor of Benj. A. Botkin*, 1–9. Seeger added commentary to the piece in his *Studies in Musicology, 1935–1975*. Botkin's essay, which inspired Seeger's title, "The Folkness of the Folk," appeared in *The English Journal* 26, College Edition, June 1937, 461–69.

142. Seeger, Reviewed Work(s), 216.

143. Seeger, Reviewed Work(s), 217.

144. Seeger, Reviewed Work(s), 216.

145. Seeger, Reviewed Work(s): "A Collection of Ballads and Folk Songs" by Burl Ives; "Ballads and Blues" by Josh White; "Ballads and Folk Songs" by Burl Ives; Richard Dyer-Bennet, "Twentieth Century Minstrel," *Journal of American Folklore* 62, no. 243. "Hick stuff," p. 69. "Data (fact)" comes from "Folkness of the Nonfolk," in *Studies in Musicology*, 340.

146. Seeger, "Folkness of the Nonfolk."

147. Seeger, "Folk Music in the Schools of a Highly Industrialized Society," 334.

148. Seeger, Reviewed Work(s), 216.

149. Freeman, quoted in Cohen, "County Records," 48, 51.

150. Hawes to author, personal correspondence, Oct. 20, 1993.

151. The Carter Family's "Worried Man Blues" and "East Virginia Blues" appear on *Smoky Mountain Ballads.*

152. This visit with Ralph Rinzler occurred on May 4, 1983. From handwritten notes in my journal.

153. Wilgus, album notes to *Mike Seeger.*

154. Baker, *Blues, Ideology, and Afro-American Literature*, 3.

CHAPTER 11. A STORYTELLER'S STORY

An earlier and far shorter version of this essay appeared in the album notes to *A Storyteller's Story: Sources of Banjo Dancing,* Patuxent CD-333, 2019. I previously used this chapter's title in a presentation I made on September 3, 1984, for the Society of American Archivists, Washington, D.C. That paper subsequently appeared in *American Archivist,* vol. 48, no. 2, Spring 1985, 217–221. Thanks to Leonard Rapport of the National Archives for this title. Leonard, a former member of the North Carolina unit of the Federal Writers' Project, was an extraordinary source of knowledge and encouragement.

1. Mencken, "Civilized Chicago," 51.

2. Mencken, "The Literary Capital of the United States," *Nation of London,* April 17, 1920, and reprinted on the Wednesday Book Page, *Chicago Daily News,* May 12, 1920.

3. Ade, quoted in Kriebel, *Ross-Ade*, 54.

4. Cited by Mencken, *The American Language*, 377. From Duncan, *The Rise of Chicago as a Literary Center from 1885 to 1920*, 178.

5. Dunne, "History," 271. Quoted in Ware, *The Cultural Approach to History*, 3.

6. Mencken, "Literary Capital of the United States."

7. Dewey, *Democracy and Education*, 4.

8. Mencken, "Literary Capital of the United States."

9. Howells, "Certain of the Chicago School of Fiction," 740.

10. Algren, *Chicago*, 77.

11. Algren, *Never Come Morning*, 62.

12. "Staff Conference in Industrial Folklore," July 13, 1939.

13. Botkin, "The Folk and the Writer: Introduction to Folklore Craft Section," June 4, 1939, Third American Writers Congress, New York, 1. The quote also appears in Stewart, *Fighting Words*, 11.

14. Conroy, interview, Mar. 18, 1980.

15. Sandburg, foreword to Botkin, *A Treasury of American Folklore*, v.

16. Douglas Wixson reports Harold Sullivan's father-in-law as Jack Conroy's source for "Slappy Hooper" in *Worker-Writer in America*, 440, and Jack told Studs Terkel both on March 28, 1962, and again on November 30, 1973, during two of their WFMT radio interviews, that his source was an old sign painter he had met on north Clark Street in Chicago, presumably at one of the taverns that Jack frequented for his "research," as he described it to me. Indeed, Jack's May 11, 1939, Illinois Writers' Project interview with itinerant sign painter Frank DeSoto contains germs of the tale, and DeSoto employs certain technical terminology that Jack called attention to when "Slappy Hooper" first appeared in Botkin's *Treasury* (see "pounce" that Jack defines in a footnote on p. 547). The DeSoto interview can be found at the Library of Congress's American Memory website, *American Life Histories: Manuscripts from the Federal Writers' Project*.

17. For more on *Banjo Dancing*, see this book's Preface.

18. Allsopp, *Folklore of Romantic Arkansas*, 88. Mack McCormick includes a bawdy version in his LP collection, *The Unexpurgated Folksongs of Men*.

19. Hackett, *New York Evening Post*. Cited in Hodge, *Yankee Theatre*, 118.

20. Paulding, *The Lion of the West* in Botkin, *A Treasury of American Folklore*, 14. Subsequently, a recovered edition of the play, titled *The Lion of the West: A Farce in Two Acts*, came to light and on p. 55 of this edition, "Ain't I" becomes "I'm," and "aquafortis" appears as "aky fortis." The string of brags quoted in the succeeding sentence appears in Botkin, p. 14.

21. Schultz, *Travels on an Inland Voyage Through the States of New York, Pennsylvania, Virginia, Ohio, Kentucky and Tennessee and Through the Territories of Indiana, Louisiana, Mississippi and New Orleans*, 145.

22. See Poore, "Hackett and Crockett," 181.

23. Diddley, "Who Do You Love."

24. Botkin, *Treasury of American Folklore*, 272. However, as Dorothy Dondore writes in "Big Talk! The Flyting, the Gabe, and the Frontier Boast," this kind of epic brag reaches back centuries and extends far beyond the North American continent.

25. Allsopp, *Folklore of Romantic Arkansas*, 89. Spelling as in original.

26. Stracke, *The Old Town School of Folk Music*, 8.

27. For more on the history of the off-Loop movement in Chicago, see Christiansen, *A Theater of Our Own*. Also, thanks to Sharon Ferguson Phillips, who succeeded Jim Shiflett, founding director of the Body Politic, in its leadership. Sharon coordinated the original production of *Banjo Dancing* at the Body Politic, sharing initial directorial responsibility with Milton Kramer. In later years, she and I discussed the theater's founding. Specifically, our correspondence occurred on Sept. 7, 2010, followed by a telephone conversation, Sept. 10, 2010.

28. For more on Bughouse in this book, see chapter one, "Our Common Life," and also the discussion of "Worthy of Estimation" in chapter nine, "Hands on the Tune."

29. Bruns, *The Damndest Radical*, 248.

30. Steve Maxwell, quoting a 1999 letter he received from Saul Bellow, noted that he used the term "hobo intellectual" to describe individuals of this sort who, in Bellow's words, had "disappeared from the scene just before the outbreak of the World War II." In *Speaker's Corners, The Bughouse Square.*

31. Bellow, "A Sermon by Doctor Pep," 456.

32. Bruns, *The Damndest Radical*, 232.

33. Jones, quoted by Anderson in "Jack Jones, The Pickler."

34. For a rewarding study of female elocutionists, see Kimber, *The Elocutionists.*

35. At the second annual meeting of the American Humor Studies Association in December 1975, Arlin Turner acknowledged the "dynasty of scholars working in this humor at Chicago," and led by Meine and Blair. Indeed, in 1930, Meine published his landmark *Tall Tales of the Southwest*, and "Burlesques in Nineteenth Century American Humor," a portion of Blair's University of Chicago 1931 doctoral dissertation, "The Background of Bill Nye in American Literature," appeared in *American Literature* in November 1930. Blair himself used the word "pioneer" to describe Meine's place in American humor studies, cited in Hamlin Hill's "Walter Blair Through the Ages," in *Studies in American Humor*, p. 21. In the same issue, its editor, M. Thomas Inge, identifies Blair as "the founding father of the study of American humor." (p. 1). Personal thanks to Tom Inge, Larry Mintz, and to Walter Blair himself, all of whom warmly abetted my studies of American humor. Arlin Turner, quoted above, appears in "Texts of Two Addresses," published in *Studies in American Humor*, 117.

36. Fountain-Pen Salesman, recorded by Tony Schwartz. In Botkin, *Sidewalks of America*, 296.

37. See *The Beautiful Music All Around Us*, ix to xiv.

38. The workshop also included Canadian banjoist Paul Hornbeck.

39. See Lydie McFarland's protectiveness of her Buell Kazee records in *The Beautiful Music All Around Us*, p. 33. Lydie lived in Magoffin County, Kentucky, Buell Kazee's homeplace.

40. Didlake in Carlin, "An Apprentice with the Ghosts," 14.

41. Stover, in *Banjo Spirits*. See note below on John Paulson's film.

42. Stover, liner notes to *Things in Life*.

43. John Paulson's 1997 film, *Banjo Spirits*, is a half-hour study of Don Stover and myself. It can be accessed on the Folkstreams website. Don's song, which he performs in the film, appears earlier on his album, *Things in Life*, cited above.

44. Reed, quoted in the album notes to *My Epitaph: A Documentary in Song and Lyric*.

45. Reed, liner notes to *Mariposa Folk Festival 1975*.

46. Bud Reed and David Reed, quoted in notes to Ola Belle Reed, *Rising Sun Melodies*.

47. Accompanying materials about *Catching the Music*, its making and reception, can be found at the film's website

48. See Bobby Fulcher's notes to "The French Waltz," in *Gettin' Up the Stairs*.

49. Virgil Anderson in *Catching the Music*.

50. Kalem, "Pipes of Pan," 75.

51. Twain, *The Adventures of Tom Sawyer*, 29. Emphasis as in original.

52. Carter, "Labor Day Remarks at a White House Picnic."

53. Jackson, "I Don't Want that Hen to Suffer," quoted in Perdue, "'I Swear To God It's The Truth if I Ever Told It,'" 27.

54. Bronson, "Habits of the Ballad As Song," 105–7. Cited in Buchan, "Ballad Tradition and Hugh Spencer," 174.

55. Botkin, *Treasury of American Folklore*, 819.

56. Steinbeck, *The Grapes of Wrath*, 32.

Works Cited

ARCHIVAL COLLECTIONS

Alan Lomax Collection, Association for Cultural Equity, Hunter College, New York.

Archive of Folk Culture, American Folklife Center, Library of Congress, Washington, D.C.

Arthur Kyle Davis Jr. Papers, Alderman Library, University of Virginia, Charlottesville, Va.

Berea College, Hutchins Library, Special Collections, Berea, Ky.

Center for Popular Music, Audio Collections, Middle Tennessee State University, Murfreesboro, Tenn.

Frist Library and Archive, Country Music Hall of Fame and Museum, Nashville, Tenn.

Hanna Holborn Gray Special Collections Research Center, University of Chicago Library, Chicago, Ill.

League of American Writers Archives, University of California, Berkeley, Calif.

Lloyd Lewis Papers, Modern Manuscripts and Archives, Newberry Library, Chicago, Ill.

John A. Lomax Family Papers, Dolph Briscoe Center for American History, University of Texas, Austin, Tex.

Mary Wheeler Collection, McCracken County Public Library, Paducah, Ky.

Mississippi Department of Archives and History, Jackson, Miss.

Mississippi State Penitentiary at Parchman, convict files, Parchman, Miss.

Old Town School of Folk Music Resource Center & Archives, Chicago, Ill.

Raeburn Flerlage Collection, Chicago History Museum, Chicago, Ill. Flerlage Collection.

Ralph Rinzler Folklife Archives and Collections, Center for Folklife and Cultural Heritage, Smithsonian Institution.

Southern Folklife Collection, Southern Historical Collection, Manuscripts Department, Wilson Library, University of North Carolina, Chapel Hill, N.C. SFC.

Special Collections and University Archives, University of Illinois, Chicago, Ill.

Virginia Folklore Society, Special Collections, Alderman Library, University of Virginia, Charlottesville, Va.

WFMT Studs Terkel Radio Archive, Chicago, Ill.
Woody Guthrie Archives, Woody Guthrie Center, Tulsa, Okla.

INTERVIEWS

Unless otherwise indicated, I conducted and tape-recorded the following interviews.

Bagsby, Eugene. July 9, 1981, Franklin, Tenn.

Bledsoe, Tommy. Mar. 4, 2021.

Broadway, Opal. Interview and handwritten notes, Oct. 25, 1997, Memphis, Tenn.

Brown, Fleming. May 24, 1983. Published in *Banjo Newsletter* XI, no. 5 (March 1984).

Broyles, Ernest "Pappy." Interview and handwritten notes, Mar. 2, 1999, Aberdeen, Miss.

Burnett, Dick. Interview with Archie Green and Eugene Earle, Monticello, Ky., August 17, 1962. FT 12632. SFC.

Conroy, Jack. Mar. 18, 1980, Moberly, Mo.

Cotton, Appolonia. Interview and handwritten notes, Oct. 26, 1997, Clarksdale, Miss.

Dodge, Jeana Willingham. Feb. 2, 1997, Long Beach, Miss.

Dodge, Jeana Willingham. Feb. 27, 1999, Long Beach, Miss.

Edwards, David "Honeyboy." Telephone interview, handwritten notes, undated, ca. late 1996/early 1997.

Edwards, David "Honeyboy." Aug. 6, 1998, Chicago.

Ferriss, Abbott. Jan. 20, 1997, Atlanta.

Flerlage, Raeburn. Interview with Ron Cohen, July 15, 1992, Chicago. Ronald D. Cohen Collection, Audio Cassette FS-20239/7496. SFC.

Forster, Omer. July 9, 1982, McEwen, Tenn.

Grano, Charlie. Sept. 11, 1991, Chicago.

Green, Archie. Aug. 2, 2006.

Halpert, Herbert. Tape-recorded interview with Peggy Farber, Debora Kodish, and Gerald E. Parsons Jr., Nov. 17, 1978. AFS 19, 358. American Folklife Center, Library of Congress.

Harkreader, Sid. Aug. 19, 1979, Nashville.

Harris, Timothy Charles. Interview with Betsy Peterson, Nov. 16, 2011. American Folklife Center, Occupational Folklife Project. Library of Congress.

Haynes, Jewell Fagan. Interview with Charles Wolfe, June 7, 1977. Wolfe Recording 00372, Charles Wolfe Collection, Center for Popular Music, Middle Tennessee State University, Murfreesboro, Tenn.

Haynes, Jewell Fagan. July 11, 1982, Murfreesboro, Tenn.

Hopkins, Doc. Interview with Loyal Jones, Oct. 24, 1975. Doc Hopkins, Audio Recordings Reference Collection, BCA 0266, AC-CT-021-001. Berea College Special Collections & Archives.

Hopkins, Doc. Interview with Ray Nemec, Apr. 17, 1969. RP-OR-10-001-03 C, Side A. Doc Hopkins, Audio Recordings Reference Collection, Berea College Special Collections & Archives.

Hopkins, Doc. Tape-recorded interview with Douglas Green, June 11, 1974, Chicago. Frist Library and Archive of the Country Music Hall of Fame and Museum, Nashville, Tenn.

Hopkins, Doc. Tape-recorded interview with Ed Kahn, July 8, 1961. Canoga Park, Calif. FT 12619. SFC.

Hopkins, Doc. Tape-recorded interview with Ed Kahn, Jan. 7, 1962. Canoga Park, Calif. FT 12633. SFC.

Hopkins, Doc. Tape-recorded interview with Ed Kahn, July 7, 1962. Canoga Park, Calif. FT 12618. SFC.

Hopkins, Doc. Dec. 17, 1981, Chicago.

Hopkins, Doc. Dec. 17, 1982, Chicago.

Hopkins, Doc. July 12, 1983, Chicago.

Hopkins, Doc. Nov. 28, 1985, Chicago.

Hopkins, Doc. Sept. 15, 1986, Chicago.

Hopkins, Doc, and Stephen Wade. Interview with Studs Terkel. "Studs Terkel with Doc Hopkins and Stephen Wade." WFMT radio broadcast, Dec. 20, 1982, Chicago.

Jimison, Susan. Telephone interview, handwritten notes, May 11, 1999.

Johnson, Ted. Telephone interview, handwritten notes, June 8, 2022.

Jones, Willie "Tough." Mar. 2, 1999, Aberdeen, Miss.

Kemp, Cordell. July 8, 1981, Defeated, Tenn.

Kemp, Olean. July 8, 1981, Defeated, Tenn.

Keys, Bill. Mar. 2, 2021.

Keys, Jerry. Mar. 7, 2021.

Keys, Jerry. Mar. 28, 2021.

Keys, Will. July 1, 1986.

Lloyd, Jim. Mar. 5, 2021.

Logan, Benjamin "Tex." Telephone interviews, Oct. 4, 2001, and Oct. 18, 2001.

Lundy, Emmett. Interview, AAFS 4938, Archive of American Folk Song recording.

Macon, Dorris. Aug. 27, 1979, Woodbury, Tenn.

Mainer, Wade. Telephone interview, July 22, 1999.

McCormick, Robert Mack. Interview and handwritten notes, Feb. 21, 1994, Houston.

McGee, Kirk. July 9, 1981, Franklin, Tenn.

McGee, Kirk. July 9, 1981, Franklin, Tenn.

Melford, Michael. Telephone interview, Nov. 6, 2021.

Rowe, Helen Marie. Mar. 3, 1999, Okolona, Miss.
Rowe, Helen Marie. Mar. 4, 1999, Okolona, Miss.
Rowe, Helen Marie. Mar. 11, 1999, Okolona, Miss.
Rowe, Helen Marie. Telephone interview, May 30, 1999.
Rowe, Helen Marie. Telephone interview, July 27, 2001.
Schwall, Jim. Telephone interview, Oct. 14, 2021.
Schwall, Jim. Telephone interview, handwritten notes, Feb. 26, 2022.
Seroff, Doug. Telephone interview, handwritten notes, July 24, 2024.
Shipp, Luella. Feb. 8, 1997, Byhalia, Miss.
Thompson, Joe. Nov. 3, 1987, Mebane, N.C.
Treadway, Cecil. Telephone interview, handwritten notes, Feb. 27, 2014.
Ware, Helen Bell Rowe. Telephone interview, July 29, 2024.
Ware, Helen Bell Rowe. Telephone interview, July 30, 2024.
Ware, Helen Bell Rowe. Telephone interview, Aug. 4, 2024.
Ware, Helen Bell Rowe. Telephone interview, Aug. 6, 2024.
Ware, Helen Bell Rowe. Telephone interview, handwritten notes, Aug. 13, 2024.
Ware, Helen Bell Rowe. Telephone interview, Aug. 23, 2024.
Ware, Helen Bell Rowe. Telephone interview, Sept. 12, 2024.
Ware, Helen Bell Rowe. Telephone interview, Sept. 16, 2024.
Ware, Helen Bell Rowe. Telephone interview, Oct. 15, 2024.
Ware, Helen Bell Rowe. Telephone interview, handwritten notes, Dec. 1, 2024.
Willingham, Thaddeus. Interview with Herbert Halpert during recording session, June 10, 1939. AFS 3113 A.

OTHER SOURCES

1000 Fiddle Tunes. Chicago: M. M. Cole Publishing Company, no date, beyond the 1940 copyright, renewed in 1967.
Abbott, Lynn, and Doug Seroff. *Out of Sight: The Rise of African American Popular Music, 1889–1895.* Jackson: University Press of Mississippi, 2002, 308–12.
Abbott, Lynn, and Doug Seroff. "They Cert'ly Sound Good to Me, Sheet Music, Southern Vaudeville, and the Commercial Ascendancy of the Blues." In *Ramblin' on My Mind: New Perspectives on the Blues,* edited by David Evans. Urbana: University of Illinois Press, 2008.
Abrahams, Roger D. *Afro-American Folktales: Stories from Black Traditions in the New World.* New York: Pantheon Books, 1985.
Abrahams, Roger D. *Deep Down in the Jungle: Negro Narrative Folklore from the Streets of Philadelphia.* Chicago: Aldine Publishing Company, 1970.
Abrahams, Roger D. *Everyday Life: A Poetics of Vernacular Practices.* Philadelphia: University of Pennsylvania Press, 2005.
Ad for *Ryan's Mammoth Collection.* Reprinted in Wells, "Elias Howe, William Bradbury Ryan, and Irish Music in Nineteenth-Century Boston."

Addams, Jane. "The Subjective Necessity for Social Settlements." Chicago: Jane Addams Hull-House Museum, 1989.

AFS field notes. "Folk Music Recordings Made in Mississippi by Herbert Halpert," AFS 2735–3135. Typescript.

Akeman, David "Stringbean." "Say Old Man Can You Play the Banjo." *Hee Haw Corn Shucker*. Nashville NLP 2100, 1970.

Alden, William. "Sailor Songs." *Harper's Magazine* 65, no. 386 (July 1882): 281–86.

Algren, Nelson. *Chicago: City on the Make.* Chicago: University of Chicago Press, 1951.

Algren, Nelson. *Never Come Morning.* New York: Seven Stories Press, 1996.

Alinsky, Saul. *Reveille for Radicals.* Chicago: University of Chicago Press, 1946.

Allen, William Francis, Charles Pickard Ware, and Lucy McKim Garrison, eds. *Slave Songs of the United States.* Dover reprint edition. New York, 1995.

Allsopp, Fred W. *Folklore of Romantic Arkansas.* Vol. II. New York: Grolier Society, 1931.

Anderson, Glen Muncy, and Jane Muncy Fugate. "Two Versions of 'Rawhead and Bloodybones' from the Farmer-Muncy Family." *Journal of Folklore Research* 38, no. 1/2 (Jan.–Aug. 2001): 55–67. Special Double Issue: Perspectives on the Jack Tales and Other North American Märchen.

Anderson, Sherwood. "Jack Jones, The Pickler." *Chicago Daily News*, June 18, 1919.

Archdeacon, Kathe. "Uncle Dave Macon." *The Daily News-Journal*, Murfreesboro, Tenn., July 1, 1979.

Archer, James. "Rango." AFS 3073 A and B1.

Armstrong, Janice Gray, ed. *Catching the Tune: Music and William Sidney Mount.* The Museums at Stony Brook, 1984.

Asch, Moses, and Alan Lomax. "Old Man, Will Your Dog Catch a Rabbit?" In *The Leadbelly Songbook.* New York: Oak Publications, 1962.

Baker, Houston A., Jr. *Blues, Ideology, and Afro-American Literature: A Vernacular Theory.* Chicago: University of Chicago Press, 1984.

Ball, E. C. National Folk Festival, workshop, July 31, 1977.

"Ballads in America." *The Nation* 98 (Feb. 5, 1914): 128–29.

Barry, Phillips. "The Part of the Folk Singer in the Making of Folk Balladry." In *The Critics and The Ballad*, edited by MacEdward Leach and Tristram P. Coffin. Carbondale: Southern Illinois University Press, 1961, 59–76.

Bascom, William. "African Folktales in America: I. The Talking Skull Refuses to Talk." *Research in African Literatures* 8, no. 2 (Autumn 1977): 266–91, Special Issue on African Folklore.

Bayard, Samuel. *Dance to the Fiddle, March to the Fife.* University Park: Pennsylvania State University Press, 1982.

Bayard, Samuel P. "The Materials of Folklore." *Journal of American Folklore* 66, no. 259 (1953): 8.

Beck, Frank O. *Hobohemia*. Rindge, N.H.: Richard R. Smith Publisher, 1956.

Belden, H. M., ed. *Ballads and Songs Collected by the Missouri Folk-Lore Society.* Volume XV, no. 1. University of Missouri Studies, Jan. 1940.

Belden, H. M. "Balladry in America." *Journal of American Folklore* 25, no. 95 (Jan.–Mar. 1912): 16–17.

Belden, Henry M., and Arthur Palmer Hudson, eds. *Frank C. Brown Collection of North Carolina Folklore III.* Durham, N.C.: Duke University Press, 1952.

Bellow, Saul. "Chicago and American Culture: One Writer's View." *Chicago Guide* 22, no. 5 (May 1973): 83–84.

Bellow, Saul. "A Sermon by Doctor Pep." *Partisan Review* 16 (Jan.–June 1949).

Bellow, Saul. "Starting Out in Chicago." *American Scholar* XLIV, no. 1 (winter 1974–75): 71–77.

Bellwood Singers. "Longest Train I Ever Saw." AFS 253 A-1.

Ben-Amos, Dan. "The Seven Strands of Tradition: Varieties in Its Meaning in American Folklore Studies." *Journal of Folklore Research* 21, no. 2/3 (May–Dec. 1984): 97–131. Culture, Tradition, Identity Conference, March 26–28, 1984.

Berkow, Ira. *Maxwell Street: Survival in a Bazaar.* Garden City, N.Y.: Doubleday, 1977.

Bertrand, Michael T. "Race and Rural Identity." In *The Hayloft Gang: The Story of the National Barn Dance*, edited by Chad Berry. Urbana: University of Illinois Press, 2008.

Best, Carroll. *Say Old Man, Can You Play the Banjo?* Copper Creek Records, CCCD-0175, 1999.

Birmingham News. "Mountain Farmer, With Banjo, Plays Way Into Ranks of Vaudeville Stars." Jan. 8, 1925.

Birmingham News. "'Uncle Dave' Macon Begins His Fourth Week at Loew's Bijou." Jan. 26, 1925.

Bishop, Carolyn Willingham. Telephone conversation with author, handwritten notes, July 7, 2011.

Blair, Walter. "Burlesques in Nineteenth-Century American Humor." *American Literature* II, no. 3 (November 1930).

Blaustein, Richard. Notes to *Down Around Bowmantown, A Portrait of a Musical Community in Northeast Tennessee, Then and Now.* Now and Then Records 1001, Center for Appalachian Studies and Services, 1989.

Blow the Candle Out: "Unprintable" Ozark Folksongs and Folklore, Volume II, Folk Rhymes and Other Lore. Fayetteville: University of Arkansas Press, 1992.

Bolick, Harry. *Mississippi Fiddle Tunes and Songs from the 1930s.* Document Records DOCD-8071, 2015.

Bolick, Harry, and Stephen T. Austin. *Mississippi Fiddle Tunes and Songs from the 1930s.* Jackson: University Press of Mississippi, 2015.

Bordelon, Pamela, ed. *Go Gator and Muddy the Water, Writings by Zora Neale Hurston from the Federal Writers' Project.* New York: W. W. Norton and Company, 1999.

Botkin, B. A. "Mississippi Sounding Call." In *A Treasury of Mississippi River Folklore.* New York: Crown, 1955, 572–73.

Botkin, B. A. *Negro Work Songs and Calls*, AAFS, album 8. Folk Music of the United States, Recording Laboratory, Library of Congress AFS L-8, 1943. Reissued on Rounder CD 1517, 1999.

Botkin, B. A. *Sidewalks of America.* Westport, Conn.: Greenwood Press, 1976.

Botkin, B. A. *A Treasury of American Folklore.* New York: Crown Publishers, 1944.

Botkin, Benjamin. "The Function of a Folk Festival." *Washington Post*, "Folk Festival Edition," Apr. 25, 1938.

Botkin, Benjamin A. "The Folk and the Writer: Introduction to Folklore Craft Section," June 4, 1939, Third American Writers Congress, New York. League of American Writers Archives, University of California, Berkeley.

Botkin, Benjamin A. "The Folkness of the Folk." *The English Journal* 26, College Edition (June 1937).

Botkin, Benjamin A. *A Treasury of American Folklore.* New York: Crown Publishers, 1944.

Boyd, Luther. "Calling Trains." Recorded April 14, 1936, AFS 599-A-1 and A-2.

Bradley, William Aspenwall. "Song-Ballets and Devil's Ditties." *Harper's Monthly Magazine* 130 (May 1915): 901–14.

Brady, Erika. "Performers and the Phonograph: 'The Box That Got the Flourishes.'" In *A Spiral Way: How the Phonograph Changed Ethnography.* Jackson: University Press of Mississippi, 1999, 89–117.

Bressler, Sandra Gross. "Culture and Politics: A Legislative Chronicle of the American Folklife Preservation Act." PhD diss., University of Pennsylvania, 1995.

Brewer, J. Mason. *Dog Ghosts and Other Negro Folk Tales* and *The Word on the Brazos: Negro Preacher Tales from the Brazos Bottoms of Texas.* Austin: University of Texas Press, 1976.

Bristol Herald. Bristol, Vermont, June 19, 1902.

Brochure for "The People in Their Music" series. File 32.4, Flerlage Collection.

Bronson, Bertrand. "Habits of the Ballad As Song." In *The Ballad As Song.* Berkeley: University of California Press, 1969, 105–07.

Brooks, Tim. *The Blackface Minstrel Show in Mass Media: 20th Century Performances on Radio, Records, Film and Television.* Jefferson, N.C.: McFarland and Company, 2020.

Brown, Frank C. "Popular Beliefs and Superstitions." In *North Carolina Folklore*, volume 6. Durham, N.C.: Duke University Press, 1961.

Brown, John Mason. “Songs of the Slave.” *Lippincott’s Magazine*, December 1868, 617–22.

Brown, Matt. “Flowery Girls.” https://twofingerbanjo.com/flowerygirls, accessed Dec. 20, 2024.

Brown, Sterling A., Arthur P. Davis, and Ulysses Lee. “Folk Literature.” In Brown, *The Negro Caravan.*

Brown, Sterling A., Arthur P. Davis, and Ulysses Lee. *The Negro Caravan.* New York: Dryden Press, 1941.

Browning, Norma Lee. “Are You a Folknik in a Hootenanny.” *Chicago Tribune*, June 24, 1960.

Brubaker, Robert L. “Instrument Manufacturing.” In *Making Music Chicago Style.* Chicago Historical Society, 1985, exhibition catalog, 56–61.

Bruns, Roger A. *The Damndest Radical: The Life and World of Ben Reitman, Chicago’s Celebrated Social Reformer, Hobo King, and Whorehouse Physician.* Urbana: University of Illinois Press, 1987.

Bruynoghe, Yannick. “Chicago, Home of the Blues.” In *Just Jazz*, edited by Sinclair Traill and Gerald Lascelles. London: Peter Davies, 1958, 69–76.

Buchan, David. “Ballad Tradition and Hugh Spencer.” In *The Ballad Image: Essays Presented to Bertrand Harris Bronson*, edited by James Porter. Los Angeles: Center for the Study of Comparative Folklore & Mythology, University of California, 1983.

Bulletin of People’s Songs Inc., vol. 1, no. 1, February 1946.

Burke, Kenneth. *Counter-Statement.* Berkeley: University of California Press, 1968.

Burke, Kenneth. “Literature as an Equipment for Living.” *Direction* 1, no. 2 (April 4, 1938): 10–13.

Burke, Kenneth. *The Philosophy of Literary Form: Studies in Symbolic Action.* Baton Rouge: Louisiana State University Press, 1941.

Burman, Ben Lucien. “Mississippi Roustabout.” *Harper’s Magazine* (May 1940): 635–43.

Burnett, Richard D. *Songs Sung by R. D. Burnett, The Blind Man, Monticello, Kentucky.* “The Jolly Butchers.” ca. 1913. No pagination.

Butcher, Fanny. The Literary Spotlight. *Chicago Sunday Tribune*, June 4, 1950. In Box 7, Folder 142a, Scrapbooks. Lloyd Lewis Papers.

Cannon’s Jug Stompers. “Feather Bed.” Recorded Sept. 9, 1928, Victor V38515.

Cantwell, Robert. *Bluegrass Breakdown: The Making of the Old Southern Sound.* Urbana: University of Illinois Press, 1984.

Carlin, Bob. “An Apprentice with the Ghosts.” *Old-Time Herald* 5, no. 7 (Spring 1997).

Carter, Jimmy, President. “Labor Day Remarks at a White House Picnic.” The American Presidency Project. https://www.presidency.ucsb.edu/node/249441, accessed Dec. 26, 2018.

Carter, Thomas. Notes to *Emmett W. Lundy, Fiddle Tunes from Grayson, County, Virginia.* String Records STR, 802, 1977.

Cassidy, Frederic G., chief editor. *Dictionary of American Regional English.* Cambridge: Harvard University Press, 1985.

Charlie Sims file at Parchman, October 7, 1947.

Charters, Samuel. *Chicago/ The Blues/ Today!* Vanguard VMD 79216 (vol. 1); VMD 79217 (vol. 2); VMD 79218 (vol. 3), 1966, reissued 1999, Vanguard 172/74–2.

Christiansen, Richard. *A Theater of Our Own: A History and a Memoir of 1,001 Nights in Chicago.* Evanston, Ill.: Northwestern University Press, 2004.

Cincinnati Daily Enquirer. "River Intelligence." Jan. 27, 1868.

Claxton, P. P. "An Opportunity to Help in an Important Work." Bureau of Education, Department of the Interior, Special Inquiry, November 1913, p. 1.

Cohen, John. "County Records." *Sing Out!* 19, no. 2 (July–Aug. 1969).

Cohen, John. "John Cohen I." In Cohen, *"Wasn't That a Time!"*

Cohen, John. "A Rare Interview with Harry Smith." *Sing Out!* 19, no. 1 (April–May) 1969: 2–11, 41; and no. 2 (July–August 1969): 22–28.

Cohen, Norm. "Fiddling Sid Harkreader." *JEMF Quarterly* 8, Part 4, no. 28 (Winter 1972): 188–93.

Cohen, Norm. *Folk Song America, A 20th Century Revival.* Washington, D.C.: Smithsonian Collection of Recordings, 1990.

Cohen, Norm. *Long Steel Rail: The Railroad in American Folksong.* Urbana: University of Illinois Press, 1981 and 2000.

Cohen, Norm. "Old Man." Performed by Hally Wood, in *Folk Song America, A 20th Century Revival.* Smithsonian Recordings RC 046, 1991, 84.

Cohen, Norm. "The Sinking of The Titanic and the Floundering of American Folksong Scholarship." *Southern Folklore* 56, no. 1 (1999): 3–26.

Cohen, Norm. "The Songs of Uncle Dave Macon." In *Uncle Dave Macon.*

Cohen, Norm. "Tin Pan Alley's Contribution to Folk Music." *Western Folklore* 29, no. 1 (Jan. 1970): 9–20.

Cohen, Ronald D., ed. *Alan Lomax, Selected Writings 1934–1997.* New York: Routledge, 2003.

Cohen, Ronald D., ed. *"Wasn't That a Time!": Firsthand Accounts of the Folk Music Revival.* American Folk Music and Musicians, No. 1. Metuchen, N.J.: The Scarecrow Press, Inc., 1995.

Cohen, Ronald D., and Bob Riesman. *Chicago Folk: Images of the Sixties Music Scene: The Photographs of Raeburn Flerlage.* Toronto: ECW Press, 2009.

Conot, Robert. *Thomas A. Edison: A Streak of Luck.* New York: Da Capo, 1979.

"Continue Regular Scheduled Programs at Buck Lake Ranch." *Angola Herald*, Angola, Indiana, June 6, 1947.

Conway, Cecelia. *African Banjo Echoes in Appalachia: A Study of Folk Traditions.* Knoxville: University of Tennessee Press, 1995.

Cook, Rob. *Franks for the Memories: A History of the Legendary Chicago Drum Shop and the Story of Maurie and Jan Lishon.* Alma, Mich.: Rebeats Publications, 1993.

CORE Sit-In Songs: Songs of the Freedom Riders. Audio Fidelity Stereodisc DS 4601, Dauntless, 1962.

Corky Siegel with Seji Ozawa and the San Francisco Symphony Orchestra, Russo: Street Music; Three Pieces for Blues Band and Orchestra, featuring the Siegel/Schwall Band. Deutsche Grammophon 415 792-1/10 GV, 1977/73.

Courlander, Harold. *Terrapin's Pot of Sense.* New York: Holt Rinehart and Winston, 1957.

Cowell, Sidney Robertson. "Charles Seeger (1886–1979)." *The Musical Quarterly* 65 (April 1979): 305–07.

Cox, John Harrington. "Negro Tales from West Virginia." *Journal of American Folklore* 47, no. 186 (Oct.–Dec. 1934): 341–42.

Cronon, William. *Nature's Metropolis: Chicago and the Great West.* New York: W. W. Norton and Company, 1991.

The Cumberland Ridgerunners. *Mountain Ballads and Home Songs.* Chicago: M. M. Cole Publishing Co., 1936.

Cushing, Steve. *Pioneers of the Blues Revival.* Urbana: University of Illinois Press, 2014.

Cutler, Irving. *The Jews of Chicago: From Shtetl to Suburb.* Urbana: University of Illinois Press, 1996.

Daily Memphis. "Boats Leaving To-Day." Feb. 8, 1872.

Daily Missouri Republican. "Affray on Steamboat," unsigned article, St. Louis, Missouri, Feb. 18, 1861, 3.

"Dakota Jack." *Johnson City Staff-News*, Johnson City, Tenn., Jan. 21, 1916.

"Dakota Jack." *Maryville Times*, Maryville, Tenn., February 10, 1916.

Dalrymple, Dolly. "Tennessee Banjoist Reminisces of New Years On And Off Stage." *Birmingham News*, Jan. 1, 1926.

Davenport, Clyde. "Old Cow Died in the Forks of the Branch." *Clydeoscope, Rare and Beautiful Tunes from the Cumberland Plateau.* County 788, 1986.

Davidson, Eric. Notes to *Traditional Music from Grayson and Carroll Counties.* Folkways Records FS 3811, 1962.

Davidson, Eric H., and Paul Newman. *Band Music of Grayson and Carroll Counties, Va.: A Half-Century of Change.* Folkways Records FS 3832, 1967.

Davidson, Mark. "Recording the Nation: Folk Music and the Government in Roosevelt's New Deal 1936–1941." PhD diss., University of California–Santa Cruz, 2015.

Davis, Arthur Kyle, Jr. *Folk-Songs of Virginia: A Descriptive Index and Classification.* Durham, N.C.: Duke University Press, 1949.

Davis, Arthur Kyle, Jr. "Miscellaneous Material re Ballads & Ballad Collecting." Accession #9829, box 2, folder 8, Arthur Kyle Davis papers, Alderman Library, University of Virginia.

Davis, Arthur Kyle, Jr. "Some Recent Trends in Field of Folksong." *Southern Folklore Quarterly* 1, no. 2 (1937): 19–24.

Davis, Arthur Kyle, Jr. *Traditional Ballads of Virginia.* Cambridge: Harvard University Press, 1929.

Day, Lisa, ed. *Chicago Blues as Seen from the Inside: The Photographs of Raeburn Flerlage.* Toronto, Ontario: ECW Press, 2000.

"The Death of Harry Simms." *People's Songs* 2, no. 6 and 7 (July–Aug. 1947).

Denisoff, R. Serge. *Great Day Coming: Folk Music and the American Left.* Urbana: University of Illinois Press, 1971.

Denisoff, R. Serge. "The Proletarian Renascence: The Folkness of the Ideological Folk." *Journal of American Folklore* 82, no. 323 (Jan.–Mar. 1969): 51–65.

Dewey, John. *Democracy and Education.* Macmillan, 1916.

Diddley, Bo. "Who Do You Love." Originally issued as Checker 842, 1956. Reissued on *The Chess Box,* MCA Records, CHD2-19502, 1990.

Distler, Marion. Notes to *Work Songs of the U.S A. Sung by Lead Belly.* Asch 101–103, 1942.

Dixon, Robert M. W., John Godrich, and Howard W. Rye. *Blues and Gospel Records 1890–1943.* 4th ed. Oxford: Oxford University Press, 1997.

Dixon, Willie. With the Big Three Trio. "Signifying Monkey." Columbia 37358, March 1947.

Doc Hopkins and His Country Boys, Deluxe Edition. Chicago: M. M. Cole Publishing Co., 1945.

Dodge, Jeana Willingham. Personal communication with author, early 1997.

Dodge, Jeana Willingham. "We All Have a Past."

Doerflinger, William Main. *Songs of the Sailor and Lumberman.* New York: Macmillan, 1972.

Dondore, Dorothy. "Big Talk! The Flyting, the Gabe, and the Frontier Boast." *American Speech* 6, no. 1 (October 1930): 45–55.

Dorschug, Doug. Liner notes to Keys, *Evergreen.*

Dorsey, Thomas A. "Lead Me to the Rock That's Higher Than I." New York: Hill and Range Songs, Inc., 1951.

Dorson, Richard M. *American Negro Folktales.* Greenwich, Conn.: Fawcett Premier, 1967.

Dorson, Richard M. "Coon in a Box." In *American Negro Folktales.*

Dorson, Richard M. "Eating the Baby." In *American Negro Folktales.*

Doubler, Michael D. *Dixie Dewdrop: The Uncle Dave Macon Story.* Urbana: University of Illinois Press, 2018.

Doubler, Michael D. *Uncle Dave Macon: A Photo Tribute.* Macon-Doubler Fellowship, 2014.

Downey, Thomas. *Congressional Record,* September 8, 1975, 27920.

Duncan, Hugh Dalziel. *The Rise of Chicago as a Literary Center from 1885 to 1920: A Sociological Essay in American Culture.* Totowa, N.J.: Bedminster Press, 1964.

Dundes, Alan, ed. *Mother Wit from the Laughing Barrel: Readings in the Interpretation of Afro-American Folklore.* Englewood Cliffs, N.J.: Prentice-Hall, 1973.

Dunne, Finley Peter. "History." In *Observations by Mr. Dooley.* New York, 1906.

Eastwood, Carolyn. "The Demise of an Urban Market: Does it Matter? Who Cares?" Paper presented at 72nd Annual Meeting of the Central States Anthropological Society, March 1995.

Ebert, Roger. "A Hard Day's Night." October 27, 1996. Rogerebert.com reviews, accessed Nov. 11, 2021.

Edwards, David. Interview with Pete Welding. *Blues Unlimited* 54, June 1968.

Edwards, David "Honeyboy." Interview. *Living Blues* 1, no. 4 (Winter 1970–71): 20.

Edwards, David "Honeyboy." *The World Don't Owe Me Nothing.* Chicago Review Press, 1997.

Ellison, Ralph. *Going to the Territory.* New York: Vintage, 1986.

Ellison, Ralph. "Going to the Territory." In *Going to the Territory.*

Ellison, Ralph. *Invisible Man.* New York: Random House, 1947.

Ellison, Ralph. "The Little Man at Chehaw Station." In *Going to the Territory.*

Epstein, Dena J. *Music Publishing in Chicago before 1871: The Firm of Root & Cady, 1858–1871.* Detroit Studies in Music Bibliography. Detroit: Information Coordinators, 1969.

Eskew, Garnett L. "Coonjine in Manhattan." Manuscript/Mixed Material, 1939. Library of Congress WPA Folklore Project, Life Histories, 1936–39. https://www.loc.gov/item/wpalh000067/.

Evans, David. *Afro-American Folk Music from Tate and Panola Counties, Mississippi.* Originally issued as AFS L- 67, 1978. Reissued on Rounder 1515–2, 2000, 32–34.

Evans, David. "Afro-American One-Stringed Instruments." In *Western Folklore* 29 (1970) 229–45. Reprinted in *Afro-American Folk Art and Crafts,* edited by William Ferris. Boston: G. K. Hall, 1983, 181–96.

Evans, David. "The Guitar in the Blues Music of the South." In *Guitar Cultures,* edited by Andy Bennett and Kevin Dawe. Oxford: Berg, 2001.

Evans, David. Notes to *Deep River of Song: Mississippi: Saints & Sinners.* Rounder 11661-1824-2, 1999.

Evans, David. Notes to "Nigger Blues." *Let's Get Loose: Folk and Popular Blues Styles from the Beginnings to the Early 1940s.* New World Records NW 290, 1978.

Evans, David. "Riddling and the Structure of Context." *Journal of American Folklore* 89, no. 532 (Apr.–June 1976): 166–88.

Evans, David. To author, Sept. 28, 2020.

Evans, David. To author, Apr. 28, 2024.

Excell, E. O. *Triumphant Songs. No. 5: A Collection of Gospel Hymns for Sunday-Schools and Revivals.* Chicago: E. O. Excell, 1896.

Farr, T. J. "Riddles and Superstitions of Middle Tennessee." *Journal of American Folklore* 48, no. 190 (Oct.–Dec. 1935).

Ferriss, Abbott. Field notes to "Folk Music Recordings Made in Mississippi by Herbert Halpert, May 1939." Archive of Folk Culture, Library of Congress, 414–15.

Ferriss, Abbott. "Music Tour Remembered." In liner notes to *Great Big Yam Potatoes: Anglo-American Fiddle Music from Mississippi.* Mississippi Department of Archives and History AH-002, 1985.

Ferriss, Abbott (unsigned). *Memphis Commercial Appeal,* July 23, 1939.

Ferriss, Abbott. Notebook 7. 1939. Mississippi Department of Archives and History.

Fichandler, Zelda. "Toward a Deepening Aesthetic." In *The Long Revolution: Sixty Years on the Frontlines of a New American Theater,* edited by Todd London. New York: Theatre Communications Group, 2024.

Finster, Howard. *The Tonight Show,* August 5, 1983. https://www.youtube.com/watch?v=YweCaFHEZ50.

Flatt and Scruggs. "Down the Road." Mercury 6211, 1949.

Flerlage, Raeburn. "Folksong Street." *People's Songs* 2, no. 1 and 2 (Feb.–Mar. 1947): 5 and 9.

Flerlage, Raeburn. "Introductory Notes," March 12, 1946. "The People in Their Music," Flerlage Collection.

Flerlage, Raeburn. "Music for Democracy," in "The People's Music," May 18, 1946, *Farm Equipment Workers News.* MSS Lot F, file 32.6. Flerlage Collection.

Flerlage, Raeburn. "Note for Miss Blackwell." Flerlage Collection.

Flerlage, Raeburn. Program two, March 12, 1946. "The People in Their Music," Flerlage Collection.

Flerlage, Raeburn. Program five typescript, April 2, 1946, Flerlage Collection.

Flerlage, Raeburn. Program six, "Notes," April 9, 1946. "The People in Their Music," Flerlage Collection.

Flerlage, Raeburn. Program nine, "The People in Their Music."

Flerlage, Raeburn. "On the Record." *People's Songs* 1, no. 11 (Dec. 1946).

Flerlage, Raeburn. "On the Record." *People's Songs* 2, no. 1 and 2 (Feb.–Mar. 1947).

Flerlage, Raeburn. "On the Record." *People's Songs* 2, no. 3 (Apr. 1947).

Flerlage, Raeburn. "On the Record." *People's Songs* 2, no. 4 (May 1947).

Flerlage, Raeburn. To Pete Seeger, November 12, 1946.

Flerlage, Raeburn. Typed script for "Notes on the Records," from "The People in Their Music, Program no. 1, March 5, 1946." Flerlage Collection.

Flerlage, Raeburn. "Typescript and Manuscript drafts, 1946–1998." MSS Lot F, file 32.4, "The People in Their Music," Flerlage Collection.

Flerlage, Ray. Album notes to *Frank Hamilton Sings Folk Songs*. Folkways FA 2437, 1962.

Flerlage, Ray. To Bernie Asbell, December 29, 1946. Copy of letter courtesy of Ron Cohen.

Ford, Ira. *Traditional Music of America.* New York: Dutton, 1940.

Fowler, David C. "The Gosport Tragedy: Story of a Ballad." *Southern Folklore Quarterly* 43, nos. 3 and 4 (1979): 157–96.

Frankenstein, Alfred. *William Sidney Mount.* New York: Abrams, 1975.

Frost, O. W., ed. *Children of the Levee.* Lexington: University of Kentucky Press, 1957.

Fulcher, Bobby. Personal communication with author, handwritten notes, Sept. 28, 1996.

Fulcher, Bobby. Notes to "The French Waltz." In *Gettin' Up the Stairs: Traditional Music from the Cumberland Plateau, Vol. 1,* County 786, 1984.

Gaillard, Frye. "A Parable of Integrity and Survival," posted on Chapter 16, published by Humanities Tennessee, August 9, 2023, https://chapter16.org/a-parable-of-integrity-and-survival/, accessed August 14, 2023.

Gifford, Paul M. "Henry Ford's Dance Revival and Fiddle Contest: Myth and Reality." *Journal of the Society for American Music* 4, no. 3 (2010): 307–38.

Ginell, Cary. *The Columbia 15000-D-Series Discography (1924–1933) Familiar Tunes Old & New.* Self-published, 2021.

Glassie, Henry. "Tradition." In *Eight Words for the Study of Expressive Culture,* edited by Burt Feintuch. Urbana: University of Illinois Press, 2003.

Gleason, Philip. *Speaking of Diversity: Language and Ethnicity in Twentieth-Century America.* Baltimore: Johns Hopkins University Press, 1992.

Goins, Wayne Everett. *Blues All Day Long: The Jimmy Rogers Story.* Urbana: University of Illinois Press, 2014.

Golden, Harry. *Carl Sandburg.* Cleveland: World Publishing Company, 1961.

Gordon, Milton M. "Models of Pluralism: The New American Dilemma." *The Annals of the American Academy of Political and Social Science* 454 (March 1981): 178–88.

Gordon, Robert Winslow. "Banjo Songs." *New York Times,* Jan. 1, 1928. Reprinted in *Folk-Songs of America,* National Service Bureau publication 73-S, December 1938. Federal Theatre Project.

Gorrell, Sgt. T. L. Memo, October 28, 1947. Charlie Sims file at Parchman.

Green, Archie. "The Archive's Shores." *Folklife Annual 1985,* edited by Alan Jabbour and James Hardin, 60–73. Washington, D.C.: American Folklife Center, Library of Congress, 1986.

Green, Archie. "The Folklife Act in the Ninety-Third Congress," by the Citizens Committee for an American Folklife Center. Mimeographed report dated Dec. 31, 1974, 2.

Green, Archie. "General's Folk Albums." *JEMF Quarterly* no. 71 (Autumn 1983), Graphics 63.

Green, Archie. "Green ms." First draft, Feb. 12, 1997, second draft, undated (accompanied with a letter dated Mar. 25, 1997).

Green, Archie. Hearing on American Folklife Center. S. 1844, Senate Committee on Rules and Administration, before the Subcommittee on the Library. Ninety-Third Congress, Second Session, May 8, 1974. U.S. Govt. Printing Office, 62.

Green, Archie. "Hillbilly Music: Source and Symbol." *Journal of American Folklore* 78, no. 309 (July–Sept. 1965): 204–28.

Green, Archie. Introduction to *Folklife and the Federal Government, A Guide to Activities, Resources, Funds and Services*. Compiled by Linda C. Coe. Publications of the American Folklife Center, 1977, 1–9.

Green, Archie. *Only a Miner.* Urbana: University of Illinois Press, 1972.

Green, Archie. "P.L. 94-201—A View from the Lobby, A Report to the American Folklore Society." In *The Conservation of Culture: Folklorists and the Public Sector*, edited by Burt Feintuch. Lexington: University Press of Kentucky, 1988, 269–81.

Green, Archie. To author, Aug. 2, 1993. San Francisco.

Green, Archie. To author, memo, Feb. 12, 1997.

Green, Archie. To author, May 5, 2003.

Green, Archie. "Vernacular Music: A Naming Compass." *The Musical Quarterly* 77, no. 1 (Spring 1993): 35–46.

Green, Archie. "Vernacular Music Albums." *JEMF Quarterly* 17, no. 64 (Winter 1981): 201–14, Graphics 59.

Green, Archie. "Victor's 'P' Album Series." *JEMF Quarterly* 8, no. 26 (Summer 1972): 77–89, Graphics 21.

Green, Archie. *Wobblies, Pile Butts, and Other Heroes: Laborlore Explorations.* Urbana: University of Illinois Press, 1993.

Green, Archie. Unsigned notes for "Trouble at the Coal Creek Mines." In *Doc Hopkins*.

Green, Rayna. "Magnolias Grow in Dirt." *Southern Exposure* 4, no. 4 (Winter 1977): 29–33.

Greensmith, Bill, Mike Rowe, and Mark Camarigg, eds. *Blues Unlimited: Essential Interviews from the Original Blues Magazine*. Urbana: University of Illinois Press, 2015.

"Greetings from Allan M. Trout," item 3. *Louisville Courier-Journal*, June 11, 1966.

Gross, H. R. *Congressional Record*, December 16, 1974, 40142.

Guthrie, Woody. Review of *Smoky Mountain Ballads*. Ms. handwritten and typed.

Hackett, James Henry. *New York Evening Post*, April 24, 1830.

Halpert, Herbert. "Federal Theatre and Folksong." *Southern Folklore Quarterly* II, no. 2 (June 1938): 83.

Halpert, Herbert. To author, Jan. 28, 1997.

Halpert, Herbert. To author, Feb. 10, 1997.

Hamilton, Frank. To author, November 6, 2022.

Harkreader, Sid. *Fiddlin' Sid's Memoirs: The Autobiography of Sidney J. Harkreader*, edited by Walter D. Haden, JEMF Special Series, no. 9, 1976.

Harkreader, Sid. "Old Joe." Recorded June 1927, Paramount 3023.

Hatch, Marion Charles (as told to). "Some Green Sand Hogs and Others." In *Sidewalks of America*, edited by B. A. Botkin. Westport, Conn.: Greenwood Press, reprinted 1976, orig. 1954, 282–84.

Hawes, Bess. To author, personal correspondence, October 20, 1993.

Hay, George D. *A Story of the Grand Ole Opry.* Nashville: G. D. Hay, 1953.

Haynes, Jewell Fagan. To author, August 24, 1982.

Hayslett, Corbin F. "The Doyen of Dixie: A Survey of the Banjo Stylings of Uncle Dave Macon." Master's thesis, East Tennessee State University, 2018.

Hazel, Sam. Notes to Negro Roustabout Songs, "Folk Music Recordings made in Mississippi by Herbert Halpert," AFS 2735-3135. Typescript. Library of Congress.

Hazel, Sam. "Roustabout Heaving Song Discussion." AFS 3097 B.

Hazel, Sam. Roustabout Song (part 2). AFS 3098 B.

Hearn, Lafcadio. "Banjo Jim's Story." *Cincinnati Commercial*, October 1, 1876.

Hearn, Lafcadio. "Dolly/An Idyl of the Levee." *Cincinnati Commercial*, August 27, 1876. Reprinted in Frost, *Children of the Levee*.

Hearn, Lafcadio. "Levee Life." In *Children of the Levee*, edited by O. W. Frost. Lexington: University of Kentucky Press, 1957, 68–69.

Hemphill, Sid. "Skillet Good and Greasy." AFS 6673-B1, 1942.

Henry, Jim. "Workin' on the Levee, Sleepin' on de Ground." AFS 941-A2.

Hermann, Eric Neil. "'In the Good Old Days of Long Ago': Echoes of Vaudeville and Minstrelsy in the Music of Uncle Dave Macon." PhD diss., University of Maryland, 2016.

Hickerson, Joseph C. "Early Field Recordings of Ethnic Music." In *Ethnic Recordings in America: A Neglected Heritage.* Washington, D.C.: Library of Congress, American Folklife Center, 1982.

Hill, Hamlin. "Walter Blair Through the Ages." *Studies in American Humor*, New Series 3, No. 13, Special Issue: The Study of American Humor (2005–2006).

Hodge, Francis. *Yankee Theatre: The Image of America on the Stage, 1825–1850.* Austin: University of Texas, 1964.

Holt, George. Letter to presenters at Southern Crossroads, May 28, 1996.

The Home Folks. *Last Chance.* June Appal Recordings, JA 033, 1980.

Hood, Mantle. "The Challenge of 'Bi-Musicality.'" *Ethnomusicology* 4, no. 2 (May 1960): 55–59.

Hooker, John Lee. "Rabbit on the Log." From *The Unknown John Lee Hooker 1949 Recordings*, Flyright FLY CD 57, 2000.

Hooks, Joel. *Five Stringer* 220 (Summer 2022–2023): 4–11. Published by the American Banjo Fraternity.

Hooks, Joel. To author, May 31, 2016.

Hooper, Johnson J. *The Widow Rugby's Husband, a Night at the Ugly Man's, and Other Tales of Alabama.* Philadelphia: A. Hart, 1851.

Hopkins, Doc. *Doc Hopkins.* Birch 1945, 1971.

Hopkins, Doc. Personal communications with author, ca. 1981, Chicago.

Hopkins, Doc. Personal communication with author, ca. summer 1981.

Hopkins, Doc. Personal communication with author, ca. fall 1981.

Hopkins, Doc. Personal communication with author, summer 1982.

Hopkins, Doc. Personal communication with author, May 25, 1983. Chicago.

Hopkins, Doc. Personal communication and handwritten notes, spring 1986.

Hopkins, Doc. Personal communication with author, by telephone, spring 1987.

Hopkins, Doc. Personal communication with author, by phone, handwritten notes, Dec. 24, 1987.

Hopkins, Doc. Tape, "Jokes and Gags," Sept. 1, 1984.

Hopkins, Doc. Tape-recorded cassette titled "Tape of Doc to Steve," ca. 1986.

Hopkins, Doc. Tape-recorded letter to author, "Songs and Gags & Etc." Oct. 1983.

Hopkins, Doc. To author, Nov. 28, 1983.

Hopkins, Doc. To author, Dec. 18, 1983.

Hopkins, Doc. To author, Sept. 22, 1986.

Hopkins, Doc. To author, "Early Days at the Start of the Cumberland Ridge Runners, Doc Hopkins, Karl and Harty, and All the Others that Came into the Act Afterward," undated letter, ca. 1981.

Hopkins, Doc. To author, "To Steve from Doc," Undated tape-recorded letter, ca. 1983.

Hopkins, Doc. To author, "True History of Doc Hopkins," handwritten letter, undated ca. spring 1987.

Hopkins, Doc. Undated cassette tape letter, ca. 1983, with Doc's inscription, "From Doc to Steve."

House, Son. "Two at the Gate." *John and Old Marster, Negro Folk Tales.* Flyright EP 01, 1980.

Howells, William Dean. "Certain of the Chicago School of Fiction." *North American Review* 176, no. 558 (May 1903).

Hudson, A. P. *Journal of American Folklore* 39, no. 152 (Apr.-June 1926): 187–88.

Hudson, Wilson M. "I Want My Golden Arm." In *Folk Travelers: Ballads, Tales, and Talk*, edited by Mody C. Boatright, Wilson M. Hudson, and Allan

Maxwell. Publication XXV, Texas Folklore Society, Austin. Dallas: Southern Methodist University Press, 1953, 183–194.

Hugill, Stan. *Shanties from the Seven Seas.* Mystic Seaport, 1961.

Hughes, Langston, and Arna Bontemps. *The Book of Negro Folklore.* New York: Dodd, Meade & Company, 1965.

Hurston, Zora Neale. "High John de Conquer." In *The American Mercury Reader,* edited by Lawrence E. Spivak and Charles Angoff. Philadelphia: The Blakiston Company, 1944.

Hurston, Zora Neale. *Mules and Men.* Bloomington: Indiana University Press, 1978.

Hyde, Lewis. *Common as Air: Revolution, Art and Ownership.* New York: Farrar, Straus and Giroux, 2011.

Hyland, Robert. "Songs Sung and Played by Uncle Dave Macon on Radio and Appearances." In *Uncle Dave Macon.*

Illinois Writers' Project. Library of Congress, American Memory, *American Life Histories: Manuscripts from the Federal Writers' Project* (Frank DeSoto). https://tile.loc.gov/storage-services/service/mss/wpalh/wpalh-07060119/wpalh-07060119.pdf, accessed June 30, 1999.

"Immigrants Came to This Small Wisconsin City. So Did the Political Rhetoric," WBUR radio broadcast, aired November 5, 2024. From written transcription, accessed from internet, November 6, 2024.

Ismail, Matthew. *Blues Discovery: Reaching Across the Divide.* 2nd revised edition. Dost Publishing, 2023.

Ivey, William. Statement at the hearing on the American Folklife Center, Subcommittee on the Library of the Committee on Rules and Administration, United States Senate, 93rd Congress, second session, on S. 1844, May 8, 1974.

Jabbour, Alan. Introduction. In *Folk Roots, New Roots: Folklore in American Life,* edited by Jane S. Becker and Barbara Franco. Lexington, Mass.: Museum of Our National Heritage.

Jabbour, Alan. To Judith McCulloh, Oct. 10, 1969.

Jackson, Cora. "I Don't Want that Hen to Suffer." In Chuck Perdue, "'I Swear To God It's The Truth if I Ever Told It': John and Cora Jackson's Folktales from the Blue Ridge Mountains of Virginia." *Keystone Folklore Quarterly* XIV, no. 1 (Spring 1969).

Jack, Dakota. "Victory for Dakota Jack, and Com-Cel-Sar." *The Owensboro Messenger,* Owensboro, Ky., January 18, 1917.

Jackson, Bruce, ed. *Folklore and Society. Essays in Honor of Benj. A. Botkin.* Hatboro, Pa.: Folklore Associates, 1966.

Jackson, Emmett. "Steamboat Song." Recorded May 30, 1939, AFS 3076 B1.

Jackson, Emmet, and John Floyd. "Old Steamboat Roustabout Song." AFS 3081 A.

Jackson, John. *Don't Let Your Deal Go Down.* Arhoolie CD 378, 1992.

James, Skip. *The Complete Bloomington Concert- Part I (March 30, 1968).* DOCD-5633, track 2, titled "Skip James Talking."

Jones, Bessie Washington. "A Descriptive and Analytical Study of the American Negro Folktale." PhD diss., George Peabody College for Teachers, 1967.

Jones, Fred, Superintendent, Parchman Penitentiary, to Tony Standish of Heritage Records. March 9, 1961. Files for Wash Dennis, Mississippi Department of Corrections, Parchman penitentiary, Parchman, MS.

Jones, Lewis. "The Mississippi Delta." Typescript with handwritten title above printed notation "Social Science Institute, Fisk University, Nashville." Shelf number 309.17624 J77.

Jones, Loyal. *Minstrel of the Appalachians.* Lexington: University Press of Kentucky, 1984.

Jones, Max, Albert McCarthy, and Frederic Ramsey, eds. *A Tribute to Huddie Ledbetter.* Jazz Music Books: April 1946.

Jones, Moody, and Floyd Jones. "The Old Swing-Masters: Moody Jones, Floyd Jones, and Snooky Pryor." In Greensmith, *Blues Unlimited,* 134–35.

Jones, Tayari, and Genevieve West. *Hitting a Straight Lick with a Crooked Stick: Stories from the Harlem Renaissance.* New York: Harper Collins, 2020.

Kahn, Ed. Liner notes to *Smoky Mountain Ballads,* RCA Victor LPV-507, 1964.

Kaskowitz, Sheryl. *A Chance to Harmonize: How FDR's Hidden Music Unit Sought to Save America from the Great Depression—One Song at a Time.* New York: Pegasus Books, 2024.

Kalem, T. E. "Pipes of Pan." *Time,* June 25, 1979.

Kehrberg, Kevin, and Jeffrey A. Keith. "Somebody Died, Babe: A Musical Coverup of Racism, Violence & Greed." *The Bitter Southerner,* August 4, 2020.

Kerns, Clarence, to Eri Douglass, Apr. 21, 1939. Missouri Department of Archives and History.

Keys, Bill. To author, Mar. 4, 2021.

Keys, Bill. To author, Mar. 9, 2021.

Keys, Bill. To author, Mar. 12, 2021.

Keys, Bill. To author, Apr. 19, 2021.

Keys, Bill. To author, May 4, 2021.

Keys, Bill. To author, May 5, 2021.

Keys, Bill. To author, May 8, 2021.

Keys, Bill. To author, July 15, 2021.

Keys, Jerry. To author, July 18, 2021.

Keys, Jerry. To author, Aug. 22, 2021.

Keys, Jerry, and Will Keys. *Sycamore Shoals.* Keystone Records, 2013.

Keys, Will. *A Banjo Original.* County CO-CD 2720, 1997.

Keys, Will. Banjo workshop, July 4, 2003.

Keys, Will. *Evergreen*. Cloudlands CLC006, 1992.

Keys Will. Interview with Jerry Keys. *Banjo Newsletter* vol. XXI (Nov. 1993).

Keys, Will. Personal communication with author, July 1986, Washington, D.C.

Keys, Will. *Sweet Marie.* Bee-301, 1994

Keys, Will. To author, Sept. 18, 1986.

Keys, Will. To author, June 23, 1996.

Keys, Will, Barbara Kuhns, and Doug Smith. *Oldtime Banjo from Blackley Creek.* Video by Wayne Ingram, Cedar Glade Productions, VHS 005, 1999.

Kimber, Marian Wilson. *The Elocutionists: Women, Music, and the Spoken Word.* Urbana: University of Illinois Press, 2017.

Kincaid, Bradley. *Favorite Old-Time Songs and Mountain Ballads, Book 3.* Self-published, 1930.

Kriebel, Robert C. *Ross-Ade: Their Purdue Stories, Stadium, and Legacies.* West Lafayette, Ind.: Purdue University Press, 2019.

Kurin, Richard. "What Is It? The American South at the Olympics." In *Reflections of a Culture Broker: A View from the Smithsonian.* Washington, D.C.: Smithsonian Institution Press, 1997, 239–64.

"Kyle Creed: A 1966 Interview by Charlie Faurot with Tom Mylet and Kirk Sutphin." *The Old-Time Herald* 12, no. 2 (Dec. 2009-Jan. 2010): 23–32.

Langer, Suzanne K. *An Introduction to Symbolic Logic.* Rpt. ed. New York: Dover Publications, 1967.

"Last of the Troubadours," manuscript, Box 7, Folder 120. Lloyd Lewis Papers.

Laws, G. Malcolm, Jr. *American Balladry from British Broadsides.* Philadelphia: American Folklore Society, 1957.

Leach, Maria. *Whistle in the Graveyard: Folktales to Chill Your Bones*. New York: Viking Press, 1974.

Lead Belly. "Haul Away Joe." *Bourgeois Blues, Lead Belly Legacy Vol. 2.* Smithsonian Folkways SF CD 40045, 1997.

Lead Belly. "Monologue on Square Dances [or] Sooky Jumps." AFS 4469-B (a).

"Lead Belly Radio Show WNYC, 1/13/1944 (ACT-392)."

Legman, Gershon, ed. In *Roll Me in Your Arms, Vol. 1, Unprintable Ozark Folksongs and Folklore.* By Vance Randolph. Fayetteville: University of Arkansas Press, 1992.

Leonard, Will. "Tower Ticker." *Chicago Tribune,* December 29, 1951.

Levine, Lawrence. "The Meaning of the Slave Trickster." In *The Unpredictable Past: Explorations in American Cultural History.* New York: Oxford University Press, 1993.

Levine, Lawrence W. *Black Culture and Black Consciousness: Afro-American Folk Thought from Slavery to Freedom.* Oxford: Oxford University Press, 1977.

Lewis, Lloyd. "Chicago and the Midlands," *Survey Graphic* 23, no. 10 (October 1934). In Box 4, Folder 90. Lloyd Lewis Papers.

Lewis, Lloyd. "A Founding Father Returns." In *It Takes All Kinds.* Freeport, N.Y.: Books for Libraries Press, 1970, 215–18.

Lewis, Lloyd. *Myths After Lincoln.* New York: Harcourt, Brace and Company, 1929 and 1940.

Lewis, Lloyd. To Gertrude Stein, June 26, 1936. Box 2, Folder 80. Lloyd Lewis Papers.

Lightfoot, William. "A Regional Musical Style: The Legacy of Arnold Schultz." In *Sense of Place: American Regional Cultures,* edited by Barbara Allen and Thomas J. Schlereth. Lexington: University Press of Kentucky, 1990.

Linn, Karen. *That Half-Barbaric Twang: The Banjo in American Popular Culture.* Urbana: University of Illinois Press, 1991.

Lissak, Rivka Shpak. *Pluralism and Progressives: Hull House and the New Immigrants, 1890–1919.* Chicago: University of Chicago Press, 1989.

List of "colored" educable children. Town of Prairie, MS, Nov. 8, 1923. Mississippi Department of Archives and History.

Lomax, Alan. *Afro-American Spirituals, Work Songs, and Ballads.* Library of Congress, AFS L3, 1942. Reissued as LP, 1978.

Lomax, Alan. "America Sings the Saga of America." *New York Times Magazine,* January 26, 1947.

Lomax, Alan. Archive of American Folk Song, Annual Report of the Librarian of Congress for the Fiscal Year Ended June 30, 1940.

Lomax, Alan. "The Best of the Ballads." *Vogue,* December 1, 1946.

Lomax, Alan (unnamed here as author). "Introduction to American Folk Music Series." *Carl Sandburg, Cowboy Songs and Negro Spirituals.* Decca A-356, 1947.

Lomax, Alan. Notes to *Listen to Our Story.* Brunswick B-1012, 1947.

Lomax, Alan. *The People's Songbook.* New York: Oak 1948.

Lomax, Alan. "Sing-Along Book." Notes to *Listen to Our Story: A Panorama of American Ballads.* Brunswick b-1024, 1947, unpaginated.

Lomax, Alan. "Work Songs." In notes to *Negro Sinful Songs.* Musicraft 31, June 1939.

Lomax, John A. *Adventures of a Ballad Hunter.* New York: Macmillan, 1947.

Lomax, John A. Album notes to *Smoky Mountain Ballads.* Victor P-79, 1941.

Lomax, John A., and Alan Lomax. *The Leadbelly Legend.* TRO Folkways Music, 1959.

Lomax, John A., and Alan Lomax. *Our Singing Country: A Second Volume of American Ballads and Folk Songs.* New York: Macmillan, 1941.

Lomax, John A., and Alan Lomax. *Folk Song U.S.A.* New York: New American Library, 1975.

Lornell, Kip. "Old-Time Country Music in North Carolina and Virginia. The 1970s and 1980s." In *Hidden in the Mix: The African American Presence in Country Music,* edited by Diane Pecknold. Durham, N.C.: Duke University Press, 2013.

Lornell, Kip, and J. Roderick Moore. "Clarence Tross, Hardy County Banjoist." In

Mountains of Music, West Virginia Traditional Music from Goldenseal, edited by John Lilly. Urbana: University of Illinois Press, 1999, 81–86.

Lunsford, Bascom Lamar. "Swannanoa Tunnel." *Smoky Mountain Ballads.* Folkways FA 2040, 1953.

Lyon, Danny. *Memories of the Southern Civil Rights Movement.* Reprinted in "SNCC's Staff Photographer Reflects on Civil Rights Struggle in Mississippi," *Magnolia State Live*, Jan. 12, 2018, accessed Feb. 28, 2022.

McDowell, Mississippi Fred. "Soon One Mornin.'" *61 Highway Mississippi: Delta Country Blues, Spirituals, Work Songs & Dance Music*, Southern Journey, Vol. 3, Alan Lomax Collection, Rounder CD 1703, 1997. Recorded in September 1959.

Macon, Esten. "Rambling Views." *Daily News-Journal*, Murfreesboro, Tenn., July 28, 1942.

Macon, Uncle Dave. "All-Go-Hungry Hash House." Recorded April 14, 1925, Vocalion 15076.

Macon, Uncle Dave. "Arcade Blues." Recorded September 9, 1926, New York, Vocalion 15440 and 5002.

Macon, Uncle Dave. "Backwater Blues." Recorded May 11, 1927, Vocalion 5164.

Macon, Uncle Dave. "Bile Them Cabbage Down." Recorded July 11, 1924, Vocalion 14849.

Macon, Uncle Dave. "Comin' Round the Mountain." Recorded July 26, 1928.

Macon, Uncle Dave. "The Cross Eyed Butcher And The Cackling Hen." Recorded September 9, 1926, Vocalion 15453, 5014, and Brunswick 114.

Macon, Uncle Dave. "Death of John Henry (Steel Driving Man)." Recorded April 14, 1926, Vocalion 15320.

Macon, Uncle Dave. "Got No Silver Nor Gold Blues." Recorded May 10, 1927, Vocalion 5164.

Macon, Uncle Dave. "Heartaching Blues." Recorded May 10, 1927, Vocalion 5161.

Macon, Uncle Dave. "I'll Never Go There Any More (The Bowery)." Recorded May 11, 1927, Vocalion 5149.

Macon, Uncle Dave. "Keep My Skillet Good and Greasy." Recorded July 8, 1924, Vocalion 14848.

Macon, Uncle Dave. *Laugh Your Blues Away.* Rounder 1028, 1979.

Macon, Uncle Dave. "More Like Your Dad Every Day." Recorded May 11, 1927, Vocalion 5172.

Macon, Uncle Dave. "My Life and Experience." *Brunswick Topics.* San Diego: Southern California Music Co., 1928, 10–11.

Macon, Uncle Dave. "My Money Matters Easy," No. 21. *Songs and Stories of Uncle Dave Macon.* Nashville, 1938.

Macon, Uncle Dave. "Oh Lovin' Babe." Recorded Dec. 17, 1930, unissued on Okeh, first appeared on *Laugh Your Blues Away*, Rounder 1028, 1979.

Macon, Uncle Dave. "Over The Road I'm Bound To Go." Recorded July 25, 1928, Brunswick 329.

Macon, Uncle Dave. "Poor Sinners, Fare You Well." Recorded April 16, 1926, Vocalion 15324.

Macon, Uncle Dave. "Put Me in My Little Bed." Recorded June 20, 1929, Vocalion 5397.

Macon, Uncle Dave. "Railroadin' And Gamblin.'" Recorded January 26, 1938, Bluebird 8325.

Macon, Uncle Dave. "Rise When the Rooster Crows." Recorded April 14, 1926, Vocalion 15321.

Macon, Uncle Dave. "Rooster Crow Medley." Recorded April 13, 1925, Vocalion 15101.

Macon, Uncle Dave. "Run Nigger Run." Recorded April 13, 1925, Vocalion 15032.

Macon, Uncle Dave. "Sail Away Ladies." Recorded May 7, 1927, Vocalion 5155.

Macon, Uncle Dave. *Songs and Stories of Uncle Dave Macon.* Nashville: Uncle Dave Macon, 1938.

Macon, Uncle Dave. "Sourwood Mountain Medley." Recorded September 8, 1926, Vocalion 15443.

Macon, Uncle Dave. To Alan Lomax, November 26, 1947.

Macon, Uncle Dave. "Walking in the Sunlight." Recorded May 10, 1927, Vocalion 5160.

Macon, Uncle Dave. "When Reubin Comes To Town." Recorded May 10, 1927, Vocalion 5163.

Macon, Uncle Dave. "Whoop 'Em Up Cindy." Recorded April 16, 1926, Vocalion 15323.

Macon, Uncle Dave. "Worthy of Estimation." Recorded July 25, 1928, Brunswick 266.

Macon, Uncle Dave. "Wouldn't Give Me Sugar In My Coffee." Recorded September 8, 1926, Vocalion 15440.

Macon, David Ramsey. "Banjo Heritage." Tape-recorded letter to author, Dec. 29, 1981.

Malone, Bill C. "Music." In *High Mountains Rising: Appalachia in Time and Place,* edited by Richard A. Straw and H. Tyler Blethen. Urbana: University of Illinois Press, 2004.

Maloney, Mick. "Irish Ethnic Recordings and the Irish-American Imagination." In *Ethnic Recordings in America.*

Marshall, Howard Wight. *Play Me Something Quick and Devilish: Old-Time Fiddlers in Missouri.* Columbia: University of Missouri Press, 2012.

Maxwell, Steve. *Speaker's Corners, The Bughouse Square Debates (part 2), Soapbox Speakers, Sydney.* https://soapboxspeakers.wordpress.com/steve-maxwells-passing-parade/the-bughouse-square-debates-part-2/, accessed Oct. 18, 2023.

McCormick, Mack. Notes to "Boar Hog Blues," *The Unexpurgated Folk Songs of Men.* Raglan R-51, 1960.

McCormick, Mack. *The Unexpurgated Folksongs of Men.* Raglan R-51, 1960.
McCulloh, Judith. "'In the Pines': The Melodic-Textual Identity of an American Lyric Folksong Cluster." PhD diss., Indiana University, 1970.
McCusker, Kristine M. *Lonesome Cowgirls and Honky-Tonk Angels: The Women of Barn Dance Radio.* Urbana: University of Illinois Press, 2008.
McCutcheon, John. Headnote to "John B. Sails," in Sandburg, *The American Songbag.*
McGee, Kirk. *Mister Kirk—54 Years of Country Pickin'.* MBA Records, NR 111331, 1980.
McGee, Kirk. Personal communication with author, July 8, 1981, Franklin, Tenn.
McGee, Sam. *Grand Dad of the Country Guitar Pickers.* Arhoolie 5012, 1971.
Mead, Joan Tyler. "Roll the Cotton Down! A Worksong Goes to Sea." *Mississippi Folklore Register* XVIII, no. 1 (Spring 1984): 5–15.
Meine, Franklin J. *Tall Tales of the Southwest.* New York: Knopf, 1930
Memphis Public Ledger. "Ledger Lines." Feb. 13, 1874.
Menand, Louis. "Diversity." In *Critical Terms for Literary Study,* edited by Frank Lentricchia and Thomas McLaughlin. Chicago: University of Chicago Press, second edition, 1995.
Mencken, H. L. *The American Language: An Inquiry into the Development of English in the United States.* 3rd ed. New York: Alfred A. Knopf, 1930.
Mencken, H. L. "Civilized Chicago." *Chicago Sunday Tribune,* October 28, 1917.
Mencken, H. L. "The Literary Capital of the United States." *Nation of London,* April 17, 1920.
Menius, Art. "The Marrow of Tradition." *Bluegrass Unlimited* (September 1992): 33–35.
Merrick, George Byron. *Old Times on the Upper Mississippi, Recollections of a Steamboat Pilot from 1854 to 1863.* Minneapolis: University of Minnesota Press, 2001.
"A Message of Hope to the Sick and Afflicted." *Interior Journal,* Stanford, Ky., October 13, 1916.
Miller, Joe, and Jim Henry. "Lord, I'm in Trouble." Recorded April 15, 1936, AFS 743-B1. Published on *Mississippi: Saints & Sinners.*
Miller, Kiri. *Traveling Home: Sacred Harp Singing and American Pluralism.* Urbana: University of Illinois Press, 2008.
Milnes, Gerald. "The Banjo in West Virginia." *Goldenseal* 43, no. 1 (Spring 2017): 40–47.
Mindte, Tom. Unpublished remembrance of Will Keys, May 2006.
Minton, John. *78 Blues: Folksongs and Phonographs in the American South.* Jackson: University Press of Mississippi, 2008.

Minton, John, and David Evans. *"The Coon in the Box": A Global Folktale in African-American Tradition.* Helsinki: Academia Scientiarum Fennica, 2001. Folklore Fellows Communications, no. 277.

Mississippi Department of Corrections. Microfilm document checklist, Parchman penitentiary, Parchman, MS.

Mississippi: Saints & Sinners, From Before the Blues and Gospel. Deep River of Song series, Alan Lomax Collection, Rounder 11661-1824-2, 1999.

Mississippi Sheiks. "Bootleggers' Blues." OK 8820, 1930.

"Mississippi State Penitentiary, Physical Examination and Description." Charlie Sims file at Parchman.

Mitchell, Joseph. *McSorley's Wonderful Saloon.* New York: Penguin Books, 1945.

Monge, Luigi, and David Evans. "New Songs of Blind Lemon Jefferson." *Journal of Texas Music History* 3, no. 2 (2003).

Monge, Luigi. *Wasn't That a Mighty Day: African American Blues and Gospel Songs on Disaster.* Jackson: University Press of Mississippi, 2022.

"Monologue [The Alphabet of the Parchman Penitentiary]." AFS 598 A4.

Monseur, Mike. To author, Nov. 17, 2024.

Morning Light, no. 112, n.p. Dallas, Texas: Stamps-Baxter Music and Printing Company Co. Inc., 1949.

Morning Stars of Savannah, Nashboro 7231 (LP), ca. 1980.

Mount, Robert Nelson. To William Sidney Mount, July 28, 1840.

Mount, William Sidney. To C. M. Cady, Nov. 24, 1853.

Mountain Frolic. American Folk Music Series, Album No. B-1025, Brunswick Radio Corp., 1947.

Muir, Peter C. *Long Lost Blues: Popular Blues in America, 1850–1920.* Urbana: University of Illinois Press, 2010.

Music from the Motion Picture, The General's Daughter, Milan 73138 35885-2, 1999.

The Nashville Banner. "Large Crowd Will Seek Park Program." May 16, 1933.

"*National Barn Dance* WLS Performances." Apr. 10, 1942, broadcast. Country Music Hall of Fame and Museum, digital file TR 002380.

National Endowment for the Arts. *National Heritage Fellowships Program Book,* 1996.

National Register of Historic Places. Inventory-Nomination Form. Received April 19, 1973. Submitted and written by Mrs. Donald Drummond.

New Orleans Republican. "Boats Leaving To-Day." November 30, 1870.

Notation from listing to "Convict Groups" at "Brickyard Camp." Courtesy of Chris Smith, revisions for *Blues and Gospel Recordings 1890–1943,* forthcoming fifth edition, compiled by John Godrich and Robert M. W. Dixon, revised and expanded by Howard Rye and Chris Smith.

Odell, Scott. Email to author, Jan. 12, 2022.

Odum, Howard W. "Religious Folk-Songs of the Southern Negroes." *American Journal of Religious Psychology and Education* 3 (July 1909).

"Old Man." Asch 103 B, on *Work Songs of the U.S.A.* Author's transcription.

"Old Man, Can I Have Your Daughter." *The Hammons Family: The Traditions of a West Virginia Family and Their Friends.* Originally issued on AFS L65–66, 1973. Reissued on Rounder CD 1504/05, 1998.

"Old Man, Will Your Dog Catch a Rabbit?" *Lead Belly's Last Sessions.* Folkways 241/2941 and 242/2942. Reissued on Smithsonian Folkways SF CD 40068/71, 1994.

Old Town School of Folk Music. "Sloop John B." *Episode 8, Five from the Archives,* https://soundcloud.com/oldtownschool/ep-8-five-from-the-archives-sloop-john-b.

Old Town School of Folk Music songbook, ca. 1958.

Oldham, Paul. "Pianist Recalls Years with Macons." *The Tennessean,* July 17, 1991.

Oliver, Paul, and Mack McCormick. *The Blues Come to Texas: Paul Oliver and Mack McCormick's Unfinished Book.* College Station: Texas A & M University Press, 2019.

Olson Ted. "Fiddle Style" Banjo. In Carroll Best and the White Oak String Band, *Old-Time Bluegrass from the Great Smoky Mountains, 1956 & 1959.* Great Smoky Mountains Association 200949, 2014.

"On the Record." *People's Songs* 2, no. 5 (June 1947).

"On the Record." *People's Songs* 3, no. 8 (Sept. 1948).

"On the Record." *People's Songs* 3, no. 10 (Nov. 1948).

"On the Record." *People's Songs* 3, no. 11 (Dec. 1948).

O'Neill, Francis J. *Music of Ireland.* Chicago: Lyon and Healy, 1903.

Oster, Harry. "Negro Humor: John and Old Marster." *Journal of the Folklore Institute* 5, no. 1 (June 1968): 42–57.

Oxford English Dictionary, Compact Edition. Oxford: Oxford University Press, 1971, twentieth U.S. printing, January 1981.

"A Page of Breakdowns." *People's Songs* III, no. 6 and 7 (July–Aug. 1948).

Paine-Brooks, Leisa. "Banjo Picker's Style Earns Award." *Johnson City Press,* November 3, 1996.

Paley, Tom. "Salty Dog." *Hard Luck Papa, Old Time Picking Styles & Techniques.* Kicking Mule 201, 1976.

Palmer, Robert. *Deep Blues.* New York: Viking Press, 1981.

Palmer, Robert. Notes to Edwards, David "Honeyboy." *Mississippi Delta Bluesman.* Folkways Records FS 3539, 1979.

Palmer, Robert. "Pure Honeyboy Edwards." *Living Blues* (March/April 1990): 36–38.

Pankake, Jon. Liner notes to McGee Brothers and Arthur Smith, *Milk 'em in the Evening Blues.* Folkways Records, FT 1007, 1968.

Paredes, Américo, and Ellen J. Stekert. *The Urban Experience and Folk Tradition.* Austin: University of Texas Press, 1971.

Parsons, Elsie Clews. "Notes on Folk-Lore of Guilford County, North Carolina." *Journal of American Folklore* 30, no. 116 (Apr.–June 1917).

Parsons, Gerald E. "Phenomenology and Folklife Research." In *American Material Culture and Folklife,* edited by Simon Bronner. Ann Arbor: UMI Research Press, 1985.

Parsons, Gerald E., Jr. "Special Report: Performers, Collectors, and the People of the United States," January 7, 1991.

Patton, Charley, and Bertha Lee. "Oh Death." Vocalion 02904, 1934.

Paulding, James Kirke. *The Lion of the West: A Farce in Two Acts.* Stanford, Cal.: Stanford University Press, 1954.

Paulding, James Kirke. "The Lion of the West." In Botkin, *A Treasury of American Folklore.*

Paulson, John. *Banjo Spirits.* John's Films, 1997.

Paybarah, Azi. "Rubio Sees a 'Remaking' of the Republican Party." *Washington Post,* November 6, 2024.

Pearson, Barry Lee. "Appalachian Blues." *Black Music Research Journal* 23, no.1/2 (Spring–Autumn 2003).

Pearson, Barry Lee. Introduction, in Cushing, *Pioneers of the Blues Revival.*

Pearson, Barry Lee. Notes to *Honeyboy Edwards, Mississippi Delta Bluesman.* Smithsonian Folkways Recordings, SFW CD 40132, 2001.

Pearson, Barry Lee. *"Sounds So Good to Me": The Bluesman's Story.* Philadelphia: University of Pennsylvania Press, 1984.

Perrow, E. C. "Songs and Rhymes from the South." *Journal of American Folklore* 26, no. 100 (Apr.–June 1913).

Pescatello, Ann M. *Charles Seeger: A Life in American Music.* Pittsburgh: University of Pittsburgh Press, 1992.

Phillips, Sharon Ferguson. Personal correspondence with author, Sept. 7, 2010, telephone conversation, Sept. 10, 2010.

Pike, Martha V. "Catching the Tune." In Gray, *Catching the Tune.*

Polacheck, Hilda Satt. *I Came a Stranger: The Story of a Hull-House Girl,* edited by Dena J. Polacheck Epstein. Urbana: University of Illinois Press, 1991, 51–52.

Polacheck, Hilda Satt. Typescript, American Folk Stories, Illinois Writers' Project, 1937.

Poore, Ben Perley. "Hackett and Crockett." In *Perley's Reminiscences or Sixty Years in the National Metropolis.* Vol. 1. Philadelphia: Hubbard Brothers, 1886.

Pope's Arkansas Mountaineers. "Hog Eye." Reissued on *Echoes of the Ozarks, Volume One.* County CD-3506, 1995.

Porterfield, Nolan. *Last Cavalier: The Life and Times of John A. Lomax.* Urbana: University of Illinois Press, 1996.

Proffitt, Frank. "Sourwood Mountain." *Frank Proffitt.* Folk-Legacy FSA 1, 1962.

Psalm 61, *The Holy Bible.* Authorized King James version. Cambridge: Cambridge University Press, n.d.

Pucinski, Roman. "Ethnic Heritage Studies Centers." H.R. 14910, House General Subcommittee on Education, Committee on Education and Labor, Ninety-First Congress, Second Session, Feb. 16, 17, 18, 24, 26; March 4, 5, 19; and May 6, 1970.

Pucinski, Roman. "Ethnic Studies and Urban Reality." In Wenk, *Pieces of a Dream,* 73–88.

Puckett, Newbell Niles. *Folk Beliefs of the Southern Negro.* Chapel Hill: University of North Carolina Press, 1926.

Randolph, Vance. *Blow the Candle Out, "Unprintable" Ozark Folksongs and Folklore, Volume II, Folk Rhymes and Other Lore.* Fayetteville: University of Arkansas Press, 1992.

Randolph, Vance. *The Devil's Pretty Daughter and Other Ozark Folk Tales.* New York: Columbia University Press, 1955.

Reed, Ola Belle. *My Epitaph: A Documentary in Song and Lyric.* Folkways Records FA 2493, 1976.

Reed, Ola Belle. Liner notes to *Mariposa Folk Festival 1975.* M-75-001, 1976.

Reed, Ola Belle. Notes to *Rising Sun Melodies.* Smithsonian Folkways SFW CD 40202, 2010.

Reuss, Richard A. "American Folklore and Left-Wing Politics: 1927–1957." PhD diss., Indiana University, 1971.

Reuss, Richard A. "Woody Guthrie and His Folk Tradition." *Journal of American Folklore* 83, no. 329 (Jul.–Sept. 1970): 273–303.

Riddle, Almeda. *A Singer and Her Songs: Almeda Riddle's Book of Ballads*, edited by Roger D. Abrahams, music ed., George Foss. Baton Rouge: Louisiana State University Press, 1970, 98–100.

Rinzler, Ralph. Notes to *Uncle Dave Macon: First Featured Star of the 'Grand Ole Opry,'* Decca DL 4760, 1966.

Rinzler, Ralph. Personal communication with author, handwritten notes, May 4, 1983.

Rinzler, Ralph, and Norm Cohen. *Uncle Dave Macon: A Bio-Discography.* JEMF Special Series, No. 3. John Edwards Memorial Foundation, 1970.

Roberts, Leonard W. *South from Hell-fer-Sartin: Kentucky Mountain Folk Tales.* Berea, Ky.: Council of Southern Mountains, 1964.

Romalis, Shelly. *Pistol Packin' Mama: Aunt Molly Jackson and the Politics of Folksong.* Urbana: University of Illinois Press, 1999.

Romanoski, Steve. "Dawn Greening: The Mother of Us All." *Come for to Sing: Folk Music in Chicago and the Midwest* 6, no. 1 (Winter 1980): 6–9.

Rosenberg, Neil V. "'An Icy Mountain Brook': Revival, Aesthetics, and the 'Coal Creek March.'" In *Songs about Work: Essays in Occupational Culture for Richard A. Reuss*, edited by Archie Green, Special Publication of the Folklore Institute, no. 3. Bloomington: Folklore Institute, Indiana University, 1993, 163–83.

Rourke, Constance. *Roots of American Culture.* New York: Harcourt, Brace and Company, 1942.

Rowe, Helen Marie. Tape-recorded message, May 17, 2004.

Rowe, Mike. *Chicago Blues: The City & the Music.* New York: Da Capo, 1975.

Rowe, Mike. "Floyd Jones Interview." *Blues Unlimited* no. 137/138 (Spring 1980).

Russell, Tony. *Blacks, Whites and Blues.* New York: Stein and Day, 1970.

Russell, Tony. *Country Music Records, A Discography 1921–1942.* Oxford: Oxford University Press, 2004.

Safire, William. "The Way We Live Now." *New York Times,* March 3, 1999.

Sage, Jerome. Typed document, May 17, 1939. Mississippi Department of Archives and History.

Sandburg, Carl. 1950 memorial tribute to Lewis, p. 1, Box 1, Folder 49.P. 2, typescript. Lloyd Lewis Papers.

Sandburg, Carl. *The American Songbag.* San Diego: Harcourt Brace Jovanovich, 1927. Reprint edition, 1990.

Sandburg, Carl. Box 1, Folder 49, Incoming Correspondence, 1933–1938, n.d. Lloyd Lewis Papers.

Sandburg, Carl. *New American Songbag.* New York: Harcourt Brace, 1950.

Sandburg, Carl. *The People, Yes.* New York: Harcourt, Brace & World, Inc., 1936.

Sandburg, Carl. To John T. McCutcheon. Box 66, Folder 2152, Incoming correspondence, n.d. 1931. McCutcheon papers, Newberry Library.

Sayers, Bob. Personal communications with author, December 2019 and January 2020.

Scarborough, Dorothy. *On the Trail of Negro Folk-Songs.* Cambridge: Harvard University Press, 1925.

Scharf, John Thomas, and Thompson Westcott. *History of Philadelphia 1609–1884.* Vol 2. Philadelphia: L. H. Everts & Co., 1884.

Schrager, Samuel. "Trial Lawyers as Storytellers." In *1986 Festival of American Folklife Program Book,* 12–16.

Schultz, Christian, Jr. *Travels on an Inland Voyage Through the States of New York, Pennsylvania, Virginia, Ohio, Kentucky and Tennessee and Through the Territories of Indiana, Louisiana, Mississippi and New Orleans; Performed in the Years of 1807 and 1808.* New York: Isaac Riley, 1810.

Schulz, Edward. "A Functional Analysis of Retail Trade in the Maxwell Street Market Area of Chicago." Unpublished thesis, Northwestern University, Evanston, Illinois, 1954.

Schwartz, Tony. Fountain-Pen Salesman. West 42nd Street, New York City, July 2, 1952. Transcribed by B. A. Botkin. In Botkin, *Sidewalks of America.*

Schweiker, Richard S. "Ethnic Studies: Toward a New Pluralism in America." In Wenk, *Pieces of a Dream*, 63–71.

Scott, Mike. "Singing People." *People's Songs* 1, no. 9 (October 1946).

Second District Circuit Court. "The State vs. Charlie Sims, Murder." State of Mississippi, Chickasaw County, October 29, 1934. Files in Chickasaw County Courthouse, Okolona, MS.

Second District Circuit Court. "The State vs. Wash Dennis, Robbery with a Firearm." Signed grand jury document, no. 4238, State of Mississippi, Chickasaw County, October 30, 1934.

Seeger, Charles. "Folk Music in the Schools of a Highly Industrialized Society." In *Studies in Musicology.*

Seeger, Charles. "The Folkness of the Nonfolk and the Nonfolkness of the Folk." In *Studies in Musicology.*

Seeger, Charles. "Prescriptive and Descriptive Music Writing." In *Studies in Musicology*, 168–81.

Seeger, Charles. Reviewed Works. *Journal of American Folklore* 61, no. 240 (Apr.–June, 1948): 215–18.

Seeger, Charles. Reviewed Works. *Journal of American Folklore* 62, no. 243 (Jan.–Mar. 1949): 68–70.

Seeger, Charles. *Studies in Musicology, 1935–1975.* Berkeley: University of California Press, 1977.

Seeger, Charles. "Who Owns Folklore?—A Rejoinder." *Western Folklore* 21 (April 1962).

Seeger, Pete. Foreword to *Reprints from the People's Songs Bulletin.*

Seeger, Pete. *How to Play the 5-string Banjo.* 2nd ed. Self-published, 1954.

Seeger, Ruth Crawford. *The Music of American Folk Song and Selected Other Writings on American Folk Music*, edited by Larry Polansky with Judith Tick. Rochester, N.Y.: University of Rochester Press, 2001.

Seroff, Doug. To author, July 12, 2024.

Seroff, Doug. To author, July 22, 2024.

Shahn, Bernarda Bryson. Personal communication with author, December 9, 1994.

Shea, Mike, dir. *And This Is Free: The Life and Times of Chicago's Legendary Maxwell Street.* 1965. Shanachie 6801 DVD, 2008.

"Sheep ranching in Colorado and Utah, ca. 1925–1930." Box 10, Folder 196. Lloyd Lewis Papers.

Shores, Joe. "Roustabout Song." AFS 3094 B2 and 3095 A1.

Silber, Irwin. "Irwin Silber." In Cohen, *"Wasn't That a Time!"*

Silber, Irwin. *Reprints from the People's Songs Bulletin 1946–1949.* New York: Oak, 1961.

Simpson, Marietta. *Crooked Stick: Songs in a Strange Land.* Art Salad Productions, 2019.

Sky, Patrick, ed. *Mel Bay Presents Ryan's Mammoth Collection [of] 1050 Reels and Jigs, Hornpipes, Clogs, Walk-arounds, Essences, Strathspeys, Highland Flings and Contra Dances, with Figures, and How to Play Them.* Pacific, Mo.: Mel Bay Publications, 1995.

Smith, Arthur. "I'm Bound to Ride." Bluebird BB B-7325, 1937.

Smith, Arthur. *Milk 'em in the Evening Blues.* Folkways FTS 31007, 1968.

Smith, C. Alphonso. "Ballads Surviving in the United States." *The Musical Quarterly* 2, no. 1 (January 1916): 111.

Smith, C. Alphonso. "A Great Movement in Which Everyone Can Help." Bureau of Education, Department of the Interior, Special Inquiry, November 1913.

Smith, Charles Edward. "King of the 12 String Guitar." *Jazz Magazine* 4 (1942). Reprinted in Jones, *A Tribute to Huddie Ledbetter.*

Smith, Chris, and David Evans. "Willie and India Slayton (Also known as Will and Emma Slayden): Two Lives in Outline." *Tennessee Folklore Society Bulletin* 62, no. 2 (2006): 20–23.

Smith, Christopher J. *The Creolization of American Culture: William Sidney Mount and the Roots of Blackface Minstrelsy.* Urbana: University of Illinois Press, 2013.

Smith, Doug. To author, Mar. 9, 2021.

Smith, Harry. Album notes to *Anthology of American Folk Music.* FP 251 side B, band 8. "Condensation of lyrics," entry 8 (unpaginated).

Smith, Harry, ed. *Anthology of American Folk Music,* Folkways, FP 251, 1952.

Smyth, Willie. *Country Music Recorded Prior to 1943: A Discography of LP Reissues.* JEMF Special Series No. 14. John Edwards Memorial Forum. Los Angeles: University of California, 1984.

Snyder, Jared. "Leadbelly and His Windjammer: Examining the African American Button Accordion Tradition." *American Music* 12, no. 2 (Summer 1994): 148–66.

Southern, Eileen. *The Music of Black Americans, A History.* New York: Norton, 1971.

Spottswood, Dick. *The Blue Sky Boys.* Jackson: University Press of Mississippi, 2018.

Spottswood, Richard K. *Ethnic Music on Records, A Discography of Ethnic Recordings Produced in the United States, 1893–1942.* Urbana: University of Illinois Press, 1990.

"Staff Conference in Industrial Folklore," July 13, 1939. Reproduced in "American Life Histories: Manuscripts from the Federal Writers' Project 1936–1940," https://www.loc.gov/item/wpalh000034/, accessed June 30, 1999.

Stagner, Glenn. "Reminiscences of Uncle Dave by Smoky Mountain Glenn." In *Uncle Dave Macon.*

The Staple Singers, early Epic 9825 (45) LP/LP 24163, April 1965.

State of Mississippi, Monroe County. Handwritten grand jury document, signed by James Finley, district attorney, Oct. 24, 1927.

Stearns, Florence D. "Critic Praises Dorothy Scarborough's Song Catcher in Southern Mountains." *Richmond News Leader,* June 25, 1937.

Stearns, Harold E. *Civilization in the United States, an Inquiry by Thirty Americans.* New York: Harcourt, Brace, 1922.

Steinbeck, John. *The Grapes of Wrath.* New York: Compass Books, 1967.

Sterkert, Ellen J. "Focus for Conflict: Southern Mountain Medical Beliefs in Detroit." In *The Urban Experience and Folk Tradition,* edited by Américo Paredes and Ellen J. Stekert. Austin: University of Texas Press, 1971.

Stewart, Donald Ogden, ed. *Fighting Words.* New York: Harcourt, Brace and Company, 1940.

Stover, Don. Liner notes to *Things in Life.* Rounder 0014, 1972.

Stracke, Win. *The Old Town School of Folk Music, The First Ten Years or The Biography of a Hunch.* Chicago: Old Town School of Folk Music, 1967.

"Studs Terkel with Doc Hopkins and Stephen Wade." WFMT radio broadcast, Dec. 20, 1982, Chicago.

Szwed, John. *Alan Lomax: The Man Who Recorded the World.* New York: Penguin Books, 2010.

Talley, Thomas W. *The Negro Traditions.* Knoxville: University of Tennessee Press, 1993.

Talley, Thomas W. *Negro Folk Rhymes.* Knoxville: University of Tennessee Press, 1991.

Tamony, Peter. "'Hootenanny': The Word, Its Context and Continuum." *Western Folklore* 22, no. 3 (July 1963): 165–70.

Tate, Beulah. "Talking Bones." In Dorson, *American Negro Folktales.*

Taubman, Howard. "Records; The Smokies." *New York Times,* August 31, 1941.

The Tennessean. "Hit for Hyde's to Get Latest Musical Hits," June 22, 1924.

Thomas, Henry ("Ragtime Texas"). "Shanty Blues." Vocalion 1139, 1927.

Tick, Judith. *Ruth Crawford Seeger: A Composer's Search for American Music.* New York: Oxford University Press, 1997.

Times-Picayune. "The River: Weather and Business—Arrivals and Departures of Steamboats." January 22, 1868.

Traditional Tune Archive. "Hog Eye." https://tunearch.org/wiki/Annotation:Hog_Eye_(1), accessed Jan. 28, 2021.

Trischka, Tony. *Melodic Banjo.* New York: Oak Publications, 1976.

Tross, Clarence. "Old Man, May I Have Your Daughter." Digital Library of Appalachia.

Twain, Mark. *The Adventures of Huckleberry Finn.* New York: Heritage Reprints, 1940. Orig. 1884.

Twain, Mark. *The Adventures of Tom Sawyer.* New York: Heritage Reprints, 1936.

Tucker, Stephen B. "Hog Eye." AFS 3045 B1.

Turner, Arlin. "Texts of Two Addresses." *Studies in American Humor* 2, no. 2 (October 1975).

Tyler, Gail. To author, August 1, 2022.

Uhl, Sherley. "How Dead Is Herb-Doctoring?" *Louisville Courier-Journal,* Mar. 4, 1939.

Vlach, John. "Vernacular." In *American Folklore: An Encyclopedia,* edited by Jan Harold Brunvand. New York: Garland, 1996.

"Voice of America Broadcast with Doc Hopkins." In Wade, *A Storyteller's Story.*

Wade, Stephen. *Banjo Diary: Lessons from Tradition.* Smithsonian Folkways SFW CD 40208, 2012.

Wade, Stephen. *The Beautiful Music All Around Us: Field Recordings and the American Experience.* Urbana: University of Illinois Press, 2012.

Wade, Stephen. *Catching the Music.* WETA-TV documentary, June 23, 1987. Accessible on the Folkstreams website.

Wade, Stephen. "Chicago." In *A Storyteller's Story.*

Wade, Stephen. *Dancing Home.* Flying Fish Records FF 70543, 1990.

Wade, Stephen. "The Far-Famed Fairytale of Fenella." In *A Storyteller's Story.*

Wade, Stephen. *Hands on the Tune.* Patuxent CD-369, 2023.

Wade, Stephen. "Leadbelly's 'Old Man' and the Work Song Tradition." NPR, *All Things Considered,* Aug. 23, 2006.

Wade, Stephen. Liner notes to W. Fleming Brown, *Little Rosewood Casket and Other Songs of Joy.* Merrywang 1953.

Wade, Stephen. "A Matrix of America." *ARSC Journal* 32, no. 2 (Fall 2001): 243–49.

Wade, Stephen. "Old Town School of Folk Music" entry. In *Encyclopedia of Chicago,* edited by James R. Grossman, Ann Durkin Keating, and Janice L. Reiff. Chicago: University of Chicago Press, 2004.

Wade, Stephen. "Ora Dell Graham, A Little Black Girl from Mississippi." In *The Beautiful Music All Around Us.*

Wade, Stephen. Notes in *Across the Amerikee: Showpieces from Coal Camp to Cattle Trail.* Smithsonian Folkways SFW CD-40223, 2017, 25–26.

Wade, Stephen. Notes to *Black Appalachia: String Bands, Songsters and Hoedowns.* Rounder 1823, 1999.

Wade, Stephen. Notes to "Chatham Hill Serenade." In Smith, *In Sacred Trust.*

Wade, Stephen. Notes to Hobart Smith, *In Sacred Trust: The 1963 Fleming Brown Tapes.* Smithsonian Folkways SFW CD 40141, 2005.

Wade, Stephen. Notes to *A Treasury of Library of Congress Field Recordings.* Rounder CD 1500, 1997.

Wade, Stephen. Notes to Victor Furtado, *Dellorto Island,* Patuxent CD-319, 2018.

Wade, Stephen. “A Straight Lick and a Crooked Stick.” *Polk County*, Performance Journal 3, no. 4 (2001–2002). Published by Arena Stage.

Wade, Stephen. *A Storyteller's Story: Sources of Banjo Dancing.* Patuxent Records CD 333, 2019.

Wald, Elijah. “Banjo Strummin.'” *Boston Globe*, November 4, 1993.

Walker, Jimmy. In Greensmith, *Blues Unlimited.*

Ward, Brian, and Patrick Huber. *A & R Pioneers: Architects of American Roots Music on Record.* Nashville: Vanderbilt University Press and Country Music Foundation Press, 2018.

Ware, Caroline F. *The Cultural Approach to History.* New York: Gordon Press, 1974.

Ware, Helen Bell Rowe. To author, Facebook DM communication, Sept. 4, 2024.

Wells, Paul F. “Elias Howe, William Bradbury Ryan, and Irish Music in Nineteenth-Century Boston.” *Journal of the Society for American Music* 4, special issue 4 (Nov. 2010): 410–20.

Wells, Paul F. “'Worthy of Investigation,' Notes on the Origin of an Uncle Dave Macon Song.” *Tennessee Folklore Society Bulletin* LXIV, no. 1 (Spring 2008): 23–28.

Wenk, Michael, S. M. Tomasi, and Geno Baroni, eds. *Pieces of a Dream: The Ethnic Worker's Crisis with America.* New York: Center for Migration Studies, 1972.

Wenzel, Bertha Wheeler. *Steamboatin' Songs, Authentic Americana 1860–1900.* Recorded 1964. Reissued on CD, self-published, n.d., accompanied by Bill Small.

Wheeler, Mary. Correspondence with Joe Curtis, Memphis *Commercial Appeal,* Aug. 20, 1940. Box 4, file 23, Mary Wheeler Collection, McCracken County Public Library, Paducah, Ky.

Wheeler, Mary. Letters from Department of Commerce inspectors headquartered in New Orleans, Aug. 22 and Aug. 27, 1940. Box 4, file 23, Mary Wheeler Collection, McCracken County Public Library, Paducah, Ky.

Wheeler, Mary. *Steamboatin' Days: Folk Songs of the River Packet Era.* Baton Rouge: Louisiana University Press, 1944.

White, Lasses. *Lasses White's Book of Humor and Song.* Nashville, 1935.

Whiteis, David. *Chicago Blues: Portraits and Stories.* Urbana: University of Illinois Press, 2006.

Wilgus, D. K. Album notes to *Mike Seeger.* Vanguard VRS-9150, 1964.

Wilgus, D. K. “Bradley Kincaid.” In *Stars of Country Music: Uncle Dave Macon to Johnny Rodriguez,* edited by Bill C. Malone and Judith McCulloh. Urbana: University of Illinois Press, 1975.

Wilgus, D. K. “Country-Western Music and the Urban Hillbilly.” In Paredes, *The Urban Experience and Folk Tradition.*

Wilgus, D. K. “An Introduction to the Study of Hillbilly Music.” *Journal of American Folklore* 78, no. 309 (July–Sept. 1965).

Wilgus, D. K. Notes to *Doc Hopkins*.

Wilgus, D. K. Notes to "Wreck of the Titanic." In *Doc Hopkins*.

Wilgus, D. K. "Record Reviews." *Journal of American Folklore* 75, no. 295 (Jan.–Mar. 1962).

Wilgus, D. K. "The Text Is the Thing." *Journal of American Folklore* 86, no. 341 (Jul.–Sept. 1973).

Will Slayden, African-American Banjo Songs from West Tennessee. Tennessee Folklore Society, TPS 123, 2001.

Williams, Michael Ann. *Staging Tradition: John Lair and Sarah Gertrude Knott.* Urbana: University of Illinois Press, 2006.

Williams, Raymond. "Enclosure, Commons and Communities." In *The Country and the City.* New York: Oxford University Press, 1973, 96–107.

Williams, Raymond. *Keywords: A Vocabulary of Culture and Society, Revised Edition.* Oxford: Oxford University Press, 1983, 70–72.

Willingham, Mary Emma. "Mary's History," handwritten memoir. July 1978.

Willingham, Thaddeus. "Roll on the Ground." AFS 3113 A. *Anglo-American Shanties, Lyric Songs, Dance Tunes and Spirituals,* 1942.

Wilson, Joe. Liner notes to *The Hill-Billies.* County LP 405, 1974.

Wixson, Douglas. *Worker-Writer in America: Jack Conroy and the Tradition of Midwestern Literary Radicalism, 1898–1990.* Urbana: University of Illinois Press, 1994.

Wolfe, Charles K. "The Fiddler's Bible: A Brief History." *The Devil's Box* 21, no. 4 (Winter 1987): 37–48.

Wolfe, Charles K., ed. *Folk Songs of Middle Tennessee: The George Boswell Collection*. Knoxville: University of Tennessee Press, 1997.

Wolfe, Charles K. *A Good-Natured Riot: The Birth of the Grand Ole Opry.* Nashville: Country Music Foundation and Vanderbilt University Press, 1999.

Wolfe, Charles K. Headnote to "Old Woman." In *Folk Songs of Middle Tennessee.*

Wolfe, Charles K. Liner notes to Omer Forster, banjo, featuring Houston Daniel and The Highland Rim Boys. *Flowery Girls.* Davis Unlimited records, DU-3303.

Wolfe, Charles. "Musical Roots of the South." Atlanta: Southern Arts Federation, 1991.

Wolfe, Charles. Notes to *A Ramblin' Reckless Hobo, The Songs of Dick Burnett and Leonard Rutherford.* Rounder 1004, 1975.

Wolfe, Charles K. Notes to *Uncle Dave Macon, Keep My Skillet Good and Greasy.* Bear Family BCD 15978 JM, 2004.

Wolfe, Charles K. "Rural Black String Band Music." *Black Music Research Journal* 10, no. 1 (Spring 1990): 32–35.

Wolfe, Charles K. *Tennessee Strings: The Story of Country Music in Tennessee.* Knoxville: University of Tennessee Press, 1977.

Wolfe, Charles K. "Uncle Dave Macon." In *Stars of Country Music, Uncle Dave Macon to Johnny Rodriguez,* edited by Bill C. Malone and Judith McCulloh. Urbana: University of Illinois Press, 1975.

Wood, Hally. Notes to "Poor Howard." In *Songs to Live By.*

Wood, Hally. *Songs to Live By.* Tannehill HW 101, 1980.

Work, John W., ed. *American Negro Songs and Spirituals.* New York: Crown, 1940.

Work, John W., III. "Folk Songs of the American Negro." Master's thesis, Teachers College, Columbia University, 1930.

Work, John W., Lewis Wade Jones, and Samuel C. Adams Jr. *Lost Delta Found: Rediscovering the Fisk University-Libraryof Congress Coahoma County Study, 1941–1942.* Nashville: Vanderbilt University Press, 2005.

Index

Note: Page numbers in *italics* denote images.

Roustabout singer Rhode Bailey, Vicksburg, Mississippi, May 30, 1939. Photo by Abbott Ferriss. Courtesy of the Archives and Records Services Division, Mississippi Department of Archives and History

STEPHEN WADE is musician, author, and a Grammy-nominated recording artist best known for his long running stage performances of *Banjo Dancing* and *On the Way Home.* He is the author of the award-winning book *The Beautiful Music All Around Us: Field Recordings and the American Experience.*

The University of Illinois Press
is a founding member of the
Association of University Presses.

Text designed by Kelly Gray
in 10.75/16 Warnock Pro
with Sutro display
for the University of Illinois Press
Manufactured by Versa Press, Inc.

University of Illinois Press
1325 South Oak Street
Champaign, IL 61820-6903
www.press.uillinois.edu